THE DARKEST DAWN

THE DARKEST DAWN

Lincoln, Booth,

and the Great

American Tragedy

THOMAS GOODRICH

Indiana University Press
BLOOMINGTON AND INDIANAPOLIS

This book is a publication of
Indiana University Press
601 North Morton Street
Bloomington, IN 47404-3797 USA
http://iupress.indiana.edu
Telephone orders   800-842-6796
Fax orders   812-855-7931
Orders by e-mail   iuporder@indiana.edu

Library of Congress Cataloging-in-Publication Data

Goodrich, Th.
The darkest dawn : Lincoln, Booth,
and the great American tragedy / Thomas Goodrich.
        p.   cm.
Includes bibliographical references and index.
ISBN 0-253-32599-4 (cloth : alk. paper)
1. Lincoln, Abraham, 1809-1865—Assassination.
2. Booth, John Wilkes, 1838-1865. I. Title.
E457.5.G66 2005
973.7'092—dc22
2004015980

1 2 3 4 5 10 09 08 07 06 05

Tearfully—and joyfully—have we
witnessed these events.

—*Horatio Nelson Taft, May 30, 1865*

CONTENTS

PREFACE

WITH THE POSSIBLE EXCEPTION of one or two screaming infants, I was undoubtedly the most disgruntled and agitated person in the audience. While the excited, noisy chatter among the pre-teens and tour groups rose to a roar as the curtain call approached, I sat mostly mute. Deb and I had come to Washington the day before to conclude research on a book we'd been pounding out for nearly a year, *The Day Dixie Died*. The story unrolls with Lincoln's assassination and describes the horrific conditions in the South following the Civil War, caused in large part by the murder of the sixteenth president. We still had plenty of material to go over, perhaps several days' worth of work, and, as anyone who has spent time in the capital knows, D.C. in high season is anything but cheap. Hence, the meter was ticking. Every minute tarried added to our bills—and my woes.

At almost any other time I would have loved to be sitting in Ford's Theater—it had been a desired destination of mine for years. And at almost any other time I would have died to view a live performance on this historic stage—it is what every American historian dreams of. But today? Time was short, we needed to be busy, and here we were in a noisy theater playing tourists for a matinee musical of dubious quality. A half-hour run through the Ford's museum below would now mushroom into a half-day downtime in the theater above.

"Excuse me, sir," said a lady who had approached us earlier as we stepped from the theater onto the busy sidewalk. "I have these two tickets to *Reunion* that we can't use. . . . It's about the Civil War. Would you like to buy them?"

Before I had time to think and answer "No, thanks," Deb was counting out twenty dollars. The good lady was no scalper—the tickets were clearly marked "$10" each. But as I sat in the packed theater, not only was

I miffed at missing a day's worth of research, I also was upset that I hadn't forced Deb to dicker down the woman to, say, five dollars a ticket or, depending on her desperation, a much more appealing five dollars for both. To compound my chagrin, as we hiked back into the crowded lobby, another lady stepped forward and offered us tickets—*free* tickets! And so, when the curtain went up and the hall finally quieted, I, the historian, sat stewing in my seat, more or less determined not to enjoy myself.

Two hours later, when much of the audience had filed out, Deb and I remained in our seats, lost in thought. During those two hours, something exciting had seized both of us and stirred us to our historical bones. *Reunion* was spectacular—worth every cent of that ten-dollar ticket and more. But when, toward the end, the theater had quieted and dimmed and the spotlight had cut through the darkness upward to the box—*the box*—we, like everyone else in the audience, had sat spellbound. Since childhood, we had seen the paintings, sketches, and movies of that box; we had thought of that box and imagined that box until *that box* had become a part of ourselves as much as anything else in our history: the dark, bearded president, the happy first lady, the fatal shot, the assassin's leap, the confusion, the horror—and here, with our own eyes, we were staring into that box where perhaps the most memorable of American events took place.

Silly as it may sound, from that moment I knew I wanted to do something on Abraham Lincoln, John Wilkes Booth, and the circumstances surrounding what I have come to call Our Great American Tragedy. Despite dozens of books on the subject—some brilliant and wonderfully told—I decided to set to work. From the start, it was not my intention to unravel conspiracies, real or imagined, or to delve into hairsplitting minutiae. My hope instead was not only to add something new to the story, but also to tell the tale in such a way that the reader became emotionally invested in the drama, much as I was.

To my surprise, Deb also was fired by that day at Ford's—so much so that she went to work on *First Widows*, an account of the four women whose husbands were murdered while serving as president.

And so, indeed, that day at Ford's Theater cost us a good deal more than twenty dollars and a few hours lost. When tallied, the day drew from us a cumulative five years in research and writing time, more money than I care to consider, and thousands of miles of sometimes great and sometimes grim wandering. All said and done, it might have been better for all parties concerned had we never entered the theater that day; but for my effort, at least, you the reader will in the end decide.

PART ONE

THE OMEN

THOSE WHO WITNESSED THE PHENOMENON that day would never forget it. The sight was so sudden and unexpected that most could only look to the sky, then to their neighbors, then shake their heads in stony disbelief. Some, those of a religious strain, stared in awe and considered what they were witnessing as nothing short of a heavenly message sent from on high. Others in the throng, those earthbound souls less prone to flights of fancy, nevertheless viewed the event as utterly amazing. Whichever the persuasion, whoever the viewer, no one in the crowd that day would ever forget what they beheld at noon, Saturday, March 4, in the year of their Lord 1865.

The day was all the more remarkable because it had such an evil onset. The sun did not smile down on Washington that morning. At 6 A.M., following a week of nearly uninterrupted gray and gloom, a furious storm burst upon the nation's capital from the south.[1] Although the blast—which uprooted trees and toppled outbuildings—ended in only a matter of minutes, torrential rain soon followed in its wake.[2] When the deluge eased around nine that morning, it seemed to many as if the worst had passed. A short time later, though, as thousands of elegantly dressed men and women ventured cautiously up Pennsylvania Avenue toward the Capitol, again the rain came.[3]

"Such a wet, dirty morning as this . . . hardly ever dawned upon Washington," wrote one depressed reporter covering the day's ceremony. "[T]he proverbially filthy streets of the political metropolis [are] filthier and more unpleasant than ever."[4]

"Mud, mud everywhere," cursed another journalist, "and not a dry spot to set foot upon."[5]

For the tens of thousands of men and women who had arrived by train throughout the week from Baltimore, Philadelphia, New York, and all points north, there was little to do but tuck pants into boots or loop hoop skirts and endure the agony in mute misery. About them on the wide street, rain-soaked flags and bunting drooped in soggy silence.

For many of these Americans, some of whom had made the very same trek four years earlier, the irony was inescapable. Back then, although the weather was dry, high winds had swept the streets.[6] Even to those at the time, the dusty tempest sending dirt and grit into everyone's eyes seemed to presage an awful accounting ahead—an omen of a terrible scourge awaiting America. And for sure, a mighty maelstrom of blood, fire, and iron did indeed ravage the face of the land soon after. Now, four years later, the very heavens seemed to be frowning again, showing that, all reason and logic to the contrary, the end was not yet; that the great national trial would continue, perhaps for another four years, perhaps forever.

By noon, a great crowd of spectators stood huddled around the Capitol, silent and shivering. Among all, there was an air of dejection and defeat.[7] "Men, women and children soaked about quietly, caught cold, and waited," wrote one depressed observer. "The rain had taken all the starch out of them."[8] Contributing to the grim and gloomy mood was the knowledge that should more rain now fall, the ceremony all had come for would be held indoors, where only a favored few would be able to attend.[9]

Just when the miserable assemblage felt that it could get no worse, the black clouds above began to thin somewhat, then soften. Soon, the startled thousands pointed to streaks of blue smiling through the parting gray. Within minutes, a sweet breeze from the northwest rippled the surfaces of ponds and puddles all around and swept away the dark, dank smells that had plagued the capital all week. Color returned to the land. From a drab and seemingly lifeless landscape, the first buds on trees reappeared. Grass was green again. Almost on cue, songbirds awakened, and their beautiful music began to sparkle the world.[10]

And then, as if some unseen hand had staged the entire performance, the massive doors of the Capitol building swung open. A tall, gaunt man appeared. Dressed in black, he walked onto the portico, followed by the government of the nation. At that precise moment, the sun suddenly burst from the clouds and spread a blinding light over the entire Capitol grounds. Above, the newly completed dome glowed "snow white" in the brilliant display.[11]

"Every heart beat quicker at the unexpected omen," noted an amazed newsman, Noah Brooks.[12]

At length, the tall man in black approached the podium. As he did so, he paused for a moment, then smiled to himself, as if he, too, was aware of the miracle.[13] Around him, a loud, explosive cheer rose up from the tens of thousands who were startled by the strange and wonderful coincidence. "Finally," wrote a witness, "the tumult subsided . . . and in the universal hush, the President addressed the people as follows":

> Fellow-countrymen: At this second appearing to take the oath of the Presidential office, there is less occasion for an extended address than there was at the first. . . . The progress of our arms, upon which all else chiefly depends, is as well known to the public as to myself, and it is, I trust, reasonably satisfactory and encouraging to all. With high hope for the future, no prediction in regard to it is ventured. . . . Both parties deprecated war, but one of them would make war rather than let the nation survive; and the other would accept war rather than let it perish. And the war came.[14]

With excitement racing through the throng, many anxiously pressed forward, eager to catch every sound.[15] "His voice was singularly clear and penetrating," recalled one man mere yards away. "It had a sort of metallic ring. His enunciation was perfect."[16]

Unfortunately, only a fraction of the estimated thirty thousand in attendance could actually hear the address.[17] For most, however, mood was everything. A burst of optimism and hope had suddenly swept over the multitude, and all applauded spontaneously, though they heard not a word.[18]

"The crowd kept pushing nearer and nearer the platform," recorded a reporter for the *New York Herald*. "Negroes ejaculated 'Bress de Lord' in a low murmur at the end of almost every sentence. . . . [The president's] face glowed with enthusiasm, and he evidently felt every word he uttered."[19]

> Fondly do we hope—fervently do we pray—that this mighty scourge of war may speedily pass away. Yet, if God wills that it continue until all the wealth piled by the bondman's two hundred and fifty years of unrequited toil shall be sunk, and until every drop of blood drawn with the lash shall be paid by another drawn with the sword, as was said three thousand years ago, so still it must be said, "The judgements of the Lord are true and righteous altogether."[20]

Of all the many viewers in that vast sea of faces, of all those who felt they were witnessing the dawn of a new day, none was so swept with emotion or so flooded with words as Walt Whitman. Too old for active service, the white-haired poet served as a volunteer at a local military hospital. As he scanned the crowd around him searching for what he did not know, the old man eventually glanced toward heaven. There, to his astonishment, the poet saw that for which he sought.

"A curious little white cloud, the only one in that part of the sky, appeared like a hovering bird, right over him," wrote Whitman.[21] Whether the object was indeed a cloud, or a bird, or a God, or even a figment of the imagination, it mattered not—the poet saw it, and he, like everyone else this day, looked for signs, longed for signs, prayed for signs. To Walt Whitman, the ethereal vision meant that he would no more hear the shattering, ear-splitting screams of the broken bodies he ministered to daily. For others this day, some who spotted noonday stars overhead, the portents meant they would no longer need search the long lists of names issuing from the fields of slaughter to the south. For all, the signs meant a merciful end to the national nightmare.

> With malice toward none, with charity for all, with firmness in the right, as God gives us to see the right, let us strive on to finish the work we are in; to bind up the nation's wounds, to care for him who shall have borne the battle, and for his widow, and his orphan—to do all which may achieve and cherish a just and lasting peace among ourselves and with all nations.[22]

As the last word echoed across the crowd, the ripple of reflexive applause soon swelled to a thundering roar when the full weight of the beautiful sentiments sank in. After taking the oath of office and kissing the Bible, the president smiled warmly to his people, bowed politely, then turned and quietly departed.[23] After one final burst of cheers and shouts, the huge throng thereupon began to disperse.[24] Unlike the gloomy mood before the address, the atmosphere after it was one of emotion and joy. Many were moved to tears.[25] Most felt that they had not only witnessed but played an active role in a historical event of mystical proportions. On this day, March 4, 1865, not only the words of man but the hand of God seemed to be saying in ever so soothing terms, "The end has come and peace is nigh; the long, cruel agony is over." The day was, said one stunned viewer simply, a "bright omen of the future."[26]

But as the people departed, each aglow with renewed strength and optimism, one alone stood out from the rest. His normally pale, handsome face was not bright with happiness; instead it was black with quiet rage. To him, the words just spoken meant slavery; the songbirds were hateful crows; the sun was death. He had planned and plotted that this day might never come. But it had. Now, he would work against fate—work to ensure that the vision just glimpsed by so many happy thousands would ultimately be nothing more than a mere mirage.[27]

CHAPTER ONE

THREE ELECTRIC WORDS

CLICK, CLICK, CLICKITY-CLACK. . . . CLICK, CLICK, CLICK. . . . CLICKITY-CLACK. Staccato sounds. It was as far from glory and honor as any man or boy could get. It was here at the War Department in Washington that news from the battlefields of the South first touched the North. Along with other employees, it was the job of a "bright-faced Vermont boy," Willie Kettles, to translate the clicks and clacks into dots and dashes and the dots and dashes into words and sentences.[1] As a volunteer in the department, Kettles held a surprisingly important post for one so young. Battles won and lost, military movements, strategy, supplies, encampments, orders and counter-orders, all came rattling in on his telegraph receiver to be transcribed in pencil by the fourteen-year-old. When the clicking stopped and the scribbling was complete, the boy would then relay the message to his supervisor. If he deemed it important, Willie's boss then passed on the note to the undersecretary of war, who in turn delivered it to the office of the secretary of war if it was judged critical. Really urgent reports went straight to the president himself. Though an important task, like anything else, after weeks and months the job soon became mundane and monotonous. Each message meant more writing, more paper and pencils, more work, more war.

And then, shortly before 11 A.M. on April 3, 1865, Willie Kettles heard strange sounds coming in over the wires, sounds like he had never heard before.[2] To untrained ears, the sounds seemed like just more clicks, but to the startled teenager, these were different. These were the sounds Willie and everyone else in the North had been praying to hear for the past four years. Snatching his note, the breathless young telegrapher raced to tell his boss.

Within seconds, the news was streaking down the corridors of the War

Department. From there, the words burst through doors and flashed out windows to those on the streets below.

"The glorious news spread like a panic," wrote an excited newspaper reporter. "In a few minutes the park in front of the department was one dense mass of human beings, each one trying to see who could make the most noise. Old men cried for joy, while others hugged their companions as though they were crazed."[3]

From the War Department, the startling words raced with the speed of wind. Noah Brooks was caught in the rush:

> In a moment of time the city was ablaze with excitement the like of which was never seen before. . . . Almost by magic the streets were crowded with hosts of people, talking, laughing, hurrahing, and shouting in the fullness of their joy. Men embraced one another, "treated" one another, made up old quarrels, renewed old friendships, marched through the streets arm in arm, singing and chatting. . . . Bands of music, apparently without any special direction or formal call, paraded the streets, and boomed and blared from every public place.[4]

"We cheered, yelled, sung, and turned everything upside down," added a delirious government clerk, Newton Ferree.[5]

Among the city's black population, a jubilee soon erupted, with shouting, whooping, and dancing in the streets. At the local hospitals, wounded soldiers pulled themselves from their beds and sent up round upon round of cheers.[6] As joyous as the celebration was throughout the capital, nowhere was it more explosive than where it had begun. There, the streets surrounding the War Department were completely jammed as everyone who was anyone—and many who were not—stepped forth to make a speech.[7] Of all the dignitaries present, none was in greater demand than the secretary of war. Near tears, Edwin Stanton at last spoke:

> In this great hour of triumph, my heart, as well as yours, is penetrated with gratitude to Almighty God for his deliverance of this nation. [Tremendous and prolonged cheering.] Our thanks are due to the President, [cheers,] to the Army and Navy, [cheers,] to the great commanders by sea and land, [cheers,] to the gallant officers and men who have periled their lives upon the battle field and drenched the soil with their blood. [Great cheers.][8]

When Stanton had finished, he presented Willie Kettles to the crowd. A tremendous roar arose, and demands of "Let us hear him!" "Have him speak!" were shouted, as if the adolescent were a great general responsible for the earthshaking news, rather than the mere messenger boy who had relayed it. When the crowd finally quieted, the shy and awkward child blurted out that he "couldn't speak, he felt so." No one seemed to mind, though, and another explosion of applause greeted the stumbling words.[9]

Throughout Washington, the shouts and cheers of the people all but drowned out the din of shrill steam whistles, the blaring of bands, and the booming of cannons. So crazed by the news were the celebrants that the just-arriving report of a terrible sea disaster off Cape Hatteras in which five hundred lives were lost was treated as a "mere incident."[10] Even pickpockets, normally the bane of large capital crowds, were all but ignored in the euphoria.

That evening, far from waning, the grand celebration intensified as tens of thousands of people poured into the streets. From every window and porch, from every building high and low, candles, lamps, and gas jets flooded the night with streams of light. Along the entire length of Pennsylvania Avenue, exploding rockets sent down a blinding array of dazzling colors, and from the roof of Grover's Theater, a "perfect storm" of fireworks was unleashed, turning night into day. As evening deepened and the sky blazed even brighter, the crowds grew even thicker.[11]

"Thousands besieged the drinking-saloons, champagne popped everywhere, and a more liquorish crowd was never seen in Washington than on that night," revealed Noah Brooks.[12]

"All who did not drink were intoxicated, and those who did, were drunk," laughed one reveler.[13]

"The police allowed them to have their own way," reported the Washington *Evening Star* of the drunken celebrants. "[They] only arrested those who were committing flagrant outrages, or who were so much under the weather that they could not take care of themselves, and these in most cases, were taken to their homes—one party being taken home no less than three times."[14]

There had never been anything like it before, and most imagined there would never be anything like it after. In an instant, all the pent-up emotions of four frustrating years of war were given vent. It was the moment that all in the North had prayed for, the sounds that many had died for:

> The thunder of cannon; the ringing of bells; the eruption of flags from every window and housetop; the shouts of enthusiastic gatherings on the streets, all echo the glorious report, RICHMOND IS OURS!! Glory!!! Hail Columbia!!! Hallelujah!!! <u>RICHMOND IS OURS!!!</u>[15]

CHAPTER TWO

THE WHITE CITY

WHERE THE APPOMATTOX AND JAMES RIVERS JOIN, a long estuary is formed that eventually opens into Chesapeake Bay. Here, at the junction of the two streams, was situated City Point, Virginia. As a staging ground for Northern army operations directed at Richmond, Petersburg, and central Virginia, the site was nearly ideal. With supply lines safe and sound on the bay, the Union navy could disgorge at its leisure all the men and materiel needed to dash the last hope of the dying Confederacy. Sadly, City Point was also the perfect place to bring back the thousands of federal soldiers who had been maimed and crippled in this final attempt to crush the rebellion. Thus, in addition to the docks and warehouses that received the soldiers before they marched off to war, a great network of hospitals had sprung up to shelter the broken wrecks that came limping back again. For hundreds of men, this vast "white city" would be their last stop on earth. Except for a few fine words from their officers, and except for the satisfaction of seeing their names misspelled in hometown newspapers, there was little recognition for the sacrifice these soldiers had made for their country.

George Huron was one of the men in the hospital still able to move under his own power. On April 8, 1865, he, like everyone else in his ward, was doing nothing special. The cheers and shouts of joy over the fall of Richmond were sweet but fading memories now. Glorious as the news had been, as far as Huron or anyone else around him could see, little had changed. The war continued. For George Huron and others less seriously wounded, as soon as they had healed properly they knew that they would be sent back into that war once again, to be shot and blasted to pieces, to be soaked, starved, and wracked with malaria and diarrhea, then brought back to this very same hospital to be healed yet again—if they were lucky. Until the war was finally ended, this is the most that Huron and the others could hope for.[1]

And then, Huron turned his head toward the nearby landing at City Point. Above the normal hum of activity at the hospital, he heard something strange. "[M]y attention was attracted by cheering at the landing a mile away," the soldier remembered. "The cheering grew in volume—and like waves of the sea seemed to be rolling our way. Leaving the hospital I walked toward the landing and met an immense crowd of negroes."[2]

Among the thousands of former slaves who had congregated at City Point for work and protection, it was as if Moses or Jesus had suddenly this day stepped onto their shore, so great was their surprise and awe. Indeed, for many of these ragged, pathetic people, Abraham Lincoln was more than the above—he was the Great Deliverer, a being of mythological goodness and power.

"His progress . . . seemed almost impossible," said Huron as he watched the noisy spectacle approach:

> Another old matron dropped upon her knees and clasped her hands in adoration. The President stopped, laid his hands upon her head and said: "Don't do that, I am only a man." Then Mr. Lincoln essayed to speak. An instant hush fell upon the multitude, while he briefly told them that he had come to City Point to personally visit the hospitals, and do what he could for the brave wounded soldiers who, by their valor, had made freedom possible to the slaves. Waving his hand towards the White City he said: "There brave men are suffering,—some of them are dying,—and while I am glad to meet you, duty calls me yonder." The tumult had ceased,—and those who a moment since had been wild in expressing their joy, bowed their heads and silently returned to their camps.[3]

When word spread that the president was coming, excitement raced through the entire hospital. All those who were able stepped outside and quietly formed weak and feeble lines along the walkway.[4]

"Mr. Lincoln passed along in front, paying personal respect to each man," wrote one admiring soldier. "'Are you well, sir?' 'How do you do to-day?' 'How are you, sir?' looking each man in the face, and giving him a word and a shake of the hand as he passed."[5]

When several proud medical directors tried to steer the president toward an inspection of their facilities, they were cut short. "Gentlemen," smiled Lincoln, "you know better than I how to conduct the hospitals, but I have come here to take by the hand the men who have achieved our glorious victories."[6]

After meeting with the men outside, Lincoln and those in his group moved indoors. There, the horrors of war were visible at every turn. "We passed before all the wounded and amputated," said one aghast visitor in the presidential party. "Some had a leg cut off, some an arm. Amid this terrible mass of agony, not a cry nor a complaint."[7]

"Is this Father Abraham?" asked one patient in critical condition. With a gentle grin and a good-natured reply, Lincoln assured the young man that it was.[8]

It was not only the words that endeared Lincoln to his men; it also was his looks. The president, a friend noted, was a "plain, homely, sad, weary-looking man to whom one's heart warmed involuntarily because he seemed at once miserable and kind."[9]

"But," added another observer, "the moment he began to talk, his face lightened up."[10] And on this day Lincoln's face had reason to glow, for the end was now in sight.

When a soldier asked him when the war would end, the president thought for a moment, then assured the man it would all be over in six weeks.[11] Scanning the acres of misery all about him, Abraham Lincoln would have liked nothing more than to tell these suffering men that the war was *now* over, and they all would be heading home soon. But he knew better. Richmond had fallen, and the end was near. But Richmond was not the Confederacy. Gen. Robert E. Lee was. And Lee had not surrendered. As Lincoln well knew, so long as the man who had baffled and bewildered the best the North could give remained at large, all Union victories would ring hollow. And of necessity, the visits to such places as City Point and its white city full of crippled and broken soldiers would continue indefinitely. When the exhausted president had finally finished his visit, he turned back to the landing whence he had come, where a vessel awaited his return to Washington. Among the patients in the hospital, however, the memory of this unexpected visit was something never to be forgotten.

"The men not only reverence and admire Mr. Lincoln, but they love him," wrote one lonely, lowly private describing the day. "May God bless him, and spare his life to us for many years."[12]

CHAPTER THREE

THE LAST MAN

FOR THE PAST FOUR YEARS, the cry "On to Richmond!" had been heard throughout the North. And for the past four years, the cry had gone unheeded. Now, with the coveted prize finally in the Union's grip, many realized that the grand goal had been illusory. When the shouting, speech-making, and band music had finally faded, most soon understood that it was not the city of Richmond that had thrashed the federal army at Cold Harbor, Spotsylvania, the Wilderness, and Fredericksburg, nor was it the capital of the Confederacy that had routed the Union army at Chancellorsville, Second Manassas, and the Seven Days; it was Robert E. Lee and his magnificent Army of Northern Virginia that had done all these things. Richmond, Charleston, Atlanta, and every other city in the South might be stormed, but as long as the legendary "Gray Fox" marched and fought, the issue would always be in doubt.

Thus, one week after Richmond's fall, when news from Appomattox Court House reached the North, those who thought they had no more energy to celebrate quickly found out they were wrong. Unlike the earlier news, which arrived at midday on Monday, the latter came in the dead of night on Sunday, April 9, 1865, when most Americans were asleep.

At tiny Ottawa, Illinois, J. D. Caton was one of the few citizens still awake at 10 P.M. The wealthy judge was also one of the few men in America to have his very own telegraph office in his home. When he heard the startling news clattering over his receiver, Caton, oblivious to all dignity and decorum, ran pell-mell to a neighbor's house. In turn, the two excited men dashed away like schoolboys to the home of another friend. Together the three decided that the swiftest way to rouse the town was to illuminate their residences, which all stood on the north bank,

high above the Illinois River. In twenty minutes the three homes on the
bluff were ablaze with hundreds of sparkling candles. The owner of a
house on the opposite shore soon understood, then responded in kind.
From that point on, revealed a local correspondent, "the news spread
like wild-fire."[1]

Eighty miles to the east, the word raced through Chicago with even
greater speed. Within minutes of hearing the news, an estimated one
hundred thousand men, women, and children ignored the late hour
and the Sabbath and jammed the public square to "shout, sing, laugh,
dance, huzza, and cry for very gladness."[2]

"As we write (1 a. m.)," a newsman milling in the crowd reported, "a
band is promenading the streets playing national music, and all along
our thoroughfares resound the shouts and cheers of an enthusiastic and
excited multitude. Cannons are roaring, rockets are blazing, bonfires are
burning."[3]

At midnight, those locked in deep sleep in New York City were suddenly jarred awake. "Surrender of Lee's army, ten cents and no mistake,"
shouted newsboys "in their shrillest tones." Despite a cold drizzle, those
in the metropolis were "electrified" by the news and rushed into the
streets.[4] With the dawn, far from diminishing, the demonstrations increased in frenzy as those who had slept soundly throughout the night
joined the celebration.

"The news . . . is from Heaven. . . . I wanted to laugh and I wanted to
cry," admitted poet James Russell Lowell.[5]

In Detroit, the outburst of emotion was, said a viewer, "the most enthusiastic and joyous ever known here."[6]

"The city is perfectly wild," echoed another man from Milwaukee,
"no market, no business and no nothing but rejoicing. . . . Everybody
is intoxicated with joy and other ingredients."[7]

With a telegraph linking the continent, those in the Far West heard
the news almost as quickly as those in the East. Despite the rain, villagers
laughed and danced on the muddy streets of Kansas.[8] In Denver, hundreds braved the snow and cold to celebrate with bonfires and band
music.[9] In far-flung Portland, Oregon, the greatest celebration in the
city's brief history was staged.[10] And in the already tumultuous mining
camp of Big Bend, Nevada, nearly the entire population went on a "big
bender" upon receipt of the news. One exception was an old prospec-
tor never known to have drawn a sober breath. When pressed by shouting friends to join and "liquor up," the old man fought free.

"No, boys, no," he cried, "no, this news is too good to get drunk over;
damned if I don't get sober and enjoy it."[11]

Of all the many ways of expressing jubilation—songs, speeches, bands, rockets, liquor—none was more popular or patriotic than cannon salutes. From one end of the Union to the other, the thundering booms of artillery blasts could be heard. Unfortunately, many of the field pieces on hand were relics from previous wars, and no matter how much enthusiasm they might possess, townsmen were still only amateur artillerists. As a consequence, terrible mishaps marred the festivities.

In New York City, two men firing a cannon at dockside were blown into the harbor by a premature explosion. Both men were hideously mangled, and to the horror of bystanders, one victim was seen flailing in the bloody water just before he slipped under. Across the Hudson River at Newark, another celebrant had his face skinned to the skull when he stepped in front of the muzzle flash.[12] In New Hampshire, while ramming home another charge for a victory salute, a naval worker had both arms blown off at the elbows.[13] At Davenport, Iowa, and dozens of other towns, similar accidents had a chilling effect on the otherwise joyous occasion.

Not surprisingly, many revelers chose other means to make noise. In some muddy crossroads that had no cannon—and some that did—anvils were beaten with hammers like salvos. Steam whistles from locomotives, fire engines, and factories added to the bedlam. In New Jersey, a distraught woman who had lost a husband in the war was seen in the street with a table bell, "ringing with all her might, and throwing her body into as many shapes & contortions, as if she had been suddenly smitten with the St. Vitus' dance."[14]

Perhaps in no section of the country were the glad tidings more warmly received than in New England. In a region that rightly felt it had played a leading role in starting the war to end slavery, news of Lee's surrender was doubly satisfying. At Dartmouth College in New Hampshire, while bells rang madly and guns boomed, students and faculty crowded the Green and held a euphoric celebration.[15] In Boston, Hartford, and Burlington, those who had displayed little outward joy over the past week's news now exploded in an orgy of emotion. Explained the editor of the *Providence Daily Journal*:

> It is not often that the staid, earnest, substantial nature of our New England people is stirred to exhibit such manifestations of delirious joy. . . . When the news of the evacuation of Richmond came, gladness was depicted on every countenance, but there was no outburst of enthusiasm. The people asked eagerly, "What about Lee and his army?" . . . But on Sunday night, as soon as it

was fully understood that Lee had really surrendered his army,
the last demand of that careful, reserved New England mind was
met. There palpably was the downfall of the rebellion. . . . And if
any had supposed that the New England heart was cold as a gla-
cier, they should have seen it melt down almost in an instant, and
pour its full, swelling tide of joy, jollity, and jubilation. . . .

We never saw anything like it before here. It was . . . delirium.
It was joyous frenzy. . . . The moment any one shouted, everybody within hearing responded. If one struck up a song, everybody sang. If one started "John Brown," all were ready to declare
that "his soul's marching on." . . . Some one shouts that the recruiting booths are no longer needed, and they straightaway are
turned over into the fire to "recruit" the flame.[16]

As was the case in Providence, in Pittsburgh, Chicago, and numerous
other cities in the North, those stay-at-homes who had lived in daily
dread of the draft now vented their anger by destroying recruiting booths
and setting them alight.[17]

"No more drafting!" exclaimed a relieved man in New York. "No
more quotas! No more terror of 'notices' from provost marshals, and no
more breaking of one's neck to hunt up a substitute."[18]

In much the same spirit, others released their pent-up stress of the past
four years by engaging in violent acts. In countless towns and cities, effigies
of Jefferson Davis, Robert E. Lee, and other Confederate leaders were
hanged and burned while watching crowds roared their approval. Additionally, with virtually every loyal home and shop in the North now displaying the Stars and Stripes, those without flags came under immediate
suspicion. With seeming impunity, drunken hooligans roamed the streets
wreaking vengeance on those they considered disloyal.

At Wilmington, Delaware, a menacing mob stalked the city, forcing
Democrats and suspected dis-loyalists to display the U.S. flag. When one
physician refused, he was seized by his hair and beaten. Another doctor in the same town balked and was chased into a building. Fortunately
for the man, soldiers soon appeared and escorted him to the guard
house.[19]

When a rumor raced through Portland, Maine, that a railroad superintendent had torn down a flag placed on one of his trains by a mob, the
man was instantly seized, stripped of his clothing, dressed in a blue
soldier's uniform, then paraded through the streets waving a U.S. flag.
After being compelled to make patriotic speeches and salute the flag, the
victim was finally released.[20] A short distance south, in rainy Portsmouth,

New Hampshire, a loud and savage crowd of two thousand surrounded a democratic newspaper office. When the shaken editor thereupon displayed a flag from his window as demanded, the mob was not satisfied. With shouts of "Hang him!" and "String him up!" the surging mass burst through the doors and windows of the building. Although the journalist miraculously escaped, his office was totally destroyed. Passing by the ruins later that day, the editor of a rival Portsmouth newspaper gloated over the demise of the "miserable dirty sheet."[21]

And although the vast majority of federal soldiers were content to have merely survived the war and were more than willing to bury the hatchet with their old foe, others seemed determined to rub salt in the wounds. At Winchester, Virginia, Winfield Scott Hancock ordered the entire town illuminated to celebrate Lee's surrender. That there might be no excuses, the Union general announced that his commissary would supply candles to all who had none. "Imagine," said one heartbroken citizen, "a town full of Southern people whose hearts were bleeding and torn by the sad news . . . being compelled by military force to illuminate in token of their rejoicing over our condition."[22]

Even in victory, many in the North, high and low, were now advocating a draconian policy toward the defeated Confederacy, including wholesale executions of civil and military leaders. One of the most strident voices in support of such measures was Andrew Johnson. "Death is too easy a punishment," shouted the vice president to a crowd in Washington. Had he the power, Johnson growled, he would hang rebel leaders "twenty times higher than Haman."[23]

Viewing the violence around them, horrified by the menacing cries of summary executions, better spirits urged peace. "In mercy's name, has there not been suffering enough?" asked renowned clergyman, Henry Ward Beecher, after a New York mob threatened a wealthy banker, not for failure to show a flag but because the one displayed was too small.[24] The Union, insisted Horace Greeley's *New York Tribune*, must now demonstrate to the world its greatness by exhibiting "magnanimity in triumph."[25]

All such pleas might have gone for nothing had not the leading man in the nation agreed with Beecher and Greeley. His guidance, wisdom, patience, and, above all, his charity ensured that as long as he lived, vengeance and retribution would never find a safe haven in America. Fortunately, enough men of goodwill gratefully followed Lincoln's lead, happy to get beyond the horrors of the past.

"Glory to God, the End of bloodshed has come at last," said one government official.[26]

The *New York Times* agreed:

> The great struggle is over. . . . The history of blood—the four
> years of war, are brought to a close. The fratricidal slaughter is all
> over. The gigantic battles have all been fought. The last man, we
> trust, has been slain. The last shot has been fired.[27]

CHAPTER FOUR

STAR OF GLORY

ALTHOUGH MANY OF THE MONUMENTS, statues, and buildings would have been ornaments in any European capital, and although the promise of its future now seemed secure, by the spring of 1865 Washington, D.C., still remained a backward, rambling, shameless embarrassment on the world political map. Like a bejeweled but besotted harlot, the nation's capital was at once both beautiful and ugly—desirable, yet repellent. From a pre-war population of sixty thousand, Washington had burst its seams in four years of war, nearly doubling in size to over one hundred thousand souls. Far from keeping pace with growth, city services had fallen well behind. The hideous smells from rotting animal carcasses, as well as the festering remains from the municipal and military slaughter yards, mingled day and night with the smoke from thousands of fires and furnaces. Stagnant, motionless canals and the sluggish Potomac served as sewage dumps where all manner of offal and filth fed the stench. Hogs wandered and wallowed in the city "as freely as dogs." In the malignant Washington air, said one of those with a sensitive nose, there were "70 separate and distinct stinks."[1]

"The capital of the nation, is probably the dirtiest and most ill-kept borough in the United States," commented the well-traveled newsman Noah Brooks.[2]

Into this stifling, stinking stew were tossed some of the best, and many of the worst, people in America. Lobbyists, lawyers, clergymen, foreign ambassadors, and well-bred wives of politicians and military men jostled and elbowed for the same bit of sidewalk on Pennsylvania Avenue as prostitutes, pimps, pickpockets, thieves, thugs, thimbleriggers, drunkards, and deserters. Hundreds of saloons, bordellos, and other "dens of infamy" fed the public demand.

"Everybody has heard of the great corruption of the city of Washington," continued Noah Brooks, "but I will venture to say that its moral corruption is far exceeded by the physical rottenness of its streets."[3]

During the dry season, the byways of the capital were swirling storms of blinding, choking dust; in wet weather, they were almost bottomless quagmires. When it rained, said one man, Washington streets were "literally nothing but canals in which earth and water were mixed together for depths varying from six inches to three feet."[4] Any vehicle that foundered and sank in the yellow ooze was said to be "shipwrecked."[5] All in all, John Hay could only laugh at those smug individuals in the capital who somehow felt sophisticated and superior simply because they resided in a populous city that was the seat of power. "This miserable sprawling village imagines itself a city because it is wicked, as a boy thinks he is a man when he smokes and swears," sneered Lincoln's proper secretary.[6]

Nevertheless, on the night of April 13, 1865, all the wrinkles and warts and flaws of the bedizened lady along the Potomac were hidden by her dazzling display of jewels. Although the fall of Richmond and Lee's surrender were glorious, earthshaking events in Washington, the grand end-of-war jubilation was saved for this night. Soon after dark, the great celebration began. While cannons thundered from every part of the city and bands marched through the streets, steam fire engines, with bells clanging and whistles screaming, sent up a deafening din. Giant bonfires blazed on every corner. From virtually every home and building, candles—sometimes as many as sixty per window—sent a shower of light below, turning night into day. An estimated one million candles alone burned for the illumination.[7]

"Every tower, turret, every window in the city, from the dizzy height of the dome of the capitol, all over the immense structure; from the stairs of the Smithsonian, from every house and hovel, flashed a flood of light," wrote a reporter for the Wilmington *Delaware Republican.* "Tens of thousands of rockets were constantly mounting heavenward, with hissing sound and dazzling brightness and falling again like a rain of jewels."[8]

From the city parks, huge mortars fired enormous pyrotechnic shells into the darkness above, which, upon exploding in a grand burst, fell shimmering to earth in a shower of blue, green, and crimson stars.[9]

Wrote a dazzled Julia Shepard to her father in upstate New York:

> All along our route the city was one blaze of glorious light. From
> the humble cabin of the contraband to the brilliant White

House[,] light answered light down the broad avenue. The sky was ablaze with bursting rockets. Calcium lights shone from afar on the public buildings. Bonfires blazed in the streets and every device that human Yankee ingenuity could suggest in the way of mottoes and decoration made noon of midnight.[10]

"It looks like a city of fire," thought one spellbound spectator.[11]

To the tens of thousands in the streets that night, the celebration was an awe-inspiring event worthy of a great nation in victory. It was, said a stunned soldier simply, "the most grand exhibition that ever was witnessed in America."[12]

———

Of all the many attractions this night—the parades, the bands, the fireworks, the illuminations—there was only one individual in all of Washington who could not only rival the display but upstage it. As the presidential carriage wended its way through the sea of flame, the crowds filling the streets sent up explosions of cheers and shouts.[13] In the minds of most, the individual seated within was the man of the hour, the hero of the day, the leader whose dogged determination and iron will had gained final victory and ensured that the Union of their forefathers would continue. And Mary Lincoln was furious.

This evening was supposed to be her supreme moment and hers alone. For the better part of four years, her husband, Abraham Lincoln, had been belittled and denigrated, vilified and ridiculed by a surly public unhappy with the course of a bloody, and seemingly unwinnable, war. But despite the critics and naysayers and the overwhelming odds, she and her husband had triumphed. It was her husband and his decisions, more than any other factor, that had held the nation together to witness this final triumph. And yet, it was not her husband upon whose head the laurel of victory had been placed; nor was it he who received the delirious cheers and applause from the frenzied, yet fickle, public this night. It was instead this otherwise unremarkable, cigar-smoking little man who shared her company.

From the moment he stepped into the carriage, Ulysses Grant knew he had made a terrible, terrible mistake. What made the error doubly painful to the lieutenant general was that after the shameless spectacle of two weeks before, he should have known better.

In late March, while the Lincolns were on a business and pleasure trip to City Point, Virginia, a review of troops was planned in the president's honor. Because her husband was already on the field discussing military matters, Mary, along with Grant's wife, Julia, was forced to ride to the ceremony over a bumpy, muddy road in a lumbering ambulance. Already enraged by the slow, undignified trip, when the notoriously jealous first lady arrived at the parade ground and discovered an attractive general's wife riding next to the president, her mind became unhinged. As the unwitting young woman rode up to pay her respects, Mary unleashed a hysterical verbal assault that left those around her speechless and the startled victim in tears.[14] When Julia Grant sought to mollify Mary, the first lady's fury fell on her.

"I suppose you think you'll get to the White House yourself, don't you?" snapped the woman.[15]

And then, to cap the incident, Mary Lincoln turned her wrath on the president. To the utter pain and embarrassment of all, the maniacal display continued without letup, the husband meekly absorbing the punishment with a look of sadness and despair, as if he had suffered such tongue-lashings a thousand times before. Not repentant or shamed in the least by the outburst, that night at supper Mary all but demanded that Grant remove the general whose wife she had attacked.[16] Understandably, and in no uncertain terms, Julia Grant later that evening informed her famous husband that she would never again under any circumstances accompany the first lady anywhere. The general understood. Indeed, had Grant not been "asked" by the president, and ordered by Mary—"I want you to drive around with us to see the illumination"—he would not be enduring the agony of a carriage ride through Washington with the shrill, temperamental first lady this very moment.[17]

Hardly had the two begun their tour of the city when revelers discovered that it was the great general inside. They sent up shouts for "Grant, Grant, Grant!" Outraged that the hosannas were not for her and her husband, Mary ordered the vehicle to stop that she might get out. When the cheers from the crowd soon turned to "Lincoln, Lincoln!" the woman was appeased somewhat and allowed the carriage to continue. To Grant's mortification, Mary's tirade was repeated again and again around the city as celebrants shouted the general's name and banners proclaimed him the nation's savior—"Glory to God, who hath to U. S. Grant-d the Victory," "God, Grant, our Country, Peace."[18]

When the carriage turned off E Street to Tenth Street and passed Ford's Theater, where Laura Keene and the cast of *Our American Cousin* were giving a "rather dull" performance to a small audience, Grant's heart sank. At the insistence of both the president and his wife, the general had accepted an invitation for himself and Julia to attend Ford's Theater on the following night.[19]

Away at war these past four years, Grant must have been shocked at the first lady's insanity. The city that had endured it for years, however, was not. From her days as a poor congressman's wife in Washington, when she had suffered slights, insults, and indifference, Mary Lincoln was now firmly on top, answering to no one, and treating all as if they were her miserable, fawning subjects. Viewing herself as royalty, Mary acted as she *thought* royalty acted. Given her shallow intellect and social shortcomings, there were many ludicrous incidents.

"Her royal majesty," some sneered in secret.[20] Even one of Lincoln's secretaries, John Nicolay, referred to Mary in private as "Her Satanic Majesty."[21]

The first lady's shrill tirades and imperial posturing were revolting to common Americans. Similarly, her tasteless extravagance and styleless costumes were equally repellent to well-bred Washington society. Pompous, pretentious, and plump, Mary Lincoln, said one disgusted editor, was a "coarse, vain, unamiable woman. . . . [a] sallow, fleshy, uninteresting woman in white laces, & wearing a band of white flowers about her forehead, like some overgrown Ophelia."[22]

"[T]he weak-minded Mrs. Lincoln," added a shocked senator after attending a White House reception, "had her bosom on exhibition and a Flower pot on her head."[23]

Wrote part-time poet and full-time government functionary Benjamin French:

> [She] moved in all the insolence of pride
> as if the world beneath her feet she trod;
> Her vulgar bearing, jewels could not hide,
> And gold's base glitter was her only god![24]

With twisted logic, Mary Lincoln felt that much of the praise showered lately on her husband was rightly hers. Little did the woman realize that the applause the president received was not because of her but in spite of her. Already pathologically jealous of her husband's attention, Mary was also acutely alert to any threat to his power. Because Grant was obviously the most popular man in the land, the people must not be allowed to forget who had placed him in his current position in the first place. No matter how repugnant his presence might be to Mary Lincoln, any acclaim Grant received must be shared by the president and first lady.

Perhaps Grant had heard of Mary's jealousy and her hatred of him. "He is a butcher and is not fit to be at the head of an army," the woman had hissed to her husband after the costly victories of the summer before. When Lincoln countered that the general was successful, Mary snapped back: "Yes, he generally manages to claim victory, but such a victory! He loses two men to the enemy's one. . . . Grant, I repeat, is an obstinate fool and a butcher."[25]

Far from enjoying what should have been a triumphal ride around Washington, U. S. Grant was fidgeting in his seat, puffing nervously on a cigar, his mind preoccupied with how he might extricate both himself and his wife from enduring a similar torture the following evening.

———

Meanwhile, throughout the glowing city, the victorious merry-making continued. Bonfires blazed brighter than before, rockets soared higher, bands blared louder, revelers shouted longer, and liquor flowed freer as toasts to Grant and victory were raised again and again. Well into the following morning, the celebration continued.

But from a window in a room at the National Hotel, one dim light burned that was not of celebration. A sad young man sat at his desk writing.

April 14 2 A. M.

Dearest Mother:

> I know you expect a letter from me, and am sure you will hardly forgive me. But indeed I have nothing to write about. Everything is dull; that is, has been till last night. (The illumination.) Everything was bright and splendid. More so in my eyes if it had been a display in a nobler cause. But so goes the world. Might makes right. . . .[26]

Already a serious tippler—like his late father—the dark-haired, handsome actor was into his cups even more now, "to drive away the blues."[27] Friends who had seen him only recently noted the change. A female acquaintance who had encountered him on Pennsylvania Avenue the previous morning and had stopped to chat mentioned to him that she was on her way to buy some candy. Misunderstanding, the gloomy young man responded:

> What do you want with more candles? The windows are full of them now, and when they are lighted I wish they would burn

> every house to the ground. I would rejoice at the sight. I guess I'm
> a little desperate this morning and, do you know, I feel like
> mounting my horse and tearing up and down the streets, waving a
> Rebel flag in each hand, till I have driven the poor animal to
> death.[28]

Then, even more surprising to the young woman, the man asked,
"Don't you study at school?"

"I answered in the affirmative, where-upon he continued: 'Then tell
me this: is <u>tyrannis</u> spelled with two <u>n's</u> or two <u>r's</u>?'"[29]

Richmond, Appomattox, Lee—the end was near. The war was all but
over. The South teetered on the brink. History was rushing ahead and
passing him. Immortality was almost beyond his reach now. No blow
had been struck. And yet, even at this late hour, he knew there was still
time. Fortunes might be retrieved from one last desperate act, one final
roll of the dice. If history had taught him nothing else, it had taught him
that one must never give up. And above all else, one must be ready to
seize the moment should it arrive.

"Something decisive & great must be done," he told himself again and
again.[30]

But time was desperately short, as he well knew, and the deed must
be done soon or not at all. With one final thought, the young man
quickly scratched out the remainder of his letter.

> I only drop you these few lines to let you know I am well, and to
> say I have not heard from you. Excuse brevity; am in haste. . . .
> With best love to you all, I am your affectionate son ever, John.[31]

CHAPTER FIVE

THE PRESIDENT AND
THE PLAYER

IT WAS A BRIGHT AND BREEZY DAY ON Charleston Harbor. The sea was stirred and choppy. Those assembled inside and along the crumbling brick walls of Fort Sumter might have seen vistas of billowing whitecaps covering the blue water of the bay had it not been for the hundreds of naval vessels.

"A brilliant gathering of boats, ships, and steamers of every sort had assembled around the battered ruin of the fort," wrote one amazed viewer. "The whole bay seemed covered with the vast flotilla."[1]

The masts alone, said another witness, "was thick as A forest of trees."[2]

Inside the shattered fort itself, gusts of wind drove swirling sand and dust into the faces of those in attendance.[3] Few were discomfited. Instead, a thrill of high expectation stirred in the hearts of everyone. Today, the symbolic end of the war would be recognized on the very spot where it had begun full four years before. Adding to this startling significance was the breathtaking news of the evening preceding—news that had arrived from Appomattox Court House.[4] For the estimated three thousand blacks and whites now seated around the Fort Sumter stage, no timing had ever been more perfect. Thus, the wind and sand and dust were small concerns to a gathering that sat this day, April 14, 1865, in the very center of the hearts and minds of all throughout the reunited nation.[5]

Although many dignitaries were on hand for the occasion—Henry Ward Beecher, William Lloyd Garrison, General Abner Doubleday— the "hero" of the event was the very same man who was forced to strike the Stars and Stripes in surrender four years earlier.[6] Like Lincoln, Robert Anderson was a Kentuckian. Also like the president, the slim, silver-haired general from that hotly contested slave state was a staunch

Union man. For the past forty-eight months now, Anderson had lived daily in the knowledge that his hand was the first of the war to lower the beloved national emblem to the enemy. Hence, the ceremony this day was especially poignant for Anderson.

Shortly before noon, following prayers and the singing of a new composition, "Victory at Last," Robert Anderson stepped to the podium.[7]

"I am here, my friends and fellow-citizens, and brother soldiers, to perform an act of duty which is dear to my heart," said the handsome, devout general. "I thank God I have lived to see this day. . . . May all the world proclaim glory to God in the highest, on earth peace and good will toward men."[8]

And then, just as the bells of the surrounding ships struck noon, Anderson grabbed the halyard and hoisted the flag to the top of the staff.[9] "The whole audience sprang to their feet," recounted one writer. "Men swung their hats and grasped each other by the hand; women and children waved their handkerchiefs." Added to the thundering ovation that followed, a deafening cannon salute erupted from the fort itself and the numerous batteries along the nearby coast. When the crowd thereupon joined in the singing of "The Star Spangled Banner," the effect was "thrilling," wrote a New York newsman. "Tears of joy filled the eyes of nearly every one present."[10]

Himself on the verge of tears as he gazed upon the same flag he was compelled to haul down in 1861, Robert Anderson had but one regret. If only the man most responsible for re-raising that flag now flapping stiffly in the breeze had been there in person to see the culmination of his efforts, the day would have been perfect.[11]

———

Beyond the window, it was a pleasant though somewhat cloudy day in Washington. By noon, a balmy southern breeze had pushed the temperature into the sixties. Among the elms and maples outside, the first leaves of spring were spreading a gauzy green over the White House grounds. The sweet scent of lilacs perfumed the air. It was, remembered one who basked in the glorious warmth, "an ideal spring day."[12]

Inside the long, high-ceilinged room, the atmosphere surrounding those seated around the circular table was as mild and relaxed as the weather out the window. Around the men, maps hung so thickly that the color of the walls was difficult to discern. The carpet leading to these maps was trodden thin, so much so that most of the pattern and dyes had long since faded.[13] Less and less would the carpet be paced by anxious men, and more rarely would the maps be scanned by nervous eyes searching for strategic roads, rivers, and rails. After 1,460 days of war, this day was the first day of peace. Although several rebel armies remained in the field, including one facing General William T. Sherman in North Carolina, and although the head of the Confederate government, Jefferson Davis, was still at large, on this day President Lincoln considered the war over.[14]

"He was more cheerful and happy than I had ever seen him," said Secretary of War Edwin Stanton, whose termination of the draft spoke louder than blaring bands and booming guns in stating that, indeed, the war was closed.[15]

"He was, in fact, transfigured," added a startled Senator James Harlan of Iowa after talking with his friend earlier. "That indescribable sadness ... had been suddenly changed for an equally indescribable expression of serene joy, as if conscious that the great purpose of his life had been achieved."[16]

And with the dawn of peace came the spirit of mercy. Unlike many whose hearts hardened in victory, Lincoln's softened. Charity and peace went hand in hand, to the president's way of thinking, and on this day especially he spoke "kindly" of those who were once his enemies.[17] Lincoln, revealed Secretary of the Navy, Gideon Welles, "was for prompt and easy terms with the rebels."[18]

One of the president's private secretaries, John Hay, agreed:

> He was particularly desirous to avoid the shedding of blood, or any vindictiveness of punishment. He gave plain notice that ... he would have none of it. "No one need expect he would take any part in hanging or killing these men, even the worst of them. Frighten them out of the country, open the gates, let down the bars, scare them off," said he, throwing up his hands as if scaring sheep. "Enough lives have been sacrificed; we must extinguish our resentments if we expect harmony and union."[19]

"Let 'em up easy," was the president's simple standing order.

Though a New Englander violently opposed to slavery, white-bearded Gideon Welles—"Father Neptune," Lincoln called him—favored swift reunification with as little pain and suffering as possible. Representing the sentiments of his father, William Seward, who was recovering from a terrible carriage accident, acting secretary of state Frederick Seward's approach to reconstruction of the South most closely mirrored the president's. Ulysses Grant led by example. Invited to attend the cabinet meeting, the general's generous terms to Robert E. Lee placed both

North and South on the road to peace with a firm footing. Of all the gathering, perhaps Edwin Stanton differed most. Hard, vindictive, unforgiving, the secretary of war had such an intense hatred of treason and secession that he felt only a severe chastisement of Confederate leaders would be sufficient to warn future generations of the terrible cost of rebellion. Ever loyal to the president, however, quieted by Lincoln's popularity and wisdom, Stanton would smother his true feelings and remain the dutiful public servant.

Turning to the subject of General Sherman, who stood facing a Confederate army under Joseph Johnston near Raleigh, North Carolina, Lincoln announced that an important event was about to occur.

"I had a dream last night; and ever since this war began I have had the same dream just before every event of great importance," the president confided to his cabinet.[20] On the night prior to a number of important battles, which he listed, Lincoln imagined that he was a passenger on some unusual vessel, sailing with great speed "towards an indefinite shore." When Grant matter-of-factly pointed out that one of the engagements named was not a victory but a defeat, Lincoln shrugged the thought aside. Good news from Sherman was bound to arrive soon, the president felt. "It must relate to Sherman, my thoughts are in that direction," insisted Lincoln, "and I know no other very important event which is likely just now to occur."[21]

In all, this cabinet meeting on Good Friday, April 14, 1865, was by far the most relaxed and pleasant of Lincoln's entire administration. Everyone was in the best of spirits. But as Ulysses Grant sat contemplating the president's words, another matter, much more mundane, preoccupied the general's mind. After the torture of the night before, and after his wife's angry arguments, Grant was on the verge of doing something he had never done before. He was about to tell his boss "No." He would not attend the theater that night as requested. As an alibi, Grant and Julia would leave by train later that day to visit their children in New Jersey.[22] After facing shot and shell during the past four years and being hailed as an American hero, U. S. Grant's toughest battle perhaps was simply trying to sidestep a night at the theater and placate an angry wife.

In a room adjoining the cabinet meeting, Mary Lincoln was sealing a note and handing it to a messenger. The message—a summons—was directed at Julia Grant.

———

"Here comes the handsomest man in Washington," said one of the young men loafing outside Ford's Theater. Their eyes, full of fun and boyish admiration, followed the graceful figure as it neared the theater. Dressed in an elegant dark suit, with a cane for effect and a black silk hat tipped slightly on his head, the dashing, dapper man referred to may indeed have had the most winning face in the nation's capital. As he approached the front of the theater with an easy swagger, an air of cool confidence surrounded the young man. But there was more to this individual than mere youth and beauty. Although he was "caressed and flattered by the best people of Washington," revealed theater owner John Ford, it didn't really seem to matter; the handsome, dark-haired dandy with the trim mustache was as devoid of pretension and arrogance as any mortal man could possibly be.[23]

It was fitting that John Wilkes Booth not only received his fan mail at a theater but chose to read his letters on the steps of a theater, for the stage was his world and the world was his stage. A career in acting seemed preordained. Junius Brutus Booth had been the most celebrated actor of his day. His Shakespearean roles had electrified English audiences. After he immigrated to America in 1821, the sons he sired in the New World were determined to follow in their revered father's footsteps. Initially, one of the older sons, Edwin, seemed most likely to carry the family torch. His moody, sensuous good looks, his rich, beautiful voice, and his professional dedication made him a favorite among American audiences. By 1860, however, Edwin's role as Booth standard-bearer was being challenged by younger brother, John, or "Wilkes," as he was known in the family.

"Edwin has more poetry, John Wilkes more passion," noted one critic. "Edwin has more melody of movement and utterance, John Wilkes more energy and animation; Edwin is more correct, John Wilkes more spontaneous; Edwin is more Shakespearean, John Wilkes more melodramatic; and in a word, Edwin is a better Hamlet, John Wilkes a better Richard III."[24]

And yet, it was not the role of the hunchbacked murderer that John Wilkes preferred, and for which he was most closely identified, but that of the wronged king, and that of the selfless slayer of tyrants. "Of all Shakespeare's characters I like 'Brutus' the best, excepting only 'Lear,'" admitted the actor.[25] Nevertheless, it was Richard, the role his late father performed with such spellbinding perfection, that shot young Booth into stardom. "John has more of the old man's power in one performance than Edwin can show in a year. He has the fire, the dash, the touch of strangeness," said one who knew the father and sons well.[26] John, added another critic simply and succinctly, had more "natural genius" than Edwin.[27]

Indeed, "genius" was the term most used by critics when describing the acting ability of John Wilkes Booth.[28] The secret to the young man's success, revealed one Washington reviewer after witnessing a performance, was "intensity." And that passion, continued the critic, stemmed "not from stage rule, but from his soul."[29]

"THE PRIDE OF THE AMERICAN PEOPLE," proclaimed a playbill at Grover's Theater in Washington during the 1863 season. "THE YOUNGEST TRAGEDIAN IN THE WORLD."[30]

Booth was also one of the most athletic performers in the world. Fellow actor William Ferguson once saw his friend leap a five-foot-tall piece of scenery as if it were a footstool, and others were stunned by how easily he mastered every sport encountered.[31] Not content with merely acting his roles, the thespian *lived* them. "When he fought, it was no stage fight," remembered a friend. On more than one occasion, mock sword fights spilled real blood.[32] After watching such a realistic, energetic performance, not a few considered Booth to be "as manly a man as God ever made."[33]

As if such athletic and artistic ability in one man were not already great enough, Booth was also endowed with an almost perfect face. Some compared him to a Greek god.[34] "His coloring was unusual," recalled actress Clara Morris. "[T]he ivory pallor of his skin, the inky blackness of his densely thick hair . . . gave a touch of mystery to his face when it fell into gravity—but there was generally a flash of white teeth behind his silky moustache, and a laugh in his eyes."[35] Booth, said another acquaintance, had "the most wonderful black eyes in the world. . . . [T]hey were like living jewels. Flames shot from them."[36] In addition to dramatic dark eyes, the actor also possessed a voice that was musical, yet strong.[37] When Booth spoke, the melody in his words lingered in one's ears long after he had left.[38]

Not surprisingly, and almost in spite of himself, Wilkes Booth became the coveted object of many a lady's heart. After any given performance, the stage door was literally jammed by scores of tittering women hoping to catch a glimpse of the actor.[39] Whether at the theater, in restaurants, or at hotels, Booth was hounded by swarms of adoring females.[40]

"Such dreamy eyes," swooned one Boston lady. "I almost lose my heart when hearing him."[41]

This almost irresistible urge to catch Booth's eye and hear his voice led many a woman into potentially disastrous indiscretions. Reveals Clara Morris:

> [T]here were many handsome, well-bred and wealthy ladies in the land, married as well as unmarried, who would have done many foolish things for one of those kisses. Booth's striking beauty was something which thousands of silly women could not withstand. His mail each day brought him letters from women weak and frivolous, who periled their happiness and their reputations by committing to paper words of love and admiration which they could not, apparently, refrain from writing. . . . These fond epistles were seldom read. He instructed his dresser to burn them. Many of them were signed with the real names of the foolish women who wrote them.
>
> The dresser one day boasted that a certain lady, moving in high social circles, had written a compromising letter to Mr. Booth. The statement was treated as an absurd lie and, to prove that he had not been boasting, the dresser displayed the letter, which he had not burned as he had been instructed to do. Mr. Booth's anger was terrible when he learned the facts, and the dresser was dismissed and ever after the signatures to those letters were torn into tiny fragments by the actor.[42]

It was just such acts of kindness and mercy as the above which endeared Wilkes to those who knew him best. He was, said E. A. Emerson, who played opposite Booth in many roles, a "kind-hearted, genial person. . . . Everybody loved him."[43]

One of those who fell hopelessly under Booth's spell was Lucy Hale, daughter of a U.S. senator from New Hampshire. The couple had set a date to be wed within a year.[44] Yet another of those smitten by the actor was Abraham Lincoln. On the night of November 9, 1864, Lincoln, Mary, and several guests watched from the presidential box as the twenty-six-year-old thespian performed at Ford's Theater.[45] So impressed was the president by Booth's performance that he applauded "rapturously," then requested an interview following the play, a request that was denied. Far from being flattered by Lincoln's attention, Booth declared later that he would "sooner have applause from a negro."[46] As anyone who knew could attest, John Wilkes Booth was a Southerner through and through.

At length, when he had finished reading his mail on the steps of the theater, Booth rose and approached Harry Ford, brother of the owner.

"What's on tonight?" asked the actor.

"*Our American Cousin,*" replied Ford, "and we are going to have a big night. The president and General Grant are going to occupy the president's box."[47]

In a moment, Booth's entire demeanor changed. A dark, faraway look now swept over his handsome face, as if he was lost in deep thought.[48]

"Booth then left the theater in a kind of hurry," remembered Ford, "as if he had made up his mind about something to be done."[49]

———

Around noon, an already agitated Julia Grant heard a loud rap on her door.

"What do you want?" asked the woman when she discovered a messenger standing outside.

> "Mrs. Lincoln sends me, Madame, with her compliments to say she will call for you at exactly eight o'clock to go to the theater." To this, I replied with some feeling (not liking either the looks of the messenger or the message, thinking the former savored of discourtesy and the latter seemed like a command), "You may return with my compliments to Mrs. Lincoln and say I regret that as General Grant and I intend leaving the city this afternoon, we will not, therefore, be here to accompany the president and Mrs. Lincoln to the theater." He hesitated a moment, then urged: "Madame, the papers announce that General Grant will be with the president tonight at the theater." I said to this: "You deliver my message to Mrs. Lincoln as I have given it to you. You may go now."[50]

Concerned that her refusal was insufficient, recalling vividly the insults and humiliations she had endured via the tongue of Mary Lincoln—"How dare you be seated until I invite you!"—Julia quickly sent a note to her husband, then dispatched three staff officers to follow it up, warning her husband that she would not go to the theater under any circumstances—they must leave the city *that very day.*[51]

Other women who received theater invitations for that night were just as desperate as Julia. The wife of the secretary of war, Ellen Stanton, a woman "as white and cold and motionless as marble whose rare smiles seemed to pain her," urgently wanted to know what Julia's course of action would be. "For unless you accept the invitation," Mrs. Stanton announced, "I shall refuse. I will not sit without you in the box with Mrs. Lincoln!"[52]

CHAPTER SIX

SIC SEMPER TYRANNIS

IF ANYONE HAD THE SLIGHTEST DOUBT that the Great Rebellion was all but over, the scene on Pennsylvania Avenue would have quickly cured them of their delusion. Cordoned by guards, more than four hundred Confederate officers captured in the recent fighting around Appomattox now trudged dejectedly through Washington.[1] As word spread, hundreds, then thousands, of curious citizens lined the street to watch. In contrast to similar processions earlier in the war, which were greeted by hoots and jeers, only silence—solemn, even sad—now surrounded these prisoners, the pathetic remnant of a once mighty army.

"It was a sorrowful sight," one federal soldier wrote. "No man with the heart of a man beating in his bosom could witness it without emotion. In their old tarnished and torn uniforms they marched erect and proud, with no semblance of bravado, and yet with no apparent sense of humiliation."[2]

"Great God!" John Booth gasped to a friend as they watched. "I have no longer a country!"[3]

As the funeral-like column passed, neither Booth nor a scattering of diehard Southern sympathizers could deny that, indeed, the death of Dixie was at hand. And yet, for a few like the actor, the end had not been reached. As long as even one Confederate army remained in the field, as long as Jefferson Davis was free, as long as liberty burned in the breast of even one man, hope lived.

When the words of Harry Ford finally sank in, a sense of urgency energized John Wilkes Booth once more. In his mind, there was still time. The fortunes of the South might yet be retrieved. But the blow must be struck, and soon. As events at Richmond and Appomattox had shown, and, most recently, as the rebel prisoners on Pennsylvania Avenue had graphically illustrated, there was not a moment to spare. Over the next several hours, Booth moved swiftly about Washington, reestablishing contact with his small circle of fellow conspirators. For months, the group had plotted and planned a great stroke to save the South in its eleventh hour—the kidnapping of Abraham Lincoln. After one feeble attempt, the plan had eventually been abandoned as impossible.[4] Now, at the midnight of the Confederacy, the original organization would be activated again to attempt an even more daring, deadly mission.

"Our cause being almost lost, something great and decisive must be done," scratched Booth in his diary.[5]

The odds were long, the chances of success slim. But, should the bid prevail, the liberty of not only Southerners but also free men everywhere might be gained. In that event, millions would enshrine his name forever.

Despite the delirium sweeping the North, victory had come at a terrible price. Elected to check the spread of slavery and sustain the Union, Abraham Lincoln had been determined to do just that, no matter the cost in blood and treasure, no matter the loss of liberty. Hardly had the war begun when the writ of habeas corpus was suspended in Booth's home state, Maryland, out of what was termed "military necessity." When members of the state legislature were arrested soon after, many felt that it was a political move, pure and simple.[6] Arbitrary arrests across the nation soon followed. While many of those jailed without due process were subversives bent on sedition, others were mere political opponents of the Lincoln administration, confined for "disloyal utterances" and for daring to raise their voices against unconstitutional excess.[7] Wrote one critic:

> Citizens were arrested by thousands, and incarcerated without warrant. Judges were torn from the bench, bruised and bleeding. Ministers of the Gospel . . . were stricken down. . . . Women were incarcerated, and subjected to insult and outrage. Doctors were ruthlessly taken from the bedside of the dying patient. . . . [L]awyers [were] arrested and consigned to the same cells with their clients whose release they were endeavoring to effect. Post offices were searched; newspapers seized and suppressed, while the editors were handcuffed and secretly hurried to prison.[8]

Among those arrested was Frank Key Howard. Imprisoned with others at the same site where his famous grandfather had penned the words to

"The Star Spangled Banner" in 1814, Howard could not escape the cruel irony of his situation.

"As I stood upon the very scene of that conflict," the prisoner wrote from Fort McHenry in Baltimore, "I could not but contrast my position with his, forty-seven years before. The flag which he had then so proudly hailed, I saw waving, at the same place, over the victims of as vulgar and brutal a despotism as modern times have witnessed."[9]

By 1865, tens of thousands of Americans had been arrested and held without trial. Even more troubling, many victims had undergone torture.[10] Despite the very real threat of imprisonment, aged Supreme Court chief justice Roger Taney, ex-president Franklin Pierce, Lincoln's former attorney general Edward Bates, and others continued to criticize, in public and private, the loss of freedoms.[11] Lincoln's crimes, ventured the *Alton Telegraph* in the president's home state of Illinois, were "black enough to damn him . . . for all time to come."[12]

"How the greatest butchers of antiquity sink into insignificance when their crimes are contrasted with those of Abraham Lincoln," echoed the editor of the *Illinois State Register* from the president's hometown of Springfield.[13]

Despite the brave efforts of those who risked life and limb to rouse their countrymen to action, most Americans remained unconcerned about constitutional matters; instead, most were simply happy that the war was being won, and, more important, most were relieved that they were not required to help win it.

As if the assault on their birthright were not already troubling enough, many thoughtful Americans viewed Lincoln's reign as by far the most damaging, embarrassing, and atrocious in the nation's history. Far from being "Honest Abe," continued the *Illinois State Register*, Lincoln the lawyer was a shrewd and cunning opportunist, "the craftiest and most dishonest politician that ever disgraced an office in America."[14] Moreover, critics argued, the "railsplitter" was crude, coarse, and comical, an unworthy successor to such stately and dignified chief executives as Jefferson, Polk, and Pierce. "He is brutal in all his habits and in all his ways," sneered one New York editor. "He is filthy. He is obscene. He is vicious."[15]

Lincoln's well-known fondness for ribald jests and "smutty" stories also caused even well-wishers to shake their heads in shame.[16] According to one White House visitor, some of the president's anecdotes were revolting in the extreme, as when a young Lincoln, after a hunting trip, climbed a tree while several of his companions lay down just below:

> Golliher shut his eyes like he was asleep. . . . I thought I would
> shit in his hat[.] Golliher was watching and when I let the load
> drop he swaped [*sic*] hats and my hat caught the whole Charge.

At the telling of this tale, recalled the visitor, Lincoln "laughed heartily."[17]

But by far the greatest source of Northern antipathy toward the president was his 1863 Emancipation Proclamation and, more recently, his hint at Negro suffrage. While other issues struck at significant though smaller segments of society, this last raised concern among even those formerly void of opinions. "The simple question to be decided," announced a Kansas editor, "is whether the white man shall maintain his status of superiority or be sunk to the level of the Negro."[18] Unless Lincoln's program was thwarted, one New York editor warned, the United States would soon become a "mongrel concern of whites, negroes, mulattoes, and sambos, . . . the most degrading and contemptible the world ever saw."[19]

It was this perception among many Americans that Lincoln was now fighting for the black man, and not the white, that caused his greatest loss of support. And of all issues, the dread specter of Negro enfranchisement and miscegenation was the spark that ignited John Wilkes Booth to contemplate bloody deeds. Standing in the crowd outside the White House on the night of April 11, when the actor heard the president suggest that in the post-war world some blacks—the soldiers, the educated, the intelligent—should have the vote, he was outraged.

"That means nigger citizenship," Booth growled to his companion, David Herold. "Now, by God, I'll put him through. . . . That is the last speech he will ever make."[20]

And thus, as Booth moved swiftly ahead with his plans on the afternoon of April 14, his goal was not simply to save the South; he was spurred on by a vision that his action would strike a blow for free white men everywhere. Time, though, was against him. When a friend encountered the normally buoyant actor on a sidewalk that day, he was surprised by Booth's somber look. "What makes you so gloomy?" the man asked. Booth sidestepped the question by simply stating that he had been hard at work all day and was about to leave Washington, never to return.[21]

After he chanced to meet another friend, a journalist, the two stepped briefly into a restaurant, where Booth began plying the man with questions:

"Suppose Lincoln was killed, what would be the result?" I replied: "Johnson would succeed," and he said, "But if he was killed?" "Then Seward," I said, and he continued, "But suppose he was killed, then what?" "Then anarchy or whatever the Constitution provides," and laughing, I said, "but, what nonsense, they don't make Brutuses now days." He shook his head and said: "No they do not." I left him without a second thought of what he had said. . . .[22]

Like his father before him, John Wilkes was named for a man who placed liberty above life. From father to son, the hatred of tyranny and the love of liberty were passed along. Also like his father, Booth craved glory and honor. Although the young actor would have gladly given his life for the cause he believed in, he was, after all, human. He much preferred to *live* for that cause and savor his success on the stage of world acclaim.[23]

———

A stir was created as the carriage rolled down Pennsylvania Avenue. Shortly, word spread along the sidewalks that Ulysses Grant was inside, and curiosity-seekers paused to point, cheer, and hopefully gain a glimpse of the famous general. Much to the relief of both Grant and Julia, in a short while they would be on a northbound train, leaving Washington and all their troubles behind.

Suddenly, a horseman galloped past the carriage. After only a short distance, the man pulled up and wheeled his mount back. As the stranger came abreast of the vehicle, he peered intently at the occupants for a moment. Julia became uneasy. "That is the very man who sat near us at lunch to-day with some others, and tried to overhear our conversation," she nudged her husband. "He was so rude . . . as to cause us to leave the dining-room. Here he is again, riding after us!"

Grant dismissed the incident as idle curiosity, but Julia was troubled by the actions of the handsome, dark-haired man.[24]

CHAPTER SEVEN

TOWARDS AN
INDEFINITE SHORE

BY LATE AFTERNOON, THE WEATHER had taken a turn for the worse. When the couple had set out earlier, the day was sunny and the thermometer was reaching for seventy. Now a cold, raw wind came whistling down the streets from the north, and the dark clouds above portended rain.[1] Nevertheless, little or nothing could dampen the joy of the carriage ride.

Following an inspection of the *Montauk*, a monitor gunboat that lay at anchor in the Potomac, and a jaunt to the "Soldier's Home," their summer retreat, Abraham and Mary Lincoln turned back toward the White House.[2] As had been the case throughout the day, the president's spirits were high. His goal had been reached. The weary load he had shouldered for the past four years was now about to be set down. And Abraham Lincoln felt relief.

"Dear husband," Mary stared at her normally morose mate, "you almost startle me, by your great cheerfulness."

"[W]ell I may feel so, Mary," the president smiled. "I consider *this day*, the war has come to a close."[3]

"I never saw him so sumpremely [*sic*] cheerful—his manner was even playful," remembered the first lady.[4]

Recalled the president's secretary, John Hay:

> The day was one of unusual enjoyment to Mr. Lincoln. . . . His mood . . . was singularly happy and tender. He talked much of the past and the future. . . . He was never simpler or gentler than on this day of unprecedented triumph; his heart overflowed with sentiments of gratitude to Heaven, which took the shape usual to generous natures, of love and kindness to all men.[5]

Indeed, nothing bore out the truth of those words more than Lincoln's actions earlier that day. Visiting with his father soon after returning from duty on General Grant's staff, Lincoln's oldest son, twenty-one-year-old Robert, handed the president a prized photograph. After carefully studying the face in the image, the face of the same man who had very nearly dashed all hopes for a reunited nation, Lincoln at last spoke. "It is a good face," the president said softly as he sat gazing at Robert E. Lee. "It is the face of a noble, brave man. I am glad the war is over at last."[6]

Lincoln's words were in sharp contrast to the cry of Radical Republicans who were even then demanding the arrest and execution of the "arch-traitor" Lee. The howl for the old Virginian's blood was second only to that of Jefferson Davis. Many Northerners would have savored the spectacle of Davis and Lee being paraded through the streets of Washington in chains. Lincoln differed. Although his motives were no doubt based in part on politics, the president preferred to simply allow Lee to return to his home in peace and watch while Davis fled the country into exile.

"Now, General," the president had earlier suggested to William T. Sherman, "I'm bound to oppose the escape of Jeff. Davis; but if you could manage to let him slip out unbeknownst-like, I guess it wouldn't hurt me much!"[7]

Additionally, Lincoln hurried to save lives. Already noted for a liberal pardon policy, with the close of war the president picked up the pace. "Well, I think this boy can do more good above ground than under ground," he said while commuting a death sentence for desertion that afternoon.[8]

Coming down the staircase at the White House just prior to the carriage ride with Mary, the president overheard a one-armed soldier declare that he would almost be willing to lose the other arm if it could but shake the hand of Abraham Lincoln. "You shall do that and it shall cost you nothing, my boy!" the tall, smiling president announced as he approached the man.[9]

"I have never been so happy in my life," Lincoln admitted to Mary. Although her husband's happiness should have been a source of comfort, the words were not entirely welcome to the superstitious woman. The last time Lincoln had uttered similar sentiments, their eleven-year-old son, Willie, had died.[10] "We must *both*, be more cheerful in the future," cautioned the husband. "[B]etween the war & the loss of our darling Willie—we have both, been very miserable."[11]

For her part, Mary Todd Lincoln was more than ready to be cheerful. Indeed, much like her husband—though for vastly different reasons—

the first lady was experiencing the happiest moments of her past four years. Because of compulsive extravagance and waste while at the White House, unbeknownst to the president Mary had accrued horrific debts. Some estimates of her arrears were as high as $70,000.[12] In one month Mary had purchased eighty-four pairs of kid gloves; already this spring she had bought over $3,000 worth of jewelry. Had her husband been rich, it might not have mattered. On a $25,000 salary, however, there was no way the president's income could keep pace with the frenetic spending spree.[13] Living in mortal dread that her husband would not be re-elected to a second term and that her staggering debt would be revealed, Mary was overcome with joy to learn that she had four more years to hide her secret.

Coupled with anxiety arising from spending woes was Mary's concern for her husband's safety. Already involved in séances and the occult, the fretful woman was understandably worried about the possibility of assassination.[14] Thus, when the president shared with his wife a recent dream, the woman was horrified. Revealed Lincoln:

> There seemed to be a deathlike stillness about me. Then I heard subdued sobs, as if a number of people were weeping. I thought I left my bed and wandered downstairs. . . . I arrived in the East Room, which I entered. There I met with a sickening surprise. Before me was a catafalque, on which rested a corpse in funeral vestments. Around it were stationed soldiers who were acting as guards and there was a throng of people, some gazing mournfully upon the corpse, whose face was covered, others weeping piti-fully.
>
> "Who is dead in the White House?" I demanded of one of the soldiers.
>
> "The President," was his answer. "He was killed by an assassin!"[15]

"That is horrid!" gasped Mary. "I wish you had not told it. I am glad I don't believe in dreams, or I would be in terror from this time forth."[16]

But Mary Lincoln *did* believe in dreams, and the woman *was* in terror for her husband's life, though her fear of assassination had begun long before he told of his dream. The day he was nominated for the presidency in 1860, the death threats began. Upon reaching Washington, the letters arrived with as much regularity as the tides on the Potomac. Some were crude drawings of Lincoln being hanged; others were notes with daggers and red ink spattered about.[17]

"The first one or two made me a little uncomfortable," Lincoln confessed, "but I came at length to look for a regular instalment of this kind of correspondence in every week's mail."[18]

"God damn your god damned old Hellfire god damned soul to hell," foamed one semi-literate citizen. "[G]od damn you and your god damned family's god damned hellfired god damned soul to hell."[19]

"[H]is mail was infested with brutal and vulgar menace," revealed presidential secretary John Hay, "mostly anonymous, the proper expression of vile and cowardly minds. . . . [and] the vaporings of village bullies."[20] Not every threat was cowardly and anonymous. Risking imprisonment and mobs, a handful of intrepid Democratic politicians and editors dared criticize Lincoln and his Republican "tyranny."

At the 1864 Democratic Convention in Chicago, S. S. Cox took the podium. "For less offences than Mr. Lincoln had been guilty of," yelled the delegate to the crowd, "the English people had chopped off the head of the first Charles."[21] The editor of the *Lacrosse Daily Democrat* in Wisconsin went further and openly hoped that some assassin would stab the president in the heart, "for the public good."[22]

"The people will soon rise," assured one orator, "and if they cannot put Lincoln out of power by the ballot, they will by bullet. [Loud cheers.]"[23]

With such bloodthirsty diatribes as these, Mary's concern for her husband's safety seemed justified. Although Lincoln, too, was at times understandably despondent and felt he would indeed fall by the hand of an assassin, his approach generally tended toward the fatalistic.

> I have received a great many threatening letters but I have no fear of them. . . . I determined when I first came here I should not be dying all the while. . . . [I can] die only once; to go continually in fear would be to die over and over. . . . If anyone is willing to give his life for mine, there is nothing that can prevent it. . . . If I wore a shirt of mail, and kept myself surrounded by a body-guard, it would be all the same. There are a thousand ways of getting at a man if it is desired that he should be killed.[24]

In sum, concluded the president, "I do not believe it is my fate to die in this way."[25]

And indeed, with each hour that passed, it appeared as if Lincoln's beliefs were accurate and Mary's fears unfounded. With the conflict all but over and with peace sweeping the continent, the likelihood of harm now coming to the president seemed increasingly remote. The couple had survived the war, and now plans for a peaceful future could finally crowd out thoughts of violence and death.

"Mary," said Lincoln as the carriage cut into the raw wind and steered toward the White House, "we have had a hard time of it since we came to Washington; but the war is over, and with God's blessing we may hope for four years of peace and happiness, and then we will go back to Illinois, and pass the rest of our lives in quiet."[26]

As the couple rode through the streets, bundled against the chill, they passed motley piles of debris from the celebration of the night preceding—crumpled bunting, smoldering bonfires, whiskey bottles. Another, though smaller, victory demonstration was planned for that evening. But the president and first lady would not be among the revelers. They would instead go to Ford's Theater, as planned, and begin living that quiet life Lincoln spoke so fondly of.

Meanwhile, those with a genuine interest in the survival of the nation could only give thanks to the Almighty above that the chief executive had been spared to lead the country for another four years. A cold shudder must have swept over anyone who looked down the line of succession to see which two men would follow Lincoln in the event of his death. Even a glance would quickly reveal that neither man, politically or physically, was capable of assuming the post.

CHAPTER EIGHT

THE CLOWN AND
THE SPHINX

Prior to the 4th of March last, he stood high in the esteem of the
people of the United States. He was borne into the Vice Presidential chair by the votes of more than two millions of freemen; and
up to the day on which he took the oath of office, not a word of
reproach had ever been uttered against his character. But on the
occasion of his inauguration. . . . [w]e all felt mortified and
ashamed.[1]

SO WROTE A REPORTER FOR THE *Chicago Tribune.* As the journalist indicated, Andrew Johnson should have been one of the happiest
men in Washington. Instead, the former tailor was perhaps the most
forlorn and neglected person in America. Johnson's accession to the second seat of power in the nation also proved his downfall. As Lincoln's
running mate in the 1864 election, the former senator and governor of
Tennessee was summoned to attend the inauguration on March 4 and
take the oath of office. Despite illness, Johnson acquiesced.[2]

That morning, as he and outgoing vice president Hannibal Hamlin
stood about in the Capitol waiting for the ceremonies to commence, the
son of illiterate tavern servants was overcome by anxiety. Adding to
Johnson's nervousness was a bad hangover from the night before.[3] According to one account:

Johnson asked Mr. Hamlin if he had any liquor in the room,
stating that he was sick and nervous. . . . Brandy being indicated,
a bottle was brought by one of the pages. It was opened, a tum-
bler provided, and Mr. Johnson poured it about two-thirds full. . .
. When near 12 . . . Mr. Hamlin rose, moved to the door near
which the Sergeant-at-Arms stood, and suggested to Mr. Johnson
to come also. The latter got up and . . . said, "Excuse me a mo-

ment," and walked hastily back to where the bottle was deposited. Mr. Hamlin saw him . . . pour as large a quantity as before into the glass and drink it down like water. They then went into the Senate Chamber.[4]

"All eyes were turned to the main entrance, where, precisely on the stroke of twelve, appeared Andrew Johnson . . . arm in arm with Hannibal Hamlin," newsman Noah Brooks recorded. "They took seats together on the dais of the presiding officer, and Hamlin made a brief and sensible speech, and Andrew Johnson, whose face was extraordinarily red, was presented to take the oath."[5]

In addition to a joint session of Congress and the black-robed Supreme Court, numerous foreign ministers "in full court costume" were also on hand to witness the high American event. In the gallery above, Mary Lincoln and other gaily dressed wives looked down with approval.[6] That soon changed. Instead of taking the oath then and there, Johnson plunged straightaway into his acceptance speech.[7]

"I'm a-going' for to tell you—here today; yes, I'm a-going' for to tell you all, that I'm a plebian!" Johnson announced proudly. "I glory in it; I am a plebian! The people—yes, the people of the United States have made me what I am; and I am a-going' to tell you here today—yes, today, in this place—that the people are everything."[8]

Mumbling one moment, shouting the next, the unsteady speaker paused from time to time as if waiting for the "amens" and "huzzas" that typically accompanied a backwoods stump speech. Although allotted only seven minutes to speak, the wobbling, hiccupping vice president soon became oblivious to time. With a ludicrous mix of maudlin sentimentality and drunken defiance, Johnson's nearly incoherent harangue only occasionally touched upon something sensible, such as his "fel' cissons" and the "conshusun."[9] At one point, Johnson turned and began addressing the cabinet members by name. When he reached Gideon Welles, the vice president paused. "What is the name of the Secretary of the Navy?" he asked someone seated nearby. When told, Johnson continued as if nothing had happened.[10]

As the silence deepened and the drunken display continued, Republican senators and congressmen, noted a New York reporter, "began to hang their heads."[11]

"The study of the faces below was interesting," wrote Noah Brooks:

> Seward was as bland and serene as a summer day; Stanton appeared to be petrified; Welles's face was usually void of any ex-

pression; Speed sat with his eyes closed; Dennison was red and
white by turns. Among the Union Senators, Henry Wilson's face
was flushed; Sumner wore a saturnine and sarcastic smile; and
most of the others turned and twisted in their Senatorial chairs as
if in long-drawn agony. Of the Supreme Bench, Judge Nelson
only was apparently moved, his lower jaw being dropped clean
down in blank horror.[12]

Meanwhile, as Republicans reddened with anger and turned sideways
in their seats to avoid the spectacle, Democrats openly laughed.[13]

I'ze born in Tenssee an I'm a tailor an a plebean (hic). We're all
plebeans, an I propose to sustain (hic) the constitution, an I propose to support the constitution (hic) fer all plebeans.[14]

Soon, a smattering of shocked voices from the gallery became a disgusted roar: "He is drunk." "He is crazy—this is disgraceful." "What a
shame!" "Tell him to stop and save the country further disgrace." Finally,
wrote one relieved senator, Johnson was "suppressed."[15] Following some
tugging and no little verbal persuasion, the reeling vice president ceased
his rambling and was given the oath.

"When Johnson had repeated inaudibly the oath of office, his hand
on the Book," revealed Noah Brooks, "he turned and took the Bible in
his hand, and, facing the audience, said, with a loud, theatrical voice
and gesture, 'I kiss this Book in the face of my nation of the United
States.'"[16]

No sooner had the Tennessean acted out this ridiculous scene than
he tried to launch into another rodomontade.[17] As if the disgrace were
not already great enough, one final insult awaited. Because he was the
incoming vice president, it was Johnson's duty to swear in newly elected
senators. As the eight men approached the bar, in a melodramatic manner the drunk extended the Bible that each might touch it and bow their
heads in reverence. Before the bewildered men could be administered
the oath, Johnson simply waved them away. At length, the clerk of the
Senate recalled the senators, and all were duly sworn in.[18]

Humiliated more than any person present—with the possible exception of his wife—Abraham Lincoln "bowed his head with a look of
unutterable despondency."[19] Although deeply shamed by the incident,
Lincoln later defended his political partner against charges of chronic
drunkenness. The howl from other quarters, though, was swift and unforgiving.[20]

"[N]ot even in the presence of the United States Senate, in the presence of the American people, in the presence of the world, with millions regarding his action and awaiting his utterance, could [he] summon enough of energy and self-denial to remain sober until the brief ordeal was over," raged the *New York Daily News*. Johnson's vulgar display and his "beastly state of intoxication," concluded the editor, "would shame a rowdy at the threshold of a tavern."[21]

Certainly, sobriety was never a test for membership in the United States Senate. Shameless scenes of drunkenness had occurred with regularity.[22] But never before had the eyes of the world been so riveted on the American Capitol, and never before had such a "drunken clown" been but a heart beat from the Presidency. "[T]o know that this de-bauched demagogue is only withheld by the thread of a single life from the presidential chair, is appalling to every American," reflected one of the many horrified citizens.[23]

Because of the threat an intemperate rustic posed should he ever reach the White House, one former Lincoln opponent now openly admitted that the president's life had become "precious" to all Americans, friend or foe. Millions felt similarly.[24]

Now, holed up in his hotel room at the Kirkwood House, the nation's great victory celebration had all but passed Andrew Johnson by. Had the vice president contracted some virulent disease, he could not have been more of a pariah. After a meteoric rise to the top from the lowest begin-nings imaginable—lower even than Lincoln—Andrew Johnson saw all his decades of hard work and struggle erased in one embarrassing mo-ment. A grimace on his lips even in the best of times, the former tailor now had a scowl on his face as solid as stone.

———

William Henry Seward was one of the most powerful men in the fed-eral government, second only to Lincoln and perhaps Edwin Stanton. His three-story town home across from the White House on Lafayette Park was symbolic of his important station. Seward reportedly once boasted that if he rang a bell on his right hand, a man from Illinois would be arrested; a ring on his left, and a man in New York would be dead.[25] Whether he said such words or not didn't matter; people be-lieved he said them, and, more important, many people believed he had used such dread power.

And yet, the small, slight secretary of state could be at once both cour-teous and gracious. He was even wont to bow politely to everyone he met, including strangers.[26] Seward was also in the habit of hiding his true

emotions. One need not look to the secretary's face for a display of happiness or joy, of sorrow or sadness, or, as was the case during the Johnson
incident, of shock or anger. Although he no doubt was churning inside
during the ordeal, observers noted that Seward remained as inscrutable
as the Sphinx.

"Cool, thoughtful, sagacious, conciliatory and by no means ultra," as
one reporter characterized the New Yorker, Seward was as instrumen-
tal in the Union war effort and was as much responsible for its successful conclusion as any man in America. And yet, as with Johnson, it was
the secretary's fate to be denied his supreme moment of triumph.[27]

On the afternoon of April 5, while the rest of Washington was in a state
of euphoria following the fall of Richmond, Seward, his son Frederick,
and his teenage daughter, Fanny, along with a friend of the girl's,
climbed into a carriage for a jaunt around the jubilant city. Somewhere
along the way, a door refused to close properly, and the coachman was
ordered to stop and fix it. As the man stepped to the ground, the horses
took fright and bolted down the street. In an attempt to grab the trailing reins, Frederick leaped to the street. His effort unsuccessful, the
father also tried. Unfortunately, Seward's heel caught on the carriage,
and he fell hard to the ground. Although the runaway team was finally
halted by a daring soldier and the terrified young ladies were rescued,
the secretary of state was borne away unconscious with a broken arm,
a dislocated shoulder, lacerations on his face, and his jaw broken on
both sides.[28]

Rushing from her New York home when she heard the awful news,
Frances Seward reached her husband's side two days after the accident.
"I found him a great sufferer," said the woman, "so bruised and swollen
was his face that it was difficult to trace any resemblance to his features
as they were."[29]

Delirious much of the time, by April 14, Seward was finally able to sit
up, take solid food, and receive a few well-wishers.[30] One who visited his
bedside was the grim secretary of war. Like the patient, Edwin Stanton
was not known for displays of sympathy or kindness during his years in
Washington. Hence, his sudden appearance touched Seward deeply.

"God bless you, Stanton," whispered the injured man through his
pain. "You have made me cry for the first time in my life, I believe."[31]

Like Andrew Johnson, though for vastly different reasons, William
Henry Seward was now confined to his room. Unlike Johnson, Seward
was in the thoughts of many throughout the nation as they prayed for
his speedy recovery and return to office. "I have trembled with apprehension lest he & Mr. Lincoln might both be taken from us," wrote one

anxious man who realized that, after Johnson, Seward was next in line for the presidency.[32]

On the morning of this day, April 14, Seward had endured a shave like never before. Not only was he forced to lie flat on his back, but the barber had to steer carefully around the steel brace used to hold his jaw in place.[33]

CHAPTER NINE

ONE BOLD MAN

LIKE THE MAN ON A MISSION, impervious to his surroundings, John Wilkes Booth moved swiftly through the crowded streets of Washington. As the afternoon deepened, every minute now mattered. The life or death of his beloved Southern Confederacy rested on his shoulders and his alone. Stopping here on the Avenue to whisper with an intimate, hurrying there to an apartment where last-minute details were sorted with those privy to the plot, the handsome, worried actor was an economy of grace and motion.[1] Few who knew and saw Booth on this chilling afternoon of April 14 paid much mind to his frenzied actions.

"In looking back over the occurrences," recalled Ford's doorkeeper, John Buckingham, "I can see that Booth must have been under great stress of excitement, although his actions did not seem to me at the time to be at all strange. He was naturally a nervous man and restless in his movements."[2]

Some of Booth's actions were unusual, however, even for him. Wrote one Washington reporter:

> At about 4 P. M., he . . . made his appearance at the counter [of the National Hotel]. . . . and with a nervous air called for a sheet of paper and an envelope. He was about to write when the thought seemed to strike him that someone around him might overlook his letter, and, approaching the door of the office, he requested admittance. On reaching the inside of the office, he immediately commenced his letter. He had written but a few words when he said earnestly, "Merrick, is this year 1864 or 65?" "You are surely joking, John," replied Mr. M., "you certainly know what year it is." "Sincerely, I am not," he rejoined, and on being told, resumed writing. It was then that Mr. M. noticed something troubled and agitated in Booth's appearance, which

was entirely at variance with his usual quiet deportment. Sealing
the letter, he placed it in his pocket and left the hotel.[3]

But generally, Booth's actions seemed normal to those who met him,
and his words were in keeping with his character. Young Joseph
Hazelton, a program boy, saw Booth as he stepped from Ford's Theater:

> He smiled at me, patted my shoulder, and said, "Well, Joseph, have
> you made up your mind yet to become an actor?"
>
> "I don't know, Mr. Booth," I answered. "Perhaps I wouldn't do
> for the stage."
>
> He held me at arm's length and studied my face for some mo-
> ments.
>
> "Try it, Joseph, when the time comes," he said. "Try it. You have
> the face of an actor—the features of the young Byron. The world
> will think better of the actor some day and treat him more liber-
> ally."
>
> He seemed about to say something more, but turned away, then
> looked back. "We have been good friends, Joseph, eh?" he said.
> "Well, try to think well of me. And this will buy a stick of candy."
>
> He handed me a ten-cent "shinplaster" and walked quickly
> down Tenth Street.[4]

Once again, Booth pursued his frantic course, not sure where the trail
would ultimately lead. As he well knew, it was a desperate, perhaps mad,
bid to retrieve what may already have been irretrievable. And yet, it had
to be done—John Wilkes Booth and his associates had to follow their
fate to the end. If all did their duty and did not flinch, before another
sun set the U.S. government would be decapitated, leaving only anarchy and confusion in its place.[5]

——

Shortly after 5 P.M., in a "cold, rainy twilight," a happy but tired
Abraham and Mary Lincoln returned from their carriage ride around
the town. As they entered the White House grounds, the president spied
two old friends from Illinois leaving, and, though weary, he shouted for
the men to return and visit. Once in the reception room of the mansion,
the revitalized president shared passages from a favorite book of humor.
Several times during the visit, Lincoln was called to supper, but each
time, though he promised to obey, he found new cause to linger and
laugh with his friends. At length, the husband received a sharp summons from Mary to come to the table "at once." Sadly, the president
arose and bid his friends adieu.[6]

"I'd much rather swap stories than eat," he said regretfully.[7]

At dinner, the exhausted president insisted that the couple keep their commitment to attend Ford's Theater that night. To remain at home, Lincoln knew, would give him no rest, for he would be compelled to receive guests all evening, as usual.[8] Despite a headache and a less than promising night at the theater, Mary agreed.

Throughout the day, and despite all reason and logic, Mary Lincoln had assumed not only that General and Julia Grant would attend the theater with her and the president, but that both would be flattered to do so. When Grant nervously informed Lincoln that he and his wife were leaving for New Jersey on the afternoon train, Mary quickly sought replacements. One by one, others understandably begged off.[9] Finally, the invitation was accepted by Major Henry Rathbone and his fiancée, Clara Harris, daughter of a U.S. senator from New York—young and respectable, but obscure, and hardly glittering company for a victorious two-term president and his lady.

Despite the opprobrium of religious zealots and their condemnation of the theater as the devil's workshop, the Lincolns were the first presidential couple to make the stage steady fare. While Mary preferred opera, her husband most enjoyed Shakespeare and simple comedy.[10] "With the fearful strain that is upon me night and day," Lincoln earlier admitted, "if I did not laugh occasionally I should die."[11]

Not a few who had seen the president at stage-side over the years noted the irony. "I remember thinking," wrote the poet Walt Whitman, "how funny it was that . . . the leading actor in the greatest and stormiest drama known to real history's stage . . . should sit there and be so completely interested and absorb'd in those human jack-straws, moving about with their silly little gestures, foreign spirit, and flatulent text."[12]

The fare this night, *Our American Cousin,* promised little more than light distraction. Although wildly popular in its heyday years back, the farce was now one of the most well-worn and threadbare comedies still standing, and many Americans knew the lines by heart.[13]

He stood impatiently at the bar, rapping the counter to gain the waiter's attention. "Brandy, brandy, brandy!" he cried, as if it were his lifeblood. A short time before, at 7 P.M., as Booth came down from his room at the National Hotel, those in the lobby noted aloud the unnatural paleness in a face already naturally pale. Waving the comments aside, the actor tossed his keys on the front desk.

"Are you going to the theater tonight?" he asked the clerk, George Bunker. "You should. There will be some fine acting there tonight."[14]

"Fine acting" first needed steady nerves. Well might the actor's courage flag and need fortifying. For years, Booth had made an anonymous contribution to the cause of the Confederacy, confined to the shadows as a spy and courier. Now, only hours away from stepping onto the lighted political stage, not only cast in the most spectacular and dramatic role of his career, but starring in the singular event of the war, Booth threw down the hot liquid to steel a shaky hand. Most men would have blanched at the thought. Most men would have crumbled like chalk at the dread specter ahead, and no amount of brandy would have sufficed. But John Wilkes Booth, ninth child of the world-renowned Junius Brutus Booth, was quite unlike most men.

From the day he first became conscious of his own existence, the boy felt he was destined to accomplish some great feat. "Fame, I must have fame!" the child once proclaimed in a fit of exuberance. And to gain the glory and immortality he craved, young Wilkes confided to a friend that he was willing to do almost anything, even pull down the Colossus of Rhodes.

During the secession crisis of 1859–1860, the fire of Southern nationalism burned white-hot in Booth's breast. As was the case with other border slave states, the close proximity of Maryland to the abolitionist element in the North created a violent reaction greater perhaps than in her sister slave states farther south. But, as was also the case in other border states, never had families been more divided. Although Wilkes was an outspoken advocate of Southern rights, other siblings in the Booth family were either neutral or, as was the case with older brother Edwin, strongly pro-Union.

In 1859, when the startling news from Harpers Ferry arrived, John Booth was performing in Richmond. Begging officers to take him along, the actor joined a Virginia militia unit as it rushed north to quell the attempted slave revolt led by the abolitionist John Brown.[15] Although diametrically opposed to Brown's beliefs, Booth nevertheless came to understand and respect the grit and determination of the white-bearded Kansan. After his capture and trial, Booth was also present at Brown's execution. More than his life, it was John Brown's death that stirred the actor's greatest admiration. The image of the "rugged old hero" standing alone on the scaffold unflinchingly, moments from eternity, without a friend or rescuer in sight, was one that Booth never forgot.[16]

"He was a brave old man," the actor mused sadly. "[H]is heart must have broken when he felt himself deserted."[17]

One of the lessons Booth learned from Brown was that even in utter defeat, millions of souls might still be stirred; that one bold man with a will of iron and a heart of steel could make a difference and change the course of history. "John Brown was a man inspired, the grandest character of this century!" praised Booth.[18]

When the Southern states seceded and war began, Wilkes Booth, like many other Maryland hot-bloods, bristled to join the army and fight Yankee aggression. "So help me holy God!" he confessed to his sister, Asia, "my soul, life, and possessions are for the South."[19]

A mother's dread for the safety of her favorite child stopped young Wilkes in his tracks. Promising the woman he worshiped that he would not risk his life in the army, Booth instead continued performing, then entered the Confederate Secret Service, carrying dispatches and medicine across the lines.[20]

"He was a man so single in his devotion, so unswerving in his principles, that he would yield everything for the cause he espoused," reminisced Asia. "I knew that if he had twenty lives they would be sacrificed freely for that cause."[21]

Even twenty lives lost could not retrieve the fortunes of the South, however. As the embittered young actor watched his cause go down in defeat, he realized that all the blood of others had been for naught, and that his own pathetically small contribution amounted to nothing. As the pain deepened, the stress on the Booth family increased. Arguments, especially between Wilkes and Edwin, became heated.[22]

"That he was insane on that one point no one who knew him well can doubt," Edwin later wrote. "When I told him I had voted for Lincoln's re-election, he expressed deep regret, and declared his belief that Lincoln would be made King of America, and this, I believe, drove him beyond the limits of reason."[23]

Like millions more, young Booth felt that the country's woes, North and South, were caused by Abraham Lincoln. The war, the annulment of the Constitution, the imprisonment of free men everywhere, these were the handiwork of "King Ape the First." Explained Booth earlier:

> This man's appearance, his pedigree, his coarse low jokes and anecdotes, his vulgar similes, and his frivolity, are a disgrace to the seat he holds. Other brains rule the country. *He* is made the tool of the North, to crush out, or try to crush out slavery, by robbery, rapine, slaughter and bought armies. He is walking in the footprints of old John Brown, but . . . [not] fit to stand with [him].[24]

As the end approached, in his desperation Booth sought ways to alter the outcome. At length, with a small group of conspirators, the actor hatched several plans to kidnap Lincoln and hurry him south to Richmond. Although at least one legitimate attempt was made to capture the president, nothing further came of it, and the plot was finally dropped.[25] But then the terrible news of April arrived. Already desperate to aid the dying Confederacy, the actor now became frantic.

"If Wilkes Booth was mad," wrote Asia, "his mind lost its balance between the fall of Richmond and the terrific end."[26]

From that point, if the opportunity availed, assassination became the actor's ambition. Booth's best chance came during the second inauguration, as Lincoln stood starkly on the portico of the Capitol. While the event offered a "splendid" opportunity to kill the president, it, like the abduction schemes, passed without note.

And then, on this day, April 14, when it was learned that Lincoln would attend Ford's Theater in the evening, all the elements in Booth's nature came together at once—his hatred of tyranny, his love of liberty, his passion for the stage, his sense of drama, his lifelong quest to become immortal. He would slay a tyrant, become an American hero, and if the rest did their duty, liberty might again reign supreme throughout the land, North and South.

November, 1864

Dearest beloved Mother,

I have always endeavored to be a good and dutiful son, And even now would wish to die sooner than give you pain. But dearest Mother, though I owe you all, <u>there</u> is another duty. A noble duty for the sake of liberty and humanity due to my Country—For, four years I have. . . . cursed my wilful idleness, And begun to deem myself a coward and to despise my own existence. For four years I have borne it mostly for your dear sake, And for you alone, have I also struggled to fight off this desire to begone, but it seems that uncontrollable fate, moving me for its ends, takes me from you, dear Mother, to do what work I can for a poor oppressed downtrodden people. . . . I have not a <u>single selfish motive</u> to spur me on to this, nothing save the sacred duty I feel I <u>owe the cause I love</u>, the cause of the South. The cause of liberty & justice. So should I meet the <u>worst</u>, dear Mother, in struggling for such holy rights, I can say "Gods' will be done" and bless him in my heart for not permitting me, to outlive, our dear bought freedom. . . .

So then dearest, <u>dearest</u> Mother, <u>forgive</u> and pray for me. I feel that I am right in the justness of my cause. . . . Come weal or woe, with never ending love and devotion you will find me ever your affectionate son

John.[27]

Portsmouth, New Hampshire; mob attacking newspaper
after the fall of Richmond

*Courtesy Military Order of the Loyal Legion, Massachusetts Commandery
and the U.S. Army Military History Institute*

Mary Todd Lincoln

Courtesy Library of Congress

Andrew Johnson

*Courtesy Military Order of the Loyal
Legion, Massachusetts Commandery and
the U.S. Army Military History Institute*

William Henry Seward

*Courtesy Military Order of the Loyal
Legion, Massachusetts Commandery and
the U.S. Army Military History Institute*

John Wilkes Booth

*Courtesy Harvard Theatre Collection,
Houghton Library, Harvard College
Library*

Last photographic portrait of Abraham Lincoln, April 10, 1865

Courtesy Library of Congress

Laura Keene

Harry Ransom Humanities Research Center, University of Texas

Ford's Theater with guards posted at entrance and
funerary crape draped from windows

Courtesy Library of Congress

John Hay

Courtesy Brown University Library

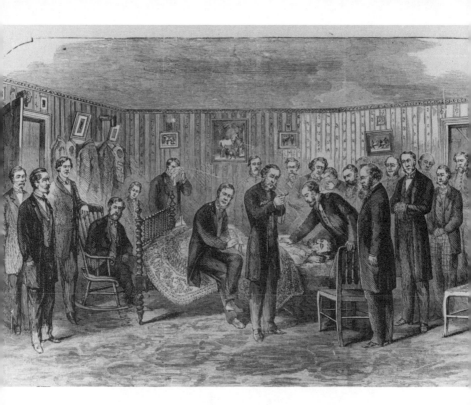

Death of Abraham Lincoln

Courtesy Military Order of the Loyal Legion, Massachusetts Commandery and the U.S. Army Military History Institute

"Assassin Sympathizers": Federal Soldiers under Arrest

Courtesy Bill Turner Collection

Jacob Haas (*left*) and John Wilkes Booth (*right*)

James F. Haas collection at U.S. Army Military History Institute

Funeral ceremony, San Francisco

Courtesy the Bancroft Library, University of California, Berkeley

Edwin Booth

Courtesy Library of Congress

The Old Capitol Prison

Courtesy Military Order of the Loyal Legion, Massachusetts Commandery
and the U.S. Army Military History Institute

(Opposite, top:) Boston Corbett

Courtesy Library of Congress

(Opposite, bottom:) Secretary of War Edwin Stanton

Courtesy Library of Congress

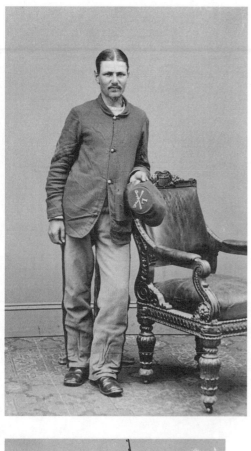

Lincoln's funeral procession in New York City, April 25, 1865

Courtesy Library of Congress

Lewis Powell, Washington Navy Yard,
D.C., April 1865

Courtesy Library of Congress

Execution of the conspirators, July 7, 1865

Courtesy Library of Congress

PART TWO

CHAPTER TEN

A NIGHT TO REMEMBER

SHORTLY BEFORE 8:30 P.M., AS drizzle began to fall softly on Washington, a carriage halted outside the imposing facade of Ford's Theater. Despite the weather, a large number of curious spectators were on hand, some to see the president, but most to view for themselves the man so much had been made of recently, Ulysses Grant. When the four occupants finally stepped down and into the light, however, the short, bearded general and his trademark cigar were nowhere to be seen. Nevertheless, the presidential party, in the "gayest spirits," was imposing enough, and Lincoln himself was more than sufficient to write home about.[1]

"I had never been so near to him before, and I remember remarking how much taller he appeared than I had previously imagined," wrote a man who boarded just across the street from Ford's. "He was engaged in animated conversation as he passed me, and I was struck with the peculiar softness of his voice. . . . As he passed through the crowd he towered a full head and shoulders above them."[2]

When the Lincolns and their guests—"young and lovely" Clara Harris and her handsome twenty-seven-year-old fiancé, Major Henry Rathbone—walked under the arched passageways and into the glittering building, they could hear the performance already in progress.[3] Young Joseph Hazelton awaited them awkwardly in the lobby:

> I was in doubt whether to hand Mr. Lincoln a program or not, but he smiled at me, nodded, said something in an aside to Mrs. Lincoln, and held out his hand. I stepped forward and gave each member of the party one of my printed sheets. Mrs. Lincoln looked at me, too, and gave me a smile. They passed within the theater, and I followed them immediately.[4]

Though some of the sheen had worn off after nearly two years of operation, Ford's Theater still had the look and feel of a building that had opened but yesterday. Ford's, praised a local newsman, was a "magnificent theater. . . . it had few superiors, even in our largest cities."[5] And seldom, if ever, in its brief existence had the playhouse been better represented than on this night. It had a seating capacity of over fifteen hundred, and most of the cane-bottomed chairs below and the wooden benches above were filled with a brilliantly attired audience.[6] Although not present this night, Walt Whitman knew and spoke with those who were:

> [T]he theater was crowded, many ladies in rich and gay costumes, officers in their uniforms, many well known citizens, young folks, the usual clusters of gas-lights, the usual magnetism of so many people, cheerful, with perfumes, music of violins and flutes— (and over all, and saturating all, that vast vague wonder, *Victory*, the Nation's Victory, the triumph of the Union, filling the air, the thought, the sense, with exhilaration more than all perfumes.)[7]

As intoxicating as the atmosphere was, most were distracted. Despite the notices in the newspapers, Lincoln and Grant, the two great architects of that heady victory, had not arrived at Ford's as announced. While many watched the doors, or looked anxiously to the box above the stage on the right, the minutes slipped by, the play continued, and it seemed that the crowning moment of the evening might be denied. By now, many in the audience were also cursing their gullibility. Aware of the demand, sharpers had bought out most of the theater's tickets earlier in the day and resold them to the avid public at twice, even thrice, the original price.[8] Nevertheless, the performance continued. Stale and hackneyed though the play may have been, it was already a historic evening of sorts. Laura Keene, the English actress who had made the comedy popular with hundreds of performances, would step down after tonight's curtain fell, never again to star as Florence Trenchard.[9] As a result, the auspicious occasion and the festive mood energized otherwise second-rate actors.

"We were giving [a] good performance that night," recalled Harry Hawk, whose rustic but witty American character, Asa Trenchard, poked holes in British society. "Both the company and the audience seemed in the best of humor."[10]

Then, around 8:30, Hawk glanced over the footlights to the dress circle on the second tier above. There was a stir toward the back, followed by a smattering of shouts and applause. Hawk continues:

> John Matthews, who was playing Lord Dundreary, had just asked
> one of his foolish conundrums, and then added in a listening
> way: "They don't see it." The people had turned and were rising
> in their seats. . . . I put in a "gag" line and said, "No, but they see
> him." The house laughed and cheered.[11]

As awareness of Lincoln's entry raced forward like a wave, the ovation
became a "storm of applause." The crowd stamped their feet, rose from
their seats, and waved hats and handkerchiefs, their cheers and shouts
soon rising to a deafening roar.[12] At his stand, the conductor, William
Withers, tapped his baton and the orchestra struck up "Hail to the
Chief."[13]

As the presidential party made their way slowly along the back wall
toward the box, those in the rear could see Lincoln clearly. "I had the
best opportunity to distinctly see the full face of the president, as the light
shone directly upon him," wrote Dr. Charles Leale. "After he had
walked a few feet he stopped for a moment, looked upon the people he
loved and acknowledged their salutations with a solemn bow. His face
was perfectly stoical, his deep set eyes gave him a pathetically sad appearance."[14]

If the president seemed largely indifferent to the tumultuous welcome, his wife Mary was not. "Mrs. Lincoln smiled very happily in ac-
knowledgment of the loyal greeting," continued Dr. Leale. "[She]
gracefully curtsied several times and seemed to be overflowing with
good cheer and thankfulness."[15]

Just as Lincoln reached the door to the private box, he paused again
and bowed formally to the people. The jubilant crowd would not be
denied, however, and the cheers and stamping of feet continued even
when the president entered and was lost to sight. At length, Lincoln
came to the rail of the box, bowed one final time, then presented to the
audience what it had demanded in the first place—one of his "never-
to-be-forgotten smiles." Only moments before, Daniel Beekman had
thought Lincoln the homeliest man he had ever seen. When the president smiled, though, "it so changed his countenance, that . . . it was the
most heavenly smile I ever saw on a man's face."[16]

"It was positively beautiful," added John Downing, Jr., as he looked up
at the happy president. "I never saw one like it on any other human face.
It seemed to come from the heart."[17]

At length, Lincoln finally took his seat, and after one last shout, the
satisfied crowd returned to theirs as well.[18] A buzz of electric excitement
continued to fill the theater as most expected to see General Grant enter
at any moment.

———

Despite encroaching bad weather, the carnival atmosphere was also in progress beyond the walls of Ford's. Even after a weeklong celebration, the denizens of the nation's capital seemed unwilling, after forty-eight months of war, to return to normal. While crowds along Pennsylvania Avenue drank, shouted, and shot off roman candles and blue lights, a huge torchlight procession of blacksmiths, carriage-makers, painters, and clerks from the Federal Arsenal, with bands blaring, marched toward Secretary Stanton's home to celebrate the flag-raising at Fort Sumter. Even after so many other parades, the spectacle of nearly fifteen hundred men carrying signs and banners was, said a viewer, "brilliant and imposing."[19]

A short distance away, outside Grover's Theater, a large transparency, glowing eerily in the mist, spelled out the epitaph of the Confederacy:

> April, 1861, the cradle.
> April, 1865, the grave.[20]

Inside Grover's, the colorful extravaganza *Aladdin, or the Wonderful Lamp* was in progress. Seated near the front with his tutor, and with his eyes riveted on the stage, was Mary and Abraham Lincoln's youngest son.[21] Ill-mannered and utterly spoiled by his indulgent parents, Tad Lincoln was both a trial and a terror to White House visitors and staff, bossing and insulting any and all who crossed his path. To gain his father's attention, the angry twelve-year-old once kicked over a game of checkers that the president and a friend were enjoying. In any other American family, such behavior would have earned the child a half-dozen strokes well laid on. Much to the shock of the checker opponent, the father merely smiled. The boy was on his best behavior tonight, though, and the colorful performance totally engaged his attention.

Not everyone in Washington was in the theaters or reveling on the streets. The Lincolns' oldest son, Robert, was spending an uneventful but restful evening at the White House, studying Spanish and joking with his friend, presidential secretary John Hay. The two also chatted at length about Robert's impressions of General Lee.

Just across from the White House, at the three-story home in Lafayette Park, all was still and subdued. While the president was receiving thunderous ovations and Edwin Stanton, who had visited the secretary of state earlier that evening, was delivering a torchlit speech to thousands, William Seward was dozing in bed with his jaw wired shut, the glory of victory passing him by. In the darkened room nearby, a nurse, Sergeant

George Robinson, watched over his patient. Elsewhere throughout the home, Seward's wife, Frances, his teenage daughter, Fanny, his grown sons, Frederick and Augustus, and a black servant, William Bell, ensured that the house remained quiet and that the secretary of state rested peacefully.[22]

In his room at the Kirkwood House, Andrew Johnson was also spending a quiet night. After his ludicrous display at the second inaugural, rumors were rife that the vice president had taken the pledge and joined the "Temperance Society." It would take much, much more than a vow of sobriety to rehabilitate Johnson's tarnished career, however, and five weeks after the fiasco, he remained, as before, the scandal of the civilized world.[23]

———

Florence: Why, what on earth has a dog's tail to do with a cart?

Lord Dundreary: When it moves about, you know. A horse makes a cart move, so does a dog make his tail move.

Florence: Oh, I see what you mean—when it's a wagon.

Lord Dundreary: Well, a wagon and a cart are the same thing, ain't they?

Florence: They are not the same. . . . there's a very great difference.

Lord Dundreary: Now I've got another. Why does a dog waggle his tail?

Florence: Upon my word, I never inquired.

Lord Dundreary: Because the tail can't waggle the dog. Ha! Ha!

Such a simpleminded script performed by a second-rate crew could hardly be expected to entertain a sophisticated audience that already knew the punch lines. And yet, with each stale pun and each corny joke, the jubilant crowd responded with round upon round of undeserved shouts and laughter.

"It was one laugh from the time the curtain went up until it fell," said Harry Hawk.[24] As the actor well knew, much of the evening's stellar success was due to its star, Laura Keene, who seemed bent on giving the greatest performance of her life.[25] Another reason for the nearly nonstop hilarity was the willingness of the cast to extemporize. Encouraged by the shouts and cheers of the crowd, the players tailored their lines to suit the moment. When humorous asides were directed at the president, Lincoln "laughed heartily" and often stood to take a bow.[26] In one scene, Harry Hawk and a young lady were chatting when the sensitive girl suggested that the two move elsewhere to avoid a chilly draft.[27] Hawk rose to the bait.

"You are mistaken," announced the actor aloud. "The draft has already been stopped by order of the President."[28]

A great shout erupted, followed by thunderous applause; those who had lived in mortal dread of conscription now laughed "long and loud" in nervous relief.[29] Many other humorous allusions were aimed at Lincoln and the war, with each drawing bursts of laughter. One line, which earned the least response and seemed ill-timed, came when Harry Hawk's character had just won the prize in an archery contest.

"[I] hadn't done nothing," said Hawk, "all it required was a steady hand [and] a clear eye — to pull the trigger & the mark was hit." As the actor finished, he stared straight up at Lincoln. The strained silence was soon broken, however, by another silly pun and renewed waves of laughter.[30]

"[T]hey laugh and shout at every clownish witticism," wrote Julia Shepard, who, like many others, seemed more amused by those around her than by the farce on stage.[31] Unfortunately for Julia and almost everyone else in the theater, little could be seen of Abraham Lincoln. Because of the position of his red rocking chair and the angle of the flag-draped box, only occasionally did the president's famous profile appear. Several times Lincoln laid his arms along the railing, resting his chin absentmindedly as he searched the crowd for familiar faces.[32] At other times, with his elbow planted on the arm of the chair and his head resting on his hand, Lincoln was visible, "looking utterly worn out and apparently in deep thought."[33] Feeling a chill, the president once arose to slip on his overcoat.[34]

But if few could actually see Lincoln, all felt his presence. "[W]e know that 'Father Abraham' is there," mused Julia Shepard, "like a father watching what interests his children, for their pleasure rather than his own."[35]

One man who did have a reasonably good view of the president was army physician Charles Taft. "[F]rom where I sat, almost under the box, I could see him plainly," recalled Taft. "Mrs. Lincoln rested her hand on his knee much of the time, and often called his attention to some humorous situation on the stage. She seemed to take great pleasure in witnessing his enjoyment. . . . [He] never applauded with his hands, but he laughed heartily on occasion."[36]

Annie Wright, wife of the stage manager, was also below the box:

> Several times I glanced up at the Presidential party from my seat below and each time Mr. Lincoln was leaning on the rail of the box, his thin, long face resting between his great hands as his elbows rested on the rail. Each time I glanced upward it seemed that Mr. Lincoln had his gaze focused upon me, and I unconsciously recalled that I had been told that I resembled Mrs. Lincoln and became embarrassed. However, I couldn't resist the temptation to look up at the President.[37]

For all practical purposes, Clara Harris and Henry Rathbone might just as well have been the furniture they sat on. In love, on their best behavior, the couple remained all but invisible. Little noticed, the guests spoke when spoken to, laughed on cue, and strained every nerve to look relaxed and happy. At around 9:30, Clara Harris's attention was distracted from the play to the rear of the box by the sound of the door opening. Glancing back, she saw in the darkness a man quickly scan the position of those in the box, then slip quietly back and close the door. The young woman dismissed the incident as little more than the rude behavior of a curious gawker.[38] Indeed, across the theater opposite the presidential box, numerous people paraded to the dress circle to stand and stare in hopes of gaining a glimpse of Grant and Lincoln.[39]

One man in particular aroused some passing attention. He seemed more intent on elbowing his way slowly along the wall toward the president's box than on watching the comedy. At times, his handsome face appeared "restless, excited"; at other times it was perfectly relaxed. He was heard humming a tune.[40] In the cast that night, Jeannie Gourlay was startled when she glanced over the footlights and saw him above. "He looked so pale," she said, "I scarcely knew him."[41]

———

At the home on Lafayette Park, a doorbell rang.

CHAPTER ELEVEN

TERROR ON
LAFAYETTE PARK

As a servant in the Seward home, William Bell's job was to ensure that the household ran smoothly. Among his many duties was screening those who called on the secretary of state. Since the carriage accident earlier in the month, the parade of friends, well-wishers, and the merely curious had been heavy, but with few exceptions most were turned away. Although he was slowly recovering, the secretary was in no condition to receive so many guests. Thus, when the young black man answered the doorbell at around ten this misty night, he knew that his response would be simple: The secretary was unavailable.

As the slightly built servant opened the door, he saw standing before him a tall, broad-shouldered figure in a light overcoat. A wide-brimmed hat was pulled low on the man's head, partly covering his eyes. In a pleasant voice, the visitor explained that the small package he held was medicine from Seward's doctor. The handsome stranger then added that he had orders to deliver the medicine and instructions to Seward in person. When Bell announced that this was out of the question, that he would deliver the packet himself, the huge man glared down at him. "Must go up—must see him—must see him," the stranger mumbled as he stepped around Bell. Fearing that the persistent intruder might indeed be an important messenger, the little servant decided that he would at the very least escort him to Frederick Seward or George Robinson. Dashing ahead, the worried employee led the way up the stairs.[1]

"I noticed that his step was very heavy," recalled Bell. "I asked him not to walk so heavy [as] he would disturb Mr. Seward."[2]

Clad only in his underwear, Frederick Seward stood waiting on the landing at the top of the stairs.[3] When the man again insisted that he must deliver the packet in person, the son was firm: "You cannot see him; you cannot see him. I am the proprietor here; I am Mr. Seward's son; if you cannot leave it with me, you cannot leave it at all."[4]

"Wouldn't you think that person would be more quiet coming up to a sickroom?" Sgt. George Robinson whispered to Fanny Seward upon hearing the commotion beyond the bedroom.[5] The secretary's teenage daughter had joined Robinson to watch over her father until an older brother, Augustus, could relieve her at eleven. The gas jets had been turned down, and her father was resting quietly. With the noise outside, however, the injured man grew restless, then finally opened his eyes.[6]

"I . . . hastened to the door, opened it a very little & found Fred standing close by it, facing me," remembered Fanny. " On his right hand, also close by the door, stood a very tall young man."

As Fanny peered through the crack, she could see that Fred was barring the way into the bedroom. Fanny also perceived that her slightly built brother was extremely nervous. When the huge stranger gruffly asked the girl if her father was asleep, Fred quickly pulled the door shut.[7]

At length, Fred Seward's determination seemed to pay off, and the unwelcome visitor turned to follow William Bell back down the stairs. After only a few steps, the servant again asked the man to walk more quietly. Hardly had Bell spoken when the stranger turned and sprang swiftly back toward the door. Pulling out a large pistol, the man brought it crashing down on Fred Seward's head. Again and again he clubbed the stunned victim.[8]

"[B]y the time I had turned clear round Mr. Fred. had fallen and thrown up his hands," said the horrified servant. Racing down the stairs, Bell threw open the front door screaming "Murder . . . Murder."[9]

"What can be the matter?" Fanny asked George Robinson. Hearing several sharp and heavy blows, the girl first thought that a rat was loose upstairs, remembering one such incident in the past.[10] Himself concerned, Robinson arose and opened the door. Hardly had the nurse glanced out and spotted Fred Seward covered in blood than he was himself knocked violently to the floor.[11]

Bursting through the door, the attacker now ran into the bedroom and leaped on the helpless form of the secretary of state. Drawing a large knife, the man began slashing at the head and neck of his victim. The blade felt cold, thought Seward in his semi-conscious state, as did the liquid running down his face, which, in his delirium, he mistook for rain. When the injured man rolled from the bed and onto the floor, the savage blows continued.[12]

"I ran beside him to the bed, imploring him to stop," remembered the horrified daughter. "I remember pacing the room back and forth from end to end screaming."[13]

Regaining his feet, George Robinson lunged at the attacker and wrestled with him on the bed. But the nurse was no match for the muscular assailant, and the brutal assault continued. Awakened by the screams and shouts, Augustus Seward rushed into the room, half-dressed and half-asleep.

> I saw what appeared to be two men, one trying to hold the other; my first impression was that my father had become delirious, and that the nurse was trying to hold him. I went up and took hold of him, but saw at once from his size and struggle it was not my father; it then struck me that the nurse had become delirious and was striking about the room at random; knowing the delicate state of my father's health I endeavored to shove the person I had hold of to the door, with the intention of putting him out of the room.[14]

"For God's sake," Robinson yelled frantically to Augustus as he fought for his life, "let go of me and take the knife out of his hand and cut his throat."[15]

Realizing his mistake, Augustus now turned to help Robinson fight the attacker. "While I was pushing him he struck me five or six times over the head with whatever he had in his left hand," said the son. "During this time he repeated . . . 'I am mad, I am mad.'"[16]

At last, the two men wrestled the assailant out of the bedroom and over Fred Seward's body. Bounding down the stairs, the man stabbed a messenger who was on his way up to help.[17] Bursting out the door, the stranger finally fled into the night.

Inside the home, all was bedlam. Screams and shouts echoed from top to bottom. On the second floor, the hallway was awash in blood. When an ailing Frances Seward finally reached the scene, she was confused by what greeted her. "What is the matter?" cried the mother to her hysterical daughter.

"I remember running back, crying out 'Where's Father,' seeing the empty bed," wrote Fanny. "At the side I found what I thought at first was a pile of bed clothes—then knew that it was my father. . . . [He] seemed to me almost dead. But he spoke to me, telling me to send for surgeons & to ask to have a guard placed around the house."[18]

CHAPTER TWELVE

THE LAST BULLET

JAMES FERGUSON WAS UPSET. The saloonkeeper had not paid good money for two tickets to simply sit all evening and watch a threadbare play that he knew almost by heart—he had come expressly to see with his own eyes the hero of the day, Ulysses S. Grant. Thus, while his female companion watched the play, for most of the night Ferguson's restless eyes peered through opera glasses at the box directly across the theater from where he sat. Throughout the evening, the anxious bartender kept his vigil, supposing that Grant—known for his aversion of the limelight—would try to slip in unnoticed. But the hours had passed, and it was now the third act of a three-act play and still no victorious general.[1]

Nevertheless, as Ferguson stared across the way, his eyes had more than enough to feast on. There was, of course, the gaunt, bearded president, at times happy, at times pensive, and at other times, as now, leaning forward with his chin on his arms as they rested along the rail, absentmindedly watching the crowd and the orchestra below. There was also the first lady, animated as always, laughing at every silly pun and jest, looking innocently to her husband to see if he was enjoying the humor as well. Increasingly, though, Ferguson's attention was focused on the peculiar and perplexing actions of John Wilkes Booth.

Even at that distance in the darkened theater, Ferguson recognized his friend and frequent patron. That very afternoon, the two had chatted about a swift horse Booth had just acquired.[2] Hence, when the bartender saw the dapper young man leaning casually against the wall near the presidential box, there was no doubt in Ferguson's mind who it was. But why an actor of Booth's caliber and dramatic nature would lounge about the theater in his spare time watching a shallow, inane comedy was puzzling to Ferguson. Even more mystifying was why John Wilkes

Booth, whose Southern sympathies were well known to everyone, would attend what amounted to a grand Union bacchanal here at Ford's.

Across from Ferguson, in the rows of seats near the president's box, others also began to feel that if Booth's actions were not bizarre, they were, at the very least, annoying. Some did not recognize the famous actor and were disgusted at being forced to move during the height of the play that an inconsiderate boor might creep ever nearer the box.[3]

George Todd, a navy surgeon, was sitting nearby:

> I heard a man say "there's Booth," and I turned my head to look at him. He was still walking very slow, and was near the box door, when he stopped, took a card from his pocket, wrote something on it, and gave it to the usher, who took it to the box. In a minute the door was opened and he walked in.[4]

"I had supposed him to be an ill-bred fellow who was pressing a selfish matter on the President in his hours of leisure," recalled another man who watched Booth close the box door behind him.[5]

Across the way, James Ferguson now aimed his glasses more intently than ever on the box, wondering who it was within that Booth was on such intimate terms with.[6] On stage, one of the play's more humorous exchanges was taking place, and the audience watched keenly as Harry Hawk delivered his hackneyed lines:

> Mrs. Mountchessington: I am aware, Mr. Trenchard, you are not used to the manners of good society, and that, alone, will excuse the impertinence of which you have been guilty. (Exit.)
>
> Asa: Don't know the manners of good society, eh? Well, I guess I know enough to turn you inside out, old gal—you sockdologizing old man trap!

While waves of laughter echoed through the theater, James Ferguson kept his eyes focused on Abraham Lincoln. Although the president joined the crowd with a "hearty laugh," his interest seemingly lay more with someone below.[7] With his right elbow resting on the arm of his chair and his chin lying carelessly on his hand, Lincoln parted one of the flags nearby that he might see better.[8]

As the laughter subsided, Harry Hawk stood on the stage alone with his back to the presidential box.[9] Before he could utter another word, a sharp crack sounded. As the noise echoed throughout the otherwise silent theater, many thought that it was part of the play. But, just as quickly, most knew that it was not.

"I stood with astonishment, thinking why they should fire off a pistol in 'Our American Cousin,'" said William Withers.[10] Around the startled conductor, the musicians glanced at one another in bewilderment.

"I at first thought it was accidentally discharged by some soldier or drunken man & looked around but saw no stir or excitement," recalled army clerk Charles Sanford.[11]

In that startling split second, some imagined that a piece of scenery had fallen. Many arose with a fright, but quickly resumed their seats when others in the rear cried "Sit down!" "Down in front!"[12]

Of all those in the theater, James Ferguson was probably the first to comprehend. Still training his glasses on the box, waiting for Booth's appearance, "I saw the flash of the pistol right back in the box," said Ferguson. As he watched in confusion, the saloonkeeper saw the president instinctively throw up his right arm and Mary Lincoln reach for her husband's neck. Then, in the swirl of blue smoke, Ferguson perceived a man standing behind them with both hands raised.[13]

Like everyone else, Helen Du Barry and her husband were startled by the sudden sound:

> We. . . . look up at the President's Box merely because that was the direction of the sound and supposing it to be part of the performance we all looked again on the stage—when a man suddenly vaulted over the railing of the box . . . then leaped to the stage—striking on his heels & falling backward but recovered himself in an instant. . . . We first thought it was a crazy man—when he jumped on to the stage we all jumped to our feet & stood spell bound.[14]

"I have done it. . . . The South is avenged!" yelled the pale, wild-eyed actor as he turned to face the audience. And then, raising a large, glittering knife above his head, in a sharp, clear voice, he shouted "*Sic Semper Tyrannis!*" Glaring at the crowd for a moment, the assassin then turned and stalked dramatically across the stage, still trailing a bit of torn flag on his spur.[15]

James Ferguson stared down at the stage, stunned and speechless:

> As he came across the stage facing me he looked me right up in the face and it alarmed me & I pulled the lady who was with me down behind the bannister. I looked right down at him & he stopped as he said "I have done it," and shook the knife.[16]

Frozen in his tracks, now sharing the stage with a knife-wielding maniac, Harry Hawk was perhaps the loneliest man in the world. "I recognized Booth as he . . . came toward me, waving his knife," said the terrified actor. "I did not know what he had done or what his purpose might be. I did simply what any other man would have done—I ran."[17]

As Booth disappeared dramatically behind the scenery, Joseph Stewart instinctively leaped from his seat near the stage and gave chase. Three times the 6'6" pursuer cried "Stop that man!" but all were too stunned to comprehend. At length, Stewart could only watch helplessly as Booth made his escape down the alley on a horse that had been waiting at the door.[18]

In the theater itself, had the audience been statues made of marble, they could not have been more quiet. "[T]here was a stillness of death," wrote one of those in the crowd.[19]

"[I]t seemed as though we were all chained to our seats, perfectly thunderstruck," said William Elmendorf.[20]

Behind the scenes, Laura Keene stood stunned and staring as if in a trance.[21] In the ten or so seconds between the shot and the disappearance of Booth, an eternity seemingly elapsed. And then, from the box above came a piercing, blood-curdling shriek that seemed to echo throughout the hall forever.[22] "Mrs. Lincoln was calling to the audience," remembered one of the actors. "I did not know what she was trying to say, nor did the audience. She exclaimed incoherently rather than spoke in words."[23]

While Mary stood shrieking, waving her arms back and forth, from the stunned crowd there was only utter silence.[24] When Clara Harris soon appeared at the box rail and screamed out the horrible words, the spectators were at last jolted from their shock. Suddenly, there came the realization. As one, the startled audience members jumped to their feet, and a roar of screams and shouts erupted. While a few people rushed to the lobby, scores climbed over the footlights and poured onto the stage.[25]

What Laura Keene saw from her vantage on the stage defied description. From a joyous, festive theater full of happy people, the audience was transformed within a matter of seconds into a wounded beast. "The crowd went mad," remembered Captain Oliver Gatch. "A wilder sight I never saw in battle, even."[26]

The tumult, thought another horrified viewer, was as terrible as Dante's description of hell.[27] So explosive was the horrible sound that it was heard far beyond Ford's. Across the street at the boarding house of William Petersen, George and Huldah Francis were just preparing for sleep. Recalled the husband:

> Huldah had got into bed. I had changed my clothes and shut off the gas, when we heard such a terrible scream that we ran to the front window to see what it could mean. We saw a great commotion — in the Theater — some running in, others hurrying out, and

we could hear hundreds of voices mingled in the greatest confusion. Presently we heard some one say "the President is shot,"
when I hurried on my clothes and ran out, across the street.[28]

Inside Ford's, the howl was deafening as the shouting, seething mass
ran aimlessly about the building.[29]

"[A]nd then the deluge," wrote Walt Whitman. "[P]eople burst
through chairs and railings and break them up—there is inextricable
confusion and terror—women faint—quiet, feeble persons fall and are
trampled on—many cries of agony are heard—the broad stage fills to
suffocation with a dense and motley crowd like some horrible carnival."[30]

Stunned like everyone else, Laura Keene was first to regain her senses.
Although the other actors and actresses ran wildly in circles, Laura, said
an amazed observer, was "the only cool person there."[31] From the foot
lamps, the actress raised her hands and at last quieted the crowd. Expecting that the woman was about to announce that the assassin had been
captured, most of the frenzied people stood in breathless anticipation.

"For God's sake have presence of mind and keep your place, and all
will be well," pleaded the actress.[32]

Surprised that no mention was made of a capture, the angry mob was
more furious than ever. "Kill him! Shoot him! Lynch him!" came the
bloodthirsty roar. "Burn the theater," cried others.[33] Again, in her familiar clipped tones, Laura begged the audience to stay calm. Her words
were quickly drowned by a ferocious roar of "Booth! Booth! Booth!"[34]

"There will never be anything like it on earth," witness Helen Truman
wrote. "The shouts, groans, curses, smashing of seats, screams of women,
shuffling of feet and cries of terror created a pandemonium that . . .
through all the ages will stand out in my memory as the hell of hells."[35]

"Strong men wept, and cursed, and tore the seats in the impotence of
their anger," Edwin Bates admitted.[36]

As the riot grew in intensity, and as many made a mad, terror-stricken
stampede toward the exits, others suddenly realized that they were in
mortal danger.[37] Said one young lady:

> The crowd behind us surged forward, and before long our party
> found itself wedged against the orchestra. As I was somewhat
> shorter in stature than those about me, my mother, fearing for my
> safety, undertook to lift me up on the stage; but the pressure from
> behind became so great that she was unable to extricate me. I
> might have been injured . . . but for the effort of a somewhat
> muscular man near by who . . . picked me up and literally threw

me over the footlights upon the stage. I could not see the President, but I could see Mrs. Lincoln and hear her shrieks and moans, as well as the loud and turbulent cries of people all over the house. . . . [S]ome well-intentioned person, seeing me in the surging mass and anxious to put me out of harm's way, lifted me into the box immediately beneath the one in which the stricken President lay.[38]

In the box above, Clara Harris was frantically screaming for both doctors and water. While Laura Keene raced for the latter, several surgeons rushed to assist. Because Booth had barred the door, for a moment the only way into the tiny room was up. "I leaped upon the stage, and was instantly lifted by a dozen pair of hands up to the President's box," said army surgeon Charles Taft.[39] Another physician was "literally dragged" up and over the rail.[40]

When the door to the box was finally forced, twenty-three-year-old Charles Leale was one of the first to enter. What the doctor saw was staggering. Both Clara Harris and Mary Lincoln were hysterical, with the latter punctuating incoherent words with hair-raising shrieks. And everywhere—on the floor, on the walls, on the furniture. . . .[41] Almost all the blood came from Major Rathbone, who had been stabbed while attempting to check the assassin's escape. Dr. Leale:

> He came to me holding his wounded arm in the hand of the other, beseeching me to attend to his wound. I placed my hand under his chin, looking into his eyes and an almost instantaneous glance revealed the fact that he was in no immediate danger, and in response to appeals from Mrs. Lincoln and Miss Harris . . . I went immediately to their assistance. . . . I grasped Mrs. Lincoln's outstretched hand in mine, while she cried piteously to me, "Oh, Doctor! Is he dead? Can he recover? Will you take charge of him? Do what you can for him. Oh, my dear husband!" . . . I soothingly answered that we would do all that possibly could be done. While approaching the President, I asked a gentleman, who was at the door of the box, to procure some brandy and another to get some water.
>
> As I looked at the President, he appeared to be dead. His eyes were closed and his head had fallen forward. He was being held upright in his chair by Mrs. Lincoln, who was weeping bitterly. . . . I placed my finger on the President's . . . pulse but could perceive no movement of the artery. . . . [W]e removed him from his chair to a recumbent position on the floor of the box, and as I held his

head and shoulders while doing this, my hand came in contact
with a clot of blood near his left shoulder. Remembering the
flashing dagger in the hand of the assassin, and the severely
bleeding wound of Major Rathbone, I supposed the President
had been stabbed, and while kneeling on the floor over his head,
with my eyes continuously watching the President's face, I asked a
gentleman to cut the coat and shirt open from the neck to the
elbow.[42]

Another who entered the increasingly crowded box was William Kent:

[P]oor Mrs. Lincoln was crying, in, oh such tones, "My husband, my husband—my God, my God—he is dead." I tried to
quiet her, but to no purpose. . . . Laura Keen [sic] . . . came
rushing into the box with a glass of water in her hand, and took
our poor President's head, from which the brains were then
slowly oozing, into her lap, and tried to force some water into
his mouth. . . . Our noble President lying there, his clothes
hanging from his body in shreds—motionless and insensible—
his precious life-blood staining the dress of the actress, and poor
Mrs. Lincoln wild with grief.[43]

Amid the noise and horror, the small group of surgeons worked feverishly to save the life of the president. Dr. Leale:

I lifted his eyelids and saw evidence of a brain injury. I quickly
passed the separated fingers of both hands through his blood
matted hair to examine his head, and I discovered his mortal
wound. The President had been shot in the back part of the head,
behind the left ear. I easily removed the obstructing clot of blood
from the wound, and this relieved the pressure on the brain.[44]

Although the pulse was faint, with the aid of artificial respiration Leale
soon started the president's heart beating again. Convinced that something more must be done if Lincoln was to live, the doctor then administered mouth-to-mouth resuscitation:

I leaned forcibly forward directly over his body, thorax to thorax,
face to face, and several times drew in a long breath, then forcibly
breathed directly into his mouth and nostrils. . . . After waiting a
moment I placed my ear over his thorax and found the action of
the heart improving. I . . . then watched for a short time, and saw
that the President could continue independent breathing and
that instant death would not occur.[45]

As the terrible life-and-death drama unfolded above, pandemonium reigned below. A hideous jumble of emotions—anger, fear, horror, sadness, hatred, confusion—all found an outlet in the most primitive way possible—violence. Chairs were smashed to splinters. Rails were ripped off and broken. Curtains were torn to shreds. Like a herd of terrified beasts, the crowd ran back and forth, crushing the smaller and weaker, heedless in their agony of the damage they wrought. Several times there were cries to clear the theater, including one from the former mayor of Washington. Although many at first obeyed the summons and moved toward the exits, a new explosion of grief, horror, and "white-faced wrath" swept the building, and again the mob surged toward the stage. In an attempt to control the situation, the theater management rung down the curtain, then dimmed and brightened the lights alternately, all to no effect.[46]

Then, when the madness was reaching its peak, hundreds of blue-clad soldiers burst through the doors. "They storm the house," wrote Walt Whitman, "through all the tiers, especially the upper ones, inflamed with fury, literally charging the audience with fix'd bayonets, muskets and pistols, shouting <u>Clear out! clear out! you sons of bitches</u>. . . ."[47] As the terrified and cowed rioters stampeded through the exits, order was quickly restored at Ford's.

In the box, however, chaos continued. When Mary Lincoln was not screaming hysterically, she sat stunned and silent, her arms uplifted for unseen help. To one side, Henry Rathbone stood holding his arm, pale as chalk from blood loss. Laura Keene, though a rock of sanity, was perhaps the most horrifying sight of all. With Lincoln's head in her lap, the actress sat mute, her dress, hands, and arms bathed in blood. Even the woman's face was streaked in red where her fingers had passed.[48]

Herself drenched in the blood of the man she hoped to marry, Clara Harris sat as if in a trance. "Poor Mrs. Lincoln," Clara remembered, "would look at me in horror and scream, 'Oh! My husband's blood,— My dear husband's blood.'"[49]

Finally, fifteen minutes or so after the bullet was fired, someone suggested that the president be carried back to the White House. Others protested, insisting that such a move would prove fatal. "It seemed, for a few moments, as if we were all paralyzed," Oliver Gatch admitted. "Then my brother broke the silence in our little group around the dying President."[50] Gatch's brother, Charles, quietly proposed that they carefully remove Lincoln to a nearby home, "or some more fitting place," rather than allow an American president to die in a mere opera house.[51] To this the others agreed.

"Accordingly," Oliver continued, "we two—my brother and I—with the aid of a couple of others, raised the President from the floor and carried him through the passage-way."[52]

Because of the dense, roiling crowds still on the stairway and in the lobby, a young lieutenant drew his sword and led the way. Although those in front were willing to give way and allow the procession to pass, the officer was forced to threaten and actually use the flat of his sword on others who were pressing forward.[53] Following behind the long column as it wound down from the dress circle, men and women sobbed like children. Horribly, on the stairs and across the lobby, a trail of blood clearly marked the president's passage. "It seemed sacrilege to step near," admitted a weeping Julia Shepard.[54]

Outside, when the head of the procession halted momentarily in the street to force back the crowd, it seemed to saloonkeeper Peter Taltavull as if those in charge were contemplating laying Lincoln in his establishment, the Star, only one door down from Ford's. "Don't bring him in here," shouted the bartender. "It shouldn't be said that the President of the United States died in a saloon."[55]

Spotting a young man beckoning from across the street, the column worked slowly through the crowd toward the three-story brick boarding house of William Petersen. A short distance behind and nearly lost in the jam was the diminutive first lady. "Mrs. Lincoln was frantic," recalled Charles Sanford. "She passed right by my side. . . . She was throwing her hands and arms about in terrible agony."[56]

As Lincoln was carried toward the home, the huge crowd watched in stunned disbelief. "There was silence as we passed," Oliver Gatch remembered. "No one spoke. As we moved slowly across the street, the only sound that was heard above the sobbing of the people was the hoofbeats of cavalry already approaching."[57]

Standing in the misty glare of the gas lamps and torches, most onlookers were horrified by the surreal scene. Although someone had thrown an overcoat across his body, Lincoln was bare from the waist up. "Pale as death," some described his face; others thought the president looked "very black." Also, as careful as those who carried him were, with every step a trail of blood and brains was left on the street.[58] To the rear, the silence was shattered by the shrill screams of Mary Lincoln. Cut off by a dense, almost impenetrable human wall, the woman cried out again and again, "Where is my husband? Where is my husband?"[59]

CHAPTER THIRTEEN

MURDER IN THE STREETS

ALTHOUGH WORD OF THE HORRIBLE DEED spread from Ford's moments after it occurred, it was only when the soldiers forced the frenzied, wild-eyed audience from the building that the city felt the full, chilling impact of the assassination.

"Every man and woman in the theater rushed forth to tell it," wrote a chronicler. "Some ran wildly down the streets, exclaiming to those they met, 'The President is killed! The President is killed!' One rushed into a ball-room, and told it to the dancers; another bursting into a room where a party of eminent public men were playing cards, cried, 'Lincoln is shot!'"[1]

As one vast crowd surged up Pennsylvania Avenue shouting "The President is shot!" they were met by another sweeping down the street yelling "Secretary Seward has been assassinated in bed."[2]

At Grover's Theater, while the stage crew was behind the scenes preparing for the fourth and final act of *Alladin*, a special interlude of the new patriotic song "When Sherman Marched Down to the Sea" had just ended. The applause was so great that the young songstress was about to offer an encore.[3] In addition to the Lincolns' little boy, Tad, young James Tanner, a soldier who had lost both legs in the war, was also in the audience. Despite boarding just across the street from Ford's, Tanner had made what was for him a long and difficult trip to the theater on Pennsylvania Avenue.[4] Just as the singer was about to begin, from the rear of the theater the door burst open with a crash.

"[A] man rushed in from the lobby and cried out, 'President Lincoln has been shot in Ford's Theater,'" Tanner recalled. "There was great confusion at once, most of the audience rising to their feet. Some one cried out, 'It is a ruse of the pickpockets; look out.' Almost everybody resumed his seat."[5] The lone exception was Tad Lincoln. When the boy heard the horrible words, he became hysterical.[6] Tearing from his seat and his tutor "like a wounded deer," the child ran screaming out the door.[7]

Staring in startled silence like everyone else, Helen Moss, sister-in-law to Grover's manager, watched as her brother stepped to the front of the lighted stage:

> [He] said he had a very grave announcement to make. 'President Lincoln has been shot in his private box at Ford's Theater. The audience will be dismissed at once, and the house closed, but every one must move out quietly and orderly without excitement." The house was as still as death. One could have heard a pin drop. The dazed look upon the faces! All were simply stunned for a moment. Then they rose as one body, and passed out toward the door, as if in the presence of death. The doors were thrown open. Sentries were stationed there with crossed bayonets to prevent a rush, but there was no rush. We stood in awe and watched the people file out one by one.[8]

As a friend helped him along, James Tanner turned up the avenue on his artificial legs, determined to learn more.[9]

With the speed of sound, the horrible word from Ford's raced over the city. In every street and alley, terrified people ran through the night screaming the awful news: "My God! The President is killed at Ford's Theater!" "Lincoln has been murdered!" "The President has been shot!"

Edwin Stanton had already locked his door for the night. Following a full day and the speech just delivered to the torchlight crowd, the secretary of war was weary and preparing for bed.[10] When he was nearly undressed, Stanton heard his wife Ellen go downstairs to answer the door. A moment later, she yelled out in a terror-filled voice, "Mr. Seward is murdered."

Startled by the words, the secretary soon collected himself. "Humbug!" he shouted back. "I left him only an hour ago."

Stomping down the stairs half-dressed—determined to deal with the prankster in person—Stanton found his hallway filling with people. "What's this story you're telling?" glared the grim secretary. Seeing in the messenger's terrified eyes that it was no hoax, Stanton quickly threw on some clothes and started for the door.

"You must'nt go out," begged a friend. "They have killed Lincoln and they will kill you if you go out. As I came up to the house I saw a man behind the tree-box, but he ran away. . . ."

Brushing the advice aside, Stanton rushed straightaway toward the home on Lafayette Park.[11]

Gideon Welles, the white-bearded secretary of the navy, had just slipped off into sleep when his wife, Mary Jane, woke him. Someone was at the door, she said. Raising a window to see what was wanted below, Welles soon heard the horrifying news.

"Damn the Rebels, this is their work!" the naval secretary cursed, something he never did in Mary's presence.

Pulling on his shirt and trousers, Welles also started in haste for Seward's home.[12]

Charles Sumner, the abolitionist courtier and confidant of Mary Lincoln, was enjoying conversation and wine with two other senators when a black servant, "his hair almost on end," burst through the door. "Mr. Lincoln is assassinated in the theater. Mr. Seward is murdered in his bed. There's murder in the streets," the frightened employee blurted out.

"Young man, be moderate in your statements. Tell us what has happened," said the startled senator.

"I have told you what has happened," insisted the servant.

Grabbing his coat, Sumner hurried toward the White House to learn for himself if there was any truth in the horrible words.[13]

As a policeman in the District of Columbia, Tom Pendel was one of several men selected for duty at the White House. With the Lincolns absent this night, the home was quiet, and there was little for Pendel to do. Even the two young men, Robert Lincoln and John Hay, had tired of their Spanish repartee and "gossiping" and had retreated to their respective rooms for the night.[14] Tom Pendel:

> I was sitting in one of the big chairs in the alcove window facing the lower part of the city, waiting to open the door for President and Mrs. Lincoln when they should arrive from the theater, when I saw a confused mass of hurrying lights approaching the White House from the direction of the theater. They came straggling up the avenue to the White House and then there came a sharp ring at the bell. I bounded out of my chair . . . and quickly opened the door. To my surprise the caller was Senator Charles Sumner of Massachusetts, whom I knew well enough by sight, and he looked pale and worried as he asked me in a rather sharp tone of voice whether the President had yet returned, and when I said that he had not, whether I had heard that anything had happened to him. He looked mighty relieved and pleased when I told him that I had heard nothing, and he said he had heard some vague rumor that something had befallen Mr. Lincoln.
>
> I closed the door, and went back to my seat by the window more anxious and nervous than ever. There seemed to be a feeling of some impending calamity hanging over me, and when I heard

quick footsteps approaching up the walk and then a violent ring at
the bell I ran to the door, feeling sure that something *had* happened. The late caller was Isaac Newton, Commissioner of Agri-
culture. He was deathly pale, and his eyes glittered as though he
had fever. His voice had a sort of strained and hoarse sound in it as
he blurted out: "O, my God, they've shot the President!" For a few
moments I could say and do nothing. I was so absolutely horror-
stricken at the news that I was unable to think or realize the situation, or even to make a move. Mr. Newton stood against the door
with his hand over his eyes, and he was shaking and quivering with
excitement and grief. It must have been nearly a minute before
either of us said anything. Then, all at once, it occurred to me that
the other occupants of the house should be made acquainted with
the terrible news.

I left Mr. Newton standing at the door, and sprang up the front
stairs, skipping two or three of them at a time in my excitement.
Hastening along the upper corridor, I came to Capt. Robert
Lincoln's room. . . . He had not gone to bed, and I remember that
he had a medicine bottle in one hand and a spoon in the other, as
though he were measuring out some medicine. . . . I shall never
forget . . . the expression that overspread his face as I shrieked out
my fearful news. He had looked up in surprise as I burst into his
room, and as I told my errand he unconsciously let the bottle drop
from one hand and then the spoon from the other. I could say
nothing more, but gazed in a sort of fascination as the medicine
slowly gurgled out over the carpet. I could only think how thick
and black it was—my mind refused to take cognizance of anything
else. But the words kept ringing through my mind in a low, monotonous song: "The President is shot—the President is shot!"[15]

Recovering his senses, Robert ordered Pendel to inform John Hay,
whose room was just down the hall. Locating the president's secretary,
the guard yelled out the news.

"I looked at him curiously as he listened," said the policeman, "and
I remember that his brilliant color—which I had often admired, it was
so curiously like a beautiful woman's—faded out so quickly that it
seemed as though some one had then and there painted his cheek a
deathly white."[16]

Racing down the stairs, Lincoln and Hay discovered a crowd at the
door, including Charles Sumner. Following the shaken senator, the two
young men climbed into a waiting carriage and lashed the horses toward
Ford's.[17]

When the naval secretary finally reached William Seward's home, he found the street outside packed with people. Pushing his way through the crowd, Gideon Welles entered the home and encountered Frances Seward at the top of the stairs. The woman, noted Welles, "was scarcely able to speak."[18] Indeed, a New York reporter on the scene recalled that such was the terror and confusion that scarcely an intelligible word could be gathered from anyone.[19]

As Welles went up the stairs, what he saw was staggering.[20] The home, according to one account, looked "like a field hospital."[21]

"It was a terrible sight—there was so much blood every where," young Fanny Seward remembered. "The stairs was sprinkled with it all the way down to the floor below."[22] Wherever one looked, one saw a "scene of horrors," said Frances Seward. On a lounge lay her frail son Fred with blood streaming over his face.[23]

"His eyes were open," Gideon Welles observed, "but he did not move them, nor a limb, nor did he speak."[24]

Elsewhere, three other men stood covered in blood, including another Seward son, Augustus, whose head had been slashed to the bone in several places.[25] It was, of course, in Secretary Seward's room where the carnival of horrors was worst. The bed, floor, walls, doors—all were awash in gore.[26]

"Where we found my father," wrote Fanny, "there was such a great pool of blood that my feet slipped in it. Some of us had our dresses drabbled in it several inches deep."[27]

When the navy secretary, now joined by Edwin Stanton, finally entered the room, he was horrified. "The bed was saturated with blood," Welles wrote. "The Secretary was lying on his back, the upper part of his head covered by a cloth, which extended down over his eyes. His mouth was open, the lower jaw dropping down."[28] Welles could also see that Seward's throat was slashed on both sides, and his right cheek had been nearly severed from his head.[29] Because he was so hacked and mangled, noted a doctor, the secretary's face was the only one in the room not stamped with terror.[30] When the horrified Edwin Stanton began chattering nervously to those around him, the physician sternly ordered him to be quiet.[31]

In suite 68 at the Kirkwood House on Pennsylvania Avenue, a troubled Andrew Johnson was awakened by a sharp knock on the door. Outside, Leonard Farwell, former governor of Wisconsin, was frantic to awaken the vice president. "I rapped," remembered Farwell, "but receiving no answer, I rapped again and said in a loud voice, 'Governor Johnson, if you are in the room, I must see you!'"[32]

"Farwell? Is that you?" asked Johnson groggily.

"Yes, let me in," came the reply.[33]

Even if the still-addled vice president could not clearly see his friend's face, there was no confusing the terror in his voice.

———

Like a mighty river fed by raging tributaries, gaining force as it swept along, a flood of stunned humanity poured from the alleys and streets of Washington and emptied into the avenues that led to Ford's Theater.[34] Around the building itself, an enormous crowd had already gathered.[35] For a brief time, the crush of people was so great that many were able to edge their way into the Petersen home on the heels of government officials. After removing these trespassers, guards eventually forced the crowd back from the house.[36] Even at that distance, however, the shrieks of Mary Lincoln were clearly heard.

"Where is my dear husband? Where is he?" cried the woman when she finally burst through the door of the Petersen home. After becoming separated from her mate by the mob outside, Mary was frantic to find him again. Spurning the arms that reached to aid her, the frenzied first lady rushed through the house until she reached a small room to the rear. Throwing herself across her husband's body, she hugged and kissed his unresponsive face. Horrified by what she saw in the light, Mary let out a startled, high-pitched scream. "Why didn't he kill me? Why didn't he kill me?" she sobbed.[37]

As best they could, physicians went to work. Charles Leale:

> While holding his face upward and keeping his head from rolling to either side, I looked at his elevated knees caused by his great height. This uncomfortable position grieved me and I ordered the foot of the bed to be removed. . . . [A]s I found this could not satisfactorily be done, I had the President placed diagonally on the bed and called for extra pillows, and with them formed a gentle inclined plane on which to rest his head and shoulders. His position was then one of repose. . . . I called the officer and asked him to open a window and . . . as I wished to see if he had been wounded in any other part of the body I requested all except the surgeons to leave the room. The Captain reported that my order had been carried out with the exception of Mrs. Lincoln, to whom he said he did not like to speak. I addressed Mrs. Lincoln, explaining my desire, and she immediately left the room.[38]

After the president was stripped of his remaining clothes, a search was made for other wounds. Finding none, Charles Taft turned his attention to the hole behind Lincoln's left ear.

> The wound was there examined, the finger being used as a probe, and the ball found to have passed beyond the reach of the finger into the brain. I put a teaspoonful of diluted brandy between his lips, which was swallowed with much difficulty; a half-teaspoon-ful administered ten minutes afterward, was retained in the throat, without any effort being made to swallow it. The respiration now became labored; pulse 44, feeble, eyes entirely closed, the left pupil much contracted, the right widely dilated; total insensibility to light in both.[39]

Meanwhile, as attention was focused on the president, and while the shrill screams of his wife sent shattered nerves to the breaking point, Henry Rathbone was swiftly bleeding to death, almost unnoticed. After ensuring that Mary Lincoln reached the Petersen home safely, the major stopped in the hallway, clutching his arm. "The wound which I had received had been bleeding very profusely," Rathbone later said.[40] Hardly had the young man seated himself when he fainted and fell to the floor, "pale as a corpse."[41] Fortunately, Rathbone's fiancée, Clara Harris, was nearby. Although bathed in blood and numbed by the night-mare all about her, the woman nevertheless had the presence of mind to quickly tie a handkerchief over the terrible wound and thus stop the bleeding.[42] As Rathbone was carried down the hall toward a waiting carriage, Mary Lincoln filled the building with unearthly shrieks and groans.[43]

"She was not weeping," wrote a witness, "but appeared hysterical, and exclaimed in rapid succession, over and over again: 'Oh! why didn't he kill me? why didn't he kill me?'"[44]

The screams piercing the walls of the house to the street beyond only added to the horror of the anxious crowd outside.[45] Standing in the cold mist with thousands of others, Julia Shepard vividly conveys the uncertainty, shock, and terror of the moment:

> We are in the street now. They have taken the President into the house opposite. He is alive, but mortally wounded. What are those people saying. "Secretary Seward and his son have had their throats cut in their own house." Is it so? Yes, and the murderer of our President has escaped through a back alley where a swift horse stood awaiting him. Cavalry come dashing up the street and

stand with drawn swords before yon house. Too late! too late!
What mockery armed men are now. Weary with the weight of
woe the moments drag along and . . . delicate women stand clinging to the arms of their protectors, and strong men throw their
arms around each other's necks and cry like children, and passing
up and down enquire in low agonized voices, "Can he live? Is
there no hope?"[46]

Another person standing outside the Petersen home was Adolphe de
Chambrun. In contrast to the sad, stunned mood that had characterized
the crowd earlier, the French traveler soon noted that with each spine-
chilling scream and each terrible report, the people began to rouse from
their stupor. "[S]uddenly," said de Chambrun, " there was a change. . .
. The city came alive; the spirit of vengeance awoke and spread like a
flame. Cries, shouts, [and] passionate exhortations rent the air."[47]

Although the Frenchman did not realize it at the time, he was witnessing the initial spark to a bloody rampage that would indeed spread over
the land like a devouring flame. In many ways, the American terror was
remarkably similar to that which had shamed de Chambrun's own
country over a half-century earlier.

CHAPTER FOURTEEN

A SPIRIT SO
HORRIBLE

A stroke from Heaven laying the whole of the city in instant ruins could not have startled us as did the word that broke from Ford's Theater a half hour ago.[1]

THUS WROTE A DAZED NEW YORK REPORTER, trying to describe the devastation the human mind suffered when it was forced to shift from happiness and hope to darkness and despair in only a heartbeat. With thousands of candles, lamps, and gas jets still glowing fiercely from the earlier celebration, the murky conditions threw a surreal and sinister shroud over the whole of Washington.

"It was so light that one could see for blocks," recalled Helen Moss as her escort hurried her home to escape the rising horror.[2] Many of those the couple met moved slowly through the mist like sleepwalkers. Others sped silently along as though they were ghosts. Some were seen to stagger, as if intoxicated.[3] Words were inadequate to describe one's emotions.

"It was one of stifling, as though someone had gripped my throat," Albert Boggs admitted when the full weight of the news finally sank in.[4]

By midnight, it seemed to many as if the entire population of Washington was in the streets, boiling and surging about aimlessly. Indeed, noted a newspaper correspondent on the scene, the city was "overwhelmed" with terror.[5] Fueling the panic, of course, was the want of reliable information. "Ten thousand rumors are afloat," stated a writer for the *New York Tribune*.[6]

Not only were Lincoln, Seward, and their entire families reportedly butchered, but as the rumors gained momentum, all the president's cabinet had been slaughtered as well.[7] "It was then reported that Gen. Grant had been killed in Philadelphia, and in a short time, they had everybody of any consequence in the city assassinated, until I almost began to doubt the fact of my own existence," added another confused man.[8]

And so, from mouth to mouth the panic grew. When a rumor raced through the city that the telegraph lines leading to Washington had been cut, men and women ran through the streets screaming that the capital was about to be attacked. John Mosby's Confederate guerrillas were infiltrating the town—Robert E. Lee had torn up the terms of Appomattox and was marching north with his army—Washington would be bombarded—thousands would be killed—the war would continue! The actions of the federal garrison seemed to confirm the reports. Files of infantry double-quicked through the streets, often passing other noisy columns marching in the opposite direction. Squadrons of cavalry, sabers clattering, dashed about the city at breakneck speed. Policemen raced across streets. Bells rang, drums rolled, carriages and ambulances tore helter-skelter through the night.[9]

Every terrifying scene seemed not only to confirm one's worst fears but to magnify them. Now at home, Helen Moss graphically conveyed her feeling of horror:

> In our eagerness to catch every sound, we huddled about the windows, not daring to have a light, lest we be made targets of by "the Rebels." A horseman would go dashing past, and down our heads would duck until we thought the danger past. Then we leaned far out to catch the first sound of news from the passers-by. Some man of the household would come dashing in to add to our terror with "The Rebels are upon us." "They have surrounded the city." "They have begun their raid." "We are in danger of being shot or made prisoners." "The President shot, and all of his cabinet." . . . [W]e were simply wild with fright.[10]

And still the rumors flew.

"A plot, a plot!" screamed a horseman as he galloped through the city. "Secretary Seward's throat is cut from ear to ear; Secretary Stanton is killed in his residence; General Grant is shot at Baltimore, and Vice President Johnson is killed at the Kirkwood House."[11]

Understandably, many individuals were paralyzed with fear. "We saw a colored man," said a reporter, "blanched with terror and trembling in every limb, his teeth chattering like one with the ague." The frightened black was not alone, as the journalist admitted: "The hair on my head stood up."[12] Others became perfectly unhinged. Overcome with excitement and fear, an army captain went "raving mad" and was placed under arrest by a lieutenant.[13]

"Rumors are so thick, the excitement of this hour is so intense," recorded a tension-filled Washington editor in the early morning hours of April 15. "Evidently conspirators are among us. To what extent does the conspiracy exist? This is a terrible question. When a spirit so horrible as this is abroad, what man is safe?"[14]

Given the fear, anger, and uncertainty, passions quickly became uncontrollable. On the streets and in hotels, huge mobs brandishing knives and pistols vowed to kill on the spot every rebel that fell into their hands.[15] According to one soldier, patrols darting about the city were not only encouraged but ordered to shoot down any who now displayed even a trace of disloyalty.[16] At such a turbulent time, many soldiers were quick to obey. Soon after entering a local hotel, Melville Stone of the Associated Press was startled by the sound of a gunshot. Running into a nearby room, the reporter saw a man lying dead on the floor. "The assailant," said Stone, "stood perfectly composed with a smoking revolver in his hand, and justified his action by saying: 'He said it served Lincoln right.' There was no arrest, no one would have dared arrest the man. He walked out a hero."[17]

Elsewhere, a federal trooper overheard a man exult over the shooting of Lincoln by exclaiming, "it was good enough for the black rascal." Without a word, the soldier immediately turned around, looked the man straight in the eye, drew a pistol, then blew his brains out.[18]

Frank Myers and his comrades were marching through the streets at the double-quick when a bystander was heard celebrating. Grabbing a musket from a private, an angry sergeant promptly ran over to the man and speared him with the bayonet. Not content with his bloody work, the enraged soldier again plunged the long blade into his victim as he lay writhing on the ground.[19]

Around the stricken city, as the mob spirit grew, others were treated similarly.[20] When someone shouted that hundreds of rebel soldiers were being held at the Old Capitol Prison, a cry of vengeance erupted. Another in the mob yelled that the prisoners were breaking out of jail at that very moment. With a roar of anger, the snarling crowd set off at a run. As the enraged mob raced forward, hundreds along the way joined. When the screaming crowd of two thousand finally reached the prison, shouts were immediately raised to burn the "Trojan wooden horse" in their midst.[21]

"'Hang 'em,' 'shoot 'em, 'burn 'em,' became the cry, and to carry this threat into execution preparations were made," recalled one of the frightened prisoners inside, Captain C. T. Allen. "Ropes were procured, knots were made, every thing ready for a general massacre of the helpless Confederate prisoners who knew nothing on earth of the occurrences of the night."[22]

Horrified by what was about to happen, Green Clay Smith, a congressman from Kentucky, and several friends rushed to place themselves between the mob and the prison. When Smith had halted the excited crowd with pleas, he left his companions and dashed off for help.[23] Continues Captain Allen:

> His friends—God bless them, whoever they were . . . responded promptly, mounted a box on the streets, and addressed the mob. When one had said all he could say, another followed him, and so on, occupying half an hour. . . . [Congressman Smith] soon found a battalion of troops on the streets, took charge of them, rushed them to the old capitol, arriving just in time . . . to save from a terrible death some three or four hundred helpless Confederate prisoners.[24]

A few others in the city—risking life and limb—kept their wits and resisted the almost irresistible tide of raging emotions.[25] Because many felt that Ford's Theater and thespians in general had played some role in the disaster, a howling mob soon surrounded the building. When a nearby storekeeper attempted to reason with the rioters, he quickly found a rope around his neck. Only the swift action of authorities saved the man's life.[26]

Walt Whitman describes another incident:

> The infuriated crowd, through some chance, got started against one man, either for words he utter'd, or perhaps without any cause at all, and were proceeding at once to actually hang him on a neighboring lamp post, when he was rescued by a few heroic policemen, who placed him in their midst and fought their way slowly and amid great peril toward the Station House. . . . [T]he attack'd man, not yet freed from the jaws of death, looking like a corpse—the silent resolute half-dozen policemen, with no weapons but their little clubs, yet stern and steady through all those eddying swarms—made indeed a fitting side-scene to the grand tragedy.[27]

While shouting mobs combed the streets searching for more victims, and while federal soldiers murdered in cold blood whomsoever they desired, many citizens looked from their windows, quaking in terror.

"Are we living in the days of the French Revolution? Will peace never come again to our dear land?" one man asked his wife that night. "[A]re we to rush on to wild ruin? It seems all a dream, a wild dream. I cannot realize it though I know I saw it only an hour ago."[28]

CHAPTER FIFTEEN

THE DARKEST DAWN

As JAMES TANNER NEARED THE STREET his boarding house sat on, he found his steps increasingly slowed. Several hundred yards from the building itself, the twenty-one-year-old former soldier found his path blocked entirely. In contrast to the riotous mobs elsewhere, a ghostly silence pervaded the dense crowd that stood outside the Petersen house. Dismayed, yet determined to reach his room, Tanner edged and slid his way forward on his shaky artificial legs. At length, he reached the military cordon encircling the Petersen home. After some intense explanation, Tanner eventually convinced the officers in charge that his quarters were indeed in the adjoining boarding house, and he was permitted to enter the building. Upon reaching his room, however, the exhausted young man was in for another surprise.[1]

"There was a balcony in front," he said, "and I found my rooms and the balcony thronged by other occupants of the house."[2]

From this high vantage, Tanner and the others had a front row seat to the drama unfolding next door. Like everyone else around him, the young man was absorbed by the coming and going at the Petersen house. As the stunned spectators watched, Edwin Stanton, Charles Sumner, and Robert Lincoln hastened up the steps, as did numerous political and military men. None, though, was more instantly recognizable than Gideon Welles, the dour, white-bearded man with the ill-fitting wig. After Welles entered the home, he hurried down the hall to the room where his beloved chief lay. Wrote the secretary of navy in his diary:

> The room was small and overcrowded. The surgeons and members of the Cabinet were as many as should have been in the room, but there were many more, and the hall and other rooms

in the front or main house were full. . . . The excitement and bad
atmosphere from the crowded rooms oppressed me physically.[3]

Indeed, the modest rooms were soon packed with scores of people,
with no fewer than sixteen doctors alone.[4] Around the fallen leader's bed
were arrayed his shaken Cabinet members, most of whom were crying
uncontrollably.[5] The normally stern and unbending Edwin Stanton, his
body now convulsed with sorrow, sat stooped beside the bed, the tears
trickling through his fingers to the floor.[6] Senator Charles Sumner was
particularly affected. "He was sobbing like a woman," noted a reporter,
"with his head bowed down almost in the pillow of the bed."[7]

When Gideon Welles, his body shaking with emotion, finally asked
a physician about Lincoln's condition, the words were heartbreaking:

> He replied the President was dead to all intents, although he
> might live three hours or perhaps longer. . . . He had been
> stripped of his clothes. His large arms . . . were of a size which we
> would scarce have expected from his spare appearance. His slow,
> full respiration lifted the clothes with each breath that he took.
> His features were calm and striking.[8]

Indeed, the president's great strength and stamina were astonishing to
those who witnessed the struggle. Among the physicians present, all
agreed that a normal man would have succumbed soon after receiving
such a grievous injury.[9] All the same, and except for some ineffectual
probing of the wound, there was little that surgeons could do but keep
the president's body warm while they waited for inevitable death.[10]

"His face looked ghastly," recalled fifteen-year-old Fred Petersen, son
of the homeowner. "He lay with his head on [the] pillow, and his eyes,
all bloodshot [were] almost protruding from their sockets. . . . [H]is jaw
had fallen down upon his breast, showing his teeth."[11] Other visitors to
the house were soon made aware that with each rise and fall of the
president's chest there issued "one of the most dismal, mournful, moaning noises ever heard."[12] Secretary of the Interior John Usher was startled
by the sound the moment he entered the home. "[H]is breathing was
deep[,] almost a snore . . . almost a moan," said Usher.[13]

Heartrending as the sounds were to those who loved him, no one felt
the impact more than his wife. Drawn from the front parlor by her
husband's suffering, her hair disheveled, her gown crumpled and
bloody, Mary entered the tiny room on the verge of total collapse.[14]
Wrote John Usher:

She implored him to speak to her[.] she did not want to go to the
theater that night but that he thought he must go because people
would expect him. . . . She called for little Tad[.] said she knew
he would speak to him because he loved him so well, and after
indulging in dreadful incoherences for some time was finally
persuaded to leave the room.[15]

But again, the crazed woman returned. "At one time, while sitting by
his bedside," recounted a viewer, "she kept saying, 'Kill me! kill me! kill
me, too! shoot me, too!' At another time I heard her exclaim in the most
piteous tones, 'Do live! do speak to me! Do live and speak to me, won't
you?'"[16]

Among the few women present in the home was Elizabeth Dixon,
daughter of a U.S. senator. Although Elizabeth sought to comfort Mary
Lincoln repeatedly, the first lady was far beyond comforting.[17] Himself
on the verge of emotional breakdown, Robert Lincoln also tried mightily
to aid his afflicted mother. Gently, though firmly, the son soothed Mary
and begged her to place her faith in God. At other times, Robert's re-
serves gave out. "Occasionally," a witness remembered, "being entirely
overcome, he would retire into the hall and give vent to the most
heartrending lamentations."[18] But then, continued the narrator, "he
would recover himself and return to his mother, and with remarkable
self-possession try to cheer her broken spirits and lighten her load of
sorrow. His conduct was a most remarkable exhibition of calmness in
the most trying hour that I have ever seen."[19]

Despite the efforts of Robert and others, as well as sedatives, nothing
seemed to ease the woman's grief and pain.[20] Almost involuntarily, Mary
limped again and again to her husband's bedside, screaming and moaning.[21]

When Edwin Stanton finally fled the room, there was little doubt in
anyone's mind that it was to escape the ear-piercing shrieks of Mary
Lincoln, a woman whom he thoroughly despised. Establishing a make-
shift office in a nearby room, Stanton and Attorney General James
Speed began orchestrating search efforts for the assassins and taking
testimony from a number of witnesses.[22] Quickly realizing that normal
transcriptions could never handle the great weight of messages and testimony, Stanton ordered Major General Christopher Auger to find
someone who took shorthand. Stepping onto the stoop, the officer
shouted for anyone in the huge crowd who might help to come forward.

Like everyone else, James Tanner and the others on his balcony were
curious about the strange summons. Whether Tanner might have vol-

unteered on his own or not would remain unknown. Before he had a chance, an acquaintance on the balcony yelled back, then pointed at Tanner.[23] Easing slowly down the stairs on his wood and steel legs, the handsome young man at last reached the Petersen home. He continues:

> Entering the house, I accompanied General Augur down the hallway to the rear parlor. As we passed the door of the front parlor, the moans and sobs of Mrs. Lincoln struck painfully upon our ears. . . . I took my seat on one side of a small library table opposite Mr. Stanton. . . . Various witnesses were brought in who had either been in Ford's Theater or up in the vicinity of Mr. Seward's residence. Among them were Harry Hawk. . . . As I took down the statements they made, we were distracted by the distress of Mrs. Lincoln, for though the folding doors between the two parlors were closed, her frantic sorrow was distressingly audible to us. . . .

Through all the testimony given by those who had been in Ford's Theater that night there was an undertone of horror which held the witnesses back from positively identifying the assassin as Booth. Said Harry Hawk, "I believe to the best of my knowledge that it was John Wilkes Booth. Still I am not positive that it was him."[24]

If Hawk and others had reservations, many more had no doubts whatsoever. "In fifteen minutes," said Tanner, "I had testimony enough to hang Wilkes Booth, the assassin, higher than ever Haman hung."[25]

The young man continues:

> Our task was interrupted very many times during the night, sometimes by reports or dispatches for Secretary Stanton but more often by him for the purpose of issuing orders to enmesh Booth in his flight. 'Guard the Potomac from the city down!' was his repeated direction. 'He will try to get south.' . . . Several times Mr. Stanton left us a few moments and passed back to the room . . . where the President lay. The doors were open and sometimes there would be a few seconds of absolute silence when we could hear plainly the stertorous breathing of the dying man. I think it was on his return from his third trip of this kind when, as he again took his seat opposite me, I looked earnestly at him, desiring, yet hesitating to ask if there was any chance of life. He understood and I saw a choke in his throat as he slowly forced the answer to my unspoken question, "There is no hope." He had impressed me through those awful hours as being a man of steel, but I knew then that he was dangerously near a convulsive breakdown.[26]

While Tanner began to transcribe his shorthand, Charles Dana, the assistant secretary of war, continued writing dispatches. Like everyone else who saw Stanton that night, Dana was impressed by the secretary's strength, especially when contrasted to others in the house.

> They seemed to be almost as paralyzed as the unconscious sufferer within the little chamber. Mr. Stanton alone was in full activity. . . . It seemed as if Stanton thought of everything. . . . The safety of Washington must be looked after. Commanders all over the country had to be ordered to take extra precautions. The people must be notified of the tragedy. The assassins must be captured. The coolness and clearheadedness of Mr. Stanton under the circumstances were most remarkable.[27]

"He was then the Master, and in reality Acting President of the United States," Dr. Leale accurately observed.[28]

———

In large part because of Stanton's efforts, much of the country quickly learned of the horrible events in Washington. During the early morning hours of April 15, Ulysses and Julia Grant stepped down from their car when it reached the banks of the Delaware. After an exhausting, though uneventful, train trip up from the capital, the Grants paused in Philadelphia for a quick meal before ferrying across the river to New Jersey. As always, and despite the late hour, a curious crowd awaited Grant's appearance at the restaurant.[29] After the usual handshakes and comments, the famished couple at last were seated.

"The General ordered some oysters, as he had had nothing to eat since nine o'clock in the morning," remembered Julia. "Before they were ready for him, a telegram was handed him, and almost before he could open this, another was handed him, and then a third."[30] Grant scanned the first telegram:

April 15, 12:30 A.M.

On night Train to Burlington

The President was assassinated at Fords Theater at 10 30 tonight & cannot live. The wound is a Pistol shot through the head. Secretary Seward & his son Frederick, were also assassinated at their residence & are in a dangerous condition. The Secretary of War desires that you return to Washington immediately. Please answer on receipt of this.

Maj. Thomas T. Eckert[31]

Stunned by the words, the general opened a second message, this from Charles Dana:

> Permit me to suggest to you to Keep a close watch on all persons who come near you in the cars or otherwise, also that an Engine be sent in front of the train to guard against anything being on the track.[32]

Julia goes on:

> The General looked very pale. "Is there anything the matter?" I inquired: "You look startled." "Yes," he answered, "something *very* serious has happened. Do not exclaim. Be quiet and I will tell you. The President has been assassinated at the theater, and I must go back at once. I will take you to Burlington (an hour away), see the children, order a special train, and return as soon as it is ready."[33]

On the brief trip up through New Jersey, Grant was silent and lost in thought.[34] "This is the darkest day of my life," the general at last muttered. "I do not know what it means. Here was the Rebellion put down in the field, and it is reasserting itself in the gutter. We had fought it as war, we have now to fight it as murder."[35]

Others were hardly less startled than Grant.

Leonard Grover was on a business trip to New York City when a sharp rap on his hotel door rudely awakened him. Leaving his partner in Washington to manage affairs at the famous theater that bore his name, Grover did not anticipate trouble of any sort now that the war was over.

> [S]ome one called, "Mr. Grover, here's a telegram for you." Thinking it was the usual message from one of the theaters (for I was then managing a Philadelphia theater as well) which would simply convey the amount of the receipts of the house, I called back: "Stick it under the door." But the rapping continued with vigor, and there were calls, "Mr. Grover, Mr. Grover, please come to the door!"
>
> I arose, hastily opened the door, when the light disclosed the long hall compactly crowded with people. Naturally, I was astonished. A message was handed to me with the request: "Please open that telegram and tell us if it's true." I opened it and read: "President Lincoln shot to-night at Ford's Theater. Thank God it wasn't ours. C. D. Hess.[36]

———

> I have just visited the dying couch of Abraham Lincoln. He is
> now in the agonies of death, and his physicians say he cannot live
> more than an hour. He is surrounded by the members of his
> Cabinet, all of whom are bathed in tears. Senator Sumner is
> seated on the right of the couch on which he is lying, the tears
> streaming down his cheeks, and sobbing like a child. All around
> him are his physicians. . . . The President is unconscious, and the
> only sign of life he exhibits is by the movements of his right hand,
> which he raises feebly.[37]

Thus wrote a correspondent to the *Chicago Tribune* at 1:30 A.M. on
April 15. So labored was Lincoln's breathing and so ghastly was the
blackening of the face and the bulging of the eyes, that all, like the reporter, felt the end was nigh. Indeed, twice during the night those
present knelt on the floor while the president's pastor, Dr. Phineas
Gurley, prayed.[38] And yet, the life force in the tall, strong Illinoisan refused to surrender.

An early end would have been merciful for Mary Lincoln. Prior to
every visit she made to the death chamber, someone hurriedly replaced
the bloody pillows with clean ones. Nevertheless, each time Mary entered the little room and beheld her husband's hideous condition, the
woman screamed and cried. On two occasions she collapsed.[39] When
the woman was revived and helped toward the front parlor, her ear-splitting shrieks and sobs again rattled the house.[40] Nearby, with his nerves
ready to shatter, Edwin Stanton somehow managed to keep the wheels
of government rolling.

"[I] dictated orders one after another, which I wrote out and sent
swiftly to the telegraph," said Charles Dana. "All those orders were designed to keep the business of the government in full motion till the
crisis should be over. It was perhaps two o'clock in the morning before
he said, 'That's enough. Now you can go home.'"[41]

Also in the early morning hours, Andrew Johnson arrived at the home.
Wisely refraining from venturing out earlier for fear of assassination, the
vice president now made his belated appearance. Johnson had been in
the building only a few minutes when Charles Sumner, knowing full
well how much Mary loathed the Tennessean, urged him to leave. Fearing his presence would indeed ignite even uglier scenes, the man destined to be president at any moment meekly left as suggested.[42]

In a house already rocked to its foundation by screams and terror,
another disturbance occurred when William Petersen returned to his
home. Outraged that his locked doors had been smashed to pieces to

accommodate Mary Lincoln and others, furious that his carpets had been destroyed by mud and blood, Petersen was also angered that dozens of pillows, towels, and sheets had been totally ruined. Additionally, souvenir-seekers who had managed to slip into the home were dismantling the building one piece at a time. With no hope of compensation in sight, the furious homeowner grabbed one of the many bloody pillows lying about and angrily flung it into the yard.[43]

As the interminable nightmare continued, Gideon Welles decided to briefly flee the stuffy building to find a quiet place where his ears would no longer be assailed by Mary's shrieks or her husband's deep groans. And so, at 6 A.M., the navy secretary walked outdoors into the dark and misty morning. As the large, white-bearded cabinet member reached the military cordon, he was instantly recognized by the waiting crowds. Wrote Welles in his diary:

> Large groups of people were gathered every few rods, all anxious and solicitous. Some one or more from each group stepped forward as I passed, to inquire into the condition of the President, and to ask if there was no hope. Intense grief was on every countenance when I replied that the President could survive but a short time. The colored people especially—and there were at this time more of these persons than of whites—were overwhelmed with grief.[44]

The navy secretary returned after only a fifteen-minute walk. Rain began to fall on him as he passed back through the military cordon.[45] One of the troopers on guard that morning was twenty-two-year-old Smith Stimmel. Awakened from a deep sleep earlier that night by the horrible news, then ordered to saddle up for duty, the young Ohio cavalryman, like everyone else, remained in a state of shock. In Stimmel's words:

> All night I rode slowly up and down the street in front of that house. Sometimes it seemed to me like an awful nightmare, and that I must be dreaming; sometimes I would . . . wonder if I was really awake and on duty, so hard was it for me to realize the fact that President Lincoln was lying in that house in a dying condition.[46]

As the gray pall from the east spread slowly over rainy Washington, and as the city bells tolled seven, Abraham Lincoln began to lose his struggle with death.

"The face of the dying had changed to a more ashy paleness," recorded a witness. "The dark patch around his right eye had spread. His breathing had become shorter and less labored. That dreadful sound had given place to a kind of wild gurgling. Occasionally for a few seconds it would entirely cease, and I would think that all was over. Then it would resume; and thus these intervals would continue."[47]

Lincoln, a correspondent of the *Chicago Tribune* added more graphically, was "breathing with great difficulty. . . . His eyes were protruding from their sockets, and suffused with blood."[48]

The president's respiration, noted Dr. Taft, would sometimes stop altogether for as long as a minute. Then, a sudden jolt from Lincoln's chest would restart the lungs, startling everyone who imagined him dead. And thus the pattern would continue. Wrote Taft:

> At these times the death-like stillness and suspense were thrilling.
> The Cabinet ministers, and others surrounding the death-bed,
> watching, with suspended breath, the last feeble inspiration, and
> as the unbroken quiet would seem to prove that life had fled, turn
> their eyes to their watches; then as the struggling life within
> would force another fluttering respiration, heave deep sighs of
> relief, and fix their eyes once more upon the face of their dying
> chief.[49]

Shortly after 7 A.M., Mary Lincoln, assisted by Elizabeth Dixon, walked down the hallway to visit her suffering husband. "At that hour," Elizabeth recalled, "just as the day was struggling with the dim candles in the room, we went in again. Mrs. Lincoln must have noticed a change, for the moment she looked at him she fainted and fell upon the floor. I caught her in my arms and held her to the window which was open, the rain falling heavily."[50]

After stimulants were administered, the woman was again helped to the bedside. "'Love,' she begged, 'live but one moment to speak to me once—to speak to our children.'"[51]

While Mary sat kissing and touching her husband's face, trying with tears to will the words from him, surgeons around the woman noted that Lincoln's breathing was growing less and less.[52] One of those watching was Dr. Charles Leale:

> As Mrs. Lincoln sat on a chair by the side of the bed with her face
> to her husband's his breathing became very stertorous and the
> loud, unnatural noise frightened her in her exhausted, agonized
> condition. She sprang up suddenly with a piercing cry and fell
> fainting to the floor. Secretary Stanton hearing her cry came in
> from the adjoining room and with raised arms called out loudly:
> "Take that woman out and do not let her in again." Mrs. Lincoln

was helped up kindly and assisted in a fainting condition from the room.[53]

When his notes were finally finished, young James Tanner stepped next door to gaze upon the president:

It was very evident that he could not last long. There was quite a crowd in the room . . . but I approached quite near the bed on which so much greatness lay, fast loosing its hold on this world. . . . At the head [of the bed] stood Captain Robert Lincoln, weeping on the shoulder of Senator Sumner. . . . Stanton was there, trying every way to be calm and yet he was very much moved. The utmost silence pervaded, broken only by the sounds of strong men's tears. It was a solemn time, I assure you.[54]

As was obvious to Tanner and everyone else in the room, the last moments of Abraham Lincoln were at hand. "His face, which had been quite pale," wrote a journalist, "began to assume a waxen transparency, the jaw slowly fell, and the teeth became exposed."[55]

The president's respirations grew farther and farther apart. Several times, when the interval between breaths was longer than usual, doctors searched for a pulse.[56]

"Such was the solemn stillness for the space of five minutes that the ticking of watches could be heard in the room," one man noted.[57]

Returning to James Tanner:

The Surgeon General [Joseph Barnes] was near the head of the bed, sometimes sitting on the edge thereof, his finger on the pulse of the dying man. Occasionally he put his ear down to catch the lessening beats of his heart. . . . [I] had full view of Mr. Stanton across the President's body. . . . [His] gaze was fixed intently on the countenance of his dying chief. He had, as I said, been a man of steel throughout the night, but as I looked at his face across the corner of the bed and saw the twitching of the muscles I knew that it was only by a powerful effort that he restrained himself.[58]

Finally, it was over. The long agony ended. After his heart "fluttered" for ten seconds or so, Abraham Lincoln was no more.[59]

"The first indication that the dreaded end had come," Tanner revealed, "was at 22 minutes past 7, when the Surgeon General gently crossed the pulseless hands of Lincoln across the motionless breast and rose to his feet."[60]

"He is gone," said Barnes simply.[61]

No one spoke. No one stirred. No one cried.

"Then I solemnly believe that for four or five minutes there was not the slightest noise or movement in that awful presence," the Reverend Dr. Gurley recalled.

> We all stood transfixed in our positions, speechless, breathless, around the dead body of that great and good man. At length the Secretary of War, who was standing at my left, broke the silence and said, "Doctor, will you say anything?" I replied, "I will speak to God." Said he, "Do it just now." And there, by the side of our fallen chief, God put into my heart to utter this petition, that from that hour we and the whole nation might become more than ever united in our devotion to the cause of our beloved, imperiled country. When I ceased, there arose from the lips of the entire company a fervid and spontanious [sic] "Amen."[62]

"Mr. Stanton raised his head, the tears streaming down his face," noted James Tanner. "A more agonized expression I never saw on a human countenance as he sobbed out the words: 'He belongs to the angels now.'"[63]

Following the prayer, Reverend Gurley went to console Mary Lincoln.

"Oh why did you not tell me he was dying," the woman burst out.[64]

Maunsell Field was standing in the hallway while Gurley sought to comfort those in the parlor:

> The prayer was continually interrupted by Mrs. Lincoln's sobs. Soon after its conclusion, I went into the parlor, and found her in a chair, supported by her son Robert. Presently her carriage came up and she was removed to it. She was in a state of tolerable composure at that time, until she reached the door, when, glancing at the theater opposite, she repeated three or four times: "That dreadful house!—that dreadful house!"[65]

Returning to the bedroom, Field continues:

> The President's eyes after death were not, particularly the right one, entirely closed. I closed them myself with my fingers, and one [of] the surgeons brought pennies and placed them on the eyes, and subsequently substituted for them silver half-dollars. In a very short time the jaw commenced slightly falling, although the body was still warm. . . . The expression immediately after death was purely negative, but in fifteen minutes there came over the mouth, the nostrils, and the chin, a smile that seemed almost

an effort of life. . . . The body grew cold very gradually, and I left
the room before it had entirely stiffened.[66]

As Lincoln's body was being placed in a coffin, one by one, those who
had maintained the horrible vigil while he yet lived now made their
sorrowful way home with his death. "I felt as though I had been engaged
all night in a terrible battle and had just strength enough left to drag
myself off the field," said a weary Reverend Gurley.[67] James Tanner, also
thoroughly drained by the ordeal, nevertheless hobbled to his apartment
next door and set to work writing another copy of the testimony taken
earlier.

> I had been thus engaged but a brief time, when hearing some
> commotion on the street, I stepped to the window and saw a cof-
> fin containing the body of the dead President being placed in a
> hearse . . . escorted by a lieutenant and 10 privates. As they passed
> with measured tread and arms reversed, my hand involuntarily
> went to my head in salute as they started on their long, long jour-
> ney back to the prairies and the hearts he knew and loved so
> well.[68]

When the hearse and its escort reached the crowds beyond the military cordon, large numbers of citizens joined the procession on its rainy
trip to the White House.[69]

His duty now done, a weary and dejected Dr. Charles Leale closed the
door on the suddenly quiet, empty Petersen home.

> I left the house in deep meditation. In my lonely walk I was
> aroused from my reveries by the cold drizzling rain dropping on
> my bare head, my hat I had left in my seat at the theater. My
> clothing was stained with blood, I had not once been seated since
> I first sprang to the President's aid; I was cold, weary and sad. The
> dawn of peace was again clouded, the most cruel war in history
> had not completely ended.[70]

CHAPTER SIXTEEN

HEMP AND HELL

IRONICALLY, THE ONE MAN IN AMERICA whose job it was to have known of the tragic developments in the capital was one of the last to learn. While events swirled madly about him, newsman Noah Brooks lay in his room, oblivious to all, bedridden by a violent bout of flu. During the night, he and his roommate were aroused by the clatter of cavalry in the streets. Other than a dry joke about rebel raids and the capture of his friend Abraham Lincoln, Brooks paid no mind to the commotion and quickly dozed off again.

> I was awakened in the early dawn by a loud and hurried knocking on my chamber door, and the voice of Mr. Gardner, the landlord, crying "Wake, wake, Mr. Brooks! I have dreadful news." I slipped out, turned the key of the door, and Mr. Gardner came in, pale, trembling . . . and told his awful story. . . . I sank back into my bed, cold and shivering with horror, and for a time it seemed as though the end of all things had come. I was aroused by the loud weeping of my comrade, who had not left his bed in another part of the room.
>
> When we had sufficiently collected ourselves to dress and go out of doors in the bleak and cheerless April morning, we found in the streets an extraordinary spectacle. They were suddenly crowded with people—men, women, and children thronging the pavements and darkening the thoroughfares. It seemed as if everybody was in tears. Pale faces, streaming eyes . . . were on every side. Men and women who were strangers accosted one another with distressed looks and tearful inquiries.[1]

For Noah Brooks—indeed, for millions more—the shock was too great, the transition too brief, the human mind too weak and simple to calculate the sudden change. With the speed of a burning bullet, the people of the North had been hurled down from the mountaintop of hope and happiness to the abyss of sorrow and despair. Around Washington, colorful flags and banners hung soaked and motionless. Slowly, sadly, these tokens of victory were taken down, and the black of mourning was hung in their place.[2]

"From lip to lip the tale of horror flew," Noah Brooks continued:

> [M]en and women went weeping about the streets; no loud voice was anywhere heard; even children's prattle was hushed; gloom, sadness, mourning sat on every countenance. . . . All shops, Government departments, and private offices were closed, and everywhere, on the most pretentious residences and on the humblest hovels, were the black badges of grief. Nature seemed to sympathize in the general lamentation, and tears of rain fell from the moist and somber sky. The wind sighed mournfully through the streets crowded with sad-faced people, and broad folds of funeral drapery flapped heavily in the wind over the decorations of the day before.[3]

As was the case in Washington, when the shattering news reached the rest of the country via the telegraph there initially was only shock and silence.

Chicago Tribune	*Boston Herald*, April 15, 1865
April 15, 1865	**GREAT NATIONAL**
TERRIBLE NEWS	**CALAMITY**
✴ ✴ ✴ ✴ ✴ ✴ ✴ ✴ ✴ ✴	✴ ✴ ✴ ✴ ✴ ✴ ✴ ✴ ✴ ✴
President Lincoln Assassinated	*ASSASSINATION OF*
at Ford's Theater	*PRESIDENT LINCOLN*
✴ ✴ ✴ ✴ ✴ ✴ ✴ ✴ ✴ ✴	✴ ✴ ✴ ✴ ✴ ✴ ✴ ✴ ✴ ✴
A Rebel Desperado Shoots Him	THE FIENDISH ACT COMMITTED
Through the Head and Escapes	AT FORD'S THEATER
✴ ✴ ✴ ✴ ✴ ✴ ✴ ✴ ✴ ✴ ✴ ✴	✴ ✴ ✴ ✴ ✴ ✴ ✴ ✴ ✴ ✴
Secretary Seward and Major Fred	**Escape of the Assassin**
Seward Stabbed by Another	
Desperado	

Ran the *Saint Louis Dispatch* of April 15:

> Many of our readers awoke this morning with a shudder, for the
> hoarse cry of the newsboy, as it was borne to them on the damp,
> chilly air, announced the "assassination of President Lincoln." . .
> . Even the voices of the vivacious, devil-may-care newsboys
> seemed hushed as they announced the sorrowful tidings.

"Men hold their breath, and turn pale at the appalling words," noted
a Boston clergyman:

> Citizens meet, and shake hands, and part in silence. Words ex-
> press nothing when uttered. All attempt to express the nation's
> grief is utterly commonplace and insignificant. . . . [A] smile
> seems irrelevant and sacrilegious. Even the fresh, green grass, just
> coming forth to meet the return of spring and the singing of birds,
> seems to wear the shadows of twilight at noonday. The sun is less
> bright than before, and the very atmosphere seems . . . a strange
> ethereal element of gloom.[4]

In Hartford, Connecticut, St. Joseph, Missouri, and countless American cities, sidewalks were packed with people milling about, mostly silent and staring, each looking desperately from face to face for an
explanation.[5] In New York City, men and women passed uncertainly
through the streets like sleepwalkers, stunned and speechless. When
reality began to sink in, even total strangers stopped on Broadway, then
"sobbed like children" with one another. "My heart is so broken . . . that
I can hardly think or write or speak," admitted Ohio congressman and
future U.S. president James A. Garfield, who was in the city on business.[6] None in the metropolis felt the shock and pain more deeply than
Walt Whitman.

"Mother prepared breakfast—and other meals afterwards—as usual,
but not a mouthful was eaten all day by either of us," the poet reminisced. "We each drank half a cup of coffee; that was all. Little was said.
We got every newspaper morning and evening, and the frequent extras
. . . and pass'd them silently to each other."[7]

Later, when rain poured from leaden skies, Whitman put pen to paper to vent his own dark and dismal emotions: "Black clouds driving
overhead. Lincoln's death—black, black, black—as you look toward the
sky—long broad black like great serpents."[8]

Across the continent, when the news reached California at 10 A.M. on
April 15, the residents were no less startled than their eastern counterparts.[9] Elkan Cohn was just about to deliver his sermon to Saturday

morning worshipers at his San Francisco church when a note was handed to him at the pulpit. As the congregation watched in suspense, the Reverend Cohn soon burst into tears, then collapsed. After recovering somewhat, Cohn announced the grim news to the gathering. His words were received "like a thunderbolt," and with sobs and groans the entire crowd was overcome with sadness.[10]

"At first," admitted an editor in the same city, "few could believe it."[11] When the truth was accepted, however, the impact on Westerners was fully as devastating as that on Easterners.[12] "Hard, stern-featured men weeping like women," wrote one witness as he walked the streets of San Francisco. "Every voice hushed to a whisper."[13]

At her home in Iowa, Marjorie Rogers first heard the incredible news when an elderly friend dropped by. "I was dumb with fear and astonishment," the Des Moines woman admitted, "we could not talk about it. . . . [E]verything looked like an eclipse of the sun, our light and hope was gone. . . . Our old friend weeping like a child rose and left me alone. I wandered listlessly about, could not realize the awfulness of the situation."[14]

When Governor Oliver Morton tried to console a large crowd gathered at the statehouse in Indianapolis, he found he could not even console himself. "[H]is grief choked his utterance so that he was obliged to sit down," said a sad witness."[15]

"And only yesterday," sighed Maggie Lindsley from the same state,

> everything was so bright and beautiful—Nature too was rejoicing in the happiness and glory of this great Nation. . . . Richmond taken! Lee surrendered! A Mighty Nation saved, purged and purified! . . . Only yesterday! And today? Alas! The terrible stroke in the midst of the Nation's triumph! O God! Our God! What does it mean? Why are we thus stricken in the midst of our paeans of praise? . . . Tears are in all eyes—sobs in every voice—old men and children—rich and poor, white and black—all feel it a personal loss. . . . God in Heaven! How hard it is to realize.[16]

Nowhere was the news from Ford's Theater more devastating than in Lincoln's hometown. To one Springfield reporter, it seemed as if the entire city was prostrated to the ground upon hearing the word—"as if," he said, "the Death Angel had taken a member from every family."[17]

"The news of his going struck me dumb," confessed Lincoln's former law partner, William Herndon, "the deed being so infernally wicked . . . so huge in consequences, that it was too large to enter my brain."[18]

Indeed, for some the awful words were simply too enormous, too terrifying to be understood and dealt with sanely. In New York City, when an unstable German heard the news and saw the horrified reaction of those around him, he drew a razor and attempted to cut his own throat.[19] In the same city, a young boy had more success. Already subject to fits, the agitated child announced to his parents that he would join Lincoln in death. Before the screaming mother could react, her son slit his throat.[20] At New Haven, Connecticut, another man dropped dead when he heard the news, and in the same state a young woman reportedly became a raving maniac.[21] After hearing of the assassination, a man in Michigan collapsed and rolled back and forth on the street in a fit. Another individual, utterly unhinged by the news, roamed the sidewalks of Detroit with a large stone in his grip. When asked his purpose, the man replied that he was going to kill two people he knew.[22]

As was the case in the nation's capital, horror and shock soon gave way to anger and violence. "Such passion, such sorrow, such indignation, I never saw before," a federal judge wrote in his journal after observing an Indiana crowd. "Every man seemed full of fury."[23]

Viewing from his office window a boiling, angry crowd, an enraged editor in Bangor, Maine, gave vent to his own explosive emotions. "Let the vengeance of an outraged people have full sway," urged the journalist. "Smite from off the earth all instigators, perpetrators—all their sympathizers. Let them die a dog's death."[24]

With prompting like the above, it is not surprising that the more excitable and unstable among the population quickly translated violent words into violent deeds. When a man on the Brooklyn ferry was overheard muttering "disloyal" sentiments, he was seized by fellow passengers and flung headfirst over the railing. The struggling victim was soon swept under the craft and smashed to death by the paddles.[25]

"Served him right!" shouted those watching from the boat.[26]

At a butcher shop in Ohio, another man clapped in elation when he heard the welcome news from Washington. According to a Cleveland newspaper:

> The shop man had raised his cleaver to strike asunder a bone in the meat as the words of levity and insane joy fell on his ears. He turned on his heels and made a pass at the man with a downward stroke of the cleaver. He sprang aside, but the corner of the blade made a gash in his face. As he was jumping out of the door he received another blow in his shoulder, the axe inflicting a savage wound.[27]

When two strangers fishing on the same stream in Connecticut first learned of Ford's Theater, one yelled that he was "damned glad he's dead." Furious, the other angler dropped his pole, beat the man sense-less, then tied him to a tree far from help.[28]

For similar comments, several were reportedly slain in Boston and Chicago.[29] In the politically divided city of St. Louis, according to one account, many men were shot down like dogs for making similar re-marks. Outside a saloon in the same city, several were wounded and the Jewish owner killed when federal soldiers opened fire.[30] In Indiana and Illinois, even in the president's hometown, those who celebrated the news from Washington were shot down on the spot. One man was lit-erally cut to ribbons by fifteen balls.[31]

Other victims in Iowa, California, and Colorado Territory "escaped up trees" after shouting mobs threw ropes around their necks.[32] In New York City, one cursing celebrant exclaimed, "Old Abe, that son of a bitch, is dead, and he ought to have been killed long ago." His joy was short-lived. A nearby policeman knocked the man cold with his club, then hauled the culprit to court, where he was promptly sentenced to six months in jail.[33] At South Camden in nearby New Jersey, police narrowly saved a black man from lynching at the hands of other blacks after a similar comment.[34]

Numerous "suicides" also were reported. Some victims were found floating in creeks, rivers, and bays. More than one victim was found mangled on railroad tracks. Others were discovered with multiple stab wounds to the heart or several bullet holes to the head. All these victims supposedly died by their own hands.[35]

When one or two boisterous individuals rashly exhibited elation at Lincoln's death, they were easily and unmercifully dealt with by snarl-ing neighbors. When entire communities celebrated, it was another matter. At Marietta, Indiana, the unexpected news from Ford's Theater propelled everyone from their homes, "crazy with joy." Reported a shocked journalist:

> In the absence of a cannon, they loaded and fired an anvil repeat-edly, shouted, danced, sang, and in every possible manner gave expression to their demoniac joy, after which they constructed an effigy of President Lincoln, with a rude representation of the bullet-hole in his head, which they carried about the streets, a big ruffian following, and ringing a bell. The effigy was afterward burnt.[36]

Though numbers and distance might insulate some anti-Lincoln communities, those areas with federal troops nearby who celebrated the president's death did so at their peril. In Green Valley, California, a full-scale battle broke out when angry soldiers moved in to suppress disloyal demonstrations following the assassination. When the smoke had cleared, several lay wounded and nearly a dozen were arrested. Else-where in California, scores of suspicious men either committed "sui-cide" or were hurled into Fort Alcatraz on San Francisco Bay.[37]

Like their civilian counterparts, federal soldiers who foolishly made public their true sentiments on Lincoln could expect short shrift from grieving comrades. One soldier at a camp near Indianapolis declared that he would "have a hoe-down" on Lincoln's grave and thereupon began dancing deliriously. Outraged onlookers seized the man and quickly strung him up. Only when the victim's face turned black did his comrades cut him down. Five other soldiers at Indianapolis were treated similarly.[38]

"Such Monsters shall not remain in my com[man]d.," swore one general, who thereupon had the heads of two soldiers shaved, then or-dered the culprits marched in front of the brigade.[39] When large num-bers of men in an Indiana regiment began a spontaneous celebration of Lincoln's death, the colonel ordered mass arrests. Some of the men were hung up by their fingers and thumbs while others were bucked and gagged.[40] At the very least, federal soldiers who displayed joy at the as-sassination could expect weeks, months, even years of prison time at hard labor.[41]

When the supply of vocal victims ran low, ever-ready rabble-rousers used the excitement to deal with political foes or anyone with a history of opposition to the war and the Republican party. In the horror and confusion following Lincoln's death, and with rumors spreading like wildfire, hundreds of pro-Confederate Northerners, or "Copperheads," as well as Democrats, neutrals, and even moderate Republicans, were seized by their frenzied neighbors to be beaten, clubbed, and sometimes killed.[42]

In Philadelphia, Boston, Battle Creek, Michigan, and other cities, victims were mobbed, then forced to perform humiliating stunts, such as singing patriotic tunes and swearing loyalty while groveling in the dirt.[43] George Stone of Swampscott, Massachusetts, was seized by an angry crowd, tarred and feathered, then dragged through the streets in a rowboat while being forced to wave an American flag.[44]

"Hemp and Hell for Traitors!" urged one journal, a religious periodi-cal that claimed to be a "high Methodist and Christian authority."[45]

On the stormy night following Lincoln's death, a shouting crowd of several hundred men and boys combed the streets of Concord, New Hampshire, searching for disloyalty and treason. After barging into a number of shops and residences, "literally driving old ladies from their houses," the mob surrounded the stately home of Franklin Pierce. "Where is your flag?" a cynical voice demanded when the former U.S. president appeared at the door. Although opposed to many of Lincoln's policies, Pierce was no traitor. After a courageous and dignified address by the Democrat, the satisfied mob left to search for sedition elsewhere.[46]

At Buffalo, when it was noticed that there were no signs of mourning on the house, an angry mob reportedly slung mud and splashed black ink on the residence of another ex-president, Millard Fillmore. Inside the home, the same man who had so cordially hosted the Lincolns on their trip to Washington in 1861 was now bedridden with a serious illness.[47] In New York City, a gang of club-wielding teenagers burst into the Staten Island home of Julia Tyler, widow of the tenth American president. Although no one was injured, before the "patriotic young men" left, they snatched from the room what was believed to be a rebel banner.

"The flag so rudely taken away," wrote Julia a short time later, "was a fancy tri-color, made some ten years ago. . . . It hung as an ornament above a picture. There was no other flag in the house but a large United States one."[48]

As these incidents illustrate, in the fury of the moment the mob's madness respected neither station, age, nor gender. Indeed, those who felt that female Copperheads had been protected from punishment over the past four years because of their sex now eagerly encouraged violence against them. "There are women among us who wept for sorrow when Richmond was taken—who lamented when Lee surrendered—who rejoiced when Lincoln was assassinated," railed the editor of an Indianapolis newspaper. "There are women in the North who, to-day say those things for which men have been imprisoned, shot and hung."[49]

At Terre Haute, Indiana, a female who reportedly shouted for Jefferson Davis was grabbed by a mob, marched through the streets waving a U.S. flag, and forced to shout for the Union.[50] In Detroit, two women were driven from their homes, with one being pounded unmercifully with a broomstick.[51] Another woman in Iowa, long suspected of disloyal sentiments, also was rumored to have cheered over the assassination. According to a Des Moines newspaper:

> Without giving the subject the least investigation . . . a number of women, among them the wife of the presiding elder of the Methodist church, visited the house of Mrs. Peterson, and compelled

her, an invalid, to leave her house and carry an emblem of mourning, which . . . was a flag, and march around the town. She protested that she had not uttered a word of exultation at the death of
the President and implored them to confront her with [the] witness; but her protestations were answered by the insulting reply
that she was lying. She assured them that she was unable to walk
the distance required, and if forced to perform the humiliating
service they must carry her. Her protestations of innocence, her
demand for the proof, her widowhood, and even the precarious
condition of her health, had no power to move their pity. Go she
must and they forced her out of the house and dragged her around
the streets to be scoffed and jeered at, tearing her dress nearly off.

Not content with inflicting this gross indignity upon the sick
woman, they attempted to compel her little daughter, thirteen
years of age, to perform the same service, and because she had
spirit enough to resist the outrage, she was beaten and bruised
until blood streamed from her nose and her arms were black and
blue.[52]

Horrifying incidents such as the above finally forced the more stable
in society to speak out. After self-appointed vigilantes gutted homes and
stores in Fall River, Roxbury, and other Massachusetts towns, then
forced citizens to perform public humiliations, the editor of the Springfield *Republican* in the same state erupted when mobs took over his
town.

"[T]he police, instead of doing anything to stop it, seem rather to go
round with the crowd, and enjoy the fun," snapped the indignant newsman. "These proceedings are too shameful to be tolerated. . . . [T]hey
are outrages and ought to be stopped. If a man blatantly thrusts disloyal
sentiments into the faces of the community, and is rash enough to insult the loyal heart of the people in this hour of its great sorrow, we are
perfectly willing, nay anxious, that he should be summarily shut up and
punished according to his deserts. . . . But as long as such men keep still,
let them severely alone."[53]

Though well-intentioned, such cries for sanity were largely lost in the
shouts for revenge.

Because the city's grand victory celebration—the greatest drunken
display in its history—had ended only hours earlier, when the awful
news from Ford's reached Cincinnati the reaction was especially violent.
Moments after hearing the word, two jubilant men stepped onto the
street and announced they were "glad" Lincoln was dead. According to

one who was there, "The words had hardly escaped their lips when a man drew a pistol and shot one dead on the spot. The other was literally cut to pieces."[54] Many others in the city fared little better.[55]

With bloodthirsty mobs controlling the streets of Cincinnati, homes and businesses of suspected Copperheads were looted and destroyed.[56] Fearing for his life, a physician who had earlier failed to display a U.S. flag during the celebration quickly hung one from his window. Unimpressed by the gesture, a howling mob now demanded that the flag be taken down. The doctor nervously refused. As bullets and rocks battered the home, police arrived and escorted the trembling inmates to safety.[57]

Unlike Cincinnati officials, who at least tried to maintain law and order, the mayor of Philadelphia announced that any who did not display symbols of mourning need expect no aid from city police.[58]

Already inhabited by some of the roughest elements in America, the West Coast was especially explosive. After the initial shock had passed, a storm of anger and violence swept through San Francisco.[59] In short order, and with employees fleeing for their lives, frenzied mobs entered the offices of several "obnoxious" Democratic newspapers and went to work.[60] When the rioters had finished, the businesses were totally destroyed.[61] To the south, the same news "fell like an avalanche" on Los Angeles, where homes were burned and many, including a black, a Jew, and a Mexican, were arrested.[62]

At Westminster, Maryland, an angry mob stormed the office of a local Democratic newspaper and smashed it to splinters. The editor, Joseph Shaw, was warned that if he returned to town he would be killed on sight. As added justification, members of the crowd insisted that the journalist was a depraved debaucher who had "led to ruin a simple-minded girl."[63]

Near Berlin, Illinois, soldiers arrested five individuals and accused them of being Missouri guerrillas. When the men were later lynched, a Springfield editor admitted that at most the victims might have been guilty of being Copperheads.[64] In far-off Washington Territory, fifteen men—"horse thieves and highwaymen"—were hung in Walla Walla, and a vigilance committee had a list of 150 more to be driven out or killed.[65] And in numerous other instances, the line separating the personal from the political became blurred as opportunists seized the moment to punish their foes.

During the height of the Cincinnati riot, one unscrupulous individual spotted an old and much-hated enemy who happened to also be a loyal Union man. Pointing at his foe, and beckoning to the mob, the man yelled: "You are not sorry, eh? You shout for Jeff. Davis, do you?" As intended, the innocent victim was swiftly set upon by the crowd.[66]

At San Francisco, a drunk who suffered from insane fits of jealousy grabbed a pistol, then chased his screaming wife into the yard and tried to kill her. Although the ball fortunately missed its mark, the man justified his murderous action by insisting that the woman was a "damned secesh bitch."[67]

Throughout the frenzied North, the madness continued as a deeply wounded nation turned savagely on itself. In the hours following Lincoln's assassination, hundreds died, thousands were beaten or jailed, and countless others were forced to flee for their lives. Indeed, for those well versed in the history of the French Revolution and the Terror that came with it, the horrors of the American terror must have seemed chillingly similar. As the nation teetered on the brink of anarchy, there was a very real fear among many sane individuals that one small ball weighing less than an ounce might accomplish that which tons and tons of rebel lead had failed to do.

CHAPTER SEVENTEEN

THIS SOBBING DAY

WITH LITTLE OR NO RESPITE, the rain that came with Lincoln's death continued throughout the day in Washington on Saturday, April 15. Despite the downpour, the streets of the capital were crowded with citizens. Little was said. Faces full of sadness said all.[1] It was if the people were compelled by some mysterious force to join with others and mourn over a loss so profound that words were meaningless. Many moved about the city as if in a stupor. Few felt the loss more sharply than soldiers. Those who had fought for years and had grown fond of Father Abraham now reacted as if they had indeed lost a parent. "It probably means more to me than it does to you," a cavalryman sobbed to a comrade. "He signed an order that saved me from being shot."[2]

Returning to the army hospital soon after his nightmarish duty at the Petersen home, Charles Leale was concerned about the terrible impact the assassination would have on his wounded men:

> One of my patients was profoundly depressed. He said to me: "Doctor, all we have fought for is gone. Our country is destroyed, and I want to die." This officer the day before was safely recovering from an amputation. I called my lady nurse, "Please closely watch Lieutenant _____; cheer him as much as possible, and give him two ounces of wine every two hours. . . ." This brave soldier received the greatest kindness and skillful care, but he would not rally from the shock and died in a short time.[3]

Of all groups, however, blacks were perhaps the most tragically stricken. Many were prostrate with grief. From "Crow Hill," "Fighting Alley," "Buzzard Town," and other communities around Washington, frightened blacks, like their white counterparts, journeyed into the rain to mourn as one and contemplate their future. "[T]hey seemed not to know what was to be their fate since their great benefactor was dead," observed Gideon Welles.[4]

"We have lost our Moses," sobbed one colored woman to a white man who tried to console her.

"God will send you another," assured the well-meaning man.

"I know that," replied the woman, "but we had him already."[5]

Amid the dreadful gloom and despondency, the only sign of normalcy was the newsboys. Feeding the public's ravenous need for news, the youngsters sold black-bordered newspapers and extras almost as fast as they were printed.[6] Many were sharp businessmen. "The newsboys raised the price to ten cents a copy (the regular price was five cents) and sold them like hot cakes," one man remembered. "I heard of one news-boy who made $56.00 selling newspapers on that Saturday."[7]

While thousands struggled inwardly with their emotions, the outward manifestations of mourning were everywhere. Within hours of Lincoln's death, down the entire length of Pennsylvania Avenue, on side streets and main thoroughfares, from the meanest hovel to the most stately mansion, hung the black symbols of grief.[8]

"Washington wears a mournful aspect from center to circumference," wrote Charles Sanford to a friend. "Miles and miles of material—from fine & expensive crape to black calico, are devoted to draping the city in mourning."[9]

Swiftly, even at drastically hiked prices, the supplies of material in the stores and shops were exhausted, and the people were reduced to hanging black aprons, scarves, ribbons, and bits of rags from doorknobs and windowsills. U.S. flags, all now lowered to half-staff, were edged in black. Those who owned portraits of the late president hung them on the outside of their homes, adding such slogans as "Our Father," "Our Savior," and "We mourn our loss."[10] At the distant forts surrounding Washington came the slow, steady salute of cannons thundering the terrible news. And in the city itself, from dozens of steeples, deep-voiced bells added to the gloom. And yet, impressive as the formality was, the outward display could in no way give a true expression of the heart.

"This frowning sky, this sobbing day, these low and agonizing words, these closed stores, offices and departments, these stern sentries, pacing to and fro in strange places, these miles of crape," wrote one reporter, "are but signs of a grief that no outward manifestations can wholly express."[11]

With each faint cannon boom and each deep bell toll, the sadness of the city was driven into each heart again and again. In rainy New York, these same sounds were a double affliction to one poor woman. The bond between her and her son was "very close, very strong," said one who knew the two well. "No matter how far apart they were, she seemed to know, in some mysterious way, when anything was wrong with him. If he were ill, or unfit to play, he would often receive a letter of sympathy, counsel, and warning, written when she could not possibly have received any news from him."[12] That morning, as the bells tolled in New York, Mary Ann Booth felt that something truly terrible had occurred to "the fondest of all my boys." A friend happened to be with the mother that morning:

> Outside the newsboys, with strident voice, were calling, "The President's death, and the arrest of John Wilkes Booth." While in answer to these words the mother moaned: "O God, if this be true, let him shoot himself, let him not live to be hung! Spare him, spare us, spare the name that dreadful disgrace!" Then came the sound of the postman's whistle, and with the ring of the doorbell a letter was handed to Mrs. Booth. It was from John Wilkes Booth, written in the afternoon before the tragedy. . . . It was an affectionate letter, such as any mother would like to receive from her son, containing nothing of particular moment, but ghastly to read now, with the thought of what the feelings of the man must have been who held the pen in writing it, knowing what overwhelming sorrow the next few hours would bring.[13]

That "overwhelming sorrow" was perhaps felt no more deeply than in the heart of another of the mother's sons:

> A fearful calamity is upon us. The President of the United States has fallen by the hand of an assassin, and I am shocked to say suspicion points to one nearly related to you as the perpetrator of this horrid deed. God grant it may not prove so![14]

Thus, from a note written by the hand of a friend, did Edwin Booth first learn of the events of the night before. Already steady fare in one of America's most cultured cities—one hundred consecutive full houses for his role as Hamlet alone—Booth was an all but adopted son in Boston. "All the women are crazy about him," one star-struck lady sighed. "[S]o silent and dark and Gawain-looking and so delightfully indifferent and so distressed. . . . [E]very one would like to do something to console him."[15] And yet, all the adulation and popularity vanished from Edwin's mind in a flash when he received the devastating news. Even as he was performing on the Boston stage Friday night and receiving waves of applause as he always had, even then the horrid act was being committed.

"Oh!" wrote the shattered actor, "How little did I dream . . . when on Friday night I was as Sir Edward Mortimer exclaiming 'Where is my honor now? Mountains of shame are piled upon me!' that I was not acting but uttering the fearful truth."[16]

"The news of the morning has made me wretched indeed," continued Booth to a friend, "not only because I have received the unhappy tidings of the suspicion of a brother's crime, but because a good man, and a most justly honored and patriotic ruler, has fallen, in an hour of national joy, by the hand of an assassin."[17]

As Edwin explained to another consoling friend:

> Lincoln was my President for in pure admiration of his noble
> career & Christian principles I did what I never did before—I
> voted & FOR HIM! I was two days ago one of the happiest men
> alive. . . . Now what am I? . . . [T]he beautiful plans I had for the
> future—all blasted now.[18]

Although at the moment it was small consolation to the distraught, sensitive actor, few in Boston were bent on harming him because of his brother's deed. No such charity was extended to another brother by the citizens of Cincinnati. Overhearing the hideous news while at rehearsal Saturday morning, Junius Brutus Booth, Jr., collapsed on stage. When he was revived and tried to stand, again he fainted.[19] During the ensuing riot that swept the city, the actor with the now infamous name was one of the first men called for by the mob. After ripping down his playbills throughout the city, several hundred rioters surrounded the hotel where he was staying. Only the quick wits of a clerk—who nervously announced that Booth had left earlier—prevented a lynching then and there.[20]

Upon hearing the horrific news, other acquaintances wisely worked to put as much distance between themselves and the assassin as possible. "I tried to persuade myself that I did not know Booth," admitted a Philadelphia theater manager. "When questioned in regard to the subject my memory was a blank."[21]

And for those who knew and loved the dashing idol, their grief was bottomless.[22] Clara Morris was in Columbus, Ohio, when word first reached her of Lincoln's murder. Although startled by the terrible news, the actress knew nothing of the details, or who the assassin was.

> My room-mate and I had, from our small earnings, bought some
> black cotton at a tripled price, as all the black material in the city
> was not sufficient to meet the demand; and as we tacked it about

our one window, a man passing told us the assassin had been
discovered, and that he was the actor Booth. Hattie laughed so
she nearly swallowed the tacks that, girl-like, she held between
her lips, and I, after a laugh, told him it was a poor subject for a
jest, and we went in.[23]

A short time later, a friend named Ellsler dropped by to deliver some
playbooks as requested.

> We heard his knock. I was busy pressing a bit of stage finery. Hattie
> opened the door, and then I heard her exclaiming: "Why—why—
> what!" I turned quickly. Mr. Ellsler was coming slowly into the
> room. He is a very dark man, but he was perfectly livid then—his
> lips even were blanched to the whiteness of his cheeks. His eyes
> were dreadful, they were so glassy and seemed so unseeing. He was
> devoted to his children, and all I could think of . . . was disaster to
> one of them, and I cried, as I drew a chair to him: "What is it? Oh,
> what has happened to them?"
>
> He sank down—he wiped his brow—he looked almost stupidly
> at me; then, very faintly, he said: "You—haven't—heard—any-
> thing?"
>
> Like a flash Hattie's eyes and mine met. We thought of the sup-
> posed ill-timed jest of the stranger. My lips moved wordlessly.
> Hattie stammered: "A man—he—lied though—said that Wi-lkes
> Boo-th—but he did lie—didn't he?" and in the same faint voice
> Mr. Ellsler answered slowly: "No—no! He did not lie—it's true!"
>
> Down fell our heads, and the waves of shame and sorrow
> seemed fairly to overwhelm us; and while our sobs filled the little
> room, Mr. Ellsler rose and laid two playbooks on the table. Then,
> while standing there, staring into space, I heard his far, faint voice
> saying: "So great—so good a man destroyed, and by the hand of
> that unhappy boy! my God! my God!" He wiped his brow again
> and slowly left the house, apparently unconscious of our pres-
> ence.[24]

"My heart feels as if it was cramped in a vise," confided another actress, Charlotte Cushman, upon hearing the news.[25]

The shock, of course, was even more devastating for those women ro-
mantically involved with Booth. Lucy Hale, the actor's fiancée, was all
but destroyed emotionally by the news. And Booth's mistress, Ella
Turner, a "rather pretty, light-haired, little woman," closed the door in
her Washington room, stared at her lover's photo one last time, then
tried to kill herself with chloroform. When she was discovered a short

time later, doctors were quickly called in and managed to save her. As the unhappy young woman came to, however, she was far from grateful for what the physicians had done.[26]

Another woman in Washington desperately prayed for the deliverance of death, but, as with Ella, her fondest hope was not to be.

———

"Not there! Oh, not there!" insisted Mary Lincoln as doctors and friends searched for a suitable room in the White House where she might lie. Every chamber, it seemed, had a painful, haunting memory of her dead husband. Finally, a little-used room was located, and the former first lady was at last eased onto a bed.[27] For the tormented woman, there would be no rest. She groaned loudly one moment and shrieked hysterically the next, and there was little anyone could do to console her. Although Mary Jane Welles, wife of the navy secretary, and Elizabeth Dixon were some comfort throughout the tortuous night, the widow repeatedly asked for her mulatto seamstress, Lizzie Keckley. When the woman was finally located later in the morning, she was swiftly driven to the White House.

> I was quickly shown to Mrs. Lincoln's room, and on entering, saw Mrs. L. tossing uneasily about upon a bed. The room was darkened, and the only person in it besides the widow of the President was Mrs. Secretary Welles. . . .
>   "Why did you not come to me last night, Elizabeth—I sent for you?" Mrs. Lincoln asked in a low whisper.
>   "I did try to come to you, but I could not find you," I answered, as I laid my hand upon her hot brow. . . .
>   Shortly after entering the room on Saturday morning, Mrs. Welles excused herself, as she said she must go to her own family, and I was left alone with Mrs. Lincoln. She was nearly exhausted with grief, and when she became a little quiet, I asked and received permission to go into the Guest's Room [across the hall] where the body of the President lay in state. . . . When I entered the room, the members of the Cabinet and many distinguished officers of the army were grouped around the body of their fallen chief. They made room for me, and, approaching the body, I lifted the white cloth from the white face of the man that I had worshipped as an idol. . . . I gazed long at the face, and turned away with tears in my eyes and a choking sensation in my throat.[28]

Soon after Lizzie left the room, an autopsy began on the dead president. Dr. Edward Curtis:

> Seated around the room were several general officers and some
> civilians, silent or conversing in whispers, and to one side,
> stretched upon a rough frame work of boards and covered only
> with sheets and towels, lay—cold and immovable—what but a
> few hours before was the soul of a great nation. The Surgeon
> General was walking up and down the room when I arrived and
> detailed me the history of the case. He said that the President
> showed most wonderful tenacity of life, and, had not his wound
> been necessarily mortal, might have survived an injury to which
> most men would succumb.[29]

"His eyes were both very much protruded—the right one most—and very black and puffy underneath," observed friend Orville Browning.[30]

During the examination, a messenger from Mary Lincoln entered the room requesting a lock of hair. When the strand had been snipped, the servant left and the procedure continued. Edward Curtis:

> Dr. [J. J.] Woodward and I proceeded to open the head and re-
> move the brain down to the track of the ball. The latter entered a
> little to the left of the median line at the back of the head, had
> passed almost directly forwards through the center of the brain
> and lodged. Not finding it readily, we proceeded to remove the
> entire brain, when, as I was lifting the latter from the cavity of the
> skull, suddenly the bullet dropped out through my fingers and
> fell, breaking the solemn silence of the room with its clatter, into
> an empty basin that was standing beneath.[31]

"There it lay upon the white china," thought Dr. Curtis as he stared at the bullet, "a little black mass no bigger than the end of my finger—dull, motionless and harmless, yet the cause of such mighty changes in the world's history."[32]

One of those mighty changes spoken of was taking place in a quiet ceremony at the Kirkwood House. At 11 A.M., Chief Justice Salmon Chase administered the oath of office to Andrew Johnson. Sharing the room were several cabinet members and senators. As he looked into the face of the soon-to-be president, a face "full of sorrow & anxiety," Chase was struck by the sudden change of fortunes.[33]

> How strange that seemed to me! I could not realize it. Just six
> weeks before . . . I administered to [Lincoln] the oath of office for
> the second term; & now I was to administer the same oath to his

successor. The duty was performed with a heart as sad, as it had
been joyous before. It all went with my lips as I said to Mr.
Johns[on] "You are President; may God support, guide & bless
you in your arduous duties.[34]

"The duties of the office are mine; I will perform them—the consequences are with God," said the new president simply. "Gentlemen, I
shall lean upon you; I feel that I shall need your support."[35]

Because of his drunken display in March and the tragic circumstances
he was now thrust into, Johnson was eyed nervously by all. Most in the
room were greatly relieved.

"All I have seen of him gives me the greatest hopes. His bearing is
modest, firm & manly," said Chief Justice Chase. "So in darkness there
is light."[36]

Unlike Chase, others present were not entirely free of apprehen-
sions.[37]

Had Mary Lincoln known of events at the Kirkwood, it would have
added to an already crushing load. Despising the man from the depth
of her heart for embarrassing her and her husband at the second inaugural, Mary's bruised and battered mind was now convinced that
Johnson had had a hidden hand in the murder. When Lizzie Keckley
finally returned to the former first lady's room, she found the woman
entering a new cycle of sadness:

> Robert was bending over his mother with tender affection, and
> little Tad was crouched at the foot of the bed with a world of
> agony in his young face. I shall never forget the scene—the wails
> of a broken heart, the unearthly shrieks, the terrible convulsions,
> the wild, tempestuous outbursts of grief from the soul. I bathed
> Mrs. Lincoln's head with cold water, and soothed the terrible
> tornado as best I could. Tad's grief at his father's death was as
> great as the grief of his mother, but her terrible outbursts awed
> the boy into silence. Sometimes he would throw his arms around
> her neck, and exclaim, between his broken sobs, "Don't cry so,
> Mamma! Don't cry, or you will make me cry, too! You will break
> my heart." . . . Every room in the White House was darkened, and
> every one spoke in subdued tones, and moved about with muffled
> tread.[38]

One of those leaving quietly, glad to escape the White House horror,
was Gideon Welles. As the secretary was descending the stairs, Tad Lincoln ran screaming after him. "Oh, Mr. Welles, who killed my father?"

cried the boy.[39] Outside, others, just as confused, were asking the same question.

"On the Avenue in front of the White House were several hundred colored people, mostly women and children, weeping and wailing their loss," noted Welles. "This crowd did not appear to diminish through the whole of that cold, wet day; they seemed not to know what was to be their fate since their great benefactor was dead, and their hopeless grief affected me more than almost anything else.[40]

For Mary Lincoln, Lizzie Keckley, Gideon Welles, and countless others, the night of April 15 was an uneasy, restless, haunted night. "I feel like a frightened child," shuddered Julia Shepard, who was at Ford's on the fateful evening,. "I wish I could go home and have a good cry. I can't bear to be alone. . . . Sleeping or waking, that terrible scene is before me."[41]

David Dorn was also tossing and turning his night away. In the audience that evening, the crippled soldier cursed the crutches and missing leg he had lost in battle and pondered what might have been. "I could have caught Booth when he started to fall on the stage," Dorn mused. "But there I was, helpless. All I could do was cry."[42]

Of all those tormented souls, none suffered more than Henry Rathbone and Clara Harris.[43] Again and again the shattered young couple replayed in their minds the last moments in the box—how promising their future appeared to be, and how happy and affectionate the Lincolns seemed.

"What will Miss Harris think of my hanging on to you so?" Mary had said playfully to her husband.

"She won't think any thing about it," the president had smiled.[44]

These thoughts, that moment, marked the end of the old life, as Clara and Henry both knew; gone forever were happiness and hope when the shadow silently entered the box. Major Rathbone:

> I heard the report of a pistol from behind me, and on looking around saw dimly through the smoke the form of a man between the President and the door. I heard him shriek out some such word as "Freedom." He uttered it in such an excited tone that it was difficult for me to understand what he said. I immediately sprang towards him and seized him. He wrested himself from my grasp, and at the same time made a violent thrust at me with a large knife. I parried the blow by striking it up and received a deep wound on my left arm. The man sprang towards the front of the box. I rushed after him but only succeeded in catching his

clothes as he leaped over the railing of the box. I instantly cried out, "Stop that man!"[45]

Before anyone could react, or even think, the shadowy figure had disappeared with "astonishing" speed. Through the swirl of smoke, Clara remembered seeing a startled and confused Mrs. Lincoln standing and looking over the balustrade, fearing that her husband had fallen to the stage.[46] For what seemed an eternity, time in the box was frozen. And then, through the smoke and flowing blood, the silence was shattered by that piercing shriek. For Clara, Henry, and the others who heard that terrible scream, the sound marked an end of lives that could never, ever be recovered.

CHAPTER EIGHTEEN

BLACK EASTER

Unlike the day before, Sunday, April 16, 1865, broke bright and beautiful over the land. From Maine to Missouri, the dark clouds and rain that had seemingly engulfed the world gave way to warmth and sunshine. All the same, in the hearts and minds of millions, no amount of blue sky or green grass could erase the deep gloom of "Black Easter." Across the nation, as if fleeing some great calamity, Americans crowded into churches until they could hold no more. In the president's hometown of Springfield, the places of worship were filled to overflowing, and many pressed close to the doors and windows to hear.[1]

On New York Avenue in Washington, the Presbyterian church that Lincoln had attended was quickly packed, and hundreds were forced to listen from outside.[2] The space where the first family normally sat was empty now, draped in black.[3]

"I sat . . . directly behind the vacant pew of the President," General Lewis Parsons wrote to his mother. "The remarks and prayers of Dr. G[urley] were impressive and solemn—but nothing so solemn to me as the recollection of seeing Mr. Lincoln in the same now vacant seat when I last attended that church—His greeting then was so kind and he so full of life."[4]

The sense of loss and sadness at Lincoln's church and thousands more throughout the land ran doubly deep, as Americans had not been given the time to say goodbye and thank the president for his accomplishments. Through four years of terrible strain and stress, Lincoln had visibly passed from youth to old age. Reviled and ridiculed by his enemies, dismissed and denounced even by many of his friends, the simple man with the common roots had succeeded when most felt he would fail. The goal was reached. The nation, *one nation*, would survive. But he who had made it possible did not live to enjoy the fruit of his labor, and those who would reap the reward now had no opportunity to show their love and appreciation.

"Just in the hour when the crowning triumph of his life awaited him," said a sad Springfield editor, "the assassin's hand at once puts a rude period to his life and to his hopes."[5]

In a world of inequity, Lincoln's sudden death seemed the most unfair blow of all. Because they had not had the chance to honor him in life, many sad and sincere individuals now rushed to honor him in death. "We knew not how much we loved him until he was gone," one clergyman tearfully admitted.[6]

Eulogized a California journalist:

> The manner of his death adds nothing to his merit, but it gives a peculiar brilliancy to his fate, and throws a halo over his memory. . . . Hot blood called him slow, and cold blood called him hot. . . . Those who would outrun the age called him too slow—those who would lag behind called him too fast; but with his steps a people kept pace.[7]

Understandably, from this heart-wrenching sadness and this desperate need to suddenly extol and exalt the slain president, deification was the next and easiest step. Explained one Washingtonian:

> He who had for years been derided by tongue and pen as a "clown," a "gorilla," and a "negro lover" was now transfigured and became immortal. People could not do enough to show their love for him and the appreciation of his memory. Booth had turned the execration and hatred of many, even of Lincoln's own party, who had been his bitterest political enemies, into the most profound reverence.[8]

Many compared Lincoln to the great American icon, George Washington; blacks considered him a modern-day Moses; not a few of both colors likened the slain president to Jesus Christ. Coming as the assassination did on Good Friday, many, especially on Easter Sunday, were quick to note the parallel. "Yes," assured a Hartford pastor, "it was meet that the martyrdom should occur on Good Friday. . . . Jesus Christ died for the world, Abraham Lincoln died for his country."[9]

The Reverend Warren Cudworth of Boston took the elevation of Lincoln to its Christ-like conclusion when he said, "[C]ould our President have spoken after he was shot, he would have forgiven the cowardly perpetrator of this inhuman act, and rounded the parallel with a final and complete imitation of our Lord's example."[10]

Some clergymen felt that the great calamity had been brought on by the nation itself—that the bacchanalian victory celebration during the days preceding Holy Week was sacrilegious, or, as one of the devout expressed it, the assassination was "the chastising rod of Providence."[11] Most ministers did not accept this argument. The attacks upon Lincoln and Seward were not proof of God's wrath, these men argued; on the contrary, the tragedy was the work of Satan. Only hearts "steeped in the venom of hell," raged an Albany preacher, could commit such acts.[12] Reasoned Sarah Hill of Norristown, Pennsylvania:

> God has permitted the thing to be [so that] the hearts of all loyal people may be filled with hatred for treason . . . and that in avenging the blood of the Martyred Lincoln [they will] root up even the smallest fibre of treason from the soil. . . . [T]he descendants of traitors and traitor sympathizers are to be shunned as a race accursed for all time to come, as were the Jews who had the blood of the Savior on their hands.[13]

With such angry words issuing from respected Christians and "men of God," it is small wonder that the already excited public was goaded into further madness. Even while preachers throughout the North were pounding their pulpits for revenge, mobs continued the violent purge. Nowhere was this more evident than in the nation's capital.

Because the whereabouts of the assassins and the extent of the conspiracy were still nebulous, Washington in effect had become a closed city, with all roads picketed and no one allowed to come and go.[14] With the city secure, the hunt for suspects was simplified. One report stated that officials were going to search every room in every building of the capital to flush out the culprits.[15] Anyone associated with Booth was, of course, under immediate suspicion. Hundreds were questioned about the popular young actor, and scores were tossed into the Old Capitol Prison.[16] After her recovery, Booth's paramour, Ella Turner, was arrested, as was everyone else in the home, "from the mistress to the cook."[17] Actors, and anyone associated with the stage, were rounded up and examined closely. A hapless Kansan who somehow blundered into town was arrested and roughly treated because he resembled the famous thespian.[18]

Some persistent rumors hinted that the assassin was still at large in the city disguised as a female. As a result, all men dressed as women were arrested; four such suspects were plucked from the streets of Georgetown alone. Another man caught in skirts was attacked by a brick-throwing mob when it was rumored that he was the assailant of Secretary Seward.[19]

Prostitutes were also jailed. Many, including a black woman, were arrested for "frisking" over Lincoln's death. One strumpet shouted with glee that Booth "deserves a crown." Under the assumption that they were celebrating, common drunks and drug addicts were taken away as well. Even halfwits and gibbering idiots were watched closely.[20]

Self-appointed vigilantes, or "street rangers," also scoured the city. Homeowners who had not illuminated during the victory celebrations and now displayed no symbols of mourning were ordered to do so within fifteen minutes or face the consequences. Likewise, those who failed to don black or dress plainly were viewed suspiciously as Southern sympathizers when they appeared in gay colors. Well-intentioned men who had urged restraint during the riots of Friday and Saturday were now pointed out and hurled into the Old Capitol Prison. In such a climate of fear and suspicion, even a smile or a jest could be construed as seditious and summon the wrath of a mob or the federal government.[21]

"No man could utter a word not of grief without proclaiming himself a partisan of the assassin," recorded one observer in the prison-like city.[22]

"Anybody and everybody was arrested on sight, if they showed the least suspicious sign," another witness wrote.[23]

Many men were reportedly beaten and killed before they reached prison. Some victims were found floating in the Potomac.[24] Once ubiquitous, paroled soldiers in Confederate uniforms now wisely sought hiding places. Those who showed themselves faced almost certain violence. When a rebel general and two aides were led through the streets Sunday by federal guards, a mob of several thousand followed close behind, chanting "Hang them up! Hang them!!" Hustling the prisoners into the provost marshal's office, troops tried to quell the riot, to no effect. Fearing that the doors would soon be forced, the men were quickly ushered out the back and ensconced in Old Capitol.[25] Later, a larger group of prisoners were led along the back streets of the city. Word soon spread, and again a rock- and brick-throwing mob attacked. When the guards themselves were hit, they halted and leveled their muskets as if to fire. As soon as the column tried to move, again the rioters pressed forward.[26] One of the rebel prisoners describes the scene:

> An angry and mongrel crowd, composed mostly of negroes and bummers, was gathering around us, uttering all kinds of threats. . . . [W]e were everywhere greeted with yells, etc., of "damned assassins," "kill them," etc. Some officer in our party seeing the

situation of himself and us all, told the sergeant of the guard that "we" (the Confederate) prisoners, did not propose to stand there and be mobbed, and that if he and his guard could not protect us, we would be forced to take their muskets and protect ourselves. . . . To the Confederate officer's request or demand, the negro sergeant replied, "Stand back dar white man. I'se gwine to pertect you." Fortunately, before the mob could find a leader, the authorities sent down some companies . . . who quickly and without any ceremony dispersed the mob.[27]

Not only were heavy reinforcements placed in and around Old Capitol, but military hospitals were patrolled to prevent the savage mobs from dragging out and murdering the Confederate wounded.[28]

Although some Americans, such as Horace Greeley, were aghast at the Jacobin spirit scourging the North, most were not. Indeed, many were elated at this settling of accounts with traitors and "home-grown rebels" in the rear. While Northern mobs were dealing out "justice" with a bloody hand, no one in the victorious Union forgot where the real roots of trouble lay. In many ways, the death of Lincoln sealed the final awful fate of the defeated Confederacy. "With malice toward none, with charity for all" died at Ford's Theater.

"[T]he South must be literally swept with the sword, all the fiends ought to be driven out or hanged," argued one leading radical to Senator Charles Sumner.[29] On this account most Northerners, high and low, generally agreed. The South and slavery had killed Abraham Lincoln, and now the South and slavery would pay.

CHAPTER NINETEEN

A DOUBLE DISASTER

WITH MUCH OF THE SOUTH'S INFRASTRUCTURE smashed by war, communications throughout the region were slowed to a crawl. News of Lincoln's death took days, even weeks, to reach many in the fast-shrinking Confederacy. As a rule, federal-held territory along waterways was first to hear. In Virginia, a steamer on the James River spread the word to both shores by displaying a huge placard on an upper deck which read: "President Lincoln Assassinated!"[1] On the Mississippi, with its whistle screaming and the unmistakable black draped from its decks, the *Sultana* carried the grim news from Kentucky to Louisiana.[2] For the most part, though, the same news that had raced across the North with the lightning speed of the telegraph now crept through the South on the slow, weary footfalls of returning rebel soldiers.

Like those in the North, most men and women in the South were stunned by the news. Unlike Northerners, however, most of those in Dixie were elated by the sudden turn of events. In fact, many Confederates felt the report was merely another false rumor stirred to keep their morale up. After four years of bloody persecution, after the deaths of husbands, fathers, and sons, most thought the news of Lincoln's death simply too good to be true. When the rumors became fact, a majority of Southerners were overjoyed.[3]

"Lincoln, Lincoln the oppressor, is dead! actually dead!" Catherine Edmondston of North Carolina excitedly jotted in her journal.[4]

"Could there have been a fitter death for such a man?" echoed Emma LeConte of Columbia, South Carolina.

> Our spirits had been so low that the least good news elevated
> them wonderfully and this was so utterly unlooked-for, took us so
> completely by surprise. I actually *flew* home and for the first time

in oh, so long, I was trembling and my heart beating with excitement. I stopped in at Aunt Josie's to talk it over. As soon as I reached the head of the stairs, they all cried, "What do you think of the news?" "Isn't it splendid," etc. We were all in a tremor of excitement. . . . The man we hated has met his proper fate.[5]

Often startled by the intensity of their hatred, most Southern women nevertheless felt in their hearts that Lincoln's death was the work of an avenging angel. Explained a Virginian:

We could not be expected to grieve . . . for Mr. Lincoln, whom we had seen only in the position of an implacable foe at the head of a power invading and devastating our land. . . . I remember how one poor woman took the news. She was half-crazed by her losses and troubles; one son had been killed in battle, another had died in prison, of another she could not hear if he were living or dead; her house had been burned; her young daughter, turned out with her in the night, had died of fright and exposure. She ran in, crying: "Lincoln has been killed! Thank God!"

I'm not glad. But, somehow, I *can't* be sorry. I believe it was the vengeance of the Lord.[6]

"We were desperate and vindictive, and whosoever denies it forgets or is false," one man candidly admitted.[7]

Intensifying Southern satisfaction was the knowledge that federal officers had received orders to murder Confederate president Jefferson Davis and his entire cabinet during an aborted cavalry raid on Richmond in 1864.[8] Most of the South felt that even if Lincoln had not signed the death papers, he had countenanced it in principle. Hence, his demise at the hand of an assassin seemed especially appropriate.[9]

In those areas of the former Confederacy occupied by federal troops, much of the celebration was understandably furtive, confined largely to parlors and diaries.[10] In regions still free of Yankee rule, emotions ran wild.

"Abe Lincoln . . . the political mountebank and professional joker, whom nature intended for the ring of a circus . . . has fallen," a Selma, Alabama, editor told his readers. "His career was as short as it was bloody and infamous."[11]

Upon receiving the news at a store in Georgia, everyone hurrahed and tossed their hats in the air.[12] In Kentucky, William Quantrill's guerrillas, still active and full of fight, set up a cheer, then galloped their horses to a nearby still house, where they celebrated "for a day or two."[13] Others throughout the hard-pressed Confederacy tied hemp on their doorknobs in mock mourning.[14] Many appreciative rebels were mad to learn more of their hero and obtain his photograph. "All honor to J. Wilkes Booth, who has rid the world of a tyrant and made himself famous for generations," cheered one woman.[15]

In the Trans-Mississippi Department, Texans were even more demonstrative. "It is certainly a matter of congratulation that Lincoln is dead," cheered a Marshall editor, "because the world is happily rid of a monster that disgraced the form of humanity."[16] On the Rio Grande, several hundred rebels in Matamoras toasted Lincoln's demise with champagne and beer, then fashioned a grave from sand and scrawled on a headboard: "To the memory of the damned Ape Lincoln."[17]

Increasingly though, the jubilation over Lincoln's death was crowded out by visions of the future. With almost certain defeat at hand, occupation could not be far behind—occupation by a wrathful enemy thirsting to avenge its fallen leader. For those joyous only a moment before, the thought was sobering indeed.[18]

Eliza Andrews was sitting on a train at a Georgia railroad station when the word from Washington arrived. "Some fools laughed and applauded," the young woman recorded, "but wise people looked grave and held their peace. It is a terrible blow to the South, for it places that vulgar renegade, Andy Johnson, in power, and will give the Yankees an excuse for charging us with a crime which was in reality only the deed of an irresponsible madman."[19]

As Eliza noted, it was now that many Confederates came to the grim realization that the vindictive "drunken ass," Andrew Johnson, had replaced the much more charitable, conciliatory Abraham Lincoln. It was also now that many Southerners began distancing themselves from their true emotions.

"We do not believe there is one intelligent citizen in Hancock County who does not deeply denounce his murder and sincerely mourn his loss," insisted one Kentuckian with a straight face.[20] From Lexington, another man announced that "every countenance was sad—even the Secessionists lamented the sad event."[21]

Though greatly exaggerated, there were indeed some Southerners who genuinely mourned Lincoln's loss. Blacks, both free and slave, felt the president's death as deeply as any. Many were uncertain of their fate now that Father Abraham was gone. "Uncle Sam is dead; have I got to go back to massa?" a little black boy asked a white lady.[22]

"Thousands of negroes were wringing their hands and in indescribable wailings were giving expression to their great grief," wrote a witness in Virginia. "[N]o one could doubt the genuiness [or] the depth of grief."[23]

Even white Southerners—Unionists in the border states, disgruntled Confederates in the mountains—were truly saddened by the death of a man who had risen from nothing to greatness.[24] "[O]ld Abe with all his apeishness was a kindhearted man disposed to treat us generously and mercifully," one North Carolinian confided.[25]

Although a majority of rebels could not force themselves to write or utter such sentiments even for self-preservation, the fear of prying eyes and certain retribution made many circumspect, even in journal entries. "Heard that Lincoln had been assassinated," scratched one secretive Virginia diarist on April 20. "Cool in the morning, pleasant day."[26] And whatever joy Mary Ford of Georgetown, Kentucky, may have felt when word arrived, little was evident in her journal entry: "Lincoln & Seward were both massacred at the theater last night. Dr. here after tea—rainy nearly all day—cleared off cooler."[27]

While the cryptic indifference of average Southern whites said much while saying nothing, the true consequences of Lincoln's murder were clearly understood by the handful of Confederate leaders.[28] "We should have regarded Mr. Lincoln's death as a calamity, even if it had come about by natural means," wrote George Cary Eggleston, "[but] coming as it did through a crime committed in our name, it seemed doubly a disaster."[29]

The fugitive Confederate president Jefferson Davis first learned of the events at Ford's Theater when he was handed an urgent telegram as he stood on the steps of a home in Charlotte, North Carolina. When the yet defiant rebel soldiers around him began to raise a cheer at the unexpected glad tidings, the somber statesman raised his hands. "It is sad news," muttered Davis. "I certainly had no special regard for Mr. Lincoln, but there are a great many men whose end I would much rather have heard than his. I fear it will be disastrous to our people, and I regret it deeply."[30]

Another Confederate leader who had real cause to rue events in Washington was Joseph Johnston. Receiving the startling news during surrender negotiations with Major General William T. Sherman near Raleigh, North Carolina, Johnston visibly reddened, broke into a cold sweat, then denounced the murder as a "disgrace to the age." While Sherman knew that neither Johnston nor his ragged army had had a hand in the assassination, the Union general also realized what the reaction of his own men would be when they heard the news. Prudently opting to withhold the information as long as possible, Sherman was determined to prevent death and destruction when the word became official.[31] By the morning of April 18, the news could no longer be held back.

Records Lieutenant John Janicke of the 4th Minnesota Infantry:

> [W]hile kneeling on the greensward around the breakfast dishes a
> newsboy came running into camp with a lot of Raleigh newspa-
> pers, shouting, "All about the assassination! President Lincoln
> assassinated! . . . " We drop knives and forks and rise, grief-
> stricken, and in solemn silence leave our breakfast. Lieutenant
> Dooley is standing behind an oak tree, the tears falling from his
> eyes. Before I get through reading I am overcome with painful
> emotion.[32]

"[A] grapeshot through the heart would not have struck me more
dumb," echoed a stunned comrade.[33]

Union soldiers elsewhere throughout the occupied South were no less
shaken. Charles Deamude heard the "lamentible nuse" while his unit
was in Cleveland, Tennessee. "I could not believe it all though it had
been con firmed by fore telegrams," the soldier wrote his father. "I
thaught it was a camp rhumer."[34]

In Morganza, Louisiana, Major Charles Hawes and his hungry men
were waiting for mess when the *Sultana,* that "dark angel of misfortune,"
hove to clad in black.[35] "[N]ot one of us could take our seats at the
table," the officer admitted upon hearing the ill tidings. "We all felt too
deeply."[36]

"Regiments were seen to weep—not a single man, here and there—
but whole regiments," reported a correspondent in Mobile.[37]

As with their civilian counterparts, after the soldiers' shock and sadness had passed, rage rushed in.[38] As Sherman had rightly feared, once
his men had been aroused, revenge on anyone at hand would be the
response. "The army is crazy for vengeance," admitted an Illinois soldier.[39] When thousands of inflamed troops, bent on murder and may-
hem, marched on Raleigh, only the superhuman efforts of Sherman's
lieutenant, General John Logan, and his threat to sweep the mutineers
with grape and canister prevented the destruction of the North Carolina
capital and a wholesale massacre.[40]

Not every Yankee commander was as conscientious as Sherman and
Logan. In northern Alabama, Brig. Gen. R. S. Granger ordered the
summary execution of anyone "who in any manner" found favor with
the assassination.[41] And elsewhere throughout the occupied South, the
emotions of Union soldiers were fully as explosive as they had been in
North Carolina. "I say hang every one of them from Jeff Davis down,"
Lieutenant Holiday Ames wrote to his wife in Ohio. "I would be in
favour of raising the black flag and not give one of them any quarters."[42]

Added to the average soldier's genuine sense of sorrow and fury at the deed was the understandable outrage that the war might be lengthened as a consequence. Such was the intense anger of Lieutenant Ames, however, that more war was actually welcomed. "I feel now like staying in the army three years more and fighting for reveng, yes fighting until every Cursed Rebble is exterminated," wrote the grim officer in his diary.[43]

When the "offle News" reached Hoosier Ivan Barr in Mississippi, his bloodlust was almost boundless. "If we had Old Jeff and his Cabanet hear [we] could cut them in mints meat[.] I could cut there heart out with my knife and lick the Blud of with my mouth. . . . I would like to get a shot at Some of them Copperheads that is rejoicing there at home[.] I could kill one of them as easy as a Hog."[44]

Unfortunately, in countless instances throughout the South, the bloody fantasies of many soldiers were more than fulfilled. At Vicksburg, Mississippi, paroled Confederate officers were chased through the town by howling Yankee soldiers.[45] Federal troops, muskets in hand, roamed the deserted streets of Memphis, anxious to slay any and all Southerners encountered.[46] In Goldsboro, North Carolina, a citizen was shot dead by an angry Union soldier.[47] Others were reportedly killed in Kentucky.[48] Perhaps as many as nine men were murdered in New Orleans alone, some for exhibiting mere "indifference" to Lincoln's death.[49]

At the numerous prison camps in the North, helpless captives were especially vulnerable. "I thought we would all be shot," remembered a rebel at Hart's Island in New York. "We were not allowed to collect in groups and the guard was to shoot if we were seen talking together."[50] South of Philadelphia, at Fort Delaware, artillery was trained on the prisoners with orders to fire if any rejoicing was observed. Understandably, far from celebrating the news, the starving, frightened inmates were cowed into silence.[51] To forestall an indiscriminate massacre, twenty-two thousand prisoners at Point Lookout in Maryland passed a resolution condemning the assassination.[52] Richard Ewell, John Marmaduke, and other general officers confined at Fort Warren in Boston Harbor did likewise.[53] Similarly, with so many murderous eyes about, many prisoners, like their civilian counterparts, were extremely circumspect in their diary entries and letters to loved ones. "I am very anxious for the *Assassin* to be captured, and the case investigated," one rebel prisoner at Johnson's Island, Ohio insisted in a letter to his brother. "I am sure, the Government I have been fighting under, for 4 years, would not be guilty of such an outrage, it was a cold, bloody murder, and can never be countenanced by any Southern man."[54]

Despite precautions such as these, there was the widespread fear that a general slaughter of Confederate inmates would occur at Castle Thunder, Belle Isle, and Libby prisons in Richmond.[55] In the military hospital at nearby City Point, wounded Yankees attacked an injured rebel for a reported anti-Lincoln comment.[56] At Elmira, New York, a Confederate was hung up by his thumbs until he fainted for cheering Lincoln's death. After a similar comment, another man at Fort Jefferson in the Dry Tortugas died from the same punishment.[57]

Nowhere in the South was the violence greater than at Nashville. Emotions were so volatile and discipline so lax that for all practical purposes, rioting soldiers ruled the streets. Soon after word from Ford's Theater reached the Tennessee capital, one man on Church Street was heard to say that he was "glad the damned abolition son of a bitch was dead; he ought to have died long ago!"[58]

"Before the words had fairly left his lips," said a bystander, "a soldier shot him through the heart, and plunging his bayonet into the falling body, pinned him to the ground!"[59] Not only was the murderer allowed to go free after the deed, but an approving witness offered him a one hundred dollar reward.[60] Another man, a federal captain, was overheard stating that Lincoln was the cause of the war. Soldiers nearby immediately jumped the officer, beat him savagely, then cut the bars and buttons from the victim's coat.[61] Numerous others in Nashville were treated like the two men above. "Every man that rejoiced over the news was doomed to death on the spot," Sergeant Hamlin Coe recorded. "Some were shot, others bayoneted, others mauled to death."[62]

At night, rampaging soldiers swarmed through the streets beating and killing suspected Confederates and destroying their homes.[63] Not satisfied with the damage already done, the rioters issued orders the following day directing that all houses and businesses in Nashville must display symbols of mourning—or face the consequences.[64]

Elsewhere throughout the South the bloody purge and enforced mourning continued. Because most Southern women were already clad in "widow's weeds" and their dwellings were draped in black, the color was an all too common sight.[65] Nevertheless, to Sarah Morgan, nothing seemed more revolting than strongly secessionist New Orleans darkening itself further for the Yankee president. "[T]he more thankful they are for Lincoln's death, the more profusely the houses are decked with the emblems of woe," said the cynical young woman.[66]

Noted one Union soldier on his march through rural Tennessee:

evry thing ever in this Rebelious country is draped in mourning[.]
Dwellings that their inmates are nown to be rebbles are draped in

mourning[.] all along our ruut from Blue Springs over 300 mills
we could see on the farm houses near and far the black crape
swing.[67]

When a large number of people were arrested and thrown into prison
for failure to festoon their homes in black, the remaining residents of
Vicksburg, Mississippi, quickly took their cue. At a meeting of citizens,
it was decided not only to continue the mourning period for a full
month, but also to solicit donations for a monument to Lincoln.[68]
Downriver at Natchez, Annie Harper's family were fired upon and
threatened with arrest for simply burning too many lights in their home.
The Harpers were also warned about playing music during the mourning period.[69] In Alabama, a home where young people were seen talking and laughing was searched and threatened with razing.[70]

For many civilians in the occupied South, it was doubly mortifying to
have been forced by federal bayonets to illuminate and celebrate their
own defeat when Lee surrendered, then shroud their homes in mourning when their conqueror was killed.[71] To save their lives and property,
most in the defeated nation would understandably yield to force. For a
very few, though, there was no compromise. Records the friend of one
Southern woman:

> Every house was ordered to be draped in black, and where the rebel
> inmates refused, it was done for them. . . . A squad of Northern boys
> organized themselves into an inspection committee and went from
> street to street to see that no house was left undraped. When I sug-
> gested to Mrs. Stuart that she had better hang out something black
> and save trouble, she turned upon me and exclaimed passionately:
> "I'd rather die first. . . ."
>
> The committee . . . came down the street upon which Mrs.
> Stuart lived, and seeing the house undraped, halted before it. There
> was a dead silence for a few moments that was more ominous than
> curses would have been. The hoarse cries of "rebel sympathizers"
> broke from the crowd. The ringleader . . . stalked forward and
> pushed open the door without ceremony and demanded to know
> why the house was not draped. I sprang forward and stood between
> him and Mrs. Stuart and tried to explain to him that my husband
> had gone down the street to get us some black, and that as soon as it
> came I would hang it out. "Yes; but she must hang it up," he cried,
> pointing threateningly at Mrs. Stuart. "Every damned rebel must
> this day kiss the dust for this dastardly act. She must do it herself. . . .
> It must be something of her own, too."

"What, I show a sign of mourning for Abraham Lincoln—I, who but for him would not be husbandless and childless today!" came from Mrs. Stuart's lips.

"Well, now, we'll see about that," he replied. "Come, boys," he called to the squad without, "some of you hold this she-devil while the rest of us search her house for something black."

The front room, dining hall and kitchen downstairs and my bedroom upstairs yielded nothing, but when they entered Mrs. Stuart's private room, just back of mine, I knew from the shouts of triumph that they had found something; but I was hardly prepared for the sight when a few minutes later they came rushing down the stairs waving with frantic gesticulations Mrs. Stuart's long crape veil; the veil that she had worn as a widow for her husband . . . [and] her son.

"Here, madame, we have found just the thing," cried the leader, "and you yourself must hang it up, right in front, too, where all may see it, or, by George, your life won't be worth a candle . . . !"

She stared at them for a few seconds with eyes in which hate, horror and revenge strove for mastery. Then, with a mighty effort, she shook herself free from her captors and in a strangely calm voice said: "Give it to me, I will hang it up where you wish. Only leave the room, leave the premises; go across the street; you can see me from there; and you, madame," she said, turning to me, "you go with them. . . ."

We all crossed the street and looked anxiously at Mrs. Stuart's front door. . . . Just then she came out on the veranda. I noticed she had changed her dress since we had come away. She was all in black—her best black; her mourning weeds. She carried a chair in one hand, while the crape veil was thrown over her shoulder and wound once about her neck. We all watched her intently. Her movements were slow and deliberate. She mounted the chair and . . . then she took the veil . . . and threw it through the opening, while at the same time she put something else through. What it was we could not tell at that distance, and then . . . she gave her chair a vigorous push with her foot and her body hung suspended in mid-air. Several seconds elapsed, in which we all stood as if frozen to the spot, staring at that dangling body across the street. Then, with a cry of horror . . . we rushed over. . . . [But] it was too late.

Under the crape veil . . . with a strong cord firmly knotted about her neck, hung all that was mortal of that once proud southern woman.[72]

CHAPTER TWENTY

IN DUNGEONS
DREADFUL

WHILE MUCH OF THE STARK HORROR and shock had lessened somewhat in the forty-eight hours following the assassination, the suspense in Washington was perhaps even greater than on the night of the murder. Rumors were rife. Most citizens felt that the full extent of the conspiracy was being withheld from a panicky public. Some believed that not only Lincoln, but most of his cabinet and many top political and military leaders had been killed as well.

Such rumors, one observer admitted, "nobody deemed . . . impossible, or even unlikely."[1]

Worse, many felt it was only the beginning.[2] Several strange men, strangely dressed, were reportedly seen lurking near the home of Chief Justice Chase.[3] Ulysses Grant, normally indifferent to personal safety during four years of bloody war, now ordered sentinels to watch his door at night.[4] "I shall only go to the Hotel twice a day for my meals and will stay indoors of evenings," the general promised his wife, Julia.[5] Formerly accessible to even the humblest of visitors, President Andrew Johnson was also surrounded by a wall of soldiers. Outside his hotel, scores of sentinels stood guard on the streets and adjoining lot. Inside the building, security was stiff, with several waves of officers probing visitors about their backgrounds.[6]

Now that he was the highest authority in the land, Andrew Johnson's worth and reputation rose dramatically. Many tried mightily to distance the president from his disaster of March 4. Some, the *New York Times* included, now insisted that Johnson was not drunk during the inaugural; on the contrary, he had suffered from poisoning by a would-be assassin.[7] This theory was eagerly accepted by many.[8]

Much like the president's hotel, the home of William Seward was also heavily guarded. And like Johnson, the secretary of state received an unexpected boon from the attack. Because of the metal jaw brace he had worn since the carriage accident, the stab wounds, though grievous, had failed to sever the artery. Indeed, the slashing blade had inadvertently relieved the terrible inflammation and actually reduced the pain.[9] No such luck blessed Seward's son. With his skull fractured in two places, Frederick remained unconscious, in critical condition. The father, unable to speak, communicated his concerns by writing on a slate.[10]

"Why doesn't the President come to see me?" Seward silently asked well-wishers. "Where is Frederick—what is the matter with him?"[11] The answers were always evasive. Finally, Edwin Stanton was selected to relay the terrible news. Sitting beside his friend, the secretary of war divulged all.

"Mr. Seward was so surprised and shocked," wrote a witness, "that he raised one hand involuntarily, and groaned."[12]

Bearing bad news was only one of Edwin Stanton's many tasks. Indeed, for all practical purposes, Stanton was not only secretary of war but also acting head of state. As the hours at the Petersen House illustrated, while the rest of the U.S. government was largely paralyzed, Stanton alone kept his wits and continued with almost superhuman focus and energy. Despite the very real threat to him, despite a bewildering storm of false reports—the French had captured New Orleans, the British were invading from Canada, Philadelphia was on fire—despite the panic of nearly everyone else around him, Stanton stood like a rock. Not only did the secretary personally oversee hundreds of pages of testimony given mere hours after the assassination, but he also orchestrated the manhunt and issued huge rewards for Booth and several collaborators.[13] Additionally, had it not been for Stanton's iron hand in the hours and days following the assassination, much of Washington might have been burned by the furious mobs as they exacted revenge on Southern sympathizers.[14] Terrible and bloody as the riots were, the outcome would have been infinitely worse had not Stanton deployed troops with orders of "shoot to kill."

"A mob raised then, even to destroy the houses of the fifty worst rebels in Washington, would not have been treated to blank cartridges or conciliatory speeches," remarked a Boston reporter, "and everybody in Washington was well aware of the fact."[15]

After the initial crisis was passed, the secretary of war remained steadfast at his post, as if the fate of the nation rested upon his shoulders and his alone. "Many nights I worked with him until the morning dawn began to steal in at the windows," General Henry Burnett reminisced, "and many nights I left the department at midnight or in the small hours of the morning completely worn out, and left him still there working."[16]

Despite his round-the-clock frenzy and his attention to a thousand details, so determined was Stanton to smoke out the conspiracy that he ordered a special performance of *Our American Cousin* in hopes of discovering some clue.[17] Although this effort provided no new leads, hundreds of other items poured into the secretary's office, including a bloody coat and a false mustache found near a cemetery.[18] Because neither the time nor the manpower was available to cull the guilty from the innocent, Stanton ordered massive arrests. As a consequence, numerous excesses occurred.

As if their horror were not already great enough, Laura Keene, Harry Hawk, and another actor were arrested in Harrisburg, Pennsylvania, · despite passes that had cleared them to leave Washington.[19] John T. Ford, owner of the fated theater, was arrested four days after the assassination and jailed.[20] "The horror of that week is indescribable," recalled Ford of his vermin-infested cell.[21] When the theater owner's wife pleaded with Stanton to release her husband, she was "brutally repulsed."[22] Along with their boss, most employees at the theater were also imprisoned.[23] Edman Spangler, a simpleminded carpenter and stagehand, was charged with complicity in the crime, even though his love of Lincoln was well known.[24]

Already eyed suspiciously by religious zealots and termed the "devil's work shop" where libertines and blasphemers consorted openly, the stage was an early and easy target following Booth's magnum opus at Ford's.[25] "The dread word 'theater,'" noted Clara Morris from Ohio, was suddenly enough to silence a room full of people.[26] For reported disloyal comments, the treasurer of a New York theater was arrested and sentenced to six months in jail.[27] A Philadelphia thespian was imprisoned for declaring that, assassin though he be, Booth had been a kind and honest man.[28] Understandably nervous that the authorities were singling them out, fifty Philadelphia actors passed a resolution stating that all should not be judged for the act of one.[29]

Because of Booth's connection with virtually every American stage from Richmond to Leavenworth, theaters were closely watched. None received more attention, of course, than Ford's. Soon after the military took control of the building, a suspicious character sporting a black mustache and red beard was seen crossing the stage. Attempts to corner the wraith-like figure proved fruitless, and the chase ended in a hopeless jumble of backdrops and scenery.[30]

With nerves already on edge and with the taxed secretary of war breathing down their necks, detectives were quick to arrest anyone who was in the least "tainted" by Booth. Females on friendly terms with the assassin were swiftly rounded up. The actor's private messenger boy was imprisoned. The hapless stable owner who had rented the horse Booth escaped on was hauled away.[31]

In the madness of the moment, anyone and everyone was subject to arrest. A well-meaning man who had discovered outside of Ford's some papers which had fallen from Lincoln's pocket that night proudly reported his find to Stanton. With a wave of the secretary's hand, the stunned citizen was tossed into prison.[32] A wealthy woman whose only apparent crime was a violent temper and a proclivity to swear was locked up, as was her brother.[33] For another luckless individual, a prominent chin, a full mustache, and a large scar under his left ear were more than enough evidence for officials to take him away.[34] Other unsuspecting victims, quietly at home one moment, found themselves in a dark, damp cell the next, simply because a neighbor felt there was "something funny" about them.[35] Scores, perhaps hundreds, were thrown into Washington prisons because of some personal grievance.[36] In his fever to unravel the conspiracy, Stanton could not be troubled with details. He would arrest everyone now, then sort them out later.

Even the dead did not escape the secretary's scrutiny. After a depressed ex-soldier killed himself while in prison, federal investigators looked into the man's past for possible links to April 14.[37] Another suicide victim was disinterred from a Baltimore grave, embalmed, then rushed to Washington, where the body was examined by government surgeons. Other than being "depressed and melancholy," there seemed no connection between the corpse and the conspiracy.[38]

Because of Stanton's actions, within days of the assassination the prisons of Washington groaned with a harlequin assortment of suspects. "It was a rare mixture," remembered prisoner Harry Ford, brother of the theater owner, "deserters, bounty-jumpers and prisoners of State, Governors, legislators and men of every station. . . . We were kept in close and solitary confinement."[39] Already in frail health, one prisoner begged a guard for food since he had not been fed in twenty-four hours. Tossing in an ear of corn, "as to a hog," the guard growled: "Damn you! that's good enough." The man—whose only offense was a Democratic voting record—soon died.[40] Asked why he was jailed and ironed, another prisoner shrugged: "I suppose because I won't say what I don't know."[41]

"There we were," said Harry Ford, "left alone in our dungeons in dreadful uncertainty."[42]

With such a fine net, numerous small fry were unavoidably caught. Stanton's broad sweep occasionally hauled in larger fish, however. One of Booth's known resorts was the three-story brick home on H Street owned by the widow Mary Surratt. Consequently, rather than act rashly, federal detectives placed the house under surveillance in hopes of bagging not only several conspirators, but perhaps the assassin himself.[43] At 11 P.M. on April 17, after hours of fruitless watch, officers finally moved in.

"I come to arrest you and all your house," Major H. W. Smith announced as he and other detectives burst into the home.[44]

Described as a large female about forty years old, "of coarse expression. . . . shabbily dressed," Mary Surratt seemed remarkably unperturbed by the intrusion; indeed, at least one witness noticed that the woman was calm, even defiant. Her daughter, Anna, as well as two nieces, were terrified, however, and quickly burst into tears.[45] While several agents searched the home for personal effects that the women would need in prison—"Everything inside was found in a filthy, disordered condition"—the captives were held in the parlor and forbidden to speak. When Anna began sobbing loudly, Mary firmly scolded the girl for displaying such weakness.[46]

Just as the officials and their prisoners were ready to leave, a loud knock was heard. Drawing their pistols, several detectives went to the hall and opened the front door. Before them stood a large young man with a pickax on his shoulder. A long stocking cap covered the stranger's head, and his boots and pants were covered in mud to the knees.

"I guess I've made a mistake," said the startled visitor as he stared at the leveled weapons.

"Who are you? What do you want here at this time of night?" demanded an officer.

Explaining that he was a homeless indigent, the man stated that Mary Surratt had hired him to dig a gutter.

"So you come to do the job at 11:30 at night?" the official stared.

"No," answered the stranger, "to see what time I should begin tomorrow morning."

"Are you a friend of Mrs. Surratt?"

"Well, I was workin' around the neighborhood. A poor man makin' his livin' with a pick. She offered me work."

When Mary was brought out to identify the caller, she threw up her hands in horror. "Before God, I have not seen that man before," the widow protested wildly. "I have not hired him; I don't know anything about him!"

"How fortunate, girls, that these officers are here," said the woman nervously; "this man might have murdered us all."

Already suspicious of anyone who would call at that hour at a known rendezvous of Booth, the detectives forced the grimy man to wash his hands. When the dirt was removed, the officers could see for themselves that the stranger had remarkably soft hands for a laborer. Together with Mary Surratt's family, the man was taken away.[47]

The following day, the mysterious young man was placed in a line-up. When William Bell, the servant in Secretary Seward's home, spotted the tall, muscular individual, he instantly walked up and pointed: "I know you, you are the man."[48]

In another part of the city, Stanton's sleuths had scored one more success. Records a witness:

> When we entered the home of Mrs. Herold, we found that good lady greatly disturbed and in tears. There was a kind-hearted man sitting near her who was endeavoring to console her, and who did everything he could to assuage her grief. Upon questioning her, it was learned that her son [David] had not been at home since the evening of the preceding day. This looked very suspicious, and confirmed our impressions that we were on the track of one of the guilty parties.[49]

Although several strong suspects were arrested and jailed, and although the trail of others was getting warmer, the lead actor of the drama remained at large. Despite shooting the president of the United States in a theater filled with friends and admirers, in a city that was a fortress, in a nation with the largest army in the world, John Wilkes Booth had vanished with hardly a trace. Ironically, the failure to track down and capture the assassin was a result not of too little help, but of too much; a case not of too few eyes and ears, but of too many.

CHAPTER TWENTY-ONE

THE WRATH OF GOD
AND MAN

SHOCKED, STUNNED, SADDENED by the daring deed at Ford's
Theater, millions of ordinary citizens willingly and eagerly joined the
largest manhunt in American history. "Let each man resolve himself
into a special detective policeman," urged the New York *Herald*, "sparing no vigilance or labor until these detested wretches are hunted down
and secured for justice. It is a duty which every man owes to his con-
science and his country."[1] Well-intentioned as such appeals were, the
result was to hinder rather than help the pursuit. Like a great wave, wild
rumors, lame reports and false leads poured into various state and federal agencies, all but swamping legitimate, valuable clues.

"[H]e is in Washington secreted Beneath Ford's Theatre," one anonymous note revealed. "he never left it but droped through a Trap Door,
& the one that road away [on] the Horse only done so to misleed justice[.]"[2] Another writer, a "semi-wakeful dreamer or clairvoyant," announced that Booth was hiding in a closet on the second floor of
number 11, J Street. Warned the psychic: "He is heavily armed & woe
to who ever tries to arrest him."[3]

"I'm still in your midst. I will remain in this city. God will'd that I
should do it. I defy detection," taunted another note signed "J. W. Booth,
Actor and the Assassin of President Lincoln."[4]

Whether well-meaning cranks or deliberately misleading pranks, all
reports of the assassin lurking about the city had to be considered. Some
outraged citizens, like the editor of the Washington *Republican*, advocated "unroofing and unearthing" every house in the city to find the
fugitive. "Seek for double partitions," the editor advised, "false walls,
secret apartments [and] under cellars."[5]

Because Booth was a famous thespian from a world-renowned family,
his face was one of the more familiar in America. Not only had tens of

thousands witnessed the actor's performances on stage, but countless shops across the land had sold his image to adoring fans. Additionally, there was no shortage of poses. Booth, noted a newsman, "has had himself daguerreotyped and photographed oftener than he has said his prayers."[6] Hence, within a very short time, journalists and members of law enforcement, as well as owners of railroad, stage, and steamboat lines, had an accurate likeness of the murderer.[7] And even those who had never viewed the actor's countenance learned from newspaper reports of his dark hair, pale face, and stunning good looks. In theory, the search should have been simple.

"Luckily for the majority of men," remarked the *Philadelphia Inquirer*, "the number of handsome fellows is small; a fact which at present is a comfortable one to the ugly fellows who form the immense majority of mankind."[8]

For the minority, though, for every natty young man of medium build who was not plain, ugly, or grotesque, life following Black Friday suddenly became one trial after another. In Pennsylvania, a breathless passenger reported to authorities in Reading that he was absolutely positive he had just shaken hands with and spoken to John Wilkes Booth on the six o'clock train to Pottsville. As a "dodge," said the shaken witness, the assassin wore mourning crape on his left arm and a Lincoln badge on his right breast. With only the above to go on, excited officials commandeered a locomotive and steamed off in pursuit.[9] When the posse—with photo in hand and reward in mind—finally caught up with the reputed assassin, the discrepancy became abundantly clear.

"[H]e is anybody but Booth," said one embarrassed official.[10]

Hardly had the Pennsylvania posse cleared one "Booth" from the board when another materialized, this sighting near Lewisburg on the Susquehanna River. In hot haste, again the same men set off.

Sitting quietly in a tavern near Lewisburg, enjoying their dinner, were Jacob Haas and a friend, William Lessig. Both men had served as Union officers in the war, and Haas, a handsome young captain, had only recently received his discharge. The pleasant meal was abruptly interrupted when the two found themselves surrounded by a circle of shouting men with drawn revolvers. When a friend propitiously entered the tavern at that moment, he soon quieted the angry intruders, explaining that although the resemblance was strong, Jacob Haas was certainly not John Wilkes Booth. Philosophical even in the worst of times, Jacob Haas was not so unsettled that he couldn't find mirth in the incident; his still-shaken companion, though, a former colonel, found nothing humorous about cocked weapons pointed at his head.

"I don't see anything so damned funny about this," snapped the man to his smiling friend.

Days later and miles away, the two men had an even closer call. Jacob Haas:

> We were taken to Philipsburg and a great crowd soon gathered, learning that the slayer of Lincoln had been caught. Cries of "Shoot him," "Lynch him," were heard and I felt a cold chill when several ruffians produced coils of rope. . . . The Colonel and myself were taken before a Lt. McDougall. He told an orderly to disarm us. A revolver was lying on the table and Lessig made a grab and secured the weapon. He levelled it at the officer's head and said, "I have served three years in the Army and will allow no man to iron me while I am alive." . . . We were later locked in a room after Lessig returned the weapon. Some men gave us an axe to defend ourselves in the event the mob would break in. All night we stayed awake.[11]

The next day, before a lynch mob could do its work, yet another friend of Haas fortuitously stepped upon the scene and vouched that the former officers were exactly who they said they were.

"On the following Tuesday, near Clarion," continues Haas, "we again heard the clatter of cavalry troops and the same scene repeated itself. We were placed in a hollow square and journeyed sixteen miles to Franklin. It was a gala day when we arrived."[12]

By now, almost beginning to doubt who he was himself, Jacob Haas stormed into the local bank.

"Who the devil am I?" Haas demanded of a cashier. " These men say I am Booth."

"No, Captain. I know you very well," replied the man.[13]

Unwilling to call off the hunt, overzealous authorities swooped up another luckless man where it had all begun, in Pottsville, simply because his middle name was "Booth." Finally, frustrated officials were forced to admit that the Pennsylvania pursuit had been nothing more than "a wild goose chase."[14]

Even more unlucky than Jacob Haas was James Chapman of Pittsfield, Massachusetts. The son of a sheriff, young Chapman bore such a strong resemblance to the assassin that he was arrested three times in one day.[15] At Sheffield in the same state, in Chicago, New York, and elsewhere, startled Booth look-alikes were surrounded by excited officers and hustled to jail.[16]

"[Is] every good-looking man . . . to be in constant danger of swinging from a lamp post because Booth is reported to be a handsome fellow?" one nervous victim wondered aloud moments after being cut down by a lynch mob in Erie, Pennsylvania.[17]

At nearby Buffalo, another suspect and his wife were arrested by police. After hours of maddening explanation and several convincing telegrams, the couple were at last allowed to continue their honeymoon. Ironically, the bridegroom was William Rathbone, a relative of the man who had tried to save Lincoln's life at Ford's Theater.[18]

Even the rough frontiersmen in far-off Kansas joined the national manhunt. When a downriver packet docked at Leavenworth—a town where Booth had performed sixteen months earlier—an excited passenger jumped ashore and dashed up the landing. Locating George Hoyt, leader of the murderous Red Legs, a Unionist guerrilla band, the informant revealed that the assassin of Abraham Lincoln was on board the boat. When the suspect was finally cornered, it was noted by a local reporter that he had "a very suspicious look." Although dressed in shabby clothes, the accused had a pale complexion and a genteel appearance. While on the voyage, offered the informant, the stranger seemed nervous and anxious to avoid everyone who came on board. After a close and potentially fatal examination, and although the accused bore a striking resemblance to Booth, the guerrilla chief finally let the man go. All agreed: The stranger was nothing more than a handsome vagabond.[19]

"So thoroughly was the national vigilance aroused," remarked one editor, "that no man who bore a remote resemblance to the doomed assassin could safely venture beyond the precincts of his immediate home."[20]

Because it was obvious that neither Booth nor anyone faintly looking like him could hope to remain at large long in a wrathful nation fully aroused, more than a few speculated that the assassin might attempt to flee disguised as a woman. As a consequence, many suspicious-looking females—and many men dressed as females—were arrested and imprisoned.[21] One report placed the fugitive in Chicago at a "house of ill fame" where he was masquerading as a prostitute.[22] Adding to the confusion were the great number of veiled widows clad in black. Joseph Hill was walking down a Washington sidewalk when he reportedly spotted a woman he thought he knew named Kate Robinson. Dressed in black and heavily veiled, the lady also hobbled on a crutch.

"Kate, when did you get hurt?" asked the surprised friend after crossing the street.

As the woman turned to respond and Hill gained a glimpse through the veil, he received another surprise.

"Hullar," the shocked man exclaimed, "Wilkes Booth, that's you, is it?"

According to Hill, the mysterious black figure thereupon vanished "in an instant."[23]

Even though the national manhunt spread to every state east of the Mississippi, and many of those west of it, government and private detectives had a sharper focus.

"There is no place of safety for them on earth except among their friends of the still rebellious South," sagely noted Colonel Lafayette Baker, chief of federal detectives. "Booth knows it and will try to reach them for his life depends upon it."[24]

As a consequence, many of the government's early efforts were directed at Maryland, especially the lower part of the state, which was considered by many to be the most disloyal region in America.[25] Because he felt the same way, Edwin Stanton sent waves of troops swarming over the section. The grim secretary of war also threatened to punish the area with fire and sword if it was caught concealing Booth and his cohorts.[26]

With scores of detectives watching the crossroads night and day, with thousands of angry soldiers and civilians feverishly searching the swamps, forests, inlets, and bays, it was tantamount to suicide for any Marylander to exhibit even a trace of Southern sympathy, much less support for Booth. When soldiers swiftly surrounded the old Booth home at Bel Air, they encountered only the new tenant, a lady from Baltimore.

"John Booth is not here," the woman indignantly informed the intruders. "But if he were, you would have found him an honored guest."

"Madame," came the deadly reply, "it is well for you that we have not found him here."[27]

Undoubtedly, many a Maryland man and woman fared not so well. Indeed, as the days passed and the fear that the murderer might miraculously escape grew, hatred intensified.

For many, simply killing Booth was not enough. "As to what should be done with the murderer when caught," a Nevada journalist revealed after hearing comments in his community, "a thousand various tortures were named, of which roasting alive was the very mildest and least enduring."[28] In a letter to his mother, a St. Louis man was even more graphic: "I hope Mr. Johnson and Secretary Stanton will give him to the populace to be put to death by slow torture, or cut to pieces inch by inch."[29] Not only Booth, of course, but anyone involved in the murder of the beloved president could expect no mercy from an inflamed public. As desperate as millions were to catch the culprits, with every pass-

ing hour the job became more difficult.[30] With the resources of a mighty
nation thrown into the hunt for the assassin, and with the days slipping
by, General Winfield Scott Hancock addressed one final appeal, to that
segment of American society who felt the loss of Lincoln more keenly,
perhaps, than any:

> Go forth, then, and watch, and listen, and inquire, and search,
> and pray, by day and by night, until you shall have succeeded in
> dragging this monstrous and bloody criminal from his hiding
> place. . . . Do this, and God, whose servant has been slain, and
> the country which has given you freedom, will bless you for this
> noble act of duty.[31]

And if any further incentive was needed, Hancock reminded the
freedmen that there was also a bonus of $100,000 in reward money.[32]

"They know that they are hunted like venomous reptiles," announced
a Massachusetts minister. "Justice will be on their track as long as they
live.[33]

Added an angry Michigan editor: "Ye slimy monsters crawl, with fear
and shame, into your dark dens, and pray the rocks and mountains may
hide you from the wrath of God and man. Henceforth, there will be no
peace for you. . . . You are marked and doomed. Blood cries to heaven
against you. Blood stains your name, your garments and your
memory."[34]

CHAPTER TWENTY-TWO

THE CURSE OF CAIN

WHILE AMERICANS, WITH VISIONS OF VENGEANCE and fabulous wealth, scanned the faces and scrutinized the actions of strangers on trains, boats, and city sidewalks hundreds of miles from Washington, the object of their search was only a proverbial stone's throw from Ford's Theater. On the ground, in a tangle of pines, surrounded by a swamp, near Port Tobacco in his native state of Maryland, lay the assassin of Abraham Lincoln—John Wilkes Booth.[1]

The pervasive stillness of this gloomy den was broken only by the nervous whispers of Booth's companion and guide, David Herold, and the occasional distant shouts of the stalkers. So intense had the hunt become that the two men could hear from time to time the neighing of horses as federal cavalry passed by.[2] Had any of those searchers ventured into the swampy hiding place, they might at first glance have dismissed their find as merely another of the many backwoods hunters and trappers who infested the area. Dirty, disheveled, a ragged growth of dark beard, grimy clothes torn and tattered, the man looked anything but the dapper, debonair figure that had captivated audiences and broken young hearts nationwide. Additionally, the once handsome face was now lined and twisted in knots of agony; dark eyes that had flashed with fire and life were now dull and dim with pain.

The cause of Booth's excruciating agony, a leg broken two inches above the ankle, was also the cause of his current predicament. Had his spur not caught on the flag adorning the box at Ford's Theater, the actor's great escape to friends farther south not only would have been possible, but, given his intelligence, daring, and athletic ability, it also would have been probable. From there, perhaps Spain, a nation that had no extradition treaty with the United States, and a nation that Booth's fiancée, Lucy Hale, was scheduled to soon reach, where her father served as ambassador to the royal court.³ But the tiny spur *had* snagged the flag, sending the actor crashing to the stage, and all his elaborate plans went for naught. Now he lay crippled and weakened, and capture and death was only a matter of time.

Joining Booth in the dismal surroundings was young David Herold. Adored and feted by thousands of America's finest, Booth now found his life in the hands of a shallow, simpleminded twenty-two-year-old jokester and braggart. Herold's worship of the stage idol easily outweighed what little good sense he possessed about getting involved in the murder of an American president. Star-struck by Booth's status, Herold was enlisted by Booth not because of his weaknesses but because of his strengths: The young man was an excellent outdoorsman and knew lower Maryland like the back of his hand.⁴

Whatever David Herold was or wasn't, his loyalty to Booth was never doubted. If not for the frivolous youth, the hunt for an assassin with a broken leg would have ended soon after it began. Navigating the tangled countryside by night, safely hiding his friend by day, young Herold begged or bought bread from farms, as well as secured whiskey to deaden his hero's mind-splitting pain. Of those residing along the escape route who suspected Booth's presence, not one attempted to collect the reward money.⁵

Grateful as Booth was for the fidelity of Marylanders, and comforting as his companion's attentions were, the actor was absorbed by only one thought: "What do the people say?" What impact had his daring deed had upon the nation, North and South? Was the Confederacy emboldened by the stroke? Was that beleaguered nation encouraged to fight on now that their persecutor was dead? Did the North rejoice? Were the enslaved millions there grateful that the tyrant of the past four years had finally been laid low? Would they now end the war and grant the South its independence? And was he, John Wilkes Booth, now hailed as the hero of the land, a modern-day Brutus or William Tell? As the hours slipped to days, the assassin, though wracked with pain, became mad to know what impact his act had upon the people.

One day, as the two lay concealed in their hiding place, a noise sounded closer than usual. Grabbing his carbine, Herold quietly left to investigate.

"As I drew near the hiding place of the fugitives," remembered Thomas Jones, "I stopped and gave the signal."

In a few moments, the secret whistle drew David Herold from the thicket with his weapon leveled squarely at Jones. "Who are you, and what do you want?" Herold demanded.

"I'm a friend. You have nothing to fear."

Watching Jones closely, the young man finally lowered his rifle and led him through the woods. Asked by the landowner to slip into the swamp and aid Booth's escape to Virginia, Jones had agreed.

"[F]ully realizing the risk I was undertaking," Jones said later, "I did not hesitate. . . . [T]he $300,000 reward [*sic*], or even $3,000,000, would not have caused me to turn traitor to the southern Confederacy, the people I loved."[6]

At length, the two men entered a small clearing. Thomas Jones:

> He was lying on the wet, cold ground, his head supported by his hand. His weapons of defense were close beside him; an old blanket was partly drawn over him. His slouch hat and crutch were lying by him, he was exceedingly pale, and his features bore traces of intense suffering. . . . Murderer though I knew him to be . . . I determined to do all I could to get him into Virginia, and so assured him. . . . He held out his hand and thanked me.[7]

Booth then asked the question he had been hoping to ask for days: "What does the world beyond this swamp think?"

Jones acknowledged that the Southerners he had spoken with were elated by the news. But when, on the following day Jones brought the latest newspapers, Booth saw to his utter chagrin that, far from being hailed in the North as a deliverer from despotism, he was instead being cast into hell as a monster, a maniac, and a fool. With a mental anguish greater, if possible, than his physical pain, Booth read the horrifying words.

"God only knows what incentive impelled this devil to the commission of this horrid and damning crime," raged the St. Louis *Republican*. "But one thing is certain—no man has ever been so effectually damned to everlasting fame as J. Wilkes Booth, the perpetrator of this cowardly, dastardly crime."[8]

"If there was a political motive in the act, it was the act of an idiot," a New York reporter added. "He has ennobled the victim of his rage, as a martyr for all history. . . . Whether he be political maniac or conspirator, or worked out some personal idea of fanaticism or revenge, he has done that which . . . makes him accursed forever."[9]

Such a reaction might be expected in the North. But even in his beloved South, although many praised him in secret and carried his photograph, others in the occupied nation now reviled him in public.

"Our expressions of disgust for the dastardly wretch who could have conceived and executed such a diabolical deed can scarcely be uttered," former South Carolina governor William Aiken announced to a large crowd in Charleston.[10]

Wrote another Southerner, expressing the fears of many:

> This is not the assassination of President Lincoln and Secretary Seward only; it is the assassination of the whole South. . . . We had come to look on the restoration of the Union as a foregone conclusion, and the whole South was on the eve of accepting the fact. We should have been friends and brothers once more but for this. . . . Now, God help us all! . . . Damned to the bottomless pit of hell the men who plotted and carried it out![11]

Although he did not regret his action and would gladly have struck again if need be, Booth could see at a glance that his efforts had gone for nothing and all his hopes had been dashed.

"And there—surrounded by the sighing pines—he read the world's just condemnation of his deed and the price that was offered for his life," remembered Thomas Jones with a note of sadness.[12]

As the dismal days in Maryland passed, while waiting to cross the wide Potomac into Virginia after an earlier unsuccessful attempt, Booth was left with little more than his thoughts and his diary:

Friday 21—

> After being hunted like a dog through swamps, woods, and last night being chased by gun boats till I was forced to return wet cold and starving, with every mans hand against me, I am here in despair. And why; For doing what Brutus was honored for, what made Tell a Hero. And yet I for striking down a greater tyrant than they ever knew am looked upon as a common cutthroat. My action was purer than either of theirs. . . . I hoped for no gain. I knew no private wrong. I struck for my country and that alone. A country groaned beneath this tyranny and prayed for this end. Yet now behold the cold hand they extend to me. . . . I think I have done well, though I am abandoned, with the curse of Cain upon me. . . . I have too great a soul to die like a criminal. Oh may he, may he spare me that and let me die bravely. . . . So ends all. For my country I have given up all that makes life sweet and Holy [and] brought misery on my family.[13]

The "misery" that the assassin feared he had caused his family was, alas, all too true. Soon after the murder, government agents and police had swarmed over the Booth homes.

"All written or printed material found in our possession, everything that bore his name was given up, even the little picture of himself hung

over my babies bed in the nursery," said Asia of her home in Philadelphia. "Not a vestige remains of aught that belonged to him; his books
of music were stolen, seized, or savagely destroyed."[14]

"Enraged and furious," more invaders returned to search and ransack
the house. When they finally departed, a heavy surveillance was kept on
the residence, and the family's mail was opened.[15]

Worse than the brutal invasion of her home was the heap of calumny
directed at the family. Asia continues:

> North, East and West the papers teemed with the most preposter-
> ous adventures, and eccentricities, and ill deeds of the vile Booth
> family. The tongue of every man and woman was free to revile
> and insult us. Every man's hand was against us; if we had friends
> they condoled with us in secret; none ventured near.[16]

Especially bitter to Asia was the sudden demand of her actor husband,
John Clarke, for a divorce. Such a separation, insisted Clarke, was his
"only salvation now."[17]

"I can give you no idea of the desolation which has fallen upon us,"
Asia wrote a friend. "I seem completely numbed and hardened in sorrow."[18]

After narrowly escaping Cincinnati with his life, the eldest brother,
Junius, Jr., fled to Philadelphia. Finding the atmosphere in the "City of
Brotherly Love" every bit as menacing as Ohio, Junius slipped from the
metropolis and took a room in the country. Although no mobs followed,
there was no peace for the Booth brother, either. "He paces his room
and pulls his hair like a man deranged," revealed a witness.[19]

Junius's brother Edwin was also locked in his own personal hell. Perhaps the most sensitive of all the siblings, Edwin was so troubled and
weighed down with gloom that he swore he would forsake his calling,
vowing never to set foot on a stage again. It was just as well, advised a
vindictive Philadelphia journalist, as "no man bearing the name of the
criminal shall, within our lifetime, be permitted to appear before an
American audience."[20] Despite his well-known love of Lincoln and his
unswerving devotion to the Union, Edwin was questioned closely about
the assassination and even had his luggage searched in Boston.[21] Ironically, it was Edwin who had, but the month before in New Jersey, saved
the son only to see a brother slay the father.[22]

> [A] group of passengers were late at night purchasing their sleep-
> ing car places from the conductor who stood on the station plat-
> form at the entrance of the car. . . . [T]here was of course a
> narrow space between the platform and the car body. There was

some crowding, and I happened to be pressed by it against the car body while waiting my turn. In this situation the train began to move, and by the motion I was twisted off my feet, and had dropped somewhat, with feet downward, into the open space, and was personally helpless . . . [when] my coat collar was vigorously seized and I was quickly pulled up and out to a secure footing on the platform. Upon turning to thank my rescuer I saw it was Edwin Booth, whose face was of course well known to me, and I expressed my gratitude to him.[23]

The grateful young man was none other than Robert Todd Lincoln, son of the American president.

Adding to Edwin's misery was a heartbreaking letter from John's fiancée, Lucy Hale. "The poor little girl to whom he had promised so much happiness," wrote Edwin, was utterly devastated by the unbelievable news.[24] Now, himself shattered to his very core, Edwin hoped only for the peace of oblivion. Wrote the actor "to the people of the United States":

Prostrated to the very earth by this dreadful event. . . . this most foul and atrocious of crimes. . . . I shall struggle on, in my retirement, with a heavy heart, an oppressed memory and a wounded name . . . to my too welcome grave.[25]

Of all those close to Wilkes, none felt the pain more sharply than Mary Ann Booth. Her dark-eyed, dark-haired Johnny, a child of love and light, her favorite son, now a felon, an assassin, a hunted fugitive without a safe haven or tender hand—the widow's heart bled a river of sorrow, her grief beyond measure. Added to the woman's already unbearable agony were the hateful words aimed at her and her family.

"Could any person that would commit such a deed have any human blood in his veins?" ran a typical comment. "Was he born of woman or devil?"[26]

For Mary Ann Booth, only death could now stop the sorrow.

———

In Washington, another woman prayed for the deliverance of death.

As workmen sawed and hammered below, erecting the catafalque for her husband's state funeral on April 19, above, Mary Lincoln suffered the tortures of the damned. Unstable in the best of times, the former first lady had now, noted a visitor, become totally "unhinged."[27] One moment she was hysterical and screaming, the next delirious and groaning.

Those intrepid individuals who visited the woman all found her inconsolable.[28]

Elizabeth Blair Lee was one of many forced to hear the painful details:

> She had her hand on his arm when he was shot[.] he never quivered — the flash of the pistol made her hold him tighter & when she first saw him after it — the "<u>head had drooped upon his chest</u>." . . . She addresses him in sleep & in her delirium from raging fever in terms & tones of the tenderest affection — She constantly refers to his religious faith — but never to her own.[29]

When friends tried to steer Mary's thoughts elsewhere, the attempts were only partially successful. Again and again, the woman would return to the last painful moments until she was once more wracked with sorrow.[30] So intense and fatiguing were the sessions that those who sought to console the widow referred to their time spent as having "served together," as if veterans of some ghastly conflict.[31]

"I shall return there again this evening & shall continue to go as long as I find I can stand it," admitted Elizabeth Lee. "I feel great pity for her now — it is a terrible thing to fall from such a height to one of loneliness & poverty."[32]

Deeply in debt, with no way now to repay it, thoughts of the future only added to Mary's insanity. Placing her fingers in her ears that she might not hear the workmen below, the woman nevertheless could not escape the sounds.[33]

"[E]very plank that dropped gave her a spasm," wrote a witness, "and every nail that was driven seemed to her like a pistol shot."[34]

On Monday night, April 17, those transporting her husband's body down to the catafalque for the ceremony on the following day kindly removed their shoes as they passed Mary's room lest she hear and begin screaming.[35]

CHAPTER TWENTY-THREE

THE MID-WEEK
SABBATH

AT NOON ON APRIL 19, the doors to the White House were closed, and the formal funeral for Abraham Lincoln, sixteenth president of the United States, began. Because of space limitations in the East Room, only a relatively small group of individuals could be accommodated. In the twenty-four hours preceding the official ceremony, however, an estimated thirty thousand citizens had passed the body while it lay in state.[1] Few anticipated such numbers, or the mania of the people to gain a glimpse of the murdered president. The "rush & jam" to enter was so great, in fact, that guards were hard-pressed to hold the crowds back.[2]

Into this crush of all ages, sexes, and races, "we were obliged to force our way," wrote Helen McCalla in her diary:

> Ladies fainted near us, and children screamed, and a violent shower marred the scene, but we had to endure it, being—to say the truth—determined to enter the President's House, after waiting for over two hours near the gate. . . . Upon entering, we marched in a slow, silent procession through the Reception Room, into the East Room, where the remains were lying in state, but we were not permitted to wait a moment near the corpse, so that it was impossible to obtain a satisfactory view.[3]

What little the viewers did see of the late American leader was generally agreeable and what many had hoped to see. Gone were the protruding eyes that nearly sprang from their sockets; also mercifully missing was the ghastly discoloration of the face. The president, noted Orville Browning, looked "as natural as life, and [as] if in a quiet sleep."[4]

Most others, such as a correspondent for the *New York World*, also thought Lincoln lay as if resting. "The hue is rather bloodless and leaden; but he was always sallow," the journalist noted. "The dark eyebrows seem abruptly arched. . . . The mouth is shut, like that of one who had put the foot down firm, and so are the eyes, which look as calm as slumber."[5]

Unlike others who gazed upon the "sleeping" figure, the New York correspondent spoke with embalmers and knew that the present image was but an illusion:

> There is now no blood in the body; it was drained by the jugular vein and sacredly preserved, and through a cutting on the inside of the thigh the empty blood-vessels were charged with a chemical preparation which soon hardened to the consistency of stone. The long and bony body is now hard and stiff, so that beyond its present position it cannot be moved any more than the arms or legs of a statue. . . . The scalp has been removed, the brain scooped out, the chest opened and the blood emptied. All this we see of Abraham Lincoln, so cunningly contemplated in this splendid coffin, is a mere shell, an effigy, a sculpture. He lies in sleep, but it is the sleep of marble.[6]

At length, public viewing of the body was reportedly cut short when it became known that the continual shuffling of feet below had so crazed Mary Lincoln that she did not even recognize her little son, Tad.[7] Nor was Mary present when the funeral services began at noon in the East Room. Although there were numerous flowers and floral arrangements, which gave the room a fresh smell, music was noticeably lacking. Additionally, the room was so heavily festooned with black material that to some the affair seemed oppressively somber.[8] Among the political and military men attending—including the normally unkempt General Grant, now looking odd in his dress uniform—only the foreign dignitaries, resplendent in colorful, courtly costumes, disturbed a scene dominated by black.[9]

Although several ministers, including Dr. Gurley from Lincoln's church, joined to eulogize the late president, the services were kept short and simple. As a result, many were emotionally moved. While tears trickled down the weathered face of Grant, Robert Lincoln sobbed quietly nearby, his face buried in a handkerchief.[10]

By 2 P.M., when all had viewed the body—including the new president, who gazed reflectively down for a few minutes—the casket was carried from the White House by Grant, Admiral David Farragut, the new vice president, Lafayette Foster, and other pallbearers.[11] Amid the sounds of booming minute guns and tolling bells, the funeral cortege moved off toward the Capitol. As the numerous bands that accompanied the procession played dirges, the thousands who lined the sunny streets viewed Lincoln's riderless horse and the torn flag from Ford's Theater.[12]

When the procession passed his home, William Seward sat painfully up in bed to catch a glimpse out the window. Even though the secretary of state was recovering far faster than anyone could have imagined, his son Fred still teetered between life and death. "He will die," Frances Seward repeated over and over again in her still-stunned state. "He will die."[13]

At length, with a regiment of black soldiers in the van and a large contingent of colored civilians bringing up the rear, the cortege reached the Capitol.[14] There, the coffin was placed on a bier beneath the rotunda, and the public was permitted once more to pass and pay their respects. The journalist and old Lincoln friend Noah Brooks was on hand to view the scene:

> While this solemn pageant was passing, I was allowed to go alone up the winding stairs that lead to the top of the great dome of the Capitol. Looking down from that lofty point, the sight was weird and memorable. Directly beneath me lay the casket in which the dead President lay at full length, far, far below; and, like black atoms moving over a sheet of gray paper, the slow-moving mourners . . . crept silently in two dark lines across the pavement of the rotunda, forming an ellipse around the coffin.[15]

———

Simultaneous with the ceremonies in Washington, similar services — called "the mid-week Sabbath" — were occurring throughout America. In San Francisco, the funeral was by far the largest and most extravagant ever witnessed on the West Coast, with a procession of thousands that stretched for miles.[16]

At Boston, the famed orator Edward Everett Hale noted that during the nationwide funeral, more people attended church than at any time before.[17] Wrote an amazed editor from the same city: "[E]ven the thoughtless idlers, who form such an element in every large city, were for the time abashed and orderly."[18] And the displays of mourning that hung from every home and business were without precedent.[19]

"To-day the tokens of mourning are even more plentiful than when I wrote yesterday," a correspondent in New York City noted on April 19:

Crape on the left arm is largely worn, while miniature portraits
and badges of the late President are seen in the bosom or on the
coat front of most of the immense throng of pedestrians. Small
flags, bound around in black, are also everywhere visible, and
pictures of the fearful scene are displayed in the streets. . . . The
rail cars that come dashing into the city from distant points are
shrouded in the dismal color of the day; steamers and sail boats
glide along the rivers with the same solemn exhibitions; the newspapers are black as ink can make them, and there is nothing the
eye can see that has not the pall of death flung over it. . . . Even
the drink to quench our thirst, and the meat from off the
butcher's stall, is handed us beneath a massive overhanging of
black.[20]

"Every body and every thing . . . look gloomy and dismal," remarked
a woman in New York.[21]

Although most throughout the nation did indeed seem somber and
sad, that did not necessarily mean that all mourned the slain president.
Nevertheless, in the deadly, dangerous climate that still existed five days
after the murder, everyone *acted* as if they did.[22] At Reading, Pennsylvania, those walking the streets displayed "the blankest faces that I ever
witnessed," thought one observer. "[N]o man could utter a word not of
grief without proclaiming himself a partisan of the assassin."[23] Elsewhere, failure to wear the prescribed black crape or mourning badge was
itself grounds for suspicion and surveillance.[24]

"O, Lord, lay not innocent blood to our charge but bring the guilty
speedily to punishment."[25]

Similar words were uttered in other churches throughout the land that
April 19. In this case, the words were not as important as how and by
whom they were spoken. Leading this prayer in a Washington church
was a small, slight man in a sergeant's uniform. With his long hair tied
back, the newcomer soon warmed to his subject and began stalking
among the pews. As the shocked church members watched in disbelief,
the shouting stranger soon steered the services away from a eulogy of the
dead president to a common revival rant on the wages of sin. There was
a shrill fervency in his cries of "Glory to God" and "Come to Jesus," and
anyone who peered into the man's wild eyes could see at a glance that
a dangerous, unbalanced mind was at work.[26]

Like many another latecomer to God, Thomas Corbett was determined to recover lost ground with fanatical intensity. Soon after emigrating from England with his parents at the age of seven, the boy had apprenticed as a hatter. While still very young, Corbett took a wife. Several years later, though, the woman died during childbirth. Despondent over his loss and deeply in debt, the young man soon turned to liquor, which only accelerated his plunge. One night in Boston, the drunk stumbled up to a street evangelist. Despite his reeling brain, Corbett heard for the first time in his life the voice of God. And with those words still echoing in his head, a miracle occurred. Casting off his old life, including his name, the reborn Christian became a crusading missionary on the spot.[27]

"In Boston I was converted; and there met my Redeemer," said the grateful man simply, "and Boston is the only name I wish to be called by."[28]

In addition to reading the Bible day and night, Corbett allowed his hair to grow long and parted it in the middle, in imitation of Christ. He also took his Savior's message to heart by sharing his meager resources with those less fortunate. As his religious verve grew, young Corbett also refused to work for any employer whom he considered "un-Godly." And even when he did find a boss who measured up to his standards, Corbett's habit of halting work to kneel and pray for profane co-workers ensured that would find himself habitually unemployed.[29]

Moving to New York City, the crusader quickly joined a Methodist church. It was not long, though, before the newest member began to "greatly annoy" others in the flock with his peculiar brand of religion. According to one account:

> He took part frequently, and in his prayers was in the habit of
> adding "er" to all his words, as "O Lord-er, hear-er our prayer-er."
> When anything pleased him he would shout, "Amen," "Glory to
> God," in a sharp, shrill voice, to the great horror of the Dutch-
> man who controls the meeting. All remonstrance was in vain, and
> he shouted to the very last.[30]

When the newcomer was especially aroused, he would whoop and scream like an Indian, startling to a panic the more sedate parishioners.[31] Boston Corbett's missionary work was not limited to the temple. Like John the Baptist of old, he took his message into the field. Remembered the Reverend J. O. Rogers:

> He often visited the docks, and places of toil, where he would
> mount some box or chair, and speak to the rough natures around
> him of Christ and the resurrection. He was frequently threatened

with mischief, and on one occasion a burly Irishman succeeded in banding a considerable force for the purpose of compelling him to leave. Corbett was not in the least dismayed. "Now you cannot scare me. I am not made of any such stuff as you suppose. You may bring all Ireland with you, and it won't frighten me in the least."[32]

Although he and the Lord may have faced down Irish mobs, inwardly Corbett was troubled by his own demons. One night, after his return to Boston, Corbett discovered two young women watching him closely with a gleam in their eyes that was anything but godly. Frightened by the carnal passions rising within, the desperate young man—now in his mid-twenties—had a "vision" right there on the spot. Racing home, Corbett reached up to a shelf, grabbed a pair of very sharp scissors, lowered his trousers, then promptly castrated himself.[33] Once purged of the devil, the fanatic went to a prayer meeting that same night and followed it up with a "hearty dinner."[34]

When war came in 1861, Corbett was initially torn between patriotism and the teachings of Christ. At length, he reached a decision.

"I have prayed over it," he told Rev. Rogers, "and I must go."[35]

"He thought it right to shoot traitors wherever they could be found. . . . [and] he had announced his willingness to 'shoot men like dogs,'" revealed a friend. "He rejoined that the rebels deserved just that; he would first say to them: 'God have mercy on your souls,' and then 'pop them off.'"[36]

Trouble began almost the moment Corbett entered the army. When a colonel cursed his men one day as they stood at attention, the new recruit was stirred to action.[37] Recorded a witness:

> Corbett stepped out of the ranks and reproved him, saying that he had violated military regulations and the laws of God, and he considered it his duty to reprimand him. Corbett then took a Bible out of his pocket and read the commandment, "Thou shall not swear." The result was that Corbett was ordered into the guard-house for punishment. He went cheerfully, declaring on the way that he had done only what was right, and that he was willing to accept what should come of it. In the guard-house he sung psalms, disturbing the other prisoners. He was then directed by the officer in charge not to sing any more, but he would not obey, and did as he pleased.[38]

This initial brush with military law would not be his last. "I have seen him often in the guard-house," recalled a comrade, "with his knapsack full of bricks as a punishment, with his Testament in his hand, lifting up his voice against swearing, preaching temperance, and calling upon his wild companions to 'seek the Lord.'"[39] Unlike other prisoners, Corbett would emerge from his numerous confinements smiling and happy, announcing that he had spent a "good time with his God and his Bible."[40]

When the incorrigible soldier abandoned his post one night, declaring that his enlistment was up at midnight, he was arrested, tried, convicted, and sentenced to be shot. The government settled on drumming the troublemaker out of the military instead.

With his patriotism soon rekindled, Corbett reenlisted, this time with the 16th New York Cavalry. In a fight with John Mosby's guerrillas in Virginia, Corbett found himself suddenly cut off from his comrades. Although his predicament was dire, surrendering to rebels never entered his head.[41]

"I faced and fought against a whole column of them," he later reminisced. Before his ammunition finally gave out, Corbett reportedly killed seven of the enemy, shouting "Amen! Glory to God!" as each man fell.[42] Soon overwhelmed, the defiant Yankee was captured and packed off to the Andersonville prison camp in Georgia. After several months of captivity, Corbett was exchanged and returned to the North. Again, unlike other prisoners who managed to survive the hellish conditions at the camp and harbored only nightmarish memories of their imprisonment, the freed man could only praise the lord.

"There God was good to me, sparing my life," he said matter-of-factly. "But bless the Lord, a score of souls were converted, right on the spot where I lay for three months without any shelter."[43]

After recovering his health at a military hospital in Maryland, Corbett found himself in Washington on Black Friday, April 14. Like everyone else, the sergeant lamented the slain president and longed to see the assassin caught and punished. Unlike most, though, Corbett prayed day and night that God might make him the instrument of his wrath by allowing him the honor of "popping off" the murderer.

CHAPTER TWENTY-FOUR

OH! ABRAHAM
LINCOLN!

EARLY ON FRIDAY, APRIL 21, after a prayer delivered by Phineas Gurley, the coffin was closed and the body of Abraham Lincoln was carried from the Capitol. One week after the assassination, the slain president at last began his long trip back to the home he had left four years before. Preceding the long column through the cold, rainy streets was a wedge-shaped detachment of cavalry.

"Very slowly they proceeded, making their way steadily into the crowds which swarmed the streets, forcing them silently back to the curb," wrote a viewer. "The horses' footfalls were the loudest sounds, while sobs punctuated the stillness of the watching multitude."[1]

When the cortege reached the railroad depot, a special train was waiting. In a beautifully ornate funeral car near the rear, the coffin was gently lowered. Nearby was placed a smaller casket. At Mary Lincoln's insistence, the body of her little son Willie had been disinterred that he might be buried alongside his father in Illinois.[2]

With a pilot engine moving in advance several miles to prevent mishaps, the long journey officially began. Lining the track as the train pulled away were thousands of federal soldiers, including large numbers of sobbing black troops. Reported a chronicler:

> They stood with arms reversed, heads bowed, all weeping like children at the loss of a father. Their grief was of such undoubted sincerity as to affect the whole vast multitude. Dignified Governors of States, grave Senators, and scar-worn army officers, who had passed through scenes of blood and carnage unmoved, lost their self control and were melted to tears in the presence of such unaffected sorrow.[3]

At 10 A.M., the funeral train reached Baltimore, its first scheduled stop.

Here, in the same city that Lincoln had secretly slipped through to avoid assassination four years earlier, the coffin was removed to the Merchants' Exchange so that loyal Marylanders might pay their respects. After only a few hours, and with thousands of viewers still waiting in the rain, the casket was returned to the train for the planned 3 P.M. departure.[4] Despite its brevity, the ceremony in Baltimore was solemn and moving.

"Today has been a funeral day in every sense," said one sad reporter. "The heavens are hung with black. . . . Not a gleam of sunlight has even for a moment burst through the heavy clouds which hang like a leaden pall over the city. All is gloom; deep, dark, impenetrable gloom."[5]

When the train reached the Pennsylvania state line, Governor Andrew Curtin boarded the cars and rode along as a gesture of honor and respect for the fallen chief.[6] After a brief stop in York, the funeral train reached the state capital, Harrisburg. There, at 8:20 P.M., during a terrible thunderstorm, the train finally halted.[7] Because of the downpour, a scheduled procession through the streets was canceled, much to the chagrin of more than a thousand soldiers who had stood in the rain for an hour.[8] From 9:30 until midnight, amid the roar and flash of both cannons and lightning, thousands defied the elements and trudged through the Capitol to view the body.[9]

Prior to reopening on the following day, April 22, an undertaker was compelled to chalk the president's rapidly discoloring face and brush away dirt and soot that had accumulated on the beard and hair.[10] When the doors opened at 8 A.M., again the people streamed in. At one point during the viewing, a terrible stampede occurred when gas jets ignited some drapery hanging from the chandeliers. Although the flames rose rapidly and fiercely, the fire was quickly brought under control.[11]

By 11:15 that morning, with forty thousand saddened citizens looking on, the train pulled away from Harrisburg and steamed east for America's second largest city, Philadelphia.[12] Now under a sunny, cloudless sky, the track was lined with mourning Pennsylvanians.[13] One of those on the funeral train was a member of the honor guard, Robert Schenck. Although in private the Union general had detested Lincoln, referring to him as "the baboon" and to his wife, Mary, as "her royal majesty," Schenck was stunned by the outpouring of emotion he witnessed.[14]

"All along the road," the general noted, "it has been affecting to see the people assembled not only at stations, but in front of farm houses, by the fences, and in the fields beside the railway, to gaze at our passing funeral train—women often weeping and men standing respectfully uncovered."[15]

At Lancaster, an immense crowd watched the cars pass slowly through town while nearby a huge sign proclaimed: "ABRAHAM LINCOLN, THE ILLUSTRIOUS MARTYR OF LIBERTY, THE NATION MOURNS HIS LOSS. THOUGH DEAD, HE STILL LIVES." On the outskirts of the crowd, sitting silently in his carriage, was Lincoln's predecessor, James Buchanan.[16]

From West Chester east, said a chronicler, those lining the track "were not counted by thousands, but by acres."[17]

At 4:30 P.M., the funeral train reached Philadelphia. During the thundering cannon salute that announced the arrival, an artillery piece exploded prematurely, critically injuring two men.[18] For more than a few, this event seemed an ill omen. Indeed, the ceremony in Philadelphia began on a tragic note, and it never got any better.

In order that the grand procession might have more daylight for public viewing, organizers had requested that the funeral train arrive two hours earlier than scheduled, which it did. Nevertheless, because of some "blunder," the huge cortege did not even manage to move until 6:30 P.M. Because of this and other mishaps, it was well past dark when the head of the column finally reached Independence Hall, where the coffin was placed near the Liberty Bell. Given the enormous length of the procession, it was after eight o'clock before those bringing up the rear finally began to move.[19] Contributing to the sloth-like pace of the parade were the unexpectedly large crowds encountered along the route; one estimate placed the figure at over 250,000.[20] But this was nothing compared to what lay ahead.

By midnight, long lines were already forming outside Independence Hall. Even though the doors would not open until the following day, many spent the night in line because there was not a vacant bed to be had in the city. Thus, with hundreds of thousands of people pouring into Philadelphia from every direction, almost all went hungry and sleepless that night.[21]

"'The Beloved remains' are knocking the machinery of social life here into a cocked hat," complained one cynical businessman. "I could not get a bed at any hotel last night—had to sleep in my shawl on some chairs—fought for my breakfast, and am inexorably parted from my baggage."[22]

When the sun rose and the doors to Independence Hall were finally opened at 6 A.M., the streets beyond were crammed "with one living mass of humanity."[23]

"The crowd around the Hall was so dense, and its extent so great, people could not move," wrote an amazed correspondent of the *Chicago*

Tribune. "They swayed back and forward like a surging ocean."[24]

Because the lines outside the building extended for miles, the wait to view the body was estimated at six to eight hours.[25] And all the while, thousands more pressed in from the side streets. Soon the crush was so intense that people became "wedged in like brick."[26] With pressure building and no hope of escape, many now realized for the first time that there was no way out. Adding to the misery and chaos, noted a New York newsman, were "rude, rough voiced hundreds, whose ambition seemed to be to create confusion for the mere sport of the thing."[27] Continues another reporter on the scene:

> About noon, there was great excitement around the Hall, many women and children having fainted. The police and the guards seemed helpless to stay the rush. Large ropes had been fastened to the street corners to keep back the moving, surging masses. Over these ropes hundreds of women were dragged by policemen and the guard to save them from being injured. The soldiers with bayonets fixed strove to drive back the crowd but it was useless. . . . Women shrieked when one of their sex fainted, and little boys cried and struggled to get out of the great jostling masses.[28]

Another who was horrified by what he saw was Henry Wilson. In a letter to his brother, Wilson described the horrible sight of humans crushing and mashing each other to death in their madness to view Lincoln's remains:

> I saw three little boys who had been smothered that were lifted up from the ground and placed upon the Heads of the People until they revied [sic], when they succeeded in crauling upon the heads of the Mass until they finally got out back from the bilding whare the Crowd was not so dense and got out barely with there lives—though quite a Number were so far gone that they could not be restored even with medical assistance.[29]

Mingled with the normal dull roar of so many thousands were the shrieks of crushed women, the shrill cries of trampled children, and the cursing and shouting of men. Silk hats, bonnets, and parasols were smashed flat, dresses were ripped, hoop skirts were broken and mangled, the neatly pinned hair of ladies now fell to their waists in a disheveled mess. Ragged and tattered debris, including destroyed mourning badges and black crape, littered the ground below.[30]

"[T]his wild, reckless, excited mass of humanity," noted one observer sadly, "looked and acted like anything else than a vast assemblage who had come to pay respects to the honored dead."[31]

Terrible as conditions were in the crowd, the situation was worse at the narrow entry gates outside Independence Hall. Here, with an irresistible force from behind, the people were pressed through as if by a giant meat grinder. Beautiful dresses and elegant suits were now ripped off entirely, and in some cases, nearly every shred of clothing was stripped from the wearer. Many who were squashed and trampled were squeezed through to the other side unconscious.[32] Others who reached the relative safety of the courtyard surrounding the Hall fled without viewing the corpse, happy simply to escape with their lives.[33]

Undermanned, under planned, there was little funeral organizers could do to halt the disaster, though many tried. Revealed one reporter:

[A] civilian, covered with dust and perspiration and wearing a badge, came down the line, entreating the people to move back. "Ladies and gentlemen," said he, "if you stay here you take a fearful responsibility. Women are fainting and suffocating up there by the gate, and the crowd is so dense that, unless you move back, there will be a half dozen killed before the next half hour. I have just been up there myself and I saw it, or I would not tell you so. I came near being crushed to death too." . . . Then a military officer appeared at a third-story window of French's Hotel and tried to get the attention of the crowd in the street below, waving his hat and hands, and shouting: "Go back; do go back, my dear people, go back. You can't get in without you go back and give more room. All go down to the end of the line and form in single file." For a long time the majority of the crowd either did not hear, or, hearing, paid no attention to him. His voice was almost lost in the buzzing of talk below, the cries of women, and the shouts of policemen. Finally they attempted to move back two or three times, and each time were pushed up again by the outside of the eager throng. . . . Then another officer appeared at the same window and added his voice to that of the other. Occasionally he would wave his hand, pointing up Park Row to an imaginary file of soldiers or policemen, and call out "Fire, fire, fire," evidently hoping to scatter the assembly.[34]

While thousands of frightened, trapped people longed only to escape—mothers raised children aloft that they might crawl to safety over the carpet of heads—tens of thousands more were "actually wild" to force their way into Independence Hall.[35] For those who did manage to survive the crushing mob and the deadly choke point at the gates, their hours of misery were rewarded when they were herded like sheep into the building. As the mourners filed by the casket, tattered and torn, looking more like survivors of a terrible storm than funeral-goers, the few seconds allotted to each—a "mere glance"—were often emotional. Many wanted to touch the body, and others had to be restrained from kissing the cold, marble-like face.[36]

"An old colored woman, 65 or 70 years of age, thrilled the spectators with her open expressions of grief," one witness wrote. "Gazing for a few moments on the face of the dead, she exclaimed, clasping her hands, 'Oh! Abraham Lincoln! He is dead! He is dead!'"[37]

Adding one final note to a day already surreal, before the doors closed at midnight, seventy-five Union veterans, each of whom had lost a leg in the war, somehow managed to hobble through the mob and pay their respects.[38] By the time the casket was finally closed early the following morning, an estimated three hundred thousand visitors had viewed Lincoln's body. Even so, with a line outside still extending for half a mile, and with roughly one million people in the city to view the remains, only a fraction had been successful.[39]

"Never before has such a corpse been brought to Independence Hall," said one editor proudly, if indelicately.[40]

When the funeral train departed the city at 4 A.M. on April 24, most of those on board were no doubt greatly relieved to escape Philadelphia. Only by the narrowest of margins had disaster of a monumental kind been averted. Several reported deaths, broken arms, legs, and ribs, a debris field that resembled the aftermath of some great battle—with the nightmarish memories of the past thirty hours racing through their minds, officials on board the train could not be blamed if they looked ahead with trepidation to the next scheduled stop: New York City.

CHAPTER TWENTY-FIVE

THE FOX AND THE HOUNDS

> Eight days have intervened since the shocking news of his assassi-
> nation fell on their startled senses, but their sorrow and anguish
> abate not. Men walk about the streets with downcast brows and
> sad features, and . . . they refuse to be comforted.[1]

SO WROTE THE EDITOR of the *Chicago Tribune*. What was true for
Chicago was generally true for the rest of the North. In many ways, even
eight days was not sufficient space for the shock to fully set in. During
the dizzy swirl of events, there simply had not been the necessary time
needed to properly understand and appreciate one earthshaking event,
much less a dozen.

Another emotion that had "abated not" in eight days was fear. Indeed,
the terror was almost as pervasive as the night of the assassination. So un-
believably bold was the stroke, and so enormous were its consequences,
that many horrified Americans felt that Lincoln's death was only the
precursor to even greater events. When a rumor raced through New
York one week after the assassination that General Grant had just been
murdered, people were shocked, but no one doubted it.[2] Much like his
slain predecessor, Andrew Johnson—"His Accidency"—continued to
receive menacing letters. Unlike Lincoln, however, the new president
placed credence in each blood-curdling threat.[3] Even Secretary Seward,
more dead than alive, was not forgotten.

"I wish I had cut your dam head off while I was at it instead of only
half doing it," wrote one well-wisher. "If I only had you and Johnson and
Stanton out of the way I would feel as if I had done my duty to my
Country."[4]

Given the terror and uncertainty abroad, it is not surprising that many
in the North continued to strike out blindly at those in their midst who

were perceived as threats. At Harrisburg, a man arrested earlier for comments made after Lincoln's death was now dragged from jail by a mob and forced to ride on a board around town while a band played the "Rogue's March."[5] When Joseph Shaw returned to Westminster, Maryland, after his newspaper had been destroyed following Black Friday, a mob was waiting. Rushing to his hotel room late at night, the shouting attackers kicked in the editor's door. Pulling a pistol, Shaw fired, wounding one of the men. An instant later, the editor was riddled by a hail of bullets and expired on the spot.[6] Accused of delivering a "secession" speech in New York earlier, another man was chased through Philadelphia by a howling mob. When he was finally overhauled and attacked, the victim broke free momentarily and drew a pistol. Before he could fire, a policeman appeared and arrested the bloody man for carrying a concealed weapon. A short time later, when the victim's brother appeared to post bail, the man was dragged from his carriage, and he too was beaten savagely.[7]

"[H]is face [was] swollen out of all human shape," wrote a friend, "his shirt & waistcoat [were] drenched in blood. . . . The policemen allowed them to do it for a time & then, merely to save his life, interfered."[8]

At Baltimore and elsewhere, unwitting storeowners who catered to the insatiable demand found their shop windows smashed and their inventory destroyed because they sold photos of the assassin. In the conquered Confederacy, not only were unrepentant Southerners imprisoned or murdered, but public humiliations had become the norm. Some white federal officers took sadistic delight in ordering their black troops to cut the coat buttons from the defeated soldiers because of the "C S," or Confederate States, imprint on them.[9] At Murfreesboro, Tennessee, a former rebel was "persuaded" to raise a United States flag above the courthouse dome. That Yankee soldiers might laugh and joke at the spectacle, the man was ordered to remain dangling from his perch for half an hour.[10] Preachers throughout the South who neglected to pay homage to Abraham Lincoln in their sermons could expect imprisonment, exile, or worse.[11]

In the emotional backwash of April 14, many rightly felt that the reunited nation had become little better than a brutal, bloody dictatorship in which the Constitution was but a scrap of worthless paper. And at the helm, feverishly working the levers of that repressive regime, was Edwin Stanton. With the burden of catching the assassin and unraveling the conspiracy placed almost entirely on his own back, the secretary of war felt that only an iron hand would suffice. Not surprisingly, the strain on

Stanton was crushing, and the long hours with little rest soon took their toll. When two suspects brought in by Brigadier General Henry Burnett were ordered released by the secretary, the officer, of course, obeyed.

"That evening," recalled Burnett, "I should think about 12 o'clock, a messenger appeared at my room at Willard's Hotel."

"The Secretary wants you, and the devil is to pay," said the messenger.

"What is it?" the surprised general asked.

"I don't know, but he is in a terrible temper."[12]

Henry Burnett:

> When I appeared before him, he was walking up and down his office apparently in a great state of excitement, and burst out with, "I hear that Weichmann and Hollahan were in your office today, and that you let them go." I said, "Yes, Mr. Secretary, but . . . " I got no further when he broke in with, "You had no business to let these men go. They are some of the conspirators, and you have them here at this office by 8 o'clock tomorrow morning, or I will deal with you." I again commenced, "But Mr. Secretary . . . " (Intending to add that it was by his instruction) but he interrupted by saying, "Not a word sir, you have those men here by tomorrow morning at 8 o'clock."[13]

Outraged by such treatment, the general nevertheless sent his men searching anew for the same suspects he had been ordered to free. After a night spent combing the city, it was only by sheer coincidence that Burnett located the two culprits the following day just before the deadline. Once more Burnett approached the secretary's office.

> As I came in, Mr. Stanton who was then seated at his desk, looked up and said, "Well have you those men?" I said, "Yes, Mr. Secretary, they are in my office." His whole manner and countenance changed from that of a grim sort of ill-nature to that of a pleased smile. I was then a good deal aroused and indignant, and I turned upon him and said, "And now, Mr. Stanton, I am through with service under you and I beg here and now to tender my resignation to take effect immediately. You would have condemned and disgraced me without a hearing for obeying your own order, and I am damned if I will serve further under any such man. . . . I am through with you and with the service."
>
> He got up from his desk, came over to where I was standing, placed one hand on my shoulder and said, "General, I ask your

pardon. I was wrong, but remember the great strain I am under in trying to save the country. In seeking to achieve the best and the public rights, sometimes individual right goes down. I am doing the best I can with all the power with which God had endowed me to save our country. Forget this matter and go back and go on with your work and help me in the great work I am trying to do."[14]

Burnett did cool down and continue as the secretary asked, but he, like everyone else who dealt with Stanton, came to expect such behavior from their overtaxed boss.

While mob violence continued throughout the North, arrests kept pace, especially in the city of prisons, Washington. Hundreds were jailed—some for tearing down mourning crape placed on their own homes, others for carrying photos of Booth, and some for possessing Confederate flags. While there may have been justification for cases such as these, none whatsoever existed for others imprisoned under the vague, though damning, charge of "disloyalty." Thomas Green had not a clue why he was arrested. "I have had no charges made against me and know not why I am imprisoned," explained the confused man. "I have committed no offense to justify it—have done nothing and have expressed no opinions that could be offensive."[15]

Orville Browning visited with another miserable captive caught in the net. "He told me," wrote Browning in his journal, "they had subjected him to several examinations, and treated him very harshly—keeping him in a close room part of the time on bread and water, and giving him no bed, he having to sleep on a board."[16] Other victims found themselves hurled into dark, smelly holding pens with dozens of others, some of whom were spies paid to listen and report what was said.[17]

Even before the paranoid hysteria that followed Lincoln's assassination, the federal government's brutal methods of interrogation were widely known.[18] Recalled one high-ranking official on the technique employed by Secret Service chief Colonel Lafayette Baker:

> He dealt with every accused person in the same manner; with a reputable citizen as with a deserter or petty thief. He did not require the formality of a written charge; it was quite sufficient for *any person* to suggest to Baker that a citizen might be doing something that was against the law. He was immediately arrested, handcuffed, and brought to Baker's office, at that time in the basement of the Treasury. There he was subjected to a browbeating examination. . . . Men were kept in his rooms for weeks, without warrant, affidavit or other semblance of authority.[19]

Those implicated in any way with the assassination itself could expect much harsher treatment. While the prisons on land filled with suspects, many of those directly linked to the conspiracy were held on water. With these prisoners, Stanton was taking no chances. Although Mary Surratt was confined at the Old Capitol Prison, Lewis Powell (alias Payne), George Atzerodt, Michael O'Laughlen, Samuel Arnold, and others were cast into the holds of the ironclad gunboats, the *Saugus* and the *Montauk*, anchored off shore in the Potomac. Each captive, the woman included, had "stiff-shackles" placed on their wrists and a seventy-five-pound ball chained to their ankles.[20] To prevent communication among the prisoners, two marines stood watch over each.[21]

Worried that they might still exchange information among themselves, Stanton ordered each captive hooded. Like something out of a medieval torture chamber, the canvas bags—drawn over the prisoners' heads and tied at the neck—had only small holes for breathing and eating. Still unhappy, Stanton later directed that new, tighter hoods be used, with cotton pads that pressed tightly over the victims' eyes and ears. These painful devices, said Samuel Arnold, tended to "push the eye balls far back in their sockets." For Arnold and the dozens more forced to wear the hoods, the treatment was nothing short of torture.[22] Concerned that in the suffocating heat and darkness the prisoners would soon lose their reason, the surgeon in charge, George Porter, requested that the hoods be loosened. The plea was ignored.[23]

Rather than concern himself with the health and sanity of traitors in hand, the secretary of war was more worried about the murderer at large. Despite the greatest, most intense dragnet in American history, John Wilkes Booth remained a free man. From Kansas and Kentucky to Minnesota and Maine, thousands of pursuers had done their best to run the assassin to earth, but to no avail. Every day that passed made it less and less likely that the murderer would be caught.

Since the assassination, thousands of tips and unsolicited advice had poured across the desks of Stanton, Andrew Johnson, and other government officials. "There are many intelligent persons who believe that Booth still lurks in some hiding place in Washington," noted a New York newsman.[24] Indeed, more than a few felt the assassin had never even left Ford's Theater, but was ensconced in some hidden nook.

"Perhaps he is in bed, with the cap and nightgown of a female, feigning sickness," offered one citizen.[25]

Some anonymous leads were designed to hinder pursuit, not help it. Ran one letter to the secretary of state's office:

> Wishing to inform you as soon as possible that you and the God
> dam Yankee government, their detectives and M P searchers can
> save their selves the trouble and expences and perhaps also their
> lives—that any further search in unnecessary and will all avail
> nothing for Booth my dearest and best friend J W Booth is now
> safe forever. He is by now over 500 miles from Washington. . . .
> You Sonofabitch.[26]

Himself seething with rage because Booth had not been snared, Yarnall Cooper felt he had a foolproof plan for netting the murderer. Writing to President Johnson, the Illinois farmer suggested that if seven rebel prisoners—preferably generals and colonels—could be executed each and every day, the assassin was sure to surrender. "Under this course I presume that the offender can be Recovered when all others will fail," Cooper reasoned. "I am fully aware that no Reward will bring him fourth although there be Milllions offerd[.] I desire the Punishment of all traitors and midnight Assassins As <u>all are in the Same category</u>[.]"[27]

Despite such "help" from around the nation, the government's effort remained focused on southern Maryland and northern Virginia. With thousands of soldiers, civilians, and detectives scouring the area, the matter might have seemed simple. But it wasn't. Not only was the area in question a region of dense woodlands and low swamps, but some of the strongest Southern sympathizers anywhere resided here. Additionally, even the enormous rewards that should have helped the hunt only hurt it by pitting private detectives against those of the government.

"They would not work with us or give us any information they may have obtained," wrote federal detective Luther Baker, cousin of the Secret Service chief. "They preferred rather to throw us off the trail, hoping to follow it successfully themselves."[28]

Nevertheless, bits of solid, accurate information did manage to surface. On the afternoon of April 24, it was learned from a reliable source that Booth was thought to be somewhere between the Potomac and Rappahanock rivers. Acting on the tip, Luther Baker, Lieutenant Edward Doherty, and detective Everton Conger, with over a score of horsemen from the 16th New York Cavalry, approached Port Conway on the latter stream.[29] Luther Baker:

> I found a fisherman sitting at the door of his hut, whose name
> was Rollins. I asked him if a lame man had crossed the river there
> with [in] a few days. "Yes," he replied, "and there was another
> man with him." I showed him my photographs. He at once
> pointed to the pictures of Booth and Harold [sic] and said, "These

are the men, but this," referring to Booth, "had no mustache." I cannot describe to you the thrill of intense satisfaction that came over me when I heard this statement. I was positive I had struck the trail; that I was the fortunate one among all the eager thousands engaged in the search.[30]

CHAPTER TWENTY-SIX

BLADE OF FATE

HE LAY CARELESSLY IN THE GRASS, stretched out on the thick, soft carpet that felt like velvet. It was a bright and warm spring day in northern Virginia. Above, the young leaves of an apple tree gave cool shade, and the fragrance from the snowy blossoms filled the air with a sweet perfume. Around him, the little children watched in fascination. Their staring eyes followed the needle of the compass as it dutifully obeyed the metal blade. The broken leg, the crutch, the rough beard and tangled black hair, the tattoo "JWB" on the back of his hand, these no longer intrigued the children; instead, the amazing magic of "Mr. Boyd" and his strange instrument was all-absorbing.

His eyes intently watched the faces of the children as their eyes in turn watched the needle. He studied their puzzled looks as they struggled to comprehend. He thought of himself as a child, and how he, too, had struggled to understand the mysteries of life. He thought about his current condition. And then, it all became clear. He understood. Suddenly, the riddle of man and his fate made sense. And he laughed. For the first time in eleven days, he actually knew pleasure and laughed aloud.[1] With a world of hate all around, with death closing in, with eternal infamy now his certain fate, he laughed. These children, like little animals, knew nothing, cared nothing, for what he had been or would be, simply accepting him as he was here and now. No matter what they were later told, this is how their hearts would remember him. It had not really been so long ago, a score of years, when he was as they were now, naive, innocent, trusting.

His earliest memories were of his father. The child worshiped the big, burly Englishman with his booming voice, his large flashing eyes, and the stories told of strange people and places. As the boy grew, his love did not lessen. Indeed, his admiration for his father increased "almost to idolatry." The little son did not see the world-renowned Shake—spearean earning thunderous applause on a nightly basis; nor did he see the hopeless, shameless drunk who had once pawned himself off in a New York shop window simply to buy another drink.[2] The little boy only felt that love which flowed unconditionally. He loved the father he knew.

Of all the children, admitted older son Edwin, "John Wilkes was his father's favorite."[3]

Perhaps the old man was subconsciously drawn to the pale, dark-haired child because he recognized in him the same restless spirit he possessed, or perhaps it was the surfeit of energy and the extreme passion for life they both shared.

Little short was the boy's love of his mother, though for different reasons. Like the father, Mary Ann, too, secretly favored the bold, impetuous son over the others.[4] Unlike her husband, the mother was quiet, soft-spoken, and, to the little boy's mind, deep and mysterious. And she had visions. Once, while sitting by the fireplace when her favorite was still a baby, the woman clearly saw words shine out from the flames; one read "blood," another read "country," and the last, "an avenging arm."[5]

On his thirteenth birthday, the boy's parents officially married. The following year, soon after his father's death, the devastated youth quit school for good and returned to the family home near Bel Air, Maryland.[6] The "Farm," as the Booths casually referred to the modest estate, was surrounded by a forest of large, ancient trees, which all but insulated it from the outside world.[7] There the mother and her children lived a quiet, idyllic life. As vegetarians, the Booths considered their own animals, as well as those of the woods, simple extensions of their family.[8] John, remembered sister Asia, was "very tender of flowers, and of insects and butterflies."[9] Thoughtful and considerate, kind in the extreme, the teenager loved everything that shared his world, it seemed, with one exception. He despised the sly predators of the neighboring farms that mercilessly stalked their prey and robbed the woods of music and beauty. Young Booth made it his mission to rid the area of prowling cats.[10] As a child, his sole murderous urge was to destroy that which he considered evil and rescue that which he considered good.

While life was generally peaceful on the Farm, there came an event that cast a dark shadow over the teenager's life and was to affect him until the day he died. One afternoon, the boy ventured into the deep woods to have his fortune told by a gypsy. When the old woman sat the youth down and scanned his palm, her face froze in horror.

Ah, you've a bad hand; the lines all cris-cras. It's full enough of
sorrow—full of trouble—trouble in plenty, everywhere I look.
You'll break hearts, they'll be nothing to you. You'll die young,
and leave many to mourn you, many to love you too, but you'll
be rich, generous, and free with your money. You're born under
an unlucky star. You've got in your hand a thundering crowd of
enemies—not one friend—you'll make a bad end, and have
plenty to love you afterwards. You'll have a fast life—short, but a
grand one. Now, young sir, I've never seen a worse hand, and I
wish I hadn't seen it, but every word I've told is true by the signs.
You'd best turn a missionary or a priest and try to escape it.[11]

"[I]f it's in the stars, or in my hand . . . how am I to escape it?" the
startled young man asked. When she explained that the only course was
to follow his fate, Booth grew frightened, then angry.

"For this evil dose do you expect me to cross your palm?" he snapped.

Booth did grudgingly pay the Gypsy but before he left the old woman
had a final word: It was well she was no longer young and beautiful, else
she would be compelled to follow his handsome face throughout the
world, no matter his fate.[12]

While Wilkes always laughed when he retold the story to friends, it
was not the same carefree laugh of old. When he left the Farm several
years later to follow in his famous father's footsteps and seek the acclaim
he so craved, the young man's life was noticeably more melancholy, and
although he remained fun-loving and unpretentious, even after he
gained fame and fortune on the stage, his life was never the same. From
the day the gypsy stared at his hand and frowned, the life of John Wilkes
Booth became a balancing act between happiness and joy and sadness
and sorrow.[13]

And yet, on this beautiful spring day, April 25, 1865, the young man
discovered the simple pleasure of watching the light in a child's eyes
when the mystery of the compass was revealed—how, like a man and
his fate, the needle must follow the blade, no matter where it led.

———

From all indications, it appeared as if the horrific conditions that had
ruined the funeral ceremonies in Philadelphia would be repeated in
New York City fourfold on the following day. As the train arrived in
Newark, New Jersey—a town of less than twenty thousand—those on
board were stunned.

"It seemed as if it contained at least 100,000," one passenger gasped. "Every spot that could contain a human being was filled."[14]

When the train reached the Hudson a short time later, the funeral car was ferried across the river to Manhattan Island. As the boat approached shore, the bells and chimes from a hundred buildings announced its arrival. Cannons also boomed. In a chilling harbinger of Philadelphia, one of the guns along the East River had several days earlier ignited prematurely. Two men who were in the process of ramming down another charge were blown to bits. Body parts were found on neighboring piers.[15]

As the ferry finally reached the opposite shore, the hearse carrying Lincoln's body joined the parade to City Hall. After the head of the cortege stepped off, it was hours before the rear of the procession even moved. Miles long, the parade was an enormous cross-section of New York's labor, commerce, and industry. Clubs, unions, and guilds marched together in military order. Doctors, lawyers, bankers, journalists, clergymen, tailors, painters, carpenters, waiters, cigar makers, Freemasons, societies of Germans, Irish, Jews, and blacks, even the "Sons of Temperance" joined in step—everyone, it seemed, wanted to march and be counted. An estimated seventy-five thousand individuals participated in the procession, eleven thousand of them soldiers.[16]

Impressive as these figures were, they were dwarfed by the incredible number of onlookers. Broadway resembled a vast living canyon swarming with people—in windows, on rooftops, in trees, up flagpoles. The sidewalks had long since been crammed tight with a dense mass of humanity that stood for hours in the hot sun, "boiling and sweating and suffering." And yet, from the surrounding suburbs, tens of thousands more continued to pour in.[17]

"Rushing and pushing, on they went, pell mell, as if their lives depended upon their success in witnessing the procession," a disgusted witness wrote.[18]

One of those elbowing and ramming his way through the crowd was a huge man with a tanned face.

"Don't walk over me," shouted one of many outraged individuals he stepped on.

"Excuse me, sir, but I must see the coffin," the man said as he muscled forward.

"Why must you see it."

"Because I love the man—he's one of my craft, I must get through, two of my brothers have died in the same cause as Old Abe. I'll never go back to the prairies till I see and bless his coffin."[19]

Of the estimated six hundred thousand to one million people in the crowd, few gained a clear view of the parade; some who did were dismayed by what they saw. Because the normally filthy streets had been scrubbed for the occasion, horses in the procession lost their footing and many serious accidents occurred. Also, with upward of one hundred bands in the cortege, each playing a doleful dirge, a dreary cacophony of tubas, horns, and drums continually oppressed the air.[20]

"The music altogether was not well chosen and the procession was not well arranged," grumbled one viewer. "It was straggled and spun out most tediously and lost all solemnity."[21]

Hours of heat and the hordes of angry, wailing infants also did little for the decorum or dignity of the occasion. Generally, there was a momentary lull in the din when the hearse finally passed by. Built to be something grand and imposing, the elaborate vehicle was really a rather "ill-looking and awkward affair," thought one Boston reporter.[22]

"Well, is that all that's left of Ould Abe?" came a woman's loud voice from a window above.

"It's more than you'll ever be!" an angry voice shot back.

"O, I've nothing against him," the woman replied. "I never knew him or cared for him, but <u>he died like a saint</u>."[23]

"[I]t <u>has</u> lacked solemnity," agreed one journalist who viewed the procession, "perhaps . . . from its very magnitude. The crowds in the streets were more curious than reverent, and very few hats were lifted as the remains passed."[24]

Upon reaching City Hall, the coffin was carefully carried within amid the sad, solemn dirge of a vast chorus.[25] When the doors were opened for public viewing at 11 A.M., the people of New York, New Jersey, and Connecticut swarmed about the building by the hundreds of thousands. Much as in Philadelphia, authorities were totally unprepared to deal with such crushing numbers. Completely overwhelmed, yet determined to maintain a semblance of order, policemen used their clubs freely and began beating line-crowders unmercifully.[26] While there was no perilous gate to pass as in Philadelphia, those who managed to enter City Hall did so through the basement, and they thus found themselves feeling their way forward like moles through the darkened hallways.[27]

For those fortunate enough to pass the coffin, the mere two or three seconds allowed offered scant opportunity to even satisfy curiosity, much less reflect on the dead president. All hoped that the man would appear as they imagined. And some even insisted, and said aloud, that Lincoln looked like "one asleep." Many more, however, were horrified by what they saw. According to a writer for the New York *Evening Post*:

President Lincoln lying in the coffin in the City Hall is but a sad
reflection of him who so recently filled the President's chair.
Those who had thought that the embalmer's art would have pre-
served his features to us almost unchanged, will be disappointed.
Death will not be cheated of his dread ravages. The eyes of the
dead President are sunken, his face is somewhat discolored, sallow about the lower part, dark around the eyes and cheeks; his
lips are so tightly compressed that the mouth seems to be but a
straight sharp line. It is not the genial, kindly face of Abraham
Lincoln; it is but a ghastly shadow. The sunken, shrunken features give the impression that the coffin which encloses them is
far too large.[28]

"A face dark to blackness," said another journalist, "features sharp to
a miracle, an expression almost horrible in its un-nature. . . . [N]one
could regard the remains with even a melancholy pleasure."[29]

Because it was rumored that, owing to decomposition, the casket
would remain closed after leaving New York, the demand among the
crowds for a final look became even greater. Although the body was
photographed while in City Hall, this was against the express wishes of
Mary Lincoln. As a consequence, Secretary Stanton ordered the plates
destroyed.[30]

Just as in Philadelphia, guards were placed near the coffin to prevent
mourners from touching and kissing the body. When some viewers
made the mistake and tried, they were jerked back violently and col-
lared. Like some urban sheep rancher, the city police superintendent
stood nearby with his cane, ready to point out any individual he thought
might prove troublesome. Another ridiculous feature of the funeral was
caused by the placement of the coffin on a raised platform. As the
crowds reached the top and filed past, each eye lingering to the last on
the dead president, few saw the steps leading down. Overworked policemen were stationed nearby to catch the people as they tumbled forward.[31]

With nightfall, tens of thousands who had smugly imagined that they
would avoid the crush of the day crowd now arrived. As a consequence,
the numbers waiting to enter City Hall actually increased.[32] A reporter
for the New York Times watched as the miserable hordes of "fagged-out
men, toil worn women, and sleepy children" crept slowly, mindlessly
forward. Adding to the crowd's agony, continued the newsman, were
those who "push and haul, elbow and knuckle violently at every opportunity" for no better reason than to gain and inch or two.[33] When the
police were inexplicably withdrawn later that night, street gangs and

pickpockets circulated freely through the crowd, creating bedlam and causing near-riots. Though intended to be solemn and inspiring, a one-thousand-voice German choir that began chanting dirges at midnight only increased the misery. As a final exclamation mark on what even the charitable considered a "poorly conceived" ceremony, the festoons draped on City Hall caught fire and had to be ripped down.[34]

When the doors were finally closed the following day, Lincoln's face was literally coated with dust and dirt brought in by the estimated 120,000 viewers. The flowers strewn about the body were almost unrecognizable as such; even the colors were lost in the grime.[35]

CHAPTER TWENTY-SEVEN

THE BAD HAND

IN THE DARK MORNING HOURS OF APRIL 26, a column of cavalrymen drew up on the road just beyond the farm of Richard Garrett. Riding rapidly back along the line, Lieutenant Edward Doherty of the 16th New York ordered his men to draw their revolvers and move quietly through the gate. When the last trooper had passed in, the charge was sounded.[1] In a matter of moments, the thundering advance had covered the short distance, and the lawn around the home was swarming with horsemen.

"I was awakened by the violent barking of my dogs," remembered old Richard Garrett. "I arose from my bed and went to the window, and found the house surrounded by armed forces. I drew on my pantaloons . . . without waiting to put on any other dressing."[2]

Caught up in the excitement, detective Luther Baker was also on the scene:

> I leaped from my horse to the piazza and was at the door in a moment rapping vigorously. A window near the door . . . was thrown up and an old man's voice asked what was wanted. I stepped to the window, seized the man's arm and said, "Open the door and get a light and be quick about it." He opened the door, I went in and shut it. A moment more and the old gentleman appeared with a lighted tallow candle in his hand. I took the candle from him before he could think of objecting and said, "Where are the men who have been staying here for the last day or two?" "Gone to the woods," said he.[3]

"I want to know where these two men are that were here this afternoon," growled Baker as he leveled his pistol at the old man's head. "They are here, and if you don't bring them, I'll blow your brains out."[4]

When detective Everton Conger burst into the home, he, too, began screaming at Garrett and threatened to kill him. Given the terrifying bedlam of shouts, screams, curses, barking dogs, and cocked revolvers, the frightened old man, who only moments before had been sound asleep, was understandably "much excited." Again and again Garrett stammered that the men had gone to the woods; they were uninvited strangers, he added, and he had nothing to do with them.[5]

"I do not want any long story out of you; I just want to know where those men have gone," shouted Conger.

When Garrett once more mumbled the same story, Conger turned to one of his soldiers and told him to bring a rope.[6] At this moment, John Garrett burst into the room.

"Don't injure father," pleaded the son. "I will tell you all about it. The men did go to the woods last evening when some cavalry went by, but . . ."[7]

The angry officers, which now included Lieutenant Doherty, swiftly turned their wrath on young Garrett. "I seized this man by the collar," said Doherty, "and pulled him out of the door and down the steps, put my revolver to his head and told him to tell me at once where the two assassins were. He replied, 'In the barn.'"[8]

As Doherty ran toward the tobacco barn, jerking and threatening his prisoner every step of the way, another Garrett son appeared.[9]

"Where are those men?" the officer shouted as he stopped and stuck his pistol into the young man's ear.

"They are in the barn," Garrett quickly replied.[10]

As his troops surrounded the building with orders not to fire, Doherty, along with Baker, Conger, and the two Garrett brothers, reached the barn door. Inside, the rustling of hay and voices were heard.[11] After kicking at the door several times, the men saw in the glow of their candles that it had been padlocked.[12] Taking the key from one of the brothers, Baker ordered the other Garrett to go in. Terrified, the young man begged for mercy. "They are desperate fellows, and are armed to the teeth," he pleaded. With a deadly stare, the detective leveled his weapon.[13] Baker continues:

> I now unlocked the door and told young Garrett to go in and get the men to surrender if he could, but at all events, bring out their arms. . . . I closed the door after him. There was a low conversation and we heard Booth say, "Damn you! You have betrayed me; get out of here or I will shoot you." I now called to the men in the barn and said, "We sent this young man. . . . Give him your arms and surrender or we shall burn the barn and have a bonfire and a

shooting match." Soon Garrett came to the door and said, "Captain, let me out. I will do anything I can for you but I can't risk my life in here. Let me out." I opened the door; he came out with a bound.[14]

"What do you want?" asked a voice from within.

"I want you!" Baker shouted back.

"Who are you, and what do you want of me?"

"We are here to make you a prisoner," replied the impatient detective. "We know who you are. I will give you five minutes to surrender. If you do not give yourself up in that time I will set the barn on fire."

After further probing, Booth realized once and for all that his end had come.

"I am lame, with only one leg," he said. "Give me some show for my life. Withdraw your men fifty yards from the door and I'll come out and fight you."

"We didn't come here to fight you, but to take you prisoner," yelled Baker, "and we will take you dead or alive."[15]

"Give me a little time to consider," begged Booth.

"Very well, you can have two minutes."

Standing in the glow of the candles, Baker was soon made aware of how vulnerable he was when Booth yelled out that he could have shot him a half-dozen times already. "I have a bead drawn on you now, but I do not wish to do it," said the actor.[16] Startled, Baker and the others stepped away from the door. The two Garretts were ordered to hold the candles at the corners of the barn so that if those inside attempted a breakout, they could be seen by the waiting troopers. Baker also directed his men to kill the Garretts if a shot was fired from the barn.[17]

"Those men are innocent," cried Booth. "They do not know who I am."[18]

"Your time is up," shouted Baker, "we shall wait no longer."[19]

Aiming his weapon at one of the Garretts, Everton Conger ordered the man to scoop up pine boughs and pile them at the rear of the barn.[20] Hearing the noise at the corner of the structure, Booth turned sharply in that direction and threatened to open fire.[21] Now overcome with fear, David Herold begged his friend to let him walk out and surrender.

"You damned coward!" snapped the actor. "Would you leave me now! Go! go! I wouldn't have you stay."[22]

When Herold reached the door, Booth shouted that his companion was innocent of all crimes.[23] Ignoring the words, Lieutenant Doherty jerked the prisoner away from the door and bound him to a nearby locust tree.[24] As soon as Herold had cleared the barn, noted a trembling

William Garrett, the door was quickly shut "as if they feared a tiger might bounce out on them."[25]

Stepping from the shadows, a slightly built sergeant, perhaps the only man present this night who was neither frightened nor excited, asked several times for permission to enter the barn and bring Booth out. "I was not afraid to go in and take him," said the sergeant later. "[I]t was less dangerous to go in and fight him than to stand before a crack exposed to his fire, where I could not see him, although he could see me." The requests were denied.[26]

Originally hoping to hold until dawn before he forced the issue, Lieutenant Doherty now relented at the urging of detective Conger.

"I went around to the corner of the barn," said Conger, "pulled some hay out, twisted up a little of it, about six inches long, set fire to it, and stuck it back through on top of the hay. . . . It was very light, and blazed very rapidly—lit right up at once."[27]

"I was at the door," Luther Baker wrote, "and the moment the light appeared I partly opened it and peered in and could see Booth distinctly. He seemed to be leaning against the mow, but in the act of springing . . . toward the fire."[28]

Now crazed by the destruction of family property, one of the Garretts yelled for "Boyd" to surrender before the barn was consumed.[29] "Don't destroy the gentleman's property," Booth shouted back, "he is entirely innocent, and does not know who I am."[30]

"[Booth] . . . started forward as if to extinguish the fire," continued Luther Baker. "An old table was nearby. He caught hold of it as though he would cast it, top down, on the fire to extinguish it, but the fire was too quick for him and he saw that this would not do."[31]

"The blaze lit up the black recesses of the great barn until every wasp's nest and cobweb in the roof was luminous," wrote another witness as he and others peeked through cracks.[32]

Realizing it would be futile to fight the flames, Booth now knew he was left with only one option.

"He dropped his arm, relaxed his muscles, turned around, and started for the door," recalled Conger.[33]

Returning to Luther Baker:

> About the center of the barn he stopped, drew himself up to his
> full height and seemed to take in the entire situation. . . . He
> forgot that he was lame; he stood erect and defiant, though one
> crutch was by his side. His hat was gone, his dark hair was pushed
> back from a high, white forehead; his lips were firmly com-
> pressed. . . . There was a carbine [in] one hand, a revolver in the

other, a belt held another revolver and a bowie knife. I can give you no idea of the expression of the features. It was the ferocity of the tiger. It was the defiance of the lion, hunted to his lair. . . . Booth was standing under and within an arch of fire, curling, leaping, roaring, hissing. . . . Suddenly he dropped his remaining crutch, threw down his carbine, raised his revolver and made a spring for the door. In an instant there was a crack of a pistol. Booth fell forward.[34]

Fearful that he was only stunned, Baker threw open the door and leaped on the body. Almost immediately, the detective could see that the man was indeed the murderer of Lincoln.

"It is Booth sure," Baker yelled excitedly to Conger.

"He must have shot himself," responded the detective.

"No, I had my eye upon him every moment," answered Baker, "but the man who did do the shooting goes back to Washington under arrest for disobedience of orders."[35]

Seeing that Booth was still alive, the men dragged the body outside away from the flames and placed it on the grass near an apple tree.[36]

"Water was dashed into his face and we tried to make him drink, but he seemed unable to swallow," said Baker. "Presently he opened his eyes and seemed to understand it all. His lips moved, and in a whisper he said, 'Tell mother, tell mother . . .'"[37]

In the meantime, a brief but earnest effort was made to remove valuables from the barn.

"Save my property! Help put out the fire!" yelled one of the frantic Garretts as he and one or two others ran into the barn. The flames were too far advanced, though, and the men were quickly forced out.[38]

Because of the intense heat, the wounded man was carried to the porch of the Garrett home. Once there, it was evident by the blood trail that Booth had been shot through the neck. The ball had severed much of the spinal cord, all but paralyzing the actor. It was also noted that the victim's broken leg was "in splinters" and had turned black. Although Booth was obviously in critical condition, a doctor was sent for in the hope that the assassin might be brought back alive.[39]

"Kill me! kill me!" Booth whispered hoarsely as he lay in terrible agony. Every few minutes the victim would convulsively gasp and his pulse would weaken. But then the heart would rekindle, and again the dying man would beg feebly, "kill me . . . kill me."[40] The females of the Garrett home, the mother and daughters, did what little they could. A mattress was carried out. Then a pillow.[41] One of the young women dipped her handkerchief in water to moisten the actor's lips.[42]

"Tell my Mother I died for my country," whispered Booth. "I did what I thought to be best."

"I again moistened his lips and he repeated the message to his mother," said the girl.[43]

The dark hours passed, and the terrible vigil on the porch continued. To the east, dawn began to filter through the trees. At what was once a tobacco barn, the embers had cooled sufficiently to allow souvenir-seeking soldiers to poke among the ruins. Booth's crutches, mere pine limbs, were ashes, but the assassin's pistols, though charred, were quickly snapped up.[44] Tired, terrified, still tied to the tree, David Herold pleaded his innocence to any who would listen. Questioned first by Lieutenant Doherty, the frantic captive denied any knowledge of the wounded man.

"You know well who it is," shouted the officer.

"No, I do not," insisted Herold. "He told me his name was Boyd."

"It is Booth, and you know it," snapped Doherty.

"No, I did not know it; I did not know that it was Booth."[45]

Later, when a menacing private approached, the trembling captive begged for mercy. "Booth told me . . . that he was going to kidnap Lincoln," pleaded the young man, "he didn't tell me he was going to kill him."

"[W]hy did you help him to escape?" came the angry reply.

"Booth threatened to kill me if I didn't help him get away."[46]

When the crazed culprit pleaded with another man, insisting that he had nothing against the dead president and actually enjoyed "Mr. Lincoln's jokes," the outraged trooper drew his knife.

"Shut up, or I'll cut off your goddam head," shouted the soldier.[47]

Still furious at the disobedience of orders, Luther Baker asked Conger if he had found the man who fired the shot.

"No, but I will," growled the detective.[48]

After narrowing down the suspects, Conger finally spotted the soldier walking across the front lawn.[49]

"Why in hell did you shoot without orders?" demanded the angry detective.[50]

Coming to attention and saluting, the strange little sergeant stared Conger in the eye for a moment, then pointed toward heaven.

"Colonel, God Almighty directed me."[51]

Seeing at a glance that he was not dealing with a balanced mind, Conger shrugged and turned. "Well," muttered the detective, "I guess He did or you couldn't have hit him through that crack in the barn."[52]

Although a physician arrived at dawn, by that time Booth was beyond help, and the eyes once so full of dash and drama now assumed a glassy appearance.[53] With his last bit of life, the actor whispered to see his hands one final time. When Luther Baker lifted the paralyzed arms, Booth stared for a moment at the palms—the same palms the old gypsy had gazed upon—then the arms dropped.

"Useless, useless," the dying man whispered sadly.[54]

"These were the last words he ever uttered," wrote a witness:

> As he began to die the sun rose and threw beams into all the tree-tops. . . . The struggle of death twitched and fingered in the fallen bravado's face.—His jaw drew spasmodically and obliquely down-ward; his eyeballs rolled toward his feet, and began to swell; livid-ness, like a horrible shadow, fastened upon him, and with a sort of gurgle and sudden check, he stretched his feet and threw his head back and gave up the ghost.[55]

Soon after his passing, Booth's body was wrapped in an army blanket and placed in a wagon, and the jubilant cavalry column headed back to Washington. With his hands bound tightly and a rope looped around his neck, David Herold followed. The greatest manhunt in American history had come to an end.

Somewhere on the way back to the capital, Boston Corbett pulled off the road and dismounted. Troubled by the detective's stern rebuke, the trooper now knelt beside a tree and prayed—prayed that God might reveal whether he had indeed done right or wrong. After a short while, the little sergeant got to his feet and remounted, greatly relieved—God, in his infinite wisdom and mercy, was not displeased. He was still smil-ing down on Boston Corbett.[56]

CHAPTER TWENTY-EIGHT

THE HATE OF HATE

AT 9 A.M. ON APRIL 26, Junius Brutus Booth, Jr., was escorted by several detectives to the War Department for questioning prior to his confinement in the Old Capitol Prison. On the previous day, the eldest Booth brother had been arrested at the home of a relative in West Phila-delphia. His nervous system already shattered by the narrow escape from Cincinnati and the abuse heaped upon his name, Booth was now "dumbfounded" by this most recent development.

"[I] wished John had been killed before the assassination, for the sake of the family name," the actor admitted on his trip down to Washington.[1]

Junius's arrest was not simply because of his relationship to the assas-sin, but because the federal government felt he might have played an active role in the conspiracy. Mundane letters exchanged between the brothers weeks and months preceding the murder, as well as esoteric allusions, were now scrutinized and suddenly took on sinister signifi-cance. Simple scribblings that had been torn up and tossed away were fished out of spittoons by eager detectives in hopes they might provide a clue. Jottings on a scrap of paper, copied from the 49th Psalms, were quickly retrieved and carefully examined.[2]

Another Booth brother, Joseph, also was jailed. So worried were gov-ernment officials that he might somehow slip their net that even before the brother landed in New York, a cutter intercepted the ship that he was returning on from Australia.[3] Even a Booth brother-in-law, John Clarke, was soon arrested. Already nervous over the future of his acting career—so much so that he demanded a divorce from Asia—Clarke now found himself accused of complicity in the assassination.[4]

"Poor old country," wrote Asia in the depth of depression, "she has seen her best days and I care not how soon I turn my back upon her shores forever."[5]

While the Booth family was being jailed, countless others also were imprisoned, most on the shakiest of evidence. "Fresh arrests are being made each day," announced one excited journalist, as if reporting on a fisherman's daily net.[6]

Two brothers, a brother-in-law, dozens of friends, and hundreds of strangers still did not equal one assassin, however. In desperation, Washington authorities intensified their search in the capital itself. Some seriously advocated dismantling and demolishing every home and building in the city to uncover the murderer.[7]

On the evening of April 26, while a huge crowd swarmed about the Kirkwood House on Pennsylvania Avenue, hundreds of policemen and soldiers poured into the hotel itself. A short time later, the searchers fanned out to neighboring buildings, going from door to door and from roof to roof. Somewhere in the crowd below, a rumor had started which stated that John Wilkes Booth—painted black, wearing a "white negro wig," clad in a dress, walking on crutches—had been recognized before limping away near the Kirkwood. "Joe, don't say anything!" Booth had supposedly said after shaking hands with the friend. "Joe," of course, promptly did and for the next several hours the furious manhunt for the murderer continued. At length, the source of the report was finally found—a local sot just released from the city holding tank. "Drunk again," growled an angry policeman. "Go home and get sober."[8]

The following day another rumor raced through Washington, and an even larger crowd hastened to the Potomac. Unlike the hoax of the night before, this report proved true.[9] At 1:45 that morning, a tug had drawn alongside the gunboat *Montauk* as it lay anchored in the river. Several men had crossed over to the warship from the tug, including the Secret Service chief, Colonel Lafayette Baker. With them came the decomposing body of John Wilkes Booth. Although there was little doubt in anyone's mind, a formal identification of the assassin's body was scheduled for later that day. David Herold also was taken aboard, then whisked below, where he was heavily secured by double irons.[10]

As the sun rose and the report spread, thousands hurried down to the river, where they stood staring in grim fascination at the black ship.[11] Hundreds of requests were made for passes, that the morbid and curious might feast their eyes on the "monster," but only a handful were granted. Most simply stared and pointed from the shoreline or peered through field glasses and powerful telescopes.[12] As frustrating as the quarantine was for a people who desperately wanted to scowl at the actor and spurn his dead body, there was soon something very tangible in which all could share.

Walking into the War Department, Lieutenant Edward Doherty presented himself to Edwin Stanton. Beside the officer stood his sergeant from the 16th New York.

"Are you sure Corbett shot Booth?" stared the stern secretary of war.

"I am," answered Doherty.

"You arrested him for firing without your order?"

"I did."

"You did right," said Stanton as he turned to the little sergeant. "Do you agree with the Lieutenant's story?"

"Yes," replied Corbett, "I shot without an order. Booth would have killed me if I had not shot first. I think I did right."

After a brief pause to study the strange little man, Stanton at last spoke: "The rebel is dead, the patriot lives; he has spared the country expense, continued excitement and trouble. Discharge the patriot."[13]

Thus did Boston Corbett narrowly avert yet another court-martial. Even greater surprises were waiting outside, however. Accepting a lunch invitation from a War Department employee named Johnson, Corbett and his host were followed by a growing crowd eager to feast their eyes on the slayer of Booth. Once at the home, the throng became so noisy, and their demands for a speech were so loud, that the hero was finally forced to step out to the porch.[14] When the cheers and applause died down, Corbett spoke.

"Fellows," shouted the sergeant, "I am glad to see you all. Johnson won't let me make a speech. Goodbye."[15]

After lunch, Corbett's host led him through the streets toward Matthew Brady's studio, where photographs of the now famous celebrity were scheduled.[16] Again, surrounded by wild, cheering crowds, the sergeant was besieged by hundreds seeking his autograph. One man offered Corbett a thousand dollars for the revolver he had used to kill Booth. Although his carbine had already disappeared while he was at the War Department, the little soldier refused the money, stating that the pistol was government property and not his to sell.[17] Others in the throng merely wanted to hear Corbett speak and tell his tale. The hero was happy to oblige:

> I aimed at his body. I did not want to kill him. . . . I think he
> stooped to pick up something just as I fired. That may probably
> account for his receiving the ball in the head.[18]

> [W]hen the assassin lay at my feet, a wounded man, and I saw the
> bullet had taken effect about an inch back of the ear, and I re-
> membered that Mr. Lincoln was wounded about the same part of

the head, I said: "What a God we have. . . . God avenged
Abraham Lincoln."[19]

His disobedience of orders and a single pistol shot had elevated Boston Corbett from a religious crank and crazy fanatic to an "eccentric" hero and man of the hour.[20]

"[H]e will live as one of the World's great avengers," praised a grateful editor.[21]

Not everyone was happy with Corbett's deed, of course. Hundreds of young women who would secretly love John Wilkes Booth for the rest of their lives, no matter what he had done, were shattered by the news. When she first heard word of the assassin's death, one such woman who was traveling on a Washington streetcar became so overcome with emotion that she wept aloud, then pulled out a small photo of the actor and kissed it.[22] Millions more were unhappy with Corbett's actions for other reasons. Most censured the deed because it deprived them of the supreme satisfaction of seeing the assassin brought back in chains; of relishing his imprisonment and trial; of savoring his last moments as he trembled on the gallows.[23]

"What a pity there was not enough life left in Booth to choke out of him by the hangman," raged one man.[24]

Had Booth indeed been captured alive, many would have been in favor of slow torture.[25] The "well-known English poet," Dr. C. Mackay, had suggested that between his capture and execution, Booth should receive a savage flogging each morning and night.[26] His agony, insisted a Washington editor, should be "long drawn out. . . . No humane man should object to apply such mental tortures to such a wretch."[27] Others argued that following the lengthy torture, Booth's body should be chopped up and the parts put on public display.[28]

Denied the sadistic satisfaction of watching his demise, active imaginations sought solace by envisioning the agony the murderer must have suffered before death.[29] Wrote a citizen to the *Chicago Tribune*:

> For ten days and nights [*sic*] the forests and swamps were his home, with pain, and dread, and anguish. When discovered, the barn was fired; before him a sea of flame, ready to engulf him; beyond the grave, a still greater sea of flame awaiting him; and at that instant he received his peculiar, his wonderful wound. . . . Could the end of such a life have been more painful, more dreadful, more appalling? Was there not in it all the hand of an overruling Providence?[30]

"Justice hunted the crippled fugitive like a starved beast from swamp to swamp," echoed a Washington editor, "and at last, exhausted by ex-

posure and hunger and pain, the wretch died the death of a. . . . mad
dog in an out-house."[31]

Aghast at the savagery evinced, repulsed by the growing mountain of
lies heaped on a dead man, some stalwart individuals could not remain
silent, even if the victim was a much-hated assassin. Protested the editor of a Canadian newspaper:

> The shooting of Booth was a cold-blooded murder—nothing more
> or less. Granted that he was a criminal of the deepest dye—that was
> no reason why he should have been shot down the way he was. He
> was a foolish man, but a brave one. He died like one who loved his
> country dearly, according to his idea of what a noble death was. It is
> very evident that the detective gang were a lot of cowards, or they
> would never have had recourse to the means they adopted to finish
> up the "brief, eventful history" of a man who was already half dis-
> abled.[32]

When others agreed and suggested that even the devil deserved his
due, that Booth had been a brilliant, beloved actor who had shown no
mean amount of boldness and bravery both in staging his deed and in
meeting his end, the voices of fairness were shouted down by a roar of
anger. Exploded a Baltimore editor:

> His whole history is a history of libertinism, baseness and dishonor.
> Any attempt to illumine a lifetime of shame and misconduct is a
> wretched sham. If he had had any redeeming qualities, he has
> swamped them all by a crime whose magnitude is not paralleled in
> the annals of human events. . . . He has left a name infamous be-
> yond expression. "Dowered with the hate of hate, the scorn of
> scorn," and any apology for his damning misdeeds should be
> crushed forever. Let him take his place where he belongs; let the
> evil he has done live after him; and let not those who he has so
> foully wronged, the good and true and loyal men of the whole na-
> tion, be sickened with pitiful attempts to make a martyr of a villain,
> to array in the garb of a hero a monster of crime, and to surround
> with fragrant flowers and rainbow colors the exit of one who died
> like a dog.[33]

While those on shore strained to see, a number of important individuals, along with a cumbersome camera, were rowed out to the *Montauk*,
and the official identification of the body began.[34] As the tarpaulin was
pulled back and the corpse was revealed, those on deck had their first
glimpse of the assassin. Accompanying his father—a physician who had
performed some minor surgery on Booth in the past—was John May, a

teenager well acquainted with the actor. The boy was shocked by what he saw. "[N]ever in a human body," May said later, "had greater change taken place . . . than in the haggard corpse which was before me with its yellow discolored skin, its unkempt and matted hair, and its whole facial expression sunken and sharpened by the exposure and starvation that it had undergone."[35]

"[T]he body looked more like that of some dirt-bearer than of the whilom fop," sneered another viewer.[36]

In addition to a growth of beard, the body was undergoing rapid decomposition. Nevertheless, the tattoo "JWB" was still visible on the left hand.[37] Also, a scar was yet plainly seen on the back of the neck. Earlier, John May's father had removed a tumor in that spot. "Booth at the time," young May recalled, "was playing with Charlotte Cushman in Romeo and Juliet and during the play she embraced him with so much ardor that she tore out the stitches and tore open the wound. It then healed . . . and left a wide large scar."[38]

With identification settled, Alexander Gardner set up his equipment and took a number of plates of the body.[39] While the camera was in place, it was decided to bring up David Herold as well. "As I stood near the hatchway," remembered Seaton Munroe, "I had my first look at him as he slowly ascended and moved forward with the sentries."

> He was not only handcuffed, but to his leg irons were attached a chain, and a 32-pound shot, the latter being carried by the sentry in the rear. As they approached the turret the gangway narrowed, and their footsteps along the iron deck were but a few feet from the water. The idea instantly seized me that at this moment had come to the unhappy wretch the first, last and only opportunity of escape from the gallows. A sudden dash to the right, and his impetus would have dragged the shot, if not the sentry, after him over the unrailed side of the "Monitor"; and in two minutes thereafter his parting breath would have bubbled to the surface from where he lay anchored, three fathoms below, on the muddy bottom of the river.[40]

Although the assassin had not been captured alive, as many had hoped, he was no longer at large; nor had he escaped retribution, as many had feared. And for this, all mourners of the martyred president were eternally grateful.[41]

And thus, concluded a Chicago editor, "the fifth act in the most imposing tragedy the world has ever seen has closed, and the curtain fallen upon the dead body of J. Wilkes Booth. The assassin and his victim have met in the presence of Him who is the Judge of the quick and the dead."[42]

CHAPTER TWENTY-NINE

THE HEART OF ISRAEL

ON THE MORNING OF APRIL 27, the Lincoln funeral train, draped in black cloth, left Buffalo, New York, and continued its slow journey west. Although an estimated one hundred thousand people, including a tearful Millard Fillmore and many Canadian visitors, passed the coffin as it lay in St. James Hall, the funeral was considered by many to be a failure.[1] Because Buffalo had earlier staged its own extravagant ceremony before it was learned that the city would be an official stop, neither the time, energy, nor resources were available for yet another funeral. Disappointing as the reception may have been to some, all else between Buffalo and New York City had been impressive.

After Manhattan Island, the entire route up the Hudson Valley was literally lined with viewers.[2] When opposite the United States Military Academy at West Point, cadets were drawn up at attention, and as the "black train" stopped briefly, the young men were allowed to pass through the funeral car.[3] At Sing Sing, the train passed under a huge black and white arch covered with evergreen boughs and capped by a statue of Liberty. "He Died for Truth, Justice and Mercy," read one inscription; "We Mourn Our Country's Loss," proclaimed another.[4]

When night darkened the valley, still the people stood.

"[A]t every town and village on the way," wrote passenger John Hay, "vast crowds were revealed in waiting by the fitful glare of torches; dirges and hymns were sung as the train moved by."[5]

When the cars reached Albany near midnight, the thousands of lamps, candles, torches, and gas jets made the New York capital "as light as day."[6] Almost immediately, and with every bell in town tolling, the public poured into the capitol to view the body. For the next twelve hours, thousands of New Yorkers and New Englanders filed past to pay their last respects. As in Philadelphia, the crowds were so great outside the building that women fainted in the jam and were passed overhead from hand to hand to safety.[7]

At noon the following day, after a scheduled circus parade of giraffes, bears, and ostriches had been postponed, the body was escorted once again to the waiting cars, and the long trip home was renewed.[8]

As was the case throughout the trip, a pilot engine preceded the train by several miles, ensuring that there were no mishaps. On board this lead locomotive were telegraph operators and mechanics with their tools. Seldom running more than twenty miles per hour, the funeral train commonly slowed to a crawl as it passed through the numerous towns and villages.[9] In some of the smaller communities where the train did indeed stop, many of those on board were surprised at how genuine and heartfelt emotions were. With limited resources, many hamlets had little more than wildflowers and tears to give; but give they did, and freely.

"The occasion is more like a funeral, less of show," passenger Ozias Hatch confided following a brief stop in Little Falls, New York.[10] After all the booming guns, trilling choirs, and soaring eulogies at Washington, Philadelphia, New York, and elsewhere, one passenger was forced to admit that the journey seemed more like the triumphal march of a mighty monarch than the funeral for a common man.[11] In their haste to honor the dead president, many communities inadvertently sacrificed dignity, decorum, and order. Sheer numbers alone precluded anything approaching solemnity. As a consequence, it was quickly observed that most of those who composed the surging, shouting mobs were mere "gawkers."

"Their grief is a fashion, their mourning a fashion," said one disgusted woman, "there is little genuine feeling of any sort amongst them. . . . [M]any . . . come to such sights as they would to a wax work show."[12]

All the same, whether curious or reverent, the desire to see the body, the coffin, or simply the train as it passed had by now become a national obsession. In the minds of millions, the need to be in some way a part of the funeral had become all-absorbing, and a trek of one, two, even three hundred miles was not uncommon.

As darkness fell over the Mohawk Valley and the torches and lamps of the waiting mourners were lit, the scene was like a "pillar of fire," thought one witness. From the dark bluffs above, the train's route as it moved west through New York looked like a burning fuse to some, or a speeding comet to others. Added to the spectacle was a dull, rolling thunder as town after town welcomed Lincoln with cannon salutes.[13]

Recorded one writer:

> Bonfires and torchlights illumined the road the entire distance.
> Minute guns were fired at so many points that it seemed almost
> continuous. Singing societies and bands of music were so numer-
> ous that, after passing a station, the sound of a dirge or requiem
> would scarcely die away in the distance, until it would be caught
> up at the town or village they were approaching. Thus through
> the long hours of the night did the funeral cortege receive such
> honors.[14]

"At every city and town, it seemed as though the entire population had
turned out," observed Ozias Hatch.[15]

Amid bonfires, bells, and cannons, as well as thunder and lightning,
thirty thousand people braved a midnight storm merely to watch the
train pass through Syracuse. At 3:30 A.M., another thirty thousand ventured out in Rochester for the same reason.[16]

Impressive though the numbers were in New York, they were nothing
compared to what lay ahead. "As the train passed into Ohio," John Hay
revealed, "the crowds increased in density, and the public grief seemed
intensified at every step westward; the people of the great central basin
seemed to be claiming their own."[17] Not only numbers but the depth of
emotion was noticeably greater as the train moved through Ohio.[18]

Although Cleveland was smaller than many of the previous cities,
virtually the entire population came out to honor Lincoln.[19] With a few
days extra to organize, the city had used its time wisely. To avoid the
chaos and crush of Philadelphia, New York, and Albany, organizers
opted to stage the event out-of-doors under a large pagoda-like shelter
in Monument Square. With this simple solution, noted one viewer, "the
size of the crowd was only limited by what all outdoors could hold."[20]
Additionally, and again with the other disasters in mind, ladies were
kindly requested to leave their hoop skirts at home.[21]

Despite a merciless downpour that came and went and came again,
ten thousand people an hour passed the coffin in orderly and quiet respect. It was this example of genuinely affected mourners in Cleveland
that caused many to realize that the funeral had by now become a religious experience of mystical proportions. Already, for millions of blacks
North and South, millions of former slaves who had never seen the living man and now never would, long since had their liberator and redeemer entered the realm of the supernatural. When one freed slave
expressed a desire to see the president, another nearby ridiculed the
notion: "No man see Linkum. Linkum walks as Jesus walk—no man see

Linkum."[22] Now, for millions of whites, a similar transfiguration was taking place. In the rush to honor and exalt, Lincoln the man was slipping away, and Lincoln the myth was taking his place. Even skeptics and former enemies were stunned to silence by the irony and the timing of his death; it was as if a mighty, mysterious force had ordained it.

So great was the growing love for Lincoln that many mourners simply would not accept the fact that a mere mortal had died. Surely all heaven and earth would acknowledge the passing of such a great and good man. When no earthquakes, eclipses, comets, or other natural phenomena were forthcoming, well-meaning mourners invented them. The torrential spring rains that marred most of the funeral ceremonies were interpreted by many as the sadness of heaven. "God is weeping," insisted citizens of Cleveland.[23] During the rare bouts of blue sky and sunshine, "the Lord was looking kindly down."

Just as some were quick to transform the natural into the supernatural, others were just as quick to turn the mundane into the mystical. During the New York funeral procession, a Saint Bernard supposedly bolted from his master and ran beneath the moving hearse. Despite all attempts to call him back, the huge canine continued to walk solemnly along under the vehicle the entire length of the route, hidden from view by the trailing black cloth. The dog, so the rumors ran, had known and loved Lincoln and had been petted by the president only the day before his death. All in all, reported the *New York Tribune* soberly, it was a "curious performance."[24]

Given the mania of the public mind, the need to take away something tangible from the martyrdom of Abraham Lincoln was almost insatiable. Whether they were simple souvenir-hunters or devout pilgrims seeking holy relics, the results were the same.

"Hundreds daily call at the house to gain admission to my room," wrote William Clark, in whose room the president died. "Everybody has a great desire to obtain some memento from my room, so that whoever comes in has to be closely watched for fear they will steal something."[25] Among other items, Clark himself had a lock of Lincoln's hair, carefully framed, as well as a piece of the president's brain.[26]

On the funeral train itself, surrounded by millions of clamorous people, the demand for keepsakes was overwhelming. Ran a typical account:

> It was necessary to set a strong guard around the car, arch and catafalque, to prevent them from being torn to pieces. Ladies eagerly picked up the leaves of the flowers which had been strewn on the coffin, and put them carefully in paper for preservation.

Scissors were pulled out to clip pieces from the drapery, and
positive roughness had to be used in many cases to prevent the
complete demolition of everything.[27]

Without alert, eagle-eyed guards nearby, the crowds, as many observers later admitted, would have quickly reduced the coffin to splinters,
then snipped away all the clothes and hair from the corpse.

For those unable to pluck something momentous, a whole array of
hucksters waited on the edge of every large crowd ready to hawk mourning badges and ribbons, flags, jewelry, rings, even books hot off the press
detailing the life and death of Lincoln.[28] Photos and sketches of the dead
president were also much-coveted souvenirs, as were images of the assassin. This last item incensed many. "People cannot pass along without seeing the unblushing countenance of the fiend who inflicted the
blow," raged one furious viewer.[29]

Ubiquitous profiteers were also on hand, ready, willing, and able to
turn calamity into cash. In some cities, windows overlooking the funeral
procession rented for as much as one hundred dollars each.[30] One unscrupulous individual in Philadelphia charged a toll of twenty-five cents
for every person who used his gate while fleeing the mobs around Independence Hall.[31] With the inventory of most stores long since exhausted of anything black, "sacrilegious wretches" slipped through
darkened streets at night stealing cloth and crape from homes and businesses, then with the dawn resold the material at marked-up prices.[32]
Railed one editor:

> We have heard of mean men—men who would steal chickens,
> rob graves of their contents, live on the earnings of prostitutes,
> abstract pennies from dead men's eyes, or pilfer acorns from a
> blind swine . . . but the meanest of all low thieves is the person
> who will go about the streets at the dead of night and steal the
> habiliments of mourning.[33]

Another scourge was pickpockets. Following the fall of Richmond and
Lee's surrender, these sly criminals lifted thousands upon thousands of
dollars from exuberant and distracted Northern crowds.[34] Now, when-
ever the funeral train passed through cities great and small, the nimble-
fingered thieves were sure to be prowling. Though some were caught,
most were not, and given the incredible density of crowds, the situation
was every pickpocket's dream. In some cases, notably Philadelphia and
New York, much of the terrible crush was caused by thieves relieving
valuables from wedged and almost helpless victims.[35] Like wolves trailing a herd of buffalo, organized gangs of pickpockets and burglars fol-

lowed the funeral train west. When the cars reached Columbus, police received a tip that a band of New York criminals would soon arrive to work the crowds in the Ohio capital. As the gang's train pulled into the station, the doors to their coach were quickly bolted. At their leisure, police thereupon arrested eleven suspects.[36]

When the funeral train left Columbus, it passed through towns that few on board had even heard of. And yet, in many cases thousands, even tens of thousands, were dutifully on hand to greet the cars. At little Piqua, Ohio, ten thousand people gathered at midnight. Across the border in Richmond, Indiana, upwards of fifteen thousand more were waiting at 3 A.M.

Because of a terrible, prolonged rainstorm, the grand demonstration planned for Indianapolis was canceled. With soaked flags hanging limp, and with black dye from the decorations streaming down buildings and onto the sidewalks, the elements visibly reduced the number of visitors. One man took advantage of the smaller crowds to view Lincoln's body three times. All the same, though fewer mourners were on hand than in other stops, Indianapolis was still packed with people.[37]

"Tremendous crowds in the city," John Jefferson jotted in his journal after making the trip up from Louisville, Kentucky, that morning. "Fell into a dense column & wended my way to the State House where I looked upon the uncovered face of Abraham Lincoln."[38]

What Jefferson and others saw when they gazed upon the president's face sixteen days after his death depended upon what they wanted to see. Some insisted that Lincoln looked natural, like one at rest; "certainly very sweet [and] amiable," wrote one viewer.[39] Others recoiled at the sight. Many thought Lincoln looked less like a man than a shriveled, shrunken mummy. Because of serious decomposition and blackening, embalmers at each halt had to apply heavier amounts of powder and rouge. The result was a waxy, artificial look. Fortunately, the tons and tons of flowers delivered to the funeral car and the floral arrangements at the various ceremonies mostly masked the increasingly foul odor.

"To me," said one revolted woman, "there was something shocking in parading the poor decomposing remains through so many towns to be gazed at by crowds."[40]

In addition to the undignified and drawn-out display of the body, many more were quietly upset by the tremendous cost to the country and the various cities involved. Already deeply in debt because of the war, the United States, grumbled one critic, was now "pouring out money like water in showing its sympathy."[41] The silver and mahogany coffin alone cost an estimated fifteen hundred dollars, and the spectacular ceremonies themselves involved enormous expenditures.[42]

At 10 P.M. April 30, the funeral train left rainy Indianapolis and steamed north. A short time later, the alert crew of the pilot engine spotted something unusual on the track ahead. Upon investigation, the men discovered and carefully removed a "torpedo," or land mine, designed to blow up the cars.[43]

Late the following morning, May 1, the funeral train pulled slowly into the station at Chicago. While the coffin was being taken from the car to the waiting hearse, bystanders noted how "oppressively" solemn and sad the crowds were. Wrote a witness:

> Every one was anxious—expectant—but there was no rush, not even the attempt at disorder. Every one in that vast crowd kept place—not a soul stirred, or spoke; the dropping of a pin might almost have been heard in the midst of the throng. The figures were immovable, almost as if placed on canvass.[44]

More than any other stop on the long journey thus far, Chicago claimed Lincoln as its own. "Illinois clasps to her bosom her slain and glorified son"; "The heart of Israel is slain upon high places"; "We mourn our loss"—just a few of the heartfelt inscriptions among the sea of banners that covered Chicago.[45]

"Many before had lost a father, brother or son," explained one eulogist. "Now we have all lost our noblest son, our bravest brother, our kindest father. Our cup is drained. The sacrifice is ended. . . . The memory of the last great martyr is embalmed forever in the hearts of the American people."[46]

Scenes witnessed elsewhere were repeated in the prairie metropolis. Chicago, with a normal population of 300,000, saw its size more than double with visitors, despite the same miserable conditions that had plagued the entire trip. An estimated 150,000 people viewed the remains during their rainy stay, and many thousands more took part in the ceremonies.[47]

Although the greater number of days allowed organizers more time to plan than in other cities, and although the advance notice was used wisely, the ceremony in Chicago was not without mishap. In addition to the hordes of thieves and sharpers preying upon the crowds, authorities also had to be especially alert to foil determined souvenir-seekers, many of whom came equipped with scissors, razors, and knives.[48] Also, as the remains were passing solemnly through the torchlit streets the following evening for the last leg of the journey home, an elevated side-walk, overflowing with spectators, suddenly collapsed. With the exception of a child who received severe head injuries, most escaped with only cuts and bruises. A few moments later, though, another such passage-way also crashed under the weight, hurling over one hundred viewers onto the jagged rocks and glass below. Scores of victims suffered broken bones and deep lacerations.[49]

Chicago was by far the most emotional ceremony of the entire trip. When the train finally pulled away from the lights of the city and slipped into the darkness, bound for its last stop in Springfield, there was a genu-ine and palpable sense of sadness left behind.

"[N]ow that the form is forever departed, and naught save the memory of the man remains," wrote one reflective journalist, "now comes the blank desolation and sorrow. . . . Lincoln has been identified with Chi-cago as no other President. He was peculiarly ours. . . . He was our Presi-dent in every sense of the word."[50]

CHAPTER THIRTY

DUST TO DUST

LATE ON THE NIGHT OF APRIL 27, Lafayette Baker and his cousin Luther stepped from a small boat near the Old Arsenal in Washington. With the help of several men waiting by the river's edge, oarsmen quietly gathered up an ungainly bundle and placed it onto a waiting cart. Silently, the procession moved off through the pitch-black darkness toward the nearby prison.[1]

Throughout the day, the two Bakers had engaged in a cat-and-mouse game with the public. Following the autopsy on Booth—in which a section of his injured vertebrae had been removed—the Secret Service chief was ordered by Edwin Stanton to take charge of the corpse.[2]

"The secretary of war wishes me to dispose of Booth's body," explained the elder Baker as he asked Luther for help. "He says he don't want the Rebs to get it and make an ado over it. He does not care where it is put, only let it be where it won't be found until Gabriel blows his last trumpet."[3]

After the body had been ostentatiously placed in a gig earlier that day, a heavy ball and chain were noisily dropped into the craft that the thousands of curious ears on shore might hear. Shortly after 2 P.M. the party cast off from the *Montauk*.[4]

"A few touches of the oars and we had parted company with the gun boat and were half rowing, half drifting down the river," recalled Luther Baker. "Crowds of people were all along the shore. It went from lip to lip that we had with [us] a heavy ball and chain and that, of course, we were going to sink the body. Many followed as far as they could."[5]

After two or three miles, and when they were lost to the crowds, the men eased the craft into a hidden cove and awaited darkness.[6] Finally, when Lafayette Baker was certain that the moonless, starless night would cloak their return back up the Potomac to the arsenal, the men cast off again.

Aware of the moment's historic significance, Dr. George Porter was on hand as the cart carried the body toward the prison:

> Not a word was spoken by a member of our party. The only sounds to disturb the stillness of the night were the crunching of the wheels, the shuffling of our feet and the fall of the horse's hoofs on the gravel road. As we followed the body of the assassin in that midnight march, I realized . . . its awe and solemnity . . . [N]othing was lacking to complete the dramatic closing of the "Tragedy of the Nation," and the historic ending of the event, the place, the circumstances, the time.[7]

Without ceremony, the body was removed from the wagon and placed in a large room once reserved for felons. Concludes Lafayette Baker:

> The stone slab which covered the floor had been lifted and a grave dug under it, and down into the black, dismal hole; into that unhonored grave we lowered the once proud, aristrocratic [sic], but now despised and hated J. Wilkes Booth. The stone was replaced and we turned shudderingly from a sepulchre on which no tear of sympathy could ever fall.[8]

For good reason did the federal government stage the elaborate subterfuge. As the curious thousands who watched from shore all day had illustrated, a morbid fascination for the assassin's remains was gaining momentum. Rightly fearing that a grave would become a magnet for sightseers, or worse, a shrine of rebel pilgrimage, many in the government, and many out of it, favored dismembering the body and dumping the parts at sea. "Certainly," argued the *Chicago Tribune*, "it should not be permitted to be buried on any soil over which the Federal flag waves. Equally certain is it that we have no right to thrust it upon any other people, or permit it to pollute in honorable exile any foreign country. There, remains, only the sea and the dissecting room."[9]

Adding stock to the reports of a sea burial, planted government liars sold their voices and pens. More than a few "eyewitnesses" soon came forward to claim that they had been members of the party that had sunk Booth's body far down the Potomac.[10] That public demand to view the assassin's corpse was great became clear in the days following his burial, when ambitious entrepreneurs were seen dragging the river.[11] Concern that Booth's grave might become a rebel memorial was also well warranted. Tens of thousands in the South now venerated his name and viewed the actor as a martyr to the Lost Cause. "Poor Booth," a sad woman wrote in her diary from Texas, "to think that he fell at last. Many a true heart at the South weeps for his death."[12] And even in the North, those who felt that their birthrights had been trampled into the dust over the past four years secretly revered the assassin's photo and wreathed it in laurel.[13]

For every individual longing to honor Booth, though, two more were determined that his name would forever remain entombed in infamy.

"It was a dog's death—dog that he was, and fitted him well," insisted one Northern editor.[14]

"I think he had too easy a death," offered another, "he ought to have been tortured to death."[15]

Meanwhile, as Booth's body was being reviled and cast into a criminal's grave, that of his victim was being gently escorted to martyrdom and immortality.

———

Slowly, at 9 A.M. on May 3, the black train rolled into Springfield for its last stop of the long journey. Because the arrival was an hour late, anticipation among the huge crowd was correspondingly high. Even though the streets surrounding the station were crammed for blocks and all the windows and rooftops were covered with people, when the cars finally screeched to a halt, there was only a "breathless silence" among the crowd.[16] Stirred by the scene, one witness touchingly wrote:

> In the mellow air and bright sunlight of this May morning sweetened by the rain of last night, when those prairies are clothed in flowers, and the thickets of wild fruit trees, and blossoming orchards are jubilant with birds, *he comes back.* His friends and neighbors are here to receive him, not with banners and triumphal music, not with congratulations and grasping of hands, as they had hoped to do, not so, but in mourning. And his oldest and dearest friends come to meet him to be the pallbearers at his funeral.[17]

With a degree of sadness and loss unlike any other stage of the journey, the coffin bearing Abraham Lincoln was ever so carefully transferred to a waiting hearse. As six black horses topped by white plumes led the way, the procession passed slowly through the crowds of silent onlookers until it reached the capitol. Here the body would lie in state. Around the square and on the capitol itself, all was profusely decorated in crape and cloth of black and white.[18]

"Ours in life; the Nation's in death," read one of the many banners.[19]

As elsewhere, the condition of the corpse was cause for concern. With the doors scheduled to open at 10 A.M., undertaker Thomas Lynch was horrified at how utterly black the president's face had become. Dashing across the street to a drug store, Lynch returned in haste with amber and rouge. Realizing the severity of the case, the desperate official was forced to apply the coloring so thickly as to almost paint a face on Lincoln. Even so, there was simply no way to hide the fact that the president's body was rapidly decaying. Nevertheless, at promptly ten o'clock, the public was allowed to enter.[20]

While she herself did not go to view the body, Anna Ridgely's little sister, who sang with the choir, was compelled to remain near the casket for almost an hour. "The room was close and the gas lighted," said Anna, "the air was scented with evergreen which was placed all around the room and the poor child came near fainting."[21]

Another problem that had plagued the journey surfaced yet again in the Illinois capital. Despite the obvious solemnity of Springfield, predatory pickpockets were utterly merciless in their quest for ill-gotten gain. With thousands of farmers and unsophisticated rustics swarming the streets, the thieves had a field day. Although many were arrested by plainclothes policemen, for every criminal locked in jail, two more seemed to materialize.[22] So pervasive was the problem that when General Joseph Hooker spied a pickpocket in the act, he angrily ran over to the man.

"[H]e gave the thief a kick that sent him not less than ten to fifteen feet," laughed an appreciative onlooker.[23]

Hordes of shameless hucksters were also on hand, peddling the normal mementos, with images of the president's old horse, his dog, and the former Lincoln home added to the mix. At the residence itself, though the current owners graciously allowed thousands of curiosity-seekers to enter and even carry away a leaf or flower as a token of the visit, a strong guard eventually had to be posted when relic-hunters were caught hacking off pieces of fence and prying bricks from the house.[24]

Although Lincoln's interment was scheduled for the following day, late into the evening of May 3 there still was doubt among many as to just where the remains would rest. On its own volition, Springfield had spent over five thousand dollars to purchase a beautiful six-acre tract in the heart of town to bury its most beloved son. Mary Lincoln vetoed the plan. Favoring the more remote Oak Ridge Cemetery, the widow threatened to inter her husband in Chicago if this demand was not met.[25] Already tested sorely by her actions in the past, the citizens of Springfield were furious at this latest fit of temper and the woman's refusal to accept a well-intentioned gift.

"The people are in a rage about it and all the hard stories that were ever told about her are told over again," revealed attorney Henry Bromwell. "She has no friends here."[26]

Two days before the funeral train reached Springfield, Mary's son, Robert, had sent a sharp telegram to Illinois governor Richard Oglesby:

> There seems to be a disposition at Springfield to disregard my mother's wishes in regard to the internment. Both the temporary and final interment must take place in the Oak Ridge Cemetery. We have reasons for not wishing to use the [other] place for either purpose and we expect and demand that our wishes should be consulted.[27]

While rumors that the widow was on her way to Springfield to handle affairs were untrue, those regarding Robert Lincoln were not. Arriving at ten that night, the angry son settled the matter for good.[28]

Throughout the night, thousands of mourners continued to tramp in and out of the capitol building. At the same time, noisy trains arrived at the depot disgorging thousands more. As a result, an already crowded city soon became packed, forcing most to sleep on floors, in barns, or not at all.[29]

The following day, May 4, almost three weeks after the murder, the coffin containing Lincoln's body was finally sealed for good.[30] When the casket was placed in the hearse, the grand, solemn procession started for the cemetery three miles to the north. The day was clear, but humid and hot—"almost intolerably hot," thought a Chicago reporter.[31] There was the promise of more rain in the air. Already the spring had been so unusually wet in central Illinois that farmers could not enter their fields. As a result, hundreds of idle yeomen joined the huge procession as it moved through the countryside. The wet weather had been kind to nature, however, and not only were the surrounding fruit trees leafed out, but sweet-smelling lilacs were also in full bloom.[32] As the cortege entered the rolling cemetery, it was greeted by a three-hundred-voice choir that delivered a sad and deeply felt dirge.[33]

"He made all men feel a sense of himself—a recognition of individuality—a self-relying power," praised Bishop Matthew Simpson in his eulogy.

> They saw in him a man who they believed would do what is right, regardless of all consequences. It was this moral feeling that gave him the greatest hold on the people, and made his utterances

almost oracular. . . . Chieftain, farewell! The nation mourns thee.
Mothers shall teach thy name to their lisping children. The youth
of our land shall emulate thy virtues. Statesmen shall study thy
record, and from it learn the lessons of wisdom. . . . We crown
thee as our martyr, and humanity enthrones thee as her trium-
phant son. Here, Martyr, Friend, farewell.[34]

"As the speaker uttered the last words," wrote a witness, "peals of thunder broke through the black clouds which had been gathering over
head, and heavy rain drops spattered upon the ground as if the very
clouds were weeping. The cortege resumed its order of march and alone
in the last sleep we left all that was mortal of this great and good man,
the pure patriot, the immortal martyr, ABRAHAM LINCOLN."[35]

Lincoln was left not quite alone. Indeed, in the days following his
funeral, the crowds of visitors became so great that soldiers were stationed at the grave to prevent souvenir-hunters from carting off everything "living and dead."[36] Far from fading with time, the fascination for
the sixteenth president gained an inexorable momentum from the cross-
country funeral that would never diminish. In twelve days and sixteen
hundred miles, from Washington to Springfield, perhaps as many as ten
million Americans, or roughly one-half the population of the North,
viewed either the train, the coffin, or the body itself.[37] Despite the rain
and the sun, the dust and the distance, Americans had trekked to see
their fallen chief in numbers never before witnessed in the history of
man.

"I can say I had the honor of seeing the remains of the greatest man
that ever lived," explained one visitor simply.[38] Millions more could
make the same claim, and someday they would thrill their children and
their children's children with tales of that terrible time and the role they
played in it.

By the time of his burial, the memory of Abraham Lincoln—his life,
his death—had become for many almost a state religion. In their rush
to deify, Lincoln the man was all but lost. Rather than accept that in him
which was simply good and decent and that which each and every one
of them shared to some degree, well-meaning men and women chose
instead to gild the common and create an impossible paragon: Lincoln—the Great Emancipator, Lincoln—the Martyr, Lincoln—"the
greatest man that ever lived," Lincoln—the American Christ.

PART THREE

CHAPTER THIRTY-ONE

OLD SCORES

The April just closing has been crowded with memorable events.
. . . Had ever any April more of alternating sunshine and gloom?[1]

THUS WROTE THE EDITOR OF THE *St. Louis Democrat* after reviewing in amazement the past thirty days. From the fall of Richmond to the burial of Lincoln, it seemed to many as if an eon had elapsed, and yet, when people looked back as did the above journalist, they found to their astonishment that all had been encompassed within the span of one short month. Earthshaking events had come so fast and furious that eventually they were as looked for each day as the sun or rain.[2] Other incidents—the fall of Mobile, the flag-raising at Fort Sumter, the death of fifteen hundred Union soldiers when the *Sultana* sank in the Mississippi, the surrender of Joe Johnston's rebel army—were each momentous in their own right, yet in the dizzy swirl of events they were all but forgotten.

"This has been a most eventful month," concurred Horatio Taft from Washington. "The most eventful in the history of our Country."[3]

Although Taft's comment was true, those who imagined that Lincoln's burial had closed the book on stirring times were wrong. Much lay ahead. On May 10, near Irwinville, Georgia, federal soldiers finally captured the fugitive president of the Confederacy, Jefferson Davis. As news spread, there was instant celebration throughout the North. After so much sadness, when word reached Springfield on Sunday morning there was an outburst of applause from every church in town.[4]

"For a month past the body of the rebellion has lain helpless at our feet," exulted a Springfield editor, "now its head is in our power."[5]

Not only was the capture of Davis symbolic proof that the war was won, but now the "arch-traitor" would answer for his bloody crimes. For at least one angry Northern diarist, the list of those sins was almost infinite:

> A man Starver, A soal killer, A dastard Rascal, A midnight assassin, A thief, A Rober, A Liar, A forsworn vilian, A Confirmed Traitor, A Slave Driver, A nigger breeder, A negro Equality man mixing his own Blood with niggers. . . . He has made fatherless Children by tens of thousands and widows by thousands [and] has Caused the Spilling of Rivers of Blood. Hang him I say . . . and Leave him on the Gallows for Crows and vultures to feed on.[6]

Davis, concluded the upset writer, was "two mean to Live, two mean to Dy."[7]

Not content with his capture and imprisonment, those who blamed Davis for the past four years of death and destruction now began a deliberate attempt to denigrate and vilify not only the man, but also the cause for which he fought.

"Jeff Davis captured in women's clothes! Jeff Davis captured in women's clothes!" cried newsboys soon after the arrest.[8]

A simple shawl and cloak thrown on in the confusion of the moment were gleefully transformed by an eager and excited press into Davis flying through the woods disguised as a female.[9] "The Rebel President in Petticoats"; "The Hero of the Last Ditch Betrayed by his Boots!!" "Full Particulars of the Capture of the Old Lady"—these were just a few of the fanciful Northern headlines.[10]

"What an end of all the boastings of chivalry," laughed Julia Trumbull of Springfield. "Could tragedy end in a greater farce than has this . . . ? [T]he would be hero of a great Confederacy . . . takes to the woods in his wife's petticoats! to preserve a little longer . . . his miserable contemptible life! Degradation & chivalry are henceforth synonymous."[11]

As the above example illustrates, most in the North uncritically accepted the lies as truth. Despite the fact that even Union soldiers involved in the capture were men enough to admit that there was no substance to the story, most Northerners desperately wanted to believe the tale, and believe it they did.[12] One fair-minded individual who didn't, and who quickly saw through the "humbug," was the editor of the *New York News*. Jefferson Davis was forced into the dress, said the incensed journalist, "because there was danger of the appearance of some little sympathy with the fallen Confederate Chief; and it was necessary to quash and drown any expression of that nature with an universal roar of scornful laughter."[13]

Nevertheless, the story stuck. And in a nation anxiously seeking laughter, no one could have been happier than Edwin Stanton. At the same time that he was promising Chicagoans he would send the "dress" Davis was captured in for public viewing, the secretary of war also was charging the ex-Confederate president and other rebel leaders with complicity in the assassination. Perhaps to draw attention away from his own role in the scheme to murder Davis and his cabinet during the 1864 raid on Richmond, Stanton was well aware that there were no hard facts to support such a charge. And yet, in the overheated atmosphere following Lincoln's death, such things as facts were small matters.

Even as Davis was being imprisoned and chained at Fortress Monroe, Virginia, the cry for a swift and savage accounting was being raised. Edward Goodwin, a Congregationalist clergyman from Ohio, favored hanging Southern leaders high and low, "if it took a string of gallows from M[ain]e. to Cal[ifornia]."[14] Other preachers were equally bloodthirsty. Seventeen Massachusetts ministers from Newburyport signed a petition informing President Andrew Johnson that he was now the Lord's thunderbolt and that he must smite the defeated "without respect to persons."[15]

Many Northerners felt as did George Armstrong Custer, when he matter-of-factly urged a massacre across the board. Wrote the "Boy General" to a Detroit newspaper:

> Extermination is the only true policy we can adopt toward the political leaders of the rebellion, and at the same time do justice to ourselves and to our posterity. . . . Let all of those who have occupied prominent positions in the rebel State Governments or the so-called Confederate Government—all the editors and others, who, by their traitorous harangues or speeches, have stirred up the people to revolt, be condemned as traitors and punished with unrelenting vigor, until every living traitor has been swept from our land, and our free government and free institutions shall be purged from every disloyal traitor. Then, and not till then, may the avenging angel sheathe his sword.[16]

Fortunately for the future, older and much wiser generals, such as Grant and Sherman, had seen quite enough bloodshed over the past four years and were more than willing to call a halt to the slaughter. Indeed, few vices were more repugnant to Sherman's mind than vindictiveness. Especially galling to the general were the Radical Republican politicians—"invisible in war, invincible in peace"—who were now using Lincoln's death as a pretext to foist a cruel, crushing "peace" on the defeated and disarmed South. The bloodthirsty speeches and cries for mass executions, said Sherman, were nothing more than "the howlings of a set of sneaks who were hid away as long as danger was rampant, but now shriek with very courage."[17]

Though truly terrible in war, Sherman was also magnanimous in victory. Thus, following Lincoln's death, when he extended to his adversary, Joe Johnston, virtually the same charitable surrender terms that Grant had offered to Lee, the document was rescinded by a federal government still stunned and angry over the assassination. Though stung by the censure, Sherman was especially outraged by the accusations of treason and treachery that followed. One Washington editor suggested that the "erratic, ambitious" general was planning to seize power in a coup.[18]

Erratic though he may have been, few generals in the Union Army were less ambitious politically, and fewer still had done more to win the war than Sherman. Thus, with Edwin Stanton leading the Radical chorus against him, the red-headed hero exploded. Wrote Sherman to a friend on May 19:

> It is amazing to observe how brave and firm some men become when all danger is past. I have noticed on fields of battle brave men never insult the captured or mutilate the dead; but cowards and laggards always do. . . . Falstaff, the prince of cowards and wits . . . stabbed again and again the dead Percy, and carried the carcass aloft in triumph to prove his valor. So now, when the rebellion in our land is dead, many Falstaffs appear to brandish the evidence of their valor and seek to win applause, and to appropriate honors for deeds that never were done.[19]

Four days later, the greatest military display ever witnessed in the New World was staged when the victorious Union Army marched in a final grand review through the streets of Washington. The second day of the pageant was reserved for Sherman's tough army, fresh from its triumph in the Carolinas. As the victor of Atlanta and the march to the sea, the commanding general received a thunderous ovation when he was recognized by the tens of thousands of spectators gathered. Just prior to the parade, Sherman—still smarting from Stanton's reprimand—dismounted and climbed up to the grandstand, where he might watch his troops pass in review. There, the top military and political leaders in the land arose to greet the general, including Andrew Johnson and Ulysses Grant. As Sherman moved down the line shaking hands, Edwin Stanton stood and extended his. With a sharp turn on his heel, the fiery commander ignored the gesture and seated himself at the end of the stage.

"The slight was no sooner given," noted a reporter, "than it was noticed by the multitude, who in the enthusiasm of the moment loudly applauded the act, and even laughed at the Secretary's discomfiture."[20]

With their commander's honor vindicated in dramatic style, Sherman's rugged veterans now stepped off up Pennsylvania Avenue on their last march of the war. Only the month before, in the depth of depression, the same crowds had watched silently in the rain as Lincoln's coffin had passed; now, all were joyous once again in the euphoria of victory.

"The shouts of the multitude rent the air," remembered one of the soldiers. "Garlands of flowers were strewed in our pathway, and blessings showered upon us."[21]

It was, indeed, a thrilling spectacle, a glorious celebration to close out four years of war. As impressive as the Grand Review was, though, in the minds of most it would always be incomplete.

"O! If Mr. Lincoln could only live again, how glorious it would all be!" stated one young woman of the bittersweet times. "[B]ut with the gladness comes the sadness of the thought 'Too late!' and takes with it all the enthusiasm—at least from me."[22]

No one in America felt these sentiments more painfully than the lonely widow waiting at the depot on the evening of May 23.

———

Out of deference to the dead president, Mary Lincoln had been allowed to remain in the White House for more than five weeks while the new president shifted as best he could. During that entire period, the widow was all but bedridden with grief.[23] She was, noted Noah Brooks, "more dead than alive."[24] Again and again, despite the best efforts of those around her, the distraught woman would dwell upon the final agonizing moments at Ford's. Nights in the great, empty home were the worst. Remembered Mary's dressmaker and confidant, Lizzie Keckley:

> Often at night, when Tad would hear her sobbing, he would get
> up, and come to her bed in his white sleeping-clothes: "Don't cry,
> Mamma; I cannot sleep if you cry! Papa was good, and he has
> gone to heaven. He is happy there. He is with God and brother
> Willie. Don't cry, Mamma, or I will cry too."[25]

Between her uncontrollable fits of sobbing, Mary did manage to receive several reluctant well-wishers, although Julia Grant was denied entrance many times.[26] One group that gained egress into Mary's quarters were female "spiritualists."

"They poured into her ears pretended messages from her dead husband," recalled bodyguard William Crook. "Mrs. Lincoln was so weakened that she had not force enough to resist the cruel cheat. These women nearly crazed her."[27]

Because of the startling circumstances surrounding her fall from power and the public's love of Lincoln, many of Mary's sharpest critics demonstrated a remarkable capacity to forgive, if not entirely forget, her past behavior. "Whatever indiscretions she may have committed in the abrupt transition from plainness to power are now forgiven and forgotten," soothed one well-intentioned editor. "She and her sons are the property of the nation."[28] In numerous cities throughout the North, subscriptions were started to ease the widow's financial load.

This natural sympathy and willingness to forgive was short-lived. Unstable in the best of times, Mary now became completely and utterly unhinged. When not sobbing and moaning her loss, the former first lady was ranting and raving, accusing everyone from "that miserable inebriate," Andrew Johnson, to mere messenger boys of complicity in her husband's death.[29] And of all Mary's characteristics, her strident vindictiveness had abated not one jot, as when she learned of the arrest of the Confederate president.

"The news of the capture of Davis, almost overpowers me!" she wrote to Charles Sumner. "In my crushing sorrow, I have found myself almost doubting the goodness of the Almighty!"[30]

The woman, admitted one who knew her well, was now "crazier than she used to be."[31]

And thus, when the black-clad widow of Abraham Lincoln, "in a daze . . . almost a stupor," finally vacated her home of the previous four years and journeyed to the railroad depot on a warm evening in May, and while the city was alive with the music and celebration of the Grand Review, "there was scarcely a friend to tell her good-by," recorded Lizzie Keckley. "The silence was almost painful."[32] Indeed, only grudgingly did the Washington *Evening Star* devote five lines buried on a back page to the woman's more-than-welcome departure. Even pickpockets fleecing the crowds at the Grand Review received more ink.[33] Mary's acerbic tongue, her fits of anger, rage, and jealousy, and her haughty, high-handed demeanor and imperious posturing while her husband had lived now came rushing home with a mighty vengeance after his death. Few noted the former first lady's departure from Washington, and fewer still cared.

For the tens of thousands of federal soldiers mustering out of the service in the capital following the Grand Review, the opportunity to see the sites they had heard so much about was overwhelming. Ford's Theater drew most of the blue-clad tourists. Although it was now off limits to visitors, souvenir-seekers had earlier all but destroyed the famous box at the theater, cutting up the curtains one piece at a time and even peeling off the wallpaper.[34] With memories all too fresh, many in Washington favored razing the building entirely. Though the fire was extinguished, one angry arsonist took it upon himself to do just that.[35]

In contrast to Ford's, at the home just across the street where Lincoln had died, William Petersen welcomed any and all into his house—at fifty cents a head.[36] Despite what some considered an outrageous fee, thousands felt compelled to enter. Outside Willie Clark's rented room, where the president had breathed his last, were placed a pillow and several slips, each smeared with dried blood. Inside the room, Lincoln's shoes rested on a chair.

"The same mattress is on my bed, and the same coverlid covers me nightly that covered him while dying," Clark told his sister, and no doubt hundreds of gaping tourists as well.[37]

Even with the hawk-eyed homeowner and his son watching for scavengers, the Petersens could not be everywhere at once. "[I]f they do not tear down the house by inches I shall be very much surprised," laughed one observer.[38]

At the homes of Mary Surratt, Secretary of State Seward, and others, the situation was much the same, as the desire for some souvenir of the assassination seemed insatiable.[39] Even the Lincoln log cabin from Macon County, Illinois, uprooted and headed for display in Boston, had already been hacked of its doors and shutters.[40] Indeed, hardly had the president's body cooled when a booming industry sprang up involving relics related to Black Friday.

Mere moments after the dead president was removed from the house, and before the clamorous hordes had entered, those in the Petersen home began cutting up the bloody shirt, sheets, and towels into smaller, more manageable pieces. Even the hair that surgeons had clipped to reveal the mortal wound were counted and divided one by one.[41] Outside, a little boy was discovered rubbing white paper on the Petersen steps, then delicately placing each in his pocket. When asked by an onlooker what he was doing, the child's answer was simple: "Don't you see those dark stains on the board? It is the blood of the President, and I want to save it."[42]

So frenzied became the quest for anything associated with the assassination that even the screws on the coffin that had carried Lincoln from the Petersen home to the White House were stolen.[43] When the rowboat used by Booth and Herold to cross the Potomac was hauled back to Washington, relic-hunters began chopping away so industriously that the craft had to be impounded.[44] After nearly being lynched by a Washington mob, the Garretts were eventually cleared of any complicity with Booth, and they soon returned to their Virginia home. Quick to capitalize on the swarm of tourists visiting their farm, the family began selling boards purportedly from their bloodstained porch, as well as chips of Booth's crutch and locks of his hair.[45] Although Laura Keene and Clara Harris refused offers to buy their gowns, numerous blood-soaked dresses were sold nonetheless.[46]

"I also send You Enclosed in this letter a piece of the Shirt Bosom worn By the President on the Night of his Murder," wrote one excited young man. "I wish you to give a piece of it to Billy Denver and Tom Greene, I could Sell every inch of it for $5."[47]

"I have several relics of the awful event," another man admitted to his mother. "Among them are a piece of the President's collar stained with his blood and several pieces of the sheet and pillow case on which he died; these are also stained with his blood."[48]

As these typical letters indicate, so much clothing and blood was being peddled that to some it must have seemed as if a score of presidents had been shot at Ford's and a hundred women had held their heads. Obviously, much claiming to be *bona fide* was fake. With men like P. T. Barnum offering one thousand dollars for the death pillow, however, and with hundreds more willing to pay from five to ten dollars for what they thought were patches of cloth stained by Lincoln's blood, the market for assassination artifacts grew and grew, with no end in sight.[49]

For those unwilling to gamble on the authenticity of relics, ever-ready vendors were on hand to hawk mourning badges, mourning rings, mourning shrines, mourning flags, and mourning mementos of every description. So great was the demand for some keepsake, even after Lincoln's burial, that a "Depot for Mourning Goods" opened in Washington. "This house is now making a specialty of black goods," announced a city newspaper, "and they are prepared to exhibit the largest and best selected stock."[50]

"I am going to have [a photo of Lincoln,] let it cost what it will," said one determined woman, explaining in a sentence why the market was so strong.[51]

———

One Washington attraction that drew tourists but did not charge a fee was the assassin of the assassin. Since his great feat, Boston Corbett had remained a popular, if curious, celebrity. Wherever the hero trod, people were sure to stop and stare and crowds were sure to follow. In keeping with his character, Corbett eagerly used his new notoriety to save souls and spread the Lord's mighty message. Wrote the sergeant in one lady's album: "Andersonville, the blackest spot on earth was made bright and glorious by the saving presence of God. His providence also was manifest in delivering me from that place, and making me the agent of His swift retribution on the assassin of our beloved President, Abraham Lincoln."[52]

So far had Corbett's renown spread that Chicago was preparing a life-size photo of the little hero to exhibit at the upcoming Sanitary Fair.[53] As Corbett soon discovered, though, fame had its price.

Despite persistent requests to buy his pistol, Corbett refused, insisting that it was not his to sell. And so, someone simply stole it.[54] Also, the sergeant began receiving crank letters and hate mail. For the moment, Corbett was too preoccupied to trouble himself with death threats. Instead, he spent much of his time trying to secure his share of the reward money—of which he had not seen a cent—and using his sudden status to badger Edwin Stanton into granting him an early discharge from the army, a request the secretary refused.[55] Soon, though, Corbett's concern for his personal safety became all-consuming. Increasingly, the famous sergeant considered himself a "marked man," imagining that mysterious men were dogging his trail—men who definitely were not interested in his autograph.[56]

"My life has been threatened in a most blood-thirsty manner, but God is well able to protect me," announced the hero in public.[57] In private, however, Corbett began withdrawing from the limelight. When newspapers reported his murder near Baltimore, the sergeant saw it as a terrible portent and became even more neurotic.[58] After pulling his new pistol on another sergeant who had angrily ordered him from a military stable, Corbett was court-martialed yet again. The defendant's only alibi—"[I was] on the alert for anyone that might molest me"—was not good enough; he was convicted and received a reprimand.[59]

With his revolver capped and ready for action, Corbett turned in each night with the weapon under his pillow, expecting a visit from either stealthy assassins, the ghost of John Wilkes Booth, or the devil himself. Because those individuals still seeking his signature could expect a pistol pointed at their heads and a lengthy examination, autograph-seekers became fewer and fewer.[60] Delusions, self-mutilations, dementia, orders from God—Boston Corbett could now add chronic paranoia to his growing list of mental maladies.

The slayer of Booth was not the only one to conjure plots. One month after the assassination, lurid minds saw them at every turn. Whether there was any substance to the reports was unimportant. Some people simply wanted to see such conspiracies, and see them they would.

"The mob spirit is very rife, and what is more, it is encouraged by the authorities," explained a St. Louis diarist. "These seem to profit eagerly of these occasions to overawe and silence the opposition."[61]

At Philadelphia and Annapolis, Maryland, fires that in normal times would have been shrugged off to carelessness were now the diabolical work of diehard rebels. As a result, innocent men were arrested. In California, a newspaper that had somehow survived the first purge of democratic journals did not survive the second. The editors were jailed.[62] Because he was found in possession of "suspicious papers," a New Haven, Connecticut, man was arrested and charged with aiding Booth, though no evidence existed.[63] After attending Lincoln's funeral in Springfield on Thursday, Dr. Francis Tumblety was accused of being a Booth conspirator on Friday.[64] A self-proclaimed "Indian Herb Doctor," Tumblety was considered a harmless quack by some, but many in the St. Louis medical establishment were, according to the culprit, "jealous of my increasing fame and practice."[65] Whatever, the stunned prisoner was hauled back to Washington and hurled into the Old Capitol Prison. Protested the doctor:

> It was a persecution worthy the dark epoch of the middle ages, or the bloody era of the French Revolution. . . . Myself and fellow-inmates . . . were prohibited looking from our bars upon the outer world. One day we were startled by the crash of martial music. . . . A lady, who was imprisoned for some political offense, or at least she was charged with such . . . , looked from the casement, when one of the lynx-eyed guards witnessing the breach of Old Capitol Prison discipline, raised his piece and fired, the bullet taking effect upon a brick, a few inches from the fair one's head.[66]

Although Tumblety was set free after a three-week stay, and others were similarly released, so many more were arrested that new prison space was always being added.[67] In Chestnut Hill, Pennsylvania, in Sheffield, Massachusetts, in the mining camps of Nevada, and throughout the nation at large, the roundup continued.[68] In such a chaotic climate of hatred, fear, and suspicion, even one month after the assassination opportunists found it a "soft snap" to inflame passions and eliminate personal or political foes.

Meanwhile, as the purge continued apace, most of America's attention was suddenly directed elsewhere—for much of the next two months it would be the all-absorbing focus of attention.

CHAPTER THIRTY-TWO

THE LIVING DEAD

On May 10, 1865, the same day that Jefferson Davis was captured in Georgia, the "trial of the century" began in Washington. The site chosen for the event was the prison at the Old Arsenal, located on a point of land where the Potomac and Anacostia rivers joined. Prior to that day, the only momentous event to occur on this spot had come in 1814, after Washington was captured and burned by the British. With orders to raze the arsenal, one of the redcoats assigned the task made the mistake of tossing a torch into a dry well where a stash of powder had been concealed. The resulting explosion not only killed many of the troops nearby but also ignited an adjacent magazine. When the smoke had cleared, the area was strewn with arms, legs, heads, and other body parts.[1]

Now, half a century later, the eyes of the nation were once again focused on this otherwise insignificant spit of land. Despite the arcane efforts of the Secret Service, rumors were already afloat that the assassin himself was buried beneath the prison floor.[2] It was the large prison building itself, however, where attention was sharpest, for the structure not only would provide a seat to the trial and a home for the eight culprits charged in the conspiracy, but it would also be a place of execution should the verdicts prove guilty.

A decade earlier, two common criminals had managed an escape from the prison, but there would be no possibility of that now. To preclude a rescue of the prisoners, on the one hand, or mob violence, on the other, thousands of troops were encamped in and around the arsenal grounds. Inside the massive stone and brick walls of the prison itself, more soldiers and sentries stood guard. On the nearby Potomac, menacing gunboats lay at anchor ready to sweep either shore with shot and shell. In all, there was enough firepower in the vicinity of the prison to repel an invading army. Nevertheless, nervous officials were not satisfied.

Not only was each of the accused consigned to solitary confinement in a dark, dungeon-like cell but also the legs of all were fettered by chains, shackles, and heavy balls.[3] The hands of the prisoners were likewise held rigidly in place by a brace of iron-bar handcuffs. As an additional precaution, the canvas hoods used earlier remained on the inmates' heads night and day to foil any form of communication.[4] Only when the accused were led into the courtroom were the torturous devices removed. In sum, admitted a reporter for the Philadelphia *Inquirer*, the prisoners "are already undergoing a living death."[5]

Nothing, it seemed, had been overlooked in the federal government's effort to punish the prisoners and present to the public a show trial. And showy it was. The small number of court passes were naturally in great demand, "like opera tickets to a special performance," thought one woman. Every day carriages filled with people pulled up to the prison, she continued, "the women dressed as if for a race day. One after the other of these gay parties passed in, laughing and chatting. . . . It had become a modish thing for society to drop in for a peep at the conspirators' trial."[6]

The feature attractions, of course, were the seven men and one woman who were the defendants. Each day, as the culprits were brought into the courtroom, there was a hush of horror among those in the gallery. "Ladies of positions, culture and influence enough to be admitted sat about . . . with scowls and scorn, white teeth and scorching eyes," remembered one observer.[7]

Of the eight defendants, the four most deeply involved understandably drew the lion's share of attention, not only among the public but also among members of the press. To feed the ravenous appetites of their readers, correspondents penned colorful, and often incredible, sketches of the accused. For his role in aiding the assassin's escape, Booth henchman David Herold was cast in an especially loathsome light. Although the young man hailed from a prosperous, respected Washington family, one reporter revealed that the son was "best known for his braggadocio style and vagrant habits."[8] Journalists and spectators alike were repulsed by Herold's immaturity, unkempt appearance, and "vulgar face." The defendant, said one disgusted preacher, "looks as if he had not a particle of mind, low, retreating forehead, vacant look." Herold, concluded another viewer, was "more of a simpleton than a demon."[9]

As spiteful as the depictions of Herold were, they were nothing compared to that of George Atzerodt. "Spectators generally single out Atzerodt readily among the prisoners," noted the Washington *Evening Star:*

> His face is a terrible witness against him. A villainously low fore-head, pinched up features, mean chin, sallow complexion, snaky eyes of greenish blue, nasty twisted mustache, head sunk into his shoulders and crouching figure make up the disagreeable present-ment of George A. Atzerodt.[10]

"This fellow might safely challenge the rest of the party as the com-pletest personification of a low and cunning scoundrel," reflected news-man Noah Brooks. "It was observed that when any ludicrous incident disturbed the gravity of the court . . . Atzerot [*sic*] was the only man who never smiled."[11]

As with David Herold, more than one viewer commented on Atzerodt's low and receding profile.[12] "No forehead, shaggy[,] unkempt, with hair hanging loosely over his face," sneered a revolted spectator. "I never saw a face more utterly vacant or so without a single redeeming feature."[13]

If Atzerodt had failed in his part of the plot to kill Andrew Johnson, most felt it was not, as he insisted, a change of heart, but rather simple cowardice that caused him to do so. In sum, said the *New York Times,* "George A. Atzeroth [*sic*] was a coward, mentally, morally and physically . . . , and he failed to make any one care a rap whether he lived or died."[14]

Unlike the men, the lone woman, Mary Surratt, evoked a degree of sympathy, not only because she was a widow and mother but also be-cause the evidence against her seemed weakest. Although her home had been a rendezvous for Booth and the others during the earlier kidnap-ping plot against Lincoln, and although her escaped son, John, was deeply implicated, nothing but circumstantial evidence and "tainted" testimony tied her to the assassination.[15] On the rare occasions when her heavy veil was lifted, spectators could see that Mary was an average-look-ing woman, though not unattractive; "rather pretty," mused one man.[16]

Dressed in black, sitting silently with eyes closed and face turned to-ward the wall, the woman spent the days and weeks to herself, a palm leaf fan in hand, which she seldom used.[17] Adding to a growing compas-sion for Mary was the ghastly thought of a defenseless female in chains. While some insisted that she was not shackled when brought into court, others insisted that she was. All the same, many writers were determined to reveal what they saw as Mary's inherent depravity.

"She is a large, Amazonian class of woman, square built, masculine hands; full face, dark grey lifeless eyes," revealed a reporter for the *Chicago Tribune*.[18]

While he himself could see no more beneath the dark veil than his Chicago colleague, this in no way hindered one New York correspondent: "A cold eye, that would quail at no scene of torture; a close, shut mouth, whence no word of sympathy with suffering would pass . . . ; a square, solid figure, whose proportions were never disfigured by remorse or marred by loss of sleep."[19]

Mary Surratt, concluded the *Chicago Tribune* neatly, was "the perfect type of venomous Southern woman."[20]

Of all the defendants, none drew more comments or caused more ink to flow than Lewis Powell, alias Lewis Payne. Because of his bloody rampage in the home of Secretary Seward, he naturally became the focus of morbid curiosity. The first question generally asked by newcomers to the trial, was "Which is Payne?"[21] Recorded one newsman:

> He absorbs the greater part of the attention of the audience, and you hear continually such expressions as, "Did you ever see such a perfect type of the cut-throat?" What a monster he is, to be sure. Had Booth hunted the world over, he could not have found a more fitting tool for his work. He is constitutionally an assassin.[22]

"Out of a thousand men," said one spectator, "I sh'd be sure to pick him, if I wanted a tool who w'd cut a throat as readily as he w'd carve a chicken."[23]

Beginning with his alias, which he tenaciously clung to—"I don't know my name. I was stolen from my parents when quite young"—intrigue surrounded Powell from the outset of the trial.[24] While rumors hinted that the young man was the illegitimate child of Jefferson Davis, he was in fact the son of a well-to-do Florida clergyman.[25] Powell reportedly fought under Robert E. Lee in numerous engagements until he was eventually captured at Gettysburg. Escaping captivity, the rebel then joined up with Mosby's Rangers as they operated in northern Virginia.[26] Adding to the fog shrouding Powell was when and where he had become involved with Booth in the plot. The defendant himself provided almost no clues.

"When spoken to he replies with off-hand bluffness, using barely enough words to convey an answer," wrote a trial reporter.[27]

Despite the cold-blooded nature of the assault, over the days and weeks of the trial, a curious, grudging admiration grew for the powerfully built twenty-one-year-old. More than a match for the sneers and scowls that greeted his daily arrival in court, Powell's stony return stare unnerved would-be tormentors and forced all to look away confused and frightened.[28] "He sat bolt upright against the wall, looming up like a young giant above all the others," recorded Noah Brooks.[29] Even those who desperately hoped to hate him were forced to acknowledge Powell's courage, as a Philadelphia reporter did one day when a victim of the bloody rampage, nurse George Robinson, was called to testify:

> The court room was almost breathless at this moment, every eye being turned upon the prisoner . . . but he not so much as stirred. His wild stare was fixed upon the witness. His mouth was closed tightly, as if his teeth were firmly clenched together, and he stood up as straight as a statue, with no sign of fear, trembling, or trepidation.[30]

Defiant, unyielding, strong, Powell's indifference to his fate was in stark contrast to the other defendants who naturally grasped at any straw to save their lives. Although David Herold tried to maintain a stoic air in court, the pathetic youth often wept uncontrollably in his cell. Not so Lewis Powell. In court or out, he was his same stolid self.[31] "Payne does not give way in the least," confided one journalist. "There is something wonderful about this creature. . . . His face is not an ugly one; the eyes are bright and defiant, yet not maliciously so. He is the only one of the accused whose bearing has anything at all manly in it. The rest seem to be weak and detected villains."[32]

"Payne never complained—no matter what you did to him, he never said a word," remembered his jailer, Captain Christian Rath. "I grew fond of the fellow, and was sorry for his predicament."[33]

Rath was not the only person impressed with Powell. Each day, new crowds of tittering females flocked to the trial, most to feast their eyes and admire the handsome, rugged spectacle on display.[34] For the most part, Powell was inscrutable and remained as unmoved by the ogling as he had been by the scowls. One day, a Washington writer noticed the young defendant gazing wistfully toward a window and a world beyond that was now as remote and unattainable as the far side of the moon. "As he looked," recorded the reporter, "a strange, listless dreaminess pervaded his face. . . . Who can tell, who imagine, what memories or what fears, what regrets or what hope, rolled in the brain behind those listless eyes?"[35]

While the case against Powell was open and shut, the evidence leveled at many other defendants was not so clear. All the same, the odds that the accused could receive a fair trial in the District of Columbia a mere month after the assassination were long at best. Although civil courts were in full operation, President Johnson, with the encouragement of Edwin Stanton, insisted that the prisoners be tried by a military commission—the trial would be shorter, the likelihood of convictions greater, the punishments certainly stiffer, and embarrassments to the federal government fewer. Additionally, court procedure would be dictated by military fiat, not the United States Constitution. As a result, many—Gideon Welles and former attorney general Edward Bates, to name but two—considered the trial little better than a farce.[36]

Dispensing with normal protocol, the tribunal placed impossible barriers before the defense. Testimony for the accused was often withheld or simply stricken from the record, while any amount of hearsay favoring the prosecution was admissible and accepted as fact. Those who might have spoken for the defense were intimidated and threatened by the government.[37] A boarder at Mary Surratt's home was warned that he would be prosecuted himself unless a statement was signed deeply implicating the woman in the crime.[38] Another man, after testifying for the defense, was led from the courtroom "through a jostling vulgar crowd, affecting to shrink away on either side of him as if from a monster ill-secured."[39] The trial, said one who faced it, was simply a "court of death." Recounts Henry Kyd Douglas:

> [F]or willful disregard of every principle of law and justice this
> tribunal has no rival. . . . If justice ever sat with unbandaged,
> blood-shot eyes, she did on this occasion. The temper, the expres-
> sions, the manners, the atmosphere pervading the Court made it
> an unprecedented spectacle. . . . [P]assion decided everything. Of
> official decorum, fairness, calmness, there was absolutely none. . .
> . Although the Court was organized to convict, the trial need not
> have been such a shameless farce.[40]

The press was as guilty as the government. In their dispatches to the various newspapers, reporters seldom referred to the eight prisoners on trial as the accused or the defendants; rather, they were "assassins," "criminals," and "conspirators." The eyes of the defendants were never blue or brown, but "dull" or "snaky" or "full of crime and treachery." A simple smile from one of the accused became a "smirk." Every feature and mannerism of a prisoner was scrutinized for signs of innate depravity. Instead of eight human beings on trial for their lives, correspondents depicted the defendants in their dispatches as "apes," "dogs," "panthers," "tigers," and "hyenas." Not surprisingly, the public was pleased with these portrayals.

"They are, taken together," proclaimed an Ohio minister who visited the court, "the most hang dog, villainous looking set of rascals one c'd wish to see. I don't believe you c'd take an equal number out of the penitentiary . . . without improving on their faces full fifty per cent."[41]

The fact that none of the eight prisoners had had any trouble moving virtually unnoticed through the world prior to the trial seemed to have escaped critics such as the clergyman quoted above.

By late June, after weeks of testimony, the trial of the conspirators began to lose its novelty. Newcomers, especially ladies, continued to irritate the court with their loud whispers and laughter, and souvenir-hunters were relentless in their attempts to whittle down the chairs and rails for relics. None could deny, though, that the trial was becoming monotonous.[42] "The community will experience a sense of relief at the termination of this tragedy," a local editor confessed. "Day after day the subject has been brought before the public until every one was weary of it."[43] Also by late June, mercifully, the wretched condition of the prisoners was alleviated somewhat. Gone for good were the hideous hoods, and in their place came pillows.[44] Additionally, the inmates were allowed an hour of outdoor exercise each day, the men received tobacco, and mail began to arrive. Wrote the worried father of defendant Edman Spangler:

> Our Family is in grate distres that your name is mentioned in so many papers A bout you in this murder of the Chief President men[.] if you will gratify us to hear of you the truth of the matter and the reason of your name in Almost everey paper in the Country you can certainly Let me no the truth about the matter. . . . [T]here is so much A bout it in the Nues that we cannot no the truth. . . . god bee with you.[45]

For none of the prisoners were the relaxed rules more welcome than for Mary Surratt. In addition to a rocking chair, the woman was allowed visits from Anna. "The daughter immediately on entering the room," wrote a witness, "ran to her mother and eagerly embraced and kissed her; tears meanwhile streaming down the daughter's cheeks."[46]

"They stayed in this position for fully ten minutes—not a word was spoken," said another moved viewer. Throughout this first meeting of mother and daughter after weeks of separation, Mary remained strong and stoic, merely chiding Anna for breaking down so completely.

"That woman is like a rock," one man later remarked to the jailer after witnessing the scene. "When she saw her daughter she acted as though she hadn't any heart."

"You think so?" replied the jailer. "Then you ought to have been here when I went to take her to her cell. She collapsed, cried terribly, and we had to carry her bodily from the room."[47]

In addition to the eight defendants, others were also imprisoned at the arsenal. One was Burton Harrison. Like the conspirators, Harrison was kept in solitary confinement. Unlike that group, the former secretary to Jefferson Davis was neither shackled nor hooded. Nevertheless, except for his brief walk each day, Harrison was totally isolated, and never, under any circumstances, was he allowed to speak to anyone. Thus, each night, the wretched, lonely prisoner looked forward with the greatest of joy to a slow, sad whistling that filtered up a ventilation shaft from some cell below. There was never any whistling during the day while the trial was in session. But each night Harrison felt a strange companionship with the inmate below who unwittingly helped him maintain his fragile connection to humanity—and his sanity.[48]

CHAPTER THIRTY-THREE

THE MOST
DREADFUL FATE

THOUGH THE FOCUS OF WASHINGTON and much of the reunited nation was naturally on the trial taking place at the Old Arsenal prison, other events crowded in as summer deepened. Most heartening of all, at least to Northerners, was the entire collapse of the former Confederacy. Only scattered guerrilla bands and a remnant of regular soldiers in Texas and Indian Territory still held out. The imprisonment and chaining of former rebel president Jefferson Davis at Fortress Monroe was welcome news, as was the word that other high officials in the Confederate government were now safely behind bars.

On a sober note, another victim was added to the casualty list of Black Friday. Although Secretary of State Seward was well on the road to recovery, as was his son, Fred, his wife did not fare so well. Frances Seward was already in frail health prior to April 14, and the shock and stress resulting from the attack on her household was simply too great for her to overcome. After successfully ministering to her husband and children, the exhausted woman finally lapsed into a fatal fever, and on the morning of June 21, three months short of her sixtieth birthday, she passed away.[1] The body of Mrs. Seward was escorted to her home in New York on the same train that had carried Lincoln.[2]

While thousands of Union soldiers had been mustered out of the service and had returned to their families, thousands more remained in Washington clamoring for discharge and transportation home. With discipline all but forgotten, roving gangs of surly soldiers created havoc in the sweltering city. Drunkenness, fistfights, shootings, theft, lewdness, indecent exposure, saloon brawls, and bawdy-house riots became so common that life in the capital became a "general terror."[3] One such incident occurred after several soldiers were duped by prostitutes in the red-light district. Calling on comrades for help, upwards of two hundred men soon responded, and the furious mob, many of whom had themselves been hoodwinked in the past, proceeded to dismantle the whorehouses and saloons in the area. Because the section was heavily populated by blacks, the situation quickly developed into a full-scale race riot, in which bottles, rocks, bricks, and firearms were used freely by both sides. A pistol-waving physician who bravely tried to restore order had his face smashed by a flying brick. When the riot was finally quelled, many lay seriously injured, including a soldier who had had his bowels ripped out.[4]

Although much of the terrible paranoia that had swept the streets of Washington had mercifully vanished, there were still enough rumors and dark whispers to keep nerves on edge.

"It is highly probable that our political assassinations are not yet over," hinted one reporter a full three months after Lincoln's death.[5]

After sending a violently threatening letter to Andrew Johnson one day, a "crazy German" was arrested on the next day as he entered the White House. The deranged man was packed off to the Government Insane Asylum.[6] More seriously, a group of men were supposedly overheard one night detailing plans to assassinate the president when he spoke at Gettysburg on July 4th. At a given signal, the men would fire from different points in the crowd.[7]

Because of threats such as the above—some real, some fanciful—the roundup continued. Many arrests were certainly warranted, as in the case of George Gayle of Alabama, who late in 1864 had placed an ad offering to kill Lincoln, Seward, and Johnson in exchange for one million dollars.[8] Most suspects though, were jailed and kept on bread and water without a particle of evidence against them, save the words of a jealous neighbor or a malicious gossip.

Unlike earlier arrests, this latest wave was met by mounting opposition. With peace established and hysteria waning, such high-handed and arbitrary actions were deemed unnecessary. Many, including Horace Greeley, now urged an "immediate clearing out of the Federal bastilles."

"We cannot doubt," argued Greeley in his New York *Tribune*, "that hundreds have been caught up and caged who were innocent and loyal, and whose estates have become the prey of the perjured villains who prompted their arrest."[9]

"It is high time that the dungeon doors were thrown open," agreed another editor.[10]

Greeley and a handful of others also protested the bloody purge that took place in the Border States following the surrender.[11] Already brutalized by years of invasion and guerrilla warfare, now further inflamed by Lincoln's assassination, vengeance-minded loyalists from Maryland to Missouri were quick to take matters into their own hands. In Wheeling, West Virginia, Cambridge, Maryland, Washington, D.C., and scores of other border communities, vindictive Unionists passed resolutions forbidding rebel neighbors from returning to their homes.[12] At Hagerstown, Maryland, Confederates who had already returned were ordered out by a mob. Similarly, Southern soldiers arriving in Martinsburg, West Virginia, were attacked and beaten on the streets.[13] To the west in that same state, the editor of the Clarksburg newspaper menacingly warned Confederates that "Judge Lynch's Court" would soon begin operations.[14]

The "court" was already in session in neighboring Kentucky. Torn apart by years of partisan activity and atrocities committed by each side, the angry victors in the Bluegrass State were in no mood to split hairs over who was a regular soldier and who was not. Scores of returning rebel soldiers were simply ambushed and murdered.

"[T]hey shoot down the returned Confederate heroes like dogs or deer," wrote one horrified woman from Perrryville. "[W]ithin my knowledge & neighborhood they have killed hundreds!!"[15]

Two such victims were Samuel Robinson and Thomas Evans. Accused of being guerrillas, the men were hauled to the fairgrounds in Lexington and hustled up to a well-worn scaffold. After hymns were sung and prayers spoken, the condemned said a few words, then bade goodbye to the world. Just as the hangman was in the act of adjusting the ropes, a horseman was seen approaching at a gallop waving a handkerchief. When the breathless rider pulled up, he blurted out that Evans had gained a reprieve. A witness continues:

> Each of the culprits received the announcement unmoved and with apparent indifference. Their hands being pinioned behind them they turned back to back and took each other by the hand. They stood thus a moment in perfect silence when Evans was untied and conducted from the scaffold to the wagon in which he came which was near by. Robinson said a few words to the crowd but I was not near enough to understand what he said. The noose was then adjusted about his neck, the black cap pulled over his face[,] the word given, the prop pulled from under him and he dangled in the air.[16]

Unfortunately, the rope was poorly adjusted, and the fall did not break Robinson's neck. Horribly, the crowd watched for over an hour as the struggling victim slowly strangled to death.[17]

In no state was the purge more savage and bloody than Missouri. Four years of nonstop guerrilla warfare in which scalpings, decapitations, and mutilations had become commonplace created wounds too deep and raw to be healed by someone somewhere signing a piece of paper. Returning rebel soldiers, many of whom had fought far beyond Missouri's borders, were as often as not the innocent victims, as were their helpless families. Judge Lewis Wright and his four sons were rounded up one day by militiamen near Rolla. The men were accused of being rebels, then simply slaughtered by the roadside.[18] Other Missouri victims were dragged from their beds at midnight by vigilantes and hanged from tree limbs.

"I . . . fought for things I thought was right," protested one former guerrilla. "When the war was over and I wanted to settle down they would not let me, but pursued me with a malignant hatred."[19]

Though the bloodshed and death was greatest in the ravaged border states, no Southern state escaped the savage sweep following Lincoln's death. Remembered one embattled Texan:

> I suffered more hardships and trials and experienced more dangers after the war had ended and peace had been declared than I had ever encountered during the four years in the field. . . . I have slept on high eminences in order that I might watch for scouring search parties who were shooting down in cold blood every man that wore the Southern uniform, and for no other reason. I have seen the horizon at night lit up with the burning houses of my friends whose only offense was that they had been soldiers in the Confederate army.[20]

And even in the Northern states, the spirit of violence that had erupted following Lincoln's death was still very much alive throughout the summer. "The rage for blood, now that the war is over, increases," admitted a federal judge in Indiana five weeks after Lee's surrender.[21] Near Glenwood, Iowa, a mob reportedly lynched a man believed to be a Copperhead. In neighboring Illinois, a Democrat was assassinated at his front door near Madison. At Quincy in the same state, soldiers and civilians broke into the jail, dragged out a man accused of being a bushwhacker, and promptly hanged him.[22]

When an earthquake struck the St. Louis region on the morning of June 2, the homes and shops in neighboring Alton, Illinois were rocked to their foundations. "In these startling, earthquaky, shaky times," said an Alton editor tongue-in-cheek, "timorous, trembling traitors tread quietly on free soil."[23] Indeed, in such a volatile climate, not only traitors, but Democrats and any others who had not toed the party line in the past now stepped softly on what was once free soil. Unfortunately, if not actively engaged, most Northerners quietly acquiesced in the bloody purge sweeping the continent.

"Alas," confided a horrified French immigrant to his journal, "I fear that in this country more callousness, cruelty and vindictiveness exist than in any other Christian country in the world."[24]

—

On July 4th, cannons thundered throughout the day in the nation's capital, not so much to commemorate the eighty-ninth birthday of the United States but to celebrate its rebirth. While many denizens held picnics and others tippled, little boys lit firecrackers. Adding to the noise and smoke of the day, the city dog killers, shotguns in hand, chose this opportune time to comb the streets and shoot all canines found without muzzles.[25] That evening, south of the White House, fireworks shot into the dark and made the night lurid with red, white, and blue stars.

Though the day was spent much as it always had been, the celebration was noticeably low-key and unenthusiastic. Had those in Washington known that on that very day, two thousand miles away, the last remnant of the rebel army had crossed the Rio Grande into exile, effectively ending all organized opposition to the reunited nation, perhaps the news would have created more enthusiasm—but perhaps not. After four years of bloody civil war, and after three of the most momentous months in American history, there simply was little energy left to devote to mere tradition.

On the following day, at the Old Arsenal Prison, the great conspiracy trial was scheduled to enter its ninth week. But it was not to be. After listening to over three hundred witnesses and recording forty-three hundred pages of testimony—a stack of paper more than two feet high—the military panel had finally heard enough. At noon on July 6, Major General John Hartranft entered the prison and read the verdicts to each defendant. For their role in the original kidnapping plot, Samuel Arnold and Michael O'Laughlen both received life sentences at hard labor. For his familiarity with Booth and for aiding his escape by setting the broken leg, Dr. Samuel Mudd also received life at hard labor. For innocently holding the reins to Booth's horse outside Ford's Theater, the unwitting stagehand Edman Spangler earned six years at hard labor.

As for the four main defendants, the four most deeply implicated in the April 14 plot, all were sentenced to death. Perhaps as startling to the condemned as the sentence itself was the knowledge that their execution would take place the following day, between 10 A.M. and 2 P.M.[26] Despite the gravity of the situation, none of the four at first manifested any outward concern.[27] That changed when they heard the unmistakable sounds of hammering and sawing just beyond their cell walls.

David Herold's feigned indifference quickly dissolved as reality set in. "For once," said an observer, "he seemed wholly unmanned."[28] Trusting that he would be acquitted or given a minimal sentence, George Atzerodt was initially stunned. When the shock passed, an ashy paleness spread over the stricken man's face, his limbs began trembling violently, and one who looked into his cell described him as "paralyzed with fear." The impact on Mary Surratt was greatest of all. Throughout the terrible ordeal, the woman had exhibited extreme bravery. Now alone, Anna having left shortly before the sentence was read, Mary crumbled completely.[29] Like George Atzerodt, the woman had felt that innocence would set her free. With a horrible fate now clearly before her, Mary wept uncontrollably and begged for a reprieve.[30]

"What will become of her," she cried over and over. "What will be Anna's fate?"[31]

Of the four prisoners, only Lewis Powell seemed completely unmoved. For his murderous role at the Seward home, Powell expected nothing less than death, and the shackles on his limbs and the hammering outside did nothing to rattle his nerves or hamper his appetite.[32]

Almost as the verdicts were read to the condemned, the news swept through the hot, dusty streets of Washington. Both the sentences and the scheduled executions were the main topics of conversation throughout the day. "Scarcely anything else was talked of," revealed one man.[33] At the same time, many were stunned that a woman would scale the scaffold. Even those who earlier had hotly argued for Mary's death now had a change of heart once the widow was condemned. Should she be executed, as some were quick to point out, it would be the first time in its history that the federal government had put a woman to death. "[M]any," one correspondent acknowledged, "who had been most strenuous in asking for severe punishment upon the conspirators were willing to unite in an effort to have the sentence in Mrs. Surratt's case changed to imprisonment."[34]

Not everyone felt this way, of course. The editor of the Washington

Chronicle perhaps spoke for a majority when he gleefully announced to his readers that the "hardened and remorseless fiends"—Mary Surratt included—would now suffer "that most dreadful of all penalties allowed by the civilized world—death by hanging."[35]

Whatever the sentiment, excitement rose as the news spread. Washington hotels and saloons were thronged with buzzing crowds. "The streets were filled with restless, impatient people," wrote a New York reporter. "All day long the trains came in loaded with people from the North; all night long the country roads were lined with pedestrians, with parties hurrying on to the city."[36]

Throughout the evening, hundreds of idle curiosity-seekers strolled to the Surratt house. Many paused opposite the attractive three-story home to question neighbors, most of whom were themselves lolling about their doors or watching from windows.[37] Except for a single dim light, the residence was dark and still. Then, at 8 P.M., a carriage stopped outside the house. As the crowd looked on, Anna Surratt and a male companion stepped down. Soon after the verdict had been read to her mother that day, the daughter had visited the cell again and was devastated by the news. Along with a Catholic priest, Anna sped away to the White House to plead with Andrew Johnson. The president was unavailable and the distraught young woman returned to her home in tears.[38]

"She appeared to be perfectly crushed with grief," noted one of those in the crowd. "[Her] every look and action betrayed her anguish."[39]

Ladies standing nearby were so overcome with emotion that they, too, began sobbing. After the grief-stricken young woman was helped inside, those beyond the window could plainly see that Anna soon fainted away to the floor.[40]

Sometime during the night, the chained prisoners at the Old Arsenal were removed from the upper cells they had occupied for the past two months and placed under a death watch on the ground floor.[41] Clergymen of various denominations were allowed to enter and minister to the condemned. An Episcopal priest sat with David Herold as the young man "whined and simpered." Adding to Herold's distress were several of his sisters, who crowded the tiny cell and wept uncontrollably. Now overcome himself, the boy burst into tears.[42]

Although a Lutheran minister tried to soothe him, George Atzerodt was as inconsolable as Herold. The shaken man groaned without letup, insisting again and again that he never had any intention of killing Andrew Johnson. In the same breath, Atzerodt pleaded for more time to prepare for his end. A guard who looked into the condemned man's cell described him as "pitiable in the extreme."[43]

The two Catholic priests attending Mary Surratt were also having no impact. So shattered was the woman, so wracked with cramps and pains was she by her fate, that the prison physician administered wine and "other stimulants." Over and over Mary insisted that she had had no hand in the assassination.[44]

Lying in his cell stolid and silent, "doubly ironed, doubly guarded," Lewis Powell was hardly aware of the two Baptist preachers nearby. "Declining to participate in any religious mummery," wrote a journalist, "with the clergymen he had but little to say."[45] Although he may not have heard the words of salvation being chanted in his cell, Powell did hear all too clearly the moans and sobs of Mary Surratt echoing off the walls. With a sense of desperation, Powell asked to see the only man in the prison he considered a friend, even though in a matter of hours that man's job would be to kill him. Christian Rath:

> He talked to me about Mrs. Surratt. He wanted to know if he could not suffer punishment for her. He really seemed to feel badly. He said that he was largely to blame for her incarceration. The fact that he was captured in . . . her house led to her arrest. He said he would willingly suffer two deaths if that would save Mrs. Surratt from the noose. He denied that she was implicated in the foul plot to murder.[46]

"She knew nothing about the conspiracy at all, and is an innocent woman," insisted Powell with uncharacteristic emotion.[47]

Promising to help, Rath sent word to the War Department about Powell's obviously sincere statement.[48] Already impressed by the condemned man's courage and honesty, Christian Rath had now discovered his selfless nature as well.

In his cell above, Burton Harrison had also heard the hammering and sawing throughout the night. When the guards failed to come for his customary walk that evening, he rightly guessed the reason. The prisoner was elated when later that night his "companion," as always, began whistling in his melancholy way. But then suddenly, after only a few notes, the whistling stopped and was not resumed. It was, thought Harrison, as if it was beyond the power of the man to continue.[49]

CHAPTER THIRTY-FOUR

BEADS ON A STRING

DAWN BROKE BRIGHT AND CLEAR, but exceedingly hot, in Washington on July 7, 1865. In contrast to typical Fridays in the throes of summer, the dusty streets of the capital were already astir with activity at an early hour. At the railroad station, noisy trains continued to unload hundreds of excited passengers, as they had throughout the night. Along the Potomac, ferries from Alexandria and points below brought hundreds more. Unbeknownst to these tourists and to thousands of others flocking to the city along the highways, only a relative handful of tickets to the hangings—one hundred or so—were to be had.

As commander of the military district, Winfield Scott Hancock was determined to limit the number of individuals at the execution site to the military, members of the press, and those directly involved in the trial. None would be admitted simply because they were curious.[1] All the same, the general's hotel was "besieged" by hordes of clamorous people, many willing to pay hundreds of dollars for the coveted tickets.[2] The fact that a woman was about to die did not drive down the price in the least. Indeed, resentment in the North against the women of the South, who, by their words and deeds had encouraged and prolonged the war, was so great that many now found in Mary Surratt the perfect symbol of their hatred.

Not only was Hancock hounded by those hoping to view the executions, but anyone who in any way was connected with the government was "tortured and annoyed" as well. Such badgering mattered naught. "They might as well have come to see George Washington, the one as easy as the other," laughed a *New York Times* reporter.[3]

Frustrated, though determined, the visitors swarmed toward the Arsenal grounds in the hope that somehow they might at least gain a glimpse of death. From Pennsylvania Avenue to the prison, a distance of two miles, the surging crowds were framed by double guards of soldiers along the entire route. Once the Arsenal grounds were reached, all individuals were stopped at a checkpoint, and the fortunate few with tickets were allowed to walk the remaining distance.[4]

At the penitentiary itself, those who had already arrived were not permitted to enter the courtyard until final preparations were complete. Nevertheless, ticket-holding newspaper reporters and artists were already busily at work in the prison offices, asking questions, writing dispatches, and sketching scenes.[5] Gazing through the grated windows, the journalists got their first glimpse of the scaffold. It was a frail-looking structure and had a "very primitive appearance," thought one reporter; and yet, to any who had scaled its thirteen steps, it was quickly apparent that a good many more people than four might be hanged on its sturdy platform.[6] Two hinged drops would each accommodate two of the condemned. On the beam high above, workmen were seen adjusting the four hemp nooses and finishing last-minute details. Just several paces beyond the gallows, the startled reporters could also see four wooden boxes, and next to these, four graves already dug.[7]

Among all journalists present, indeed, among all the thousands waiting outside, was the great question of the fourth grave. Many felt, many hoped, it would never be filled. It was known that Mary Surratt's attorney, Frederick Aiken, had petitioned the civil courts to issue a writ of habeas corpus in a last-ditch effort to save the woman's life.[8] The result was as yet unknown. Inside the prison, down the dark hallway and inside an even darker cell, those around Mary Surratt were also praying for a miracle. While priests sought to comfort and console her, Mary lay groaning on a mattress in a semiconscious state. Despite a mix of alcohol and opiates, the woman had passed a sleepless night weeping and moaning. Unlike others, Mary entertained no hope of a reprieve, and thus did she tearfully advise Anna on the disposal of her property.[9] Now crazed with grief, shortly after 8 A.M. Anna stepped from the cell and ran sobbing down the hallway. With what little time she had left, the frantic girl was determined to make a last desperate bid to save her mother's life.

Although he had made several attempts at sleep, George Atzerodt's last night on earth was also spent in wakeful terror.[10] During most of the dark hours, Atzerodt prayed and wept by turns. With dawn, the condemned man found a sliver of inner strength, and for a brief time he became surprisingly composed.[11] In addition to the two clergymen in his cell, Atzerodt's brother had joined him, as had his aged mother, dressed in deep mourning.[12]

"The meeting of the condemned man and his mother was very affecting, and moved some of the officers of the prison . . . to tears," one witness revealed.[13]

Sobbing, Atzerodt begged his mother to forgive him for the shame and sorrow he had caused. Again the son insisted that he never had any intention of killing Andrew Johnson.[14] While the words of the ministers in his cell seemed to have little effect, as Atzerodt sat on his cot he would from time to time scan the Bible before him. Occasionally, when a particular noise from the gathering crowd beyond caught his attention, the condemned man would stare at the window with a "wild look." At moments such as these, when the terrible reality of his situation struck home, Atzerodt seemed riven to the core. Tossing restlessly on his cot one moment, wringing his hands in despair the next, the pathetic prisoner again and again sobbed out his innocence.[15]

After managing several hours of sleep, David Herold awoke to find that his preacher had joined him in the cell. "With the clergyman he was ever respectful," a viewer noted, "but beyond a routine repetition of words and phrases seemed to know and care little more about the coming than the present world. Impressible to a remarkable degree, but equally elastic, he talked and wept with the ministers, but was as ready for a quib or a joke immediately after as ever." The light-hearted, frivolous youth, concluded the witness, was "more like a butterfly than a man."[16] Now Herold's cell was crowded with a handful of wailing sisters dressed in black. Another sister and his mother were too prostrated with grief to visit the prison.[17]

Of all the condemned, only Lewis Powell ate his breakfast; more than that, said an observer, he ate it "heartily."[18] Like Herold, the handsome Floridian had managed three hours of sleep during the night. But unlike Herold and the rest, Powell seemed untroubled by the ordeal ahead. With no friends or relatives to comfort him, the young man spent his last hours chatting quietly with the Reverend Abram Gillette, a Baptist minister, with whom he spoke of his childhood.[19]

———

At 8:30 A.M., Anna Surratt burst through the doors of the White House. The doorkeeper stopped the sobbing young woman at the foot of the stairs and informed her that the president was unavailable. When Johnson's military secretary, R. D. Mussey, came down the steps, the girl fell to her knees. Grasping the man by his coat, Anna begged and pleaded to be allowed to see the president. Explaining that such a request was out of the question, the secretary thereupon returned to his office, leaving the hysterical girl crumpled on the steps. When strangers ventured near, the red-faced young woman begged for their help. "Crying and tearing her hair and exhibiting all the evidences of insanity," Anna screamed over and over again that her mother was innocent of the crime and was too precious to die. Many who witnessed the horrible scene themselves began to weep.[20] After she had quieted somewhat, Anna was helped to a seat in the East Room. Each time someone entered the White House, however, the grief-stricken girl sprang to her feet and ran to the door.[21]

Two of David Herold's sisters also sought an audience with the president to plead for their only brother's life. The girls were no more successful than Anna. Similar appeals to speak with Mrs. Johnson or her daughter were likewise refused.[22]

———

By 11 A.M., a huge throng had gathered at the upper gate of the Arsenal grounds. To the disappointment of all, a strong guard around the entire perimeter prevented most from entering.[23] Outside the gates, enterprising vendors set up stalls and sold iced lemonade and cakes.[24] As the crowd stood staring at those who came and went, a stir was created when Mary Walker passed by. Not only was Walker the sole female physician in the Union Army, but she was the only woman admitted to the execution. Loathed by some, laughed at by others, Dr. Walker shocked all, male and female alike, due to her penchant for wearing men's trousers. On this day, the young woman added to her scandals by riding a horse through the crowd astraddle like a man.[25]

In the maddening heat and excitement, tempers soon became explosive. As a soldier attempted to pass through the Arsenal gate to fill his canteen, he was halted by the sentry. Sharp words were exchanged between the two when a sergeant of the guards suddenly appeared. Cutting the argument short, the angry officer simply drew his sword and stabbed the thirsty soldier in the eye. With blood streaming down his face, the wounded man was quickly carried away. Learning of the incident, the victim's brother, also a soldier, raced to the scene. As the stunned crowd watched in horror, the outraged brother raised his musket and shot the sergeant dead in his tracks.[26]

In addition to those guarding the perimeter of the Arsenal grounds, an extra two thousand soldiers were spread around the prison itself, as well as along the Potomac. Placed there not just to forestall rescue attempts, the men were also on the lookout for curiosity-seekers who might rush the building. Also on duty just outside the prison was Sergeant Boston Corbett's regiment, the 16th New York Cavalry.[27] Despite the blistering heat, many soldiers inside the prison yard were in a festive mood, fully aware that not only would they be mustered out of the military soon, but they were now a part of history in the making. With each sliver of wood chipped from the "assassins derrick" and each strand of hemp pulled from the "treason chokers," there was a mad, laughing scramble among the men to pocket the tossed souvenirs. One group of soldiers discovered a large rat in the yard and quickly chased it down.

"He was immediately court-martialed," an amused lieutenant laughed, "and a miniature gallows being erected and a piece of fish line procured [the rat was] hung up [and] his carcase [*sic*] chucked into one of the pits near the coffins."[28]

By eleven o'clock, the number of people in the prison offices had grown significantly. "Reporters are scribbling industriously," wrote one suspense-filled correspondent. "A suppressed whisper is audible all over the room and the hall as the hour draws nearer, and the preparations begin to be more demonstrative."[29] Nearby, the heavy iron door leading to the cells creaked and groaned loudly time and again as priests and visitors came and went.[30] When a dry-eyed Anna Surratt appeared and silently passed through the huge door, reporters excitedly speculated that her changed demeanor might indicate that she had received a reprieve for her mother.[31]

Suddenly, a loud sound beyond the window echoed through the prison and hushed the buzzing reporters.[32] To ensure that there were no mishaps, Christian Rath had wisely decided to test the drops by placing four huge cannon balls on the scaffold. When the props were knocked out, one trap had come down with a crash as planned, but the other had stuck. Carpenters immediately went to work.[33]

One of the four soldiers assigned to push out the props from under the drops already was having misgivings. When Christian Rath had requested volunteers for an unspecified task the previous day, many had stepped forward, but only William Coxshall and three others were chosen.

"None of us waited to hear what the duty was. We were eager for anything to vary the routine," Coxshall admitted.[34] Now acutely aware that he was on the verge of performing "one of the grimmest events I ever participated in," the young soldier and his stomach were having second thoughts.[35]

Shortly after 11 A.M., the door was opened, and the ticket-holding spectators were at last allowed to enter the prison yard.[36] Although many milled about, briefly inspecting the scaffold or the graves with the four boxes stacked nearby, most visitors quickly returned indoors or sought the few patches of shade. With the temperature already approaching one hundred degrees, and with virtually no wind behind the walls, the sun struck the yard "like the blasts from a fiery furnace."[37] For those who were anchored on the Potomac and had scaled masts in hopes of viewing the executions, a slight breeze offered some relief.[38] Occasionally a whiff of wind off the water would reach the scaffold, causing the dangling ropes to "writhe as I have seen wounded snakes," thought one man.[39]

As noon approached, some of the several hundred soldiers who would form a guard within the courtyard began arriving. And from a window on an adjacent building, Alexander Gardner began adjusting his clumsy apparatus to gain the best photographs possible of the grim ceremony.[40]

Inside the prison offices, "the bustle increases," wrote a correspondent for the *Philadelphia Inquirer*:

> Officers are running to and fro calling for orderlies and giving orders. General Hartranft is trying to answer twenty questions at once from as many different persons. The sentry in the hall is becoming angry because the crowd will keep intruding on his beat, when suddenly a buggy at the door announces the arrival of General Hancock. He enters the room hurriedly, takes General Hartranft aside, and a few words pass between them in a low tone, to which Hartranft nods acquiescence; then, in a louder voice, Hancock says, "Get ready, General; I want to have everything put in readiness as soon as possible." This was the signal for the interviews of the clergymen, relatives and friends of the prisoners to cease, and for the doomed to prepare for execution. . . .
>
> Mr. Aiken approaches Gen. Hancock and a few minutes' conversation passes between them. Aiken's countenance changes perceptibly at Gen. Hancock's words. The reason is plain; there is no hope for Mrs. Surratt. The habeas corpus movement, from which he expected so much, has failed, and Aiken, in a voice tremulous with emotion, said to your correspondent, "Mrs. Surratt will be hung." The bright hopes he had cherished had all vanished, and the dreadful truth stood before him in all its horror.[41]

Outside, the last loud test of the trap doors had proven successful. "The rattle echoes around the walls, it reaches the prisoners' cells close by, and penetrates their inmost recesses," continued the Philadelphia reporter.[42]

The horrible sounds did nothing to calm the nerves of the wretched living dead. When the guards came at 12:30 and ordered all visitors to leave, everyone knew that the end was at hand. Rocking back and forth on his mattress, George Atzerodt again begged his mother, and a sister who had now joined them, to forgive him for bringing such shame on the family. His life, admittedly, had never amounted to much, but now he wanted desperately to say something important and meaningful as he stood on the scaffold.[43]

David Herold's sisters, weeping uncontrollably, also said their final goodbyes.[44]

Bidding his client farewell, Lewis Powell's attorney asked if he could pass on any last message. "None," replied Powell, "except I want you to give my love to my parents, and tell them that I die in peace with God and man. I do not want to live, even if the President will spare my life; I do not want it." The condemned man then stared at his attorney. "My only regret," he said softly, "is that in leaving the world now, I will not be able to reward or show my gratitude to you for your services in my behalf."[45]

Turning to Rev. Gillette, Powell again expressed his deepest regret that his actions had harmed Mary Surratt. "She does not deserve to die with us," he said sadly.[46]

With her last shred of strength, Mary Surratt managed one final time to put on a bold, brave front for her daughter. When the moment came to say their goodbyes, however, Anna fell once more into "hysterics of grief." As the shattered young woman was led from the cell, her screams could be heard throughout the prison and beyond.[47]

By one o'clock, most of the reporters and spectators had filed through the door and moved into the fiery yard. In the windows surrounding the enclosure as well as on top of a nearby building, the onlookers were densely packed.[48] Several hundred soldiers had also taken their places and formed ranks around the scaffold. The wall of bayonets was so thick, thought one of those troops, that nothing but the president's pardon could have slipped through.[49] As with this soldier, speculation on a stay for Mary Surratt increased among all. Because less than an hour remained before the two o'clock deadline, some now felt certain that the woman would not hang, and many heads turned to the rear, as if expecting a courier to arrive at any moment announcing as much. Others wondered aloud if not only Mary but also one or more of the others had received a reprieve.[50]

All speculation abruptly ceased shortly after 1 P.M., when General Hartranft appeared in the yard. Behind him, trudging along in a row, came the condemned, including Mary Surratt. When the prisoners' weakened eyes finally adjusted to the searing light, the first sight that greeted them was the great killing machine looming just ahead; the next vision to meet their gaze was the coffins and graves ready to receive them.

Although she was dressed in black and lightly veiled, those nearest Mary Surratt could see that her lips were moving rapidly, as if in prayer. Already hampered by her shackles, the terrified woman had to be almost lifted along by her guards.[51] George Atzerodt shuffled behind wearing a "glaring, haggard look." His eyes, one soldier thought, seemed to be desperately searching the crowd for someone who might save him.[52] Following Atzerodt, appearing "filthy" and unkempt, came young David Herold, his face darting nervously to every feature of the scaffold. A soldier nearby noticed that Herold trembled and shook and seemed on the verge of fainting.[53] Calm and collected as usual, Lewis Powell brought up the rear, showing no sign whatsoever of nervousness or fear.[54]

Slowly, solemnly, the condemned scaled the stairs to the platform, their chains clanking with every step. Once on the scaffold, the four were led to chairs and seated. Flanked by Catholic priests, Mary Surratt rested for a moment; but when her eyes fastened on the dangling noose just above, she again began to mumble a prayer.[55] "She sunk in a collapsed condition in her seat," noted a reporter, "leaning feebly upon her right arm."[56] Someone thoughtfully held an umbrella above Mary to shield her from the blazing sun. Sharing the drop with the woman was Lewis Powell, who sat bolt upright, gazing curiously at the crowd below.

Stepping quickly to the front of the scaffold, General Hartranft read the order of execution in a clear voice heard throughout the yard. While he did so, a priest held a small crucifix before Mary's face, which she kissed fervently again and again.[57]

"[At] times," wrote another newsman watching David Herold, "he trembled violently." At other times, "he looked wildly around and his face had a haggard, anxious, inquiring expression."[58]

When Hartranft had finished, Abram Gillette knelt beside Lewis Powell and prayed aloud:

> Almighty God, our Heavenly Father, we pray thee to permit us to commit this soul into thy hands, not for any claim we have to make for it in ourselves, but depending as we do upon the merits of our Lord Jesus Christ, grant, O Heavenly Father . . .[59]

Looking around for a moment during the long prayer, as if trying to awaken from a bad dream, Mary Surratt then closed her eyes again and softly laid her head upon an arm when the horrible reality did not disappear. Mercifully, umbrellas appeared, and each of the condemned was soon shielded from the sun. As Gillette finished, for the first and last time throughout his long captivity, Powell's eyes briefly filled with tears. Next, as the minister prayed for his soul, the lips of David Herold could be seen silently repeating the words.[60]

Below the gallows, steadying the prop that held one of the trap doors in place, William Coxshall was becoming physically ill. The heat, the delays, the ghastly spectacle above, all were proving too much. The prayers "seemed to me interminably [long]," remembered the soldier. "The strain was getting worse. I became nauseated . . . and taking hold of the supporting post, I hung on and vomitted."[61]

At length, it was the Lutheran minister's turn:

> And now, George A. Atzeroth [sic], may God have mercy upon you. The ways of the transgressor is hard. The wages of sin is death; but if we freely confess our sins, God will in mercy pardon them. Christ came into the world to save sinners—even the chief of sinners. Believe in the Lord Jesus Christ, and thou shalt be saved. The blood of the blessed Redeemer, Jesus Christ, cleanseth from all sin. You profess to have. . . .[62]

While the prayer was in progress, Dr. George Porter watched the condemned closely:

> Mrs. Surratt was very feeble and leaned her head upon alternate sides of her armchair in nervous spasms. Her general expression was that of acute suffering, vanishing at times as if by the conjuration of her pride, and again returning in a paroxysm, as she looked at the dangling rope before her. [Powell], the strongest criminal of our history, was alone dignified and self-possessed. . . . He looked at death as for one long expected; not a tremor of a shock stirred his long stately limbs. . . . Herold, although whimpering, showed more grit than was anticipated. . . . Atzerodt . . . was the picture of despair.[63]

With the prayers finally finished, the three men were helped up and led onto the drops. While Mary was allowed to remain seated momentarily, the executioners quickly began binding the arms and legs of the condemned, including the woman, with white cloth.

"It hurts," cried Mary when the cinch was pulled too tightly.

"Well," came the sympathetic reply, "it won't hurt long."[64]

A reporter for the New York *World* shuddered when he saw Mary bound, realizing only now that, despite earlier optimism, there would be no last-second reprieve. The federal government was actually about to murder a woman.[65] A moment later, when she was lifted to her unsteady legs, another observer was sickened by the sight of two men delicately removing Mary's bonnet and veil, then ever so gently adjusting the noose around her throat.[66]

As the rope was placed around his own neck, a trembling George Atzerodt knew he must say something soon, or it would never be said. Wrote a reporter for the Washington *Evening Star*:

> Atzerodt, who seemed to grow excited as his last moments approached, just before the white cap was placed over his head, attempted in a gasping manner to address the spectators. His parched lips would not obey the helm, and it was distressing to see him convulsively endeavoring to make himself intelligible. At last he managed to get out the words: "Gentlemen, take ware," meaning evidently, "take warning." The white cap was drawn over his head, as was done with the others.[67]

Because of her unsteady legs, Mary was helped forward on the drop. "Please don't let me fall," came the stifled plea from beneath her hood.[68]

A few seconds later, at 1:25 P.M., Christian Rath silently motioned to General Hartranft that all was ready.[69] In turn, William Coxshall and his three comrades below moved back and grabbed their long poles. At the signal, they would push out the props.[70]

In the breathless silence of the yard, Mary Surratt's low, frightened voice could be heard reciting Latin prayers. Of the four, none was visibly shaking save George Atzerodt, whose legs began to buckle.[71]

"Good-by, gentlemen, who are before me now," came the pathetic muffled voice behind Atzerodt's hood, "may we all meet in the other world. God help me now. Oh! Oh! Oh!"[72]

The sounds of General Hartranft clapping his hands, once, twice, caused Atzerodt to try and step back from the drop. Mary Surratt was just in the process of stepping onto it. At Hartranft's third clap, William Coxshall and the others, "with all our might," pushed their poles and shoved out the props. Instantly, the trap doors fell with a heavy slam. The three men came down with a sickening thud, then rebounded upward "like a ball attached to a rubber." Because of her angle, Mary merely slid down the trap and was therefore sent swinging "like a pendulum."[73]

Although she briefly tried to free her left arm to reach the tight noose, Mary's struggle was short.[74] Likewise, except for leg spasms and a powerful heaving of the stomach, George Atzerodt's suffering was also mercifully brief. Not so with Lewis Powell and David Herold. With tremendous strength, Powell's massive body quaked violently; then, in a terrific effort to break the binding, his legs doubled up several times almost to a sitting position. Those close by noticed that Powell's hands and neck quickly turned purple.[75]

Surprisingly, the youngest and smallest put up the greatest struggle of all. As David Herold fought desperately to reach the rope that was slowly strangling him to death, his tortured body began discharging urine.[76]

Among the stunned spectators, there was only "breathless silence" for several minutes as the two victims waged a mighty struggle between life and death.[77]

"It was an awful sight," one of those in the crowd said later.[78]

At length, except for brief spasms of the legs and hands, the bodies of Powell and Herold, like those of Surratt and Atzerodt, were still. For almost half an hour the corpses were allowed to dangle and twist in the blistering sun, while shaken spectators silently moved to the shade or left the yard entirely. Finally, several soldiers were ordered up to cut down the bodies. In his haste, one corporal slashed the rope suspending George Atzerodt before those below were ready to catch him. The body dropped to the ground with a ghastly thump, causing a "swift and sharp shudder" among onlookers. The careless soldier was ordered down and reprimanded.[79] When Mary Surratt was gently lowered and her limp head fell to her breast, another soldier jokingly commented that "she makes a nice bow." An outraged officer nearby was not amused and hotly rebuked the callous individual.[80]

While physicians began their medical examinations, those seeking souvenirs of the event were busily at work. Already the gallows itself was being hacked and carved for mementos. Those irreverent soldiers who had cut the bodies down now whacked off as much of the ropes as they could reach and began laughingly tossing pieces to friends below.[81]

"The scramble for the twine far exceeded that for the blocks and scraps of wood," wrote an officer. "The men scuffling good humoredly for a 'rope-relic' rolled into one of the freshly dug graves, and before they could extricate themselves half a dozen shovel fulls of earth had been thrown upon them by laughing comrades."[82]

The noose that had strangled Mary Surratt was removed from her neck and presented to an officer with pieces of flesh still clinging to the fiber. During an unguarded moment, when the officer laid his trophy down, it was promptly stolen by another soldier.[83]

"After we were relieved from guard," recalled a friend of the thief, "he divided it up among us. Then some of the boys went down town and bought some rope like it, cut it into pieces two inches long, and labeled them for each of those executed and sold them for 50 cents each."[84]

After the medical examination—not one neck had been broken—the bodies were placed in the coffins along with bottles containing their names.[85]

As the dirt was being shoveled onto the boxes, many naturally saw this act as the final page in a seemingly endless tragedy that had begun so far back that it seemed from another age. And yet, even as the coffins were disappearing beneath the dust, a divisive debate spread across the United States that would continue for years. Raged the editor of the Washington *Daily Times*:

> Of the many dark deeds which disgrace the pages of history, the infliction of the extreme penalty of the law upon females is the most debasing. No gentleman of refinement . . ., no man who is mindful of the fact that to woman he is indebted for his existence—no man in whose breast the true fire of manhood burns—no matter what his position in life may be, could be guilty of affixing his name to an order for the execution of a woman upon the gallows. . . .
>
> But much as we, in common with all true men, deprecate the hanging of females, there was nevertheless, a woman hung in this city. . . . The capital of this fair nation has thus been disgraced. . . . [I]n conclusion, we will say, that for the men we had no sympathy. It is for the woman that we speak; her sex pleaded for mercy in her behalf. . . . Has manhood departed from the earth?[86]

Some blamed the grim officers who composed the military tribunal. "That nine men of ordinary respectable character in the Federal army, colonels, brigadiers, and major-generals," wrote one critic, "should have been so lost to all sense of duty and humanity, so ineffably brutal, as to sentence a woman to death for nothing, is a very strong proposition."[87]

As many more, though, including the editor of the Washington *Evening Star*, felt that justice had been served.

> The last act of the tragedy of the 19th century is ended, and the curtain dropped forever upon the lives of four of its actors. Payne [*sic*], Herold, Atzerodt and Mrs. Surratt, have paid the penalty of their awful crime. . . . In the bright sunlight of this summer day . . . the wretched criminals have been hurried into eternity; and tonight, will be hidden in despised graves, loaded with execrations of mankind.[88]

Some editors, such as those at the Philadelphia *Ledger*, the *Newark Advertiser*, and the Alton *Illinois Telegraph*, were especially elated that the "she-rebel," Mary Surratt, had paid for her crimes.[89] It was Southern females, they argued, who had encouraged the war and helped prolong it in the first place, and it now seemed fitting that one, at least, should pay, not only for these sins, but for the most atrocious crime of the war. For these angry people, Mary Surratt was a "burnt offering" — the most visible symbol of all Southern womanhood.

"I cannot see, for my life, why a woman who commits the same crime as a man, is not as guilty," reasoned a Massachusetts teenager in his journal. "Mrs. Surratt was the great cause of Mr. Lincoln's murder, and Mrs. Seward's death."[90]

For the above reasons and more, that evening following the executions, huge crowds of morbid curiosity-seekers surrounded the Surratt house, drawn not only by the hope of seeing Mary's body brought back, but also by the hysterical shrieks of Anna within. The surging mass became so great that a detail of policemen were dispatched to prevent the more brazen from entering the home. Already, before police arrived, relic-hunters had chopped pieces from the porch for souvenirs.[91]

Also that evening, Burton Harrison was taken out of his cell at the prison for his customary walk around the courtyard. As he stepped through the door, Harrison was horrified to see, near the path he had worn down over the weeks, a scaffold rising from the ground. And just beyond that, also in his path, he saw the horrible mounds—"like beads upon a string," he thought to himself over and over, "like beads upon a string."[92]

As with Harrison, the four conspirators who had escaped with their lives—Samuel Arnold, Dr. Mudd, Michael O'Laughlen, and Edman Spangler—were unaware in their isolation who had died that day and who, other than they, had lived. And for others in the prison, for those like Burton Harrison who were ignorant of their own fate, all aged "ten years in a day," fully expecting that their turn on the drop would come with each minute that passed. That night, as Harrison lay in his cell, he listened carefully for the sound he was sure would never come again—the faint, melancholy whistle that had been his only salvation as he struggled with his sanity in solitary confinement. Throughout the night he prayed for the sound. And then, echoing ever so weakly up the ventilation shaft, he heard it—a "faint, tremulous, dejected whistle." For Burton Harrison, the sound seemed the greatest of miracles. In a moment, the whistle was drowned out by his own loud and delirious laughter.[93]

THE HAUNTED STAGE

"THE CURTAIN HAS FALLEN upon the most solemn tragedy of the nineteenth century," wrote the relieved editor of the Washington *National Intelligencer*. "God grant that our country may never again witness such another one."[1]

As the words above attest, after four years of terrible war, which had ended on the most tragic note imaginable, Americans desperately longed to put the past behind them and get on with a normal life of peace and prosperity. And yet, for millions of ordinary people, particularly in the South, it would be decades before the impact of the Lincoln assassination began to release its terrible hold on their lives. And for those directly involved in the events of April–July 1865, the curtain had certainly not rung down for them. Indeed, in many ways their ordeal had just begun.

July 8, 1865

Secretary,

I make my <u>last</u> appeal to the authorities, that is, that they will allow me to receive the remains of my mother. She lived a Christian life, died a Christian death, and NOW don't refuse her a Christian burial. If it be in your power I know you will allow me her body <u>immediately</u>.

Yours Respectfully,

Anna Surratt

This favor at your hands will be rewarded.[2]

Edwin Stanton did indeed have the power. But to the tearful appeal, the secretary of war turned a deaf ear. Believing to his core that all the conspirators, including the distraught young woman's mother, deserved death, Stanton had no intention of giving up the bodies, including Booth's, out of fear that not only the curious public but rebel sympathizers would wear out a path to their graves and transform simple stones into shrines and cowardly assassins into martyrs.[3] Already, the Surratt house was becoming one of the top tourist attractions in America, as was the scene of the opening act of the tragedy, Ford's Theater. Unlike the former site, however, the latter was still under the iron grip of the U.S. military, and neither Stanton nor President Johnson had any intention of relinquishing it.

After his release from prison, the financially strapped proprietor, John Ford, tried to reopen his theater on July 10 with a sold-out performance of *The Octoroon*. Before showtime that evening, a file of soldiers appeared and promptly shut the owner down again.[4] Outraged by the act, furious that each day his theater sat vacant he was driven deeper into debt, Ford went to see the secretary of war. Curtly informing the theater owner that there would never be another performance on the fateful stage, Stanton showed Ford the door.[5]

"Nothing could be more despotic," fumed Ford's friend Orville Browning, "and yet in this free Country Mr Ford is utterly helpless, and without the means of redress[.]"[6]

With no other option left, John Ford placed his property on the block. Although many were interested, including Henry Ward Beecher, who had hoped to turn the theater into a church, all found the asking price, one hundred thousand dollars, too steep.[7]

Even without the high-handed government decree, there is every indication that Stanton was merely expressing the sentiment of a majority of Americans. The thought of reopening the theater where Lincoln was shot, announced the *New York Times*, was "an outrage upon propriety."[8] Christian zealots, already convinced that the stage was an abomination where the only fare was "profanity and pollution," were righteously indignant at Ford's attempt to reopen. To allow him to do so, said one preacher, "could only be agreeable to the enemies of the cause in which Mr. Lincoln fell."[9] There were more menacing threats as well.

"Take even fifty thousand for it, and build another . . . but do not attempt to open it again," wrote an individual to Ford who signed his threat "one of the many determined to prevent it."[10]

Wisely, John Ford did not press the issue, and when the federal government offered him fifteen hundred dollars a month to keep the building closed, the defeated theater owner at last acquiesced.[11]

The situation was reversed at the home of William Petersen. With the doors at Ford's closed, hordes of frustrated tourists simply strolled across the street, where the door was more than open. At fifty cents per person, Petersen was growing rich showing an avid public the sofa where Mary Lincoln had shrieked the night away and the bed where her husband had died. Not satisfied with this bonanza, the wily homeowner continued to press the government for remuneration for the destruction he had suffered on the night of April 14–15. Five hundred and fifty dollars was the figure Petersen advanced for all the bloody pillows and torn sheets, as well as the mud-stained rugs. Many felt such a claim bordered on sacrilege.[12]

"This latest demand is rather cool," grumbled one incensed journalist.[13]

Like Petersen, many others who thought they saw a chance to get rich quick pressed claims against the government. Although fewer than sixty individuals were directly involved in the actual apprehension of the nine main conspirators, when authorities later announced that they were ready to distribute the one hundred thousand dollars in reward money, fully five thousand persons eagerly joined the Washington gold rush.[14] The most famous of the reward claimants did eventually get his share, though it first had to be split thirty-four ways.[15]

When Boston Corbett finally received his cut of the reward, it was a mere $1,653.95. Long before that though, the destitute former soldier would have gladly swapped the money — most of which was soon stolen anyway — simply to still the demons within.[16] Already haunted by visions and voices, after Corbett left the military he was ruthlessly hounded by them.

HELL, September 1, 1874

Boston Corbett: Nemesis is on your path.

J. WILKES BOOTH[17]

Hate letters from ill-wishers like that above, which many famous people received, were pondered, then processed through Corbett's disturbed brain until they were transformed into dozens of stealthy assassins relentlessly dogging his trail. Fearing the wrath of "Booth's Avengers," the "Secret Order," and a host of other bloodthirsty organizations, Corbett remained ever vigilant and kept his pistol handy at all times. He was more likely now than ever to pull his weapon on suspicious strangers — which included virtually everyone — and fewer and fewer friends were willing to risk death by facing the fanatic's dangerous paranoia.[18]

After scratching out the most meager existence as a hatter and part-time preacher, the former army sergeant left the East for good in 1878 to stake a claim in the West. From a "little forlorn-looking house" in New Jersey, Corbett moved into a veritable hole in the ground in Kansas. Unfortunately for the novice homesteader, the letters in the mail and the voices in his head that had plagued him earlier not only followed him to Kansas, but they greatly increased.[19] As a result, Corbett began wearing two revolvers.

Almost immediately, the strange little man with the "wild look" caused trouble with his new neighbors. Whether it was warning trespassers from his land with a shotgun blast or whether it was waving his pistols at frightened youngsters who were innocently playing baseball on the Sabbath, the former soldier well earned his reputation as a dangerous, crazy hermit.[20] The few times Kansans coaxed Corbett from his muddy home to present lectures on Booth and Andersonville, the zealot spent the entire evening exhorting the crowds to repent of sin, uttering not a word of his famous exploits.[21]

Finally, in a well-intentioned, albeit misguided, attempt to parade one of the state's most celebrated heroes, a local politician managed to appoint the recluse to the position of Third Assistant Doorkeeper in the Kansas Legislature at Topeka. The plan went well for nearly a month. On February 15, 1887, however, the voices in Corbett's head became louder than usual. Pulling his pistol and a knife, the little man ran wildly through the capitol building, sending legislators, clerks, and janitors flying for cover.[22] When the culprit was finally overpowered, he was hauled into court the following day. County prosecutor Charles Curtis, a Kaw Indian and a future vice president of the United States, needed only one look to satisfy himself that the defendant was utterly mad. That very day, at age fifty-five, Corbett was judged insane and led away several blocks to the state lunatic asylum.[23]

For the next year, Corbett slipped in and out of delirium. The howls and screams of the other patients certainly did little to alleviate his paranoia or his reoccurring vision of assassins stalking the hallways.[24] On May 26, 1888, while he and other inmates were enjoying their daily exercise, Corbett spotted an unattached horse. Before attendants realized what had happened, the former cavalryman had leaped on the animal and in a cloud of dust was last seen galloping south.[25]

And thus, except for several reported sightings over the ensuing years, this was the last entry of Boston Corbett in the book of records. The famous slayer of Abraham Lincoln's assassin had come onto the world stage anonymous, and anonymous he would leave it.

Much like Corbett, others associated with the assassination were haunted by voices and visions until the day they died. The Booths, of course, were shattered beyond repair, and never would they reclaim their stature as the First Family of American acting. After his release from prison, Junius Brutus, Jr., did return to the stage, and despite his vow, Edwin was also coaxed back to acting. Unfortunately, the specter of their brother stalked every stage the two men strode, and audiences could never forget even for an instant that the actors were brothers of the infamous assassin. In 1869, Edwin opened the glittering Booth Theater in New York, reputedly the finest opera house in the nation.[26] Despite the appearance of some of the greatest names of the American stage, the venture failed.[27]

For years, Edwin and his siblings refused to even mention the name of their dead brother, much less talk of him. "The sorrow of his death is very bitter but the disgrace is far heavier," Asia Booth wrote. "[T]o us it will always be a crime."[28]

Nevertheless, when federal authorities finally surrendered their brother's body, as they did Mary Surratt's and the others, the Booths gratefully removed the remains to their private plot in Baltimore.[29] Despite the family's desire for a quiet affair, hordes of onlookers appeared, and though some had brought flowers to strew upon the grave, others brought scissors to snip off hair from the corpse when no one was looking.[30]

Although family, friends, and the federal government were satisfied that John Wilkes Booth had died in Virginia in 1865 and was buried in Baltimore four years later, others were doubtful. Unwilling to accept the notion that the same man whose single act had brought a mighty nation to the brink of ruin could simply die as did other mortals, many felt that such an incredible individual must have surely escaped and that the reputed body was a mere decoy. One "accurate" report placed Booth in the West Indies. Another breathless individual insisted that the assassin had escaped to Mexico. Others were equally positive that the murderer had fled to Texas or lived out a rich, full life in Indian Territory. Hand in hand with these apocryphal reports, various mummies toured the country, and for only a nickel the gullible and dim could gaze upon the remains of the "greatest arch-fiend" in American history.

And for most Americans, Booth remained just that—a fascinating villain, both evil and mad. For the vast majority of Northerners, it was an easy and simple step to transform a handsome, generous, kind man, a genius who many believed would have become the greatest actor of the age had he lived, into a diabolical monster who not only murdered

Father Abraham, the savior of the nation, but also robbed the victors of their supreme triumph.[31] And for many in the South, it was almost as easy to despise and curse the man who had so rashly brought down the wrath of those same victors upon themselves, adding years of untold suffering and misery to their homeland.

Eventually, as time passed, a few, and then a few more, would come to view John Booth in simpler, softer terms. Instead of a crazed, hate-filled maniac, Booth was increasingly seen as simply a passionate man whose love of liberty and the South, along with a quest for eternal fame, drove him to do desperate deeds; a pure, if miscalculating, patriot who believed so strongly in his cause that he was willing to give up every-thing—his fame, his fortune, his future, even his life—that others might be free. For those who carefully, cautiously, and impartially study his actions, the worst that might be said of John Wilkes Booth is that he was ruled by a fiery passion so intense that it caused him to tragically and fatally misjudge his life and times.

To the day he died, Edwin Booth never again set foot in Washington, D.C.[32] Strangely, the morning Edwin was buried in New York in 1893, the interior of Ford's Theater collapsed without warning, killing twenty-two government employees and injuring dozens more.[33]

Two more people who were haunted to their graves by that fateful night at Ford's were Henry Rathbone and Clara Harris. Prior to the night of April 14, 1865, the couple had had their future before them, wrote former Lincoln secretary John Hay, "with all the promise of felicity that youth, social position, and wealth could give them."[34] After that night. . . .

As planned, the two were eventually married in 1867, and for the next several years the couple led an outwardly normal life. That their souls had been altered irrevocably by the fatal night soon became abundantly clear to those who knew them, however. It was, said a friend, as if "there was a cloud always hanging over the spirit of Rathbone."[35] Haunted daily, even hourly, by the ear-splitting screams and shrieks and the vi-sion of herself drenched in blood, there was no escape for Clara. And Rathbone, a military man and officer, never forgave himself for failing to protect the president.[36]

In addition to depression, chronic indigestion, and severe headaches, Major Rathbone began suffering from bouts of paranoia. And although he was considered by many to be a model husband and father, by 1882 Rathbone had become pathologically obsessed over his wife's affection, convinced that she was unfaithful. So great grew the husband's irratio-nal jealousy that he became physically violent when any man, including relatives, approached the woman. He even went so far as to forbid Clara the simple pleasure of sitting at their apartment window. When her husband's action became even more menacing, Clara considered divorce. Because of the three children, she decided to wait.[37]

On Christmas morning 1883, while the family was living temporarily in Germany, Henry Rathbone completely snapped. After a bitter argument over the children, the demented man reached for a gun and shot his wife twice. To make absolutely certain, Rathbone then plunged a knife into her heart. Turning the blade on himself, the murderer attempted suicide but was unsuccessful.[38]

Although German courts initially placed Rathbone on trial for homicide, he was soon committed to an asylum for the criminally insane. There he lived out his last wretched days as a "raving maniac."[39]

Already considered by many to be unbalanced before April 14, Mary Lincoln dropped over the edge after her husband's death. Time, if a balm to some, only intensified the former first lady's grief and despair. "I am realizing, day by day, hour by hour, how insupportable life is, without, the presence of the One, who loved me & my sons so dearly," the woman wrote Elizabeth Blair Lee from her new home in Chicago. "[H]ow can, I live, without my Husband, any longer? This is my first awakening thought, each morning & as I watch the waves of the turbulent lake, under our windows, I sometimes feel I should like to go under them."[40]

Exacerbating her dementia was Mary's penury. Just days after the assassination, numerous American cities from St. Louis to Boston launched ambitious subscription campaigns to ease the widow's financial load. Well-intentioned as the efforts were, little or nothing came of them. Few individuals, including former "friends" and flatterers, were willing to extend charity to someone who herself had exhibited so little of it. Mary's well-known extravagance and pathological shopping sprees also did little to engender sympathy or loosen purse strings. Additionally, dark rumors hinted that she had looted the White House before she left, taking with her two full boxcars loaded with china, furniture, paintings, statuary, silverware, and other public property. Given her past performance, the charge seemed to many not only credible, but likely.[41] Although the federal government extended the remainder of her husband's salary and later provided an annual stipend, in no way did it support the widow on the level of her former lavish lifestyle. And thus, Mary Lincoln's lifelong dread of want and loneliness were now her daily realities.[42]

"What a dreary place, Lizzie!" cried Mary to her servant while she lay sobbing on the bed of her small, three-room apartment. "[A]nd to think that I should be compelled to live here."[43]

Outraged that all the eulogies, acclaim, and honors bestowed on the slain president did not translate into her own largesse, furious that Julia Grant and other wives of famous generals were being liberally rewarded by a grateful public, the widow launched into a raucous campaign designed to highlight her poverty by elevating her late husband.

> Notwithstanding my great & good husband's life, was sacrificed for his country, we are left to struggle, in a manner entirely new to us—and a noble people would pronounce our manner of life, underdeserved. Roving Generals have elegant mansions showered upon them, and the American people—leave the family of the Martyred President, to struggle as best they may! Strange justice this.[44]

Seldom referring to her husband except as the "sainted," "immortal," "martyred," "worshiped" "savior" whose image approached, and even surpassed, that of Christ, the widow flew into a rage when the slain president was not the great and all-absorbing focus of everyone's life, as he was hers.[45] Unfortunately for Mary, few now heard her words and opinions, and fewer still cared. For those who had witnessed her ridiculous, imperious pretension, for those who had stood self-conscious and embarrassed during her shrill tirades and violent temper tantrums, for those who had silently submitted to her legendary tongue-lashings, for all those who despised the woman utterly and now no longer lived in fear of her wrath, Mary's enforced exile into oblivion was welcome and long overdue.

"If I had committed murder in every city in this blessed Union,"wrote the miserable woman, "I could not be more traduced."[46]

As her anger and insanity increased over the years, Robert Lincoln finally drew up the papers, and, on May 19, 1875, he had his mother committed to a mental institution.

Mary Lincoln's self-serving attempt to vault her dead husband to immortality was unnecessary; the American pubic had already done as much, not because of Mary, but in spite of her.

"His death has made him immortal," said one admirer.[47]

"[W]hile he possessed all virtues he was free from all vices," announced a clergyman.[48]

Added an admiring poet:

A martyr to the cause of man,
His blood is freedom's eucharist,
And in the World's great hero-list
His name shall lead the van.[49]

A few sober-minded individuals were aghast at the deification of Lincoln, not because they hated him but because they preferred the plain, simple, more accurate man, with all his strengths and weaknesses—a man who achieved greatness through will and ability alone, not through divine intercession or the mysterious movement of planets. While conceding that Lincoln was a good, even great, man who would easily outstrip his contemporaries, editor Horace Greeley, for one, refused "to join in the race of heaping extravagant and preposterous laudations on our dead president as the wisest and greatest man who ever lived."[50]

The "race" to exalt that Greeley spoke of was far too advanced for any objective analysis to slow it, however. In the stampede to elevate the slain president, his virtues were magnified and his vices diminished until the one became a caricature and the other all but forgotten.

His heart was so tender that he would dismount from his horse in a forest to replace in their nest young birds which had fallen by the roadside; he could not sleep at night if he knew that a soldier-boy was under sentence of death. . . . Children instinctively loved him . . . his sympathies were quick and seemingly unlimited. He was absolutely without prejudice of class or condition. . . . [H]e was as just and generous to the rich and well born as to the poor and humble. . . . He was tolerant even of evil.[51]

This need to praise Lincoln and raise him to sainthood was understandable. Unable or unwilling to laud him in life, many were determined to do so with his death. In no one person is this sentiment better expressed than in her who most deeply felt his loss.

"If . . . I had been permitted to watch over and minister, to my idolized husband," lamented Mary Lincoln, "I could have thanked him for his lifelong . . . devotion to me & mine, and I could have asked forgiveness, for any inadvertent moment of pain, I may have caused him. . . . [Then] perhaps, _time_, could partially assuage my grief."[52]

Ridiculed and reviled during adversity by a fickle public, shamed and insulted by an ungrateful wife during his marriage, Lincoln would now be transformed into something larger than life by an unworthy people and an unworthy wife.

For millions of Americans, the assassination of Abraham Lincoln was the pivotal point in their life. No one ever forgot where they were or what they were doing when they heard the startling news. Coming as it did when Northerners were at the pinnacle of joy over victory, the plunge to the depths of despair was simply too swift and too great for the mind to comprehend.

"The sorrow and sadness caused . . . cannot be written; no pen can tell it," recalled one woman "[O]nly those who lived in those dreadful days can appreciate the pain we suffered."

In such a stunned state, it was the subtle and mundane that stood out most in the minds of many, like flashes of clarity in a night of black gloom—a sudden gust of wind on a curtain that toppled a candle; the merry notes of a mockingbird celebrating spring and life when all the world seemed sad and sobbing; or, when all appeared to be death and decay, the sweet smell of lilacs wafting on a breeze through the open window.

"I never smell lilacs without thinking of that day," wrote one resident of Springfield long after the war.[53] For millions more, including the old poet Walt Whitman, that beautiful, fragrant bloom became an eternal symbol of both the happiest and the saddest of times.[54]

> When lilacs last in the dooryard bloom'd
> I mourn'd, and yet shall mourn with ever-
>   returning spring.[55]

ACKNOWLEDGMENTS

MANY GREAT FOLKS HAD A HAND IN THIS BOOK, some of whom went far beyond their job descriptions to help me. A special thank you goes out to Dr. John Sellers at the Library of Congress, not only for making available the heretofore unpublished Horatio Nelson Taft diary but also for his friendship and critical comments upon reading the manuscript; Suzanne Kelly and the late Mike Maione at Ford's Theater, for allowing us to spend days sifting through their extensive archive; Thomas Swartz and Cheryl Schnirring, Illinois State Historic Society, Springfield; Dr. John and Ruth Ann Coski, Museum of the Confederacy, Richmond; Dennis Northcott, Missouri Historical Society, St. Louis; Gail Redmann, Washington, D.C., Historical Society; Wendy Nardi, Trentoniana Collection, Trenton (N.J.) Public Library; Randy Hackenburg, Carlisle Barracks, Pennsylvania; Nelson Lankford, Virginia Historical Society, Richmond; Fred Bauman and his superb staff in Manuscripts at the Library of Congress; Wilma Gibbs, Susan Sutton, and Michael Stauffer at the Indiana Historical Society, Indianapolis; Nancy Sherbert and Nona Williams at the Kansas State Historical Society, Topeka; Paul Plamann, Fort McHenry National Historic Site, Baltimore; Cindy Van Horn, The Lincoln Museum, Fort Wayne, Indiana; Mark Harvey, State Archives of Michigan, Lansing; and to the staffs at the West Virginia State Historical Society, Charleston; Western Historical Collection, Columbia, Missouri; Pennsylvania Historical Society, Philadelphia; Washburn University Library, Topeka, Kansas; Delaware State Archives, Dover; Washington, D.C., Public Library; Kentucky Historical Society, Frankfort; the National Archives, Washington, D.C.; and to four selfless individuals: Roger Norton, William C. Davis, Edward Steers, Jr., and Judge Bryce Benedict, each of whom gave openly and freely of his time and incredible expertise.

My greatest thanks, however, goes not to a person but to an entity. By protecting and preserving Ford's Theater and the adjacent Petersen House, the National Park Service has guaranteed that these great American shrines will be available to future generations who can come and experience and perhaps walk away with emotions similar to those felt by Deb and me on that sunny day we first visited the theater. Although Ford's, then and now, can seat a respectable fifteen hundred people, we both were stunned by how small and wonderfully intimate the theater seems. Everyone could see clearly the face of everyone else in the theater, and the stage appeared almost as if it was in your lap. Much the same might be said of the tiny room at the Petersen House where Lincoln breathed his last. Simply put, never could we have understood just how painfully personal and intimate events in these buildings were on that fateful night without being in the actual structures themselves. For the vision and will to preserve these historic treasures, my thanks again go out to the men and women of the U.S. National Park Service for a job well done.

NOTES

Prologue

1. *Newark* (N.J.) *Daily Advertiser*, March 7, 1865.
2. *New York Herald*, March 6, 1865; Washington *Evening Star*, March 4, 1865.
3. Dover *Delawarean*, March 11, 1865.
4. Ibid.
5. *New York Herald*, March 6, 1865.
6. Washington *Evening Star*, March 4, 1865.
7. Noah Brooks, *Washington, D.C. in Lincoln's Time* (New York: Rinehart, 1958), 210; Michael Burlingame, ed., *Lincoln Observed: Civil War Dispatches of Noah Brooks* (Baltimore, Md.: Johns Hopkins University Press, 1998), 165.
8. Philip Van Doren Stern, "The President Came Forward and the Sun Burst through the Clouds," *American Heritage* IX, no. 2 (February 1958): 15.
9. Ibid., 11.
10. William Owner Diary, March 6, 1865, Library of Congress; Washington *Evening Star*, March 4, 1865; *Diary of Gideon Welles — Secretary of the Navy under Lincoln and Johnson*, vol. 2 (Boston: Houghton Mifflin, 1911), 252.
11. Washington *Evening Star*, March 4, 1865; Jeremiah T. Lockwood letter, March 4, 1865, Library of Congress; *Newark* (N.J.) *Daily Advertiser*, March 7, 1865.
12. Burlingame, *Lincoln Observed*, 168.
13. Stern, "The President Came Forward," 94.
14. Washington *Evening Star*, March 4, 1865.
15. Benjamin Meyer Letter, March 8, 1865, Missouri Historical Society, St. Louis.
16. Robert W. McBride, "Lincoln's Body Guard: The Union Light Guard of Ohio with Some Personal Recollections of Abraham Lincoln," *Indiana Historical Society Publications* 5, no. 1 (1911): 29.
17. William Owner Diary, March 6, 1865; *Newark* (N.J.) *Daily Advertiser*, March 7, 1865.
18. Muriel Davies Mackenzie, *"Maggie!": Maggie Lindsley's Journal* (Southbury, Conn., 1977), March 4, 1865.
19. Stern, "The President Came Forward," 94.
20. Washington *Evening Star*, March 4, 1865.
21. Justin Kaplan, *Walt Whitman: A Life* (New York: Simon and Schuster, 1980), 301.

22. Washington *Evening Star*, March 4, 1865.

23. Burlingame, *Lincoln Observed*, 169.

24. Benjamin Meyer Letter, March 8, 1865.

25. "Lincoln's Second Inaugural: A Gala Event in Washington Society," *Lincoln Lore*, no. 1452 (February 1959): 2.

26. Louis J. Weichmann, *A True History of the Assassination of Abraham Lincoln and the Conspiracy of 1865* (New York: Alfred A. Knopf, 1975), 89.

27. Washington *Evening Star*, April 17, 1865.

1. Three Electric Words

1. Brooks, *Washington, D.C. in Lincoln's Time*, 220.

2. *Philadelphia Inquirer*, April 4, 1865.

3. Ibid.

4. Brooks, *Washington, D.C. in Lincoln's Time*, 219.

5. John K. Lattimer and Terry Alford, "Eyewitness to History: Newton Ferree, the Lincoln Assassination and the Close of the Civil War in Washington," 95, Ford's Theater Archive.

6. Washington *Evening Star*, April 3, 1865.

7. *New York Times*, April 6, 1865.

8. Washington *Evening Star*, April 3, 1865.

9. Ibid.; Brooks, *Washington, D.C. in Lincoln's Time*, 221.

10. Gordon Arthur Willett Letter, April 4, 1865, Historical Society of Washington, D.C.; Washington *Daily Constitutional Union*, April 8, 1865.

11. Edmund Leicester Poole Letter, April 5, 1865, Library of Congress.

12. Brooks, *Washington, D.C. in Lincoln's Time*, 221.

13. Wilmington *Delaware Republican*, May 4, 1865.

14. Washington *Evening Star*, April 4, 1865.

15. Ibid., April 3, 1865.

2. The White City

1. Emil and Ruth Rosenblatt, eds., *The Civil War Letters of Private Wilbur Fisk, 1861–1865* (Lawrence: University of Kansas Press, 1992), 321; "Recollection of Lincoln," George Andrew Huron Collection, Kansas State Historical Society, Topeka.

2. "Recollection of Lincoln," Huron Collection.

3. Ibid.

4. Rosenblatt, *Private Wilbur Fisk*, 322.

5. Ibid.

6. Henrietta Stratton Jaquette, *South after Gettysburg: Letters of Cornelia Hancock, 1863–1868* (New York: Thomas Y. Crowell, 1956), 179.

7. Adolphe de Chambrun, *Impressions of Lincoln and the Civil War: A Foreigner's Account* (New York: Random House, 1952), 79.

8. Rosenblatt, *Private William Fisk*, 322.

9. Victor Searcher, *The Farewell to Lincoln* (New York: Abingdon, 1965), 133.

10. Ibid.

11. Jaquette, *South after Gettysburg*, 179.

12. Rosenblatt, *Private William Fisk*, 323.

3. The Last Man

1. *Chicago Tribune*, April 11, 1865.

2. Ibid.

3. *Chicago Tribune*, April 10, 1865.

4. Harold Earl Hammond, ed. *Diary of a Union Lady, 1861–1865* (New York: Funk and Wagnalls, 1962), 351; *New York Times*, April 10, 1865; *Chicago Tribune*, April 11, 1865.

5. Ida M. Tarbell, "The Death of Abraham Lincoln," *McClure's*, December 1896, 375.

6. *Chicago Tribune*, April 11, 1865.

7. Ibid.

8. Thomas Goodrich, *Bloody Dawn: The Story of the Lawrence Massacre* (Kent, Ohio: Kent State University Press, 1991), 182.

9. *Denver Daily Rocky Mountain News*, April 11, 1865.

10. Ibid., April 15, 1865.

11. Virginia (Nev.) *Daily Territorial Enterprise*, April 18, 1865.

12. *Newark* (N.J.) *Daily Advertiser*, April 11, 1865.

13. *Portsmouth* (N.H.) *Journal*, April 15, 1865.

14. Granniss letter, Sarah to Charlie, Jr., April 11, 1865, Illinois State Historical Library, Springfield.

15. Concord *New Hampshire Statesman*, April 21, 1865.

16. *Providence Daily Journal*, April 11, 1865.

17. *Philadelphia Inquirer*, April 11, 1865.

18. Ibid., April 15, 1865.

19. Wilmington *Delaware Republican*, April 13, 1865.

20. New Orleans *Daily Picayune*, April 21, 1865.

21. *Portsmouth* (N.H.) *Journal*, April 15, 1865.

22. Laura Virginia Hale, *Four Valiant Years in the Lower Shenandoah Valley, 1861–1865* (Front Royal, Va.: Hathaway, 1986), 516.

23. *New York Times*, April 8, 1865; Thomas and Debra Goodrich, *The Day Dixie Died: Southern Occupation, 1865–1866* (Mechanicsburg, Pa.: Stackpole, 2001), 7.

24. *Philadelphia Inquirer*, April 5, 8, 1865.

25. Thomas Reed Turner, *Beware the People Weeping: Public Opinion and the Assassination of Abraham Lincoln* (Baton Rouge: Louisiana State University Press, 1982), 20.

26. Letter dated April 10, 1865, Bell Collection, Delaware Public Archives, Dover.

27. *New York Times*, April 10, 1865.

4. Star of Glory

1. George S. Bryan, *The Great American Myth* (New York: Carrick and Evans, 1940), 6; Tee Loftin, *Stranger's Guided Tour to Washington, D. C.: 1865 — The Civil War City As Mr. Lincoln Knew It* (Washington, D.C., 1967), 3.

2. Brooks, *Washington, D.C. in Lincoln's Time*, 294.

3. Ibid., 295.

4. Bryan, *The Great American Myth*, 6.

5. Ibid.

6. Ibid., 7.

7. W. Emerson Reck, *A. Lincoln: His Last 24 Hours* (Jefferson, N.C.: McFarland,

1987), 7; John Rhodehamel and Louise Taper, eds., *Right or Wrong, God Judge Me: The Writings of John Wilkes Booth* (Urbana: University of Illinois, 1997), n. 145; Justin G. Turner, ed., "April 14, 1865: A Soldier's View," *Lincoln Herald*, Winter 1964, 179.

8. Wilmington *Delaware Republican*, May 4, 1865.

9. Ibid.

10. Julia Adelaide Shepard, "Lincoln's Assassination Told by an Eyewitness," *Century Magazine*, April 1909, 918.

11. David Allen Richards, "Civil War Diary of a Male Nurse behind the Lines, September 2, 1864–July 1, 1865," *Michigan History* 39 (1955): 213.

12. Henry Colyer Letter, April 15, 1865, Ford's Theater Archive.

13. Rhodehamel and Taper, *Right or Wrong*, 145.

14. Ruth Painter Randall, *Mary Lincoln: Biography of a Marriage* (Boston: Little, Brown, 1953), 372–73; John Y. Simon, ed., *The Personal Memoirs of Julia Dent Grant* (Carbondale: Southern Illinois University Press, 1975), 146–47.

15. Ishbel Ross, *The President's Wife: Mary Todd Lincoln—A Biography* (New York: G. P. Putnam's Sons, 1973), 227.

16. Ibid.

17. Simon, *Julia Dent Grant*, 154; Justin G. Turner and Linda Levitt Turner, *Mary Todd Lincoln: Her Life and Letters* (New York: Alfred A. Knopf), 219; Bryan, *The Great American Myth*, 160.

18. Rhodehamel and Taper, *Right or Wrong*, n. 145; Margaret Leech, *Reveille in Washington, 1860–1865* (New York: Harper's Brothers, 1941), 385; Hamilton Fish Diary, November 12, 1869, Library of Congress.

19. "The Assassination of President Lincoln: Recollections of Harry Hawks," *Boston Herald*, April 11, 1897, clipping, Illinois State Historical Library, Springfield; Hamilton Fish Diary, November 12, 1869, Library of Congress.

20. Allan Peskin, "Putting the 'Baboon' to Rest: Observations of a Radical Republican on Lincoln's Funeral Train," *Lincoln Herald*, Spring 1977, 27.

21. Ross, *President's Wife*, 197.

22. Ibid., 210.

23. Wade Hall and Debra C. Reynolds, "Mary Todd Lincoln: A Life of Loss," *Louisville (Ky.) Courier-Journal Magazine*, July 11, 1982.

24. Dorothy Meserve Kunhardt and Philip B. Kunhardt, Jr., *Twenty Days: A Narrative in Text and Pictures of the Assassination of Abraham Lincoln* (New York: Harper and Row, 1965), 67.

25. Ibid., 203.

26. Rhodehamel and Taper, *Right or Wrong*, 144.

27. Statement of Mr. Henry B. Philips, Ford's Theater Archives.

28. Jesse W. Weik, "A New Story of Lincoln's Assassination: An Unpublished Record of an Eye-witness," *Century*, February 1903, 561.

29. Ibid.

30. Reinhard H. Luthin, *The Real Abraham Lincoln: A Complete One Volume History of His Life and Times* (Englewood Cliffs, N.J.: Prentice Hall, 1960), 618.

31. Rhodehamel and Taper, *Right or Wrong*, 144.

5. The President and the Player

1. Goodrich, *The Day Dixie Died*, 18.

2. John Hope Franklin, ed., *The Diary of James T. Ayers, Civil War Recruiter* (Spring-

field: Illinois State Historical Society, 1947), 93.

3. Gerald Schwartz, ed., *A Woman Doctor's Civil War* (Columbia: University of South Carolina Press, 1989), 130.

4. *New York Times*, April 18, 1865.

5. *Lafayette* (Ind.) *Daily Courier*, April 14, 1865.

6. Schwartz, *A Woman Doctor's Civil War*, 131.

7. *New York Times*, April 18, 1865.

8. Ibid.

9. Goodrich, *The Day Dixie Died*, 18.

10. *New York Times*, April 18, 1865; Schwartz, *A Woman Doctor's Civil War*, 131; Noah Andre Trudeau, *Out of the Storm: The End of the Civil War, April–June 1865* (Baton Rouge: Louisiana State University Press, 1994), 221.

11. Ibid.

12. Lattimer and Alford, "Newton Ferree," 95; Bryan, *The Great American Myth*, 149.

13. "The President's Office," *Lincoln Lore*, June 12, 1939, 1.

14. Champ Clark, *The Assassination: Death of the President* (Alexandria, Va.: Time/Life, 1987), 65; Tarbell, *Death of Abraham Lincoln*, 378.

15. Edwin Stanton Letter, transcript, April 15, 1865, Ford's Theater Archives; Tarbell, 374.

16. Tarbell, *Death of Abraham Lincoln*, 375.

17. *The War of the Rebellion: A Compilation of the Official Records of the Union and Confederate Armies* (Washington, D.C.: Government Printing Office, 1894), Series 1, XLVI, pt. 3, 780.

18. *Diary of Gideon Welles*, vol. 2, 296.

19. John G. Nicolay and John Hay, *Abraham Lincoln: A History* (New York: Century, 1890), 283–84.

20. Ross, *President's Wife*, 185.

21. Randall, *Mary Lincoln*, 341–42; Reck, *A. Lincoln*, 33.

22. Harold Hyman and Benjamin Platt Thomas, *Stanton: The Life and Times of Lincoln's Secretary of War* (New York: Alfred A. Knopf, 1962), 395.

23. John T. Ford, "Behind the Curtain of a Conspiracy," *North American Review*, April 1889, 488; Bryan, *The Great American Myth*, 106.

24. Bryan, *The Great American Myth*, 90.

25. Edward M. Alfriend, "Recollections of John Wilkes Booth," *The Era*, October 1901, 604.

26. Clara Morris, "Some Recollections of John Wilkes Booth," *McClure's Magazine*, February 1901, 302.

27. Bryan, *The Great American Myth*, 91.

28. Ibid., 98.

29. Ibid.

30. Luthin, *The Real Abraham Lincoln*, 609.

31. W. J. Ferguson, *I Saw Booth Shoot Lincoln* (Austin, Tex.: Pemberton, 1969), 16; Bryan, *The Great American Myth*, 216.

32. Luthin, *The Real Abraham Lincoln*, 608.

33. William Hanchett, *The Lincoln Murder Conspiracies* (Urbana: University of Illinois Press, 1986), 138

34. Alfriend, "Recollections of John Wilkes Booth," 604.

35. Morris, "Some Recollections," 299.

36. Rhodehamel and Taper, *Right or Wrong*, 6.

37. Alfriend, "Recollections of John Wilkes Booth," 604.

38. Weichmann, *A True History of the Assassination*, 40.

39. Luthin, *The Real Abraham Lincoln*, 609.

40. *Cincinnati Commercial*, October 20, 1868, clipping at Ford's Theater archive.

41. Untitled article, *Journal of the Illinois State Historical Society* 51 (Autumn 1958): 324.

42. Rhodehamel and Taper, *Right or Wrong*, 107.

43. Hanchett, *The Lincoln Murder Conspiracies*, 138.

44. Letter, Asia Booth Clarke to Jean Anderson, May 22, 1865, photocopy, Ford's Theater Archives.

45. Bryan, *The Great American Myth*, 99.

46. Goodrich, *The Day Dixie Died*, 29.

47. Weichmann, *A True History of the Assassination*, 136.

48. George Alfred Townsend, *The Life, Crime, and Capture of John Wilkes Booth* (New York: Dick and Fitzgerald, 1865), 27; Weichmann, *A True History of the Assassination*, 136.

49. *Cincinnati Commercial*, October 20, 1868, photocopy of article, Ford's Theater archive.

50. Simon, *Julia Dent Grant*, 155.

51. Bryan, *The Great American Myth*, 160; Simon, *Julia Dent Grant*, 155.

52. Bryan, *The Great American Myth*, 161.

6. Sic Semper Tyrannis

1. *Philadelphia Inquirer*, April 15, 1865; George A. Woodward, "The Night of Lincoln's Assassination," *United Service*, May 1889, 472, photocopy at Illinois State Historical Library, Springfield.

2. Woodward, "The Night of Lincoln's Assassination," 472.

3. Rhodehamel and Taper, *Right or Wrong*, 151.

4. Edward Steers, Jr., *Blood on the Moon: The Assassination of Abraham Lincoln* (Lexington: University Press of Kentucky, 2001), 86–87.

5. Michael Maione and James O. Hall, "Why Seward? The Attack on the Night of April 14, 1865," *Lincoln Herald*, Spring 1998, 32.

6. Mark E. Neely, Jr. *The Fate of Liberty: Abraham Lincoln and Civil Liberties* (New York: Oxford University Press, 1991), 8, 15.

7. Theodore Roscoe, *The Web of Conspiracy: The Complete Story of the Men Who Murdered Abraham Lincoln* (Englewood Cliffs, N.J.: Prentice Hall, 1959), 272; Hanchett, *The Lincoln Murder Conspiracies*, 131.

8. Hanchett, *The Lincoln Murder Conspiracies*, 131.

9. John A. Marshall, *American Bastille: A History of the Illegal Arrests and Imprisonment of American Citizens during the Late Civil War* (Philadelphia: Thomas W. Hartley, 1870), 645–46.

10. Rhodehamel and Taper, *Right or Wrong*, 9; Neely, *The Fate of Liberty*, 110–13; Roscoe, *Web of Conspiracy*, 268.

11. Hanchett, *The Lincoln Murder Conspiracies*, 10–11.

12. *Alton* (Ill.) *Telegraph*, April 21, 1865.

13. David Donald, *Lincoln's Herndon* (New York: Alfred A. Knopf, 1948), 158.

14. Ibid.

15. Hanchett, *The Lincoln Murder Conspiracies*, 12.

16. Donald, *Lincoln's Herndon*, 164; *Alton* (Ill.) *Telegraph*, April 21, 1865; *Lynchburg Virginian*, March 30, 1864.

17. Douglas L. Wilson and Rodney O. Davis, *Herndon's Informants: Letters, Interviews, and Statements about Abraham Lincoln* (Urbana: University of Illinois Press, 1998), 676.

18. Hanchett, *The Lincoln Murder Conspiracies*, 13.

19. Ibid.

20. Ibid., 37.

21. *New York Times*, April 18, 1865.

22. Maione and Hall, "Why Seward?," 32.

23. Rhodehamel and Taper, *Right or Wrong*, 7, 8; Asia Booth Clarke, *The Unlocked Book: A Memoir of John Wilkes Booth by His Sister, Asia Booth Clarke* (New York: Benjamin Blom, 1971), 139, 156–57.

24. Ward Hill Lamon, *Recollections of Abraham Lincoln, 1847–1865* (Washington, D.C.: Dorothy Lamon Teillard, 1911), 279.

7. Towards an Indefinite Shore

1. Reck, *A. Lincoln*, 47; Brooks, *Washington, D.C. in Lincoln's Time*, 229.

2. "Eye Witness Describes Lincoln Assassination in Letter to Brother," *Baltimore and Ohio Magazine*, February 1926, 11; Margarita Spalding Gerry, "Lincoln's Last Day: New Facts Now Told for the First Time by William H. Crook (His Personal Body-Guard)," *Harpers Monthly Magazine*, September 1907, 519.

3. Randall, *Mary Lincoln*, 380–81.

4. Turner and Turner, *Mary Todd Lincoln*, 284–85.

5. Nicolay and Hay, *Abraham Lincoln*, 285–86.

6. Kunhardt and Kunhardt, *Twenty Days*, 19.

7. *New York Times*, July 4, 1865.

8. Reck, *A. Lincoln*, 44.

9. Ibid., 46.

10. Kunhardt and Kunhardt, *Twenty Days*, 12.

11. Randall, *Mary Lincoln*, 381.

12. Elizabeth Keckley, *Behind the Scenes* (New York: G. W. Carleton, 1868), 204; Mark E. Neely, Jr. and R. Gerald McMurtry, *The Insanity File: The Case of Mary Todd Lincoln* (Carbondale: Southern Illinois University Press, 1986), 5.

13. Neely and McMurtry, *The Insanity File*, 5.

14. Ross, *President's Wife*, 182–83; Brooks, *Washington, D.C. in Lincoln's Time*, 66–67.

15. Clark, *The Assassination*, 9–10.

16. Randall, *Mary Lincoln*, 341.

17. Kunhardt and Kunhardt, *Twenty Days*, 5; Steers, *Blood on the Moon*, 16; Harold Holzer, *Dear Mr. Lincoln: Letters to the President* (Reading, Mass.: Addison/Wesley, 1993), 342.

18. Weichmann, *A True History of the Assassination*, 57.

19. Steers, *Blood on the Moon*, 16.

20. Nicolay and Hay, *Abraham Lincoln*, 286.

21. *Lafayette* (Ind.) *Daily Courier*, April 28, 1865.

22. Edward Noyes, "Wisconsin's Reaction to the Assassination of Abraham Lincoln," 7–8, Rare Books Collection, Library of Congress.

23. *Lafayette* (Ind.) *Daily Courier*, April 28, 1865.

24. Kunhardt and Kunhardt, *Twenty Days*, 4; Brooks, *Washington, D.C. in Lincoln's Time*, 44; Nicolay and Hay, *Abraham Lincoln*, 288.

25. Kunhardt and Kunhardt, *Twenty Days*, 4.

26. Tarbell, *Death of Abraham Lincoln*, 378.

8. The Clown and the Sphinx

1. *Chicago Tribune*, April 17, 1865.

2. Stern, "The President Came Forward," 13.

3. Albert Castel, *The Presidency of Andrew Johnson* (Lawrence: Regents Press of Kansas, 1979), 9.

4. Ibid., 14.

5. Brooks, *Washington, D.C. in Lincoln's Time*, 211.

6. Ibid., 210–11.

7. Stern, "The President Came Forward," 15.

8. Castel, *The Presidency of Andrew Johnson*, 9–10.

9. *Council Bluffs* (Iowa) *Bugle*, March 30, 1865.

10. Brooks, *Washington, D.C. in Lincoln's Time*, 211–12.

11. William Owner Diary, clipping from *New York Herald*.

12. Brooks, *Washington, D.C. in Lincoln's Time*, 212.

13. William Owner Diary, clipping from *New York Herald*.

14. *Council Bluffs* (Iowa) *Bugle*, March 30, 1865.

15. John Sherman, *Recollections of Forty Years in the House, Senate and Cabinet: An Autobiography* (Chicago: Werner, 1895), 351.

16. Brooks, *Washington, D.C. in Lincoln's Time*, 212.

17. William Owner Diary, clipping from *New York Herald*.

18. Ibid.; Stern, "The President Came Forward," 15.

19. Michael Burlingame, *The Inner World of Abraham Lincoln* (Urbana: University of Illinois Press, 1994), 168.

20. Stern, "The President Came Forward," 15; James G. Randall, ed., *The Diary of Orville Hickman Browning, 1865–1881*, vol. 2 (Springfield: Illinois State Historical Library, 1933), 9.

21. *Council Bluffs* (Iowa) *Bugle*, March 30, 1865.

22. *Newark* (N.J.) *Daily Advertiser*, March 4, 1865.

23. *Council Bluffs* (Iowa) *Bugle*, March 30, 1865.

24. William Owner Diary, clipping from *New York World*; *New York Herald*, March 22, 1865.

25. Louis Philip Fusz Diary, 72, Missouri Historical Society, St. Louis.

26. Brooks, *Washington, D.C. in Lincoln's Time*, 36.

27. New Orleans *Daily Picayune*, April 19, 1865.

28. Glyndon G. Van Deusen, *William Henry Seward* (New York: Oxford University Press, 1967), 411; *New York Times*, April 6, 1865.

29. Roscoe, *Web of Conspiracy*, 145.

30. Van Deusen, *Seward*, 412.

31. Ibid., 411.

32. Ibid., 412.

33. Kunhardt and Kunhardt, *Twenty Days*, 52.

9. One Bold Man

1. Hanchett, *The Lincoln Murder Conspiracies*, 54; New Orleans *Daily Picayune*, April 22, 1865.

2. Reck, *A. Lincoln*, 94.

3. Rhodehamel and Taper, *Right or Wrong*, n. 150.

4. Campbell MacCulloch, "This Man Saw Lincoln Shot," *Good Housekeeping*, February 1927, 115.

5. Hanchett, *The Lincoln Murder Conspiracies*, 54.

6. Luthin, *The Real Abraham Lincoln*, 629.

7. Reck, *A. Lincoln*, 52.

8. Luthin, *The Real Abraham Lincoln*, 630.

9. Ibid., 629; Kunhardt and Kunhardt, *Twenty Days*, 26.

10. Charles J. Stewart, "Lincoln's Assassination and the Protestant Clergy of the North," *Journal of the Illinois State Historical Society*, Autumn 1961, 290; Turner and Turner, *Mary Todd Lincoln*, 218.

11. Edgar Downey, *Schuykill County and Some of Its People When Abraham Lincoln Was Assassinated* (Pottsville, Pa., 1952), 16.

12. Roy P. Basler, ed., *Walt Whitman's Memoranda during the War and Death of Abraham Lincoln* (Bloomington: Indiana University Press, 1962), 46.

13. *Boston Daily Advertiser*, April 19, 1865.

14. Reck, *A. Lincoln*, 79.

15. William A. Tidwell, James O. Hall, and David Winfred Gaddy, *Come Retribution: The Confederate Secret Service and the Assassination of Lincoln* (Jackson: University Press of Mississippi, 1988), 256; Bryan, *The Great American Myth*, 87.

16. Clarke, *The Unlocked Book*, 124.

17. Rhodehamel and Taper, *Right or Wrong*, 130.

18. Clarke, *The Unlocked Book*, 124.

19. Ibid., 115.

20. Ibid., 203; Reck, *A Lincoln*, 65–66; William A. Tidwell, *April '65: Confederate Covert Action in the American Civil War* (Kent, Ohio: Kent State University Press, 1995), 137.

21. Rhodehamel and Taper, *Right or Wrong*, 11; Reck, *A. Lincoln*, 66.

22. Hanchett, *The Lincoln Murder Conspiracies*, 42–43.

23. Clarke, *The Unlocked Book*, 203.

24. Rhodehamel and Taper, *Right or Wrong*, 19.

25. Steers, *Blood on the Moon*, 86–87.

26. Ibid., 15.

27. Rhodehamel and Taper, *Right or Wrong*, 130–31.

10. A Night to Remember

1. James S. Knox, "A Son Writes of the Supreme Tragedy," *Saturday Review* (February 11, 1956), 11; William H. DeMotte, "The Assassination of Abraham Lincoln," *Journal of the Illinois State Historical Society*, October 1927, 424; New Orleans *Daily Picayune*, May 12, 1865; Frank Rathbun, "The Rathbone Connection," 1, Ford's Theater archives.

2. Clarke, *The Unlocked Book*, 171–72.

3. Bryan, *The Great American Myth*, 172.

4. MacCulloch, "This Man Saw Lincoln Shot," 116.

5. Reck, A. *Lincoln*, 72.

6. *Chicago Tribune*, April 21, 1865.

7. Basler, *Walt Whitman's Memoranda*, 47.

8. David Donald, *Lincoln* (New York: Simon and Schuster, 1995), 595.

9. E. R. Shaw, "The Assassination of Lincoln: The Hitherto Unpublished Account of an Eye-witness," *McClure's Magazine*, December 1908, 183.

10. "The Assassination of Lincoln," undated, untitled clipping, Ford's Theater archives.

11. Ibid.

12. Arthur M. Markowitz, ed., "Tragedy of an Age: An Eyewitness Account of Lincoln's Assassination," *Journal of the Illinois State Historical Society*, Summer 1973, 207; *Chicago Tribune*, April 21, 1865; Knox, "A Son Writes," 11.

13. Ronald D. Rietveld, ed., "An Eyewitness Account of Abraham Lincoln's Assassination," *Civil War History: A Journal of the Middle Period*, March 1976, n. 63.

14. Charles A. Leale, "Lincoln's Last Hours," 3, photocopy at the Illinois State Historical Library, Springfield.

15. Leale, "Lincoln's Last Hours," 3.

16. Henry Williams, Elizabeth Dixon and Daniel Dean Beekman, "A Night to Remember," *Yankee Magazine*, February 1973, 141.

17. John Downing, Jr. letter, photocopy, Ford's Theater archives.

18. Washington *Daily National Intelligencer*, April 15, 1865; William Kent letter, April 15, 1865, Ford's Theater archive; Shaw, 183.

19. Washington *Daily National Intelligencer*, April 15, 1865; Lattimer and Alford, "Eyewitness to History," 97; Washington *Evening Star*, May 11, 1865.

20. Markowitz, "Tragedy of an Age," 207.

21. Helen Moss memoir, 2, Library of Congress.

22. Hanchett, *The Lincoln Murder Conspiracies*, 57; Washington *Evening Star*, April 18, 1865.

23. Helen Du Barry, "Eyewitness Account of Lincoln's Assassination," *Journal of the Illinois Historical Society*, September 1946, 368; Gardner Brewer letter, to "Mrs. Alexander," April 17, 1865, Illinois State Historical Library, Springfield; Kunhardt and Kunhardt, *Twenty Days*, 102.

24. *Chicago Tribune*, April 20, 1865.

25. Shaw, "Assassination of Lincoln," 183.

26. Timothy S. Good, ed., *We Saw Lincoln Shot: One Hundred Eyewitness Accounts* (Jackson: University Press of Mississippi, 1995), 40.

27. Shepard, "Lincoln's Assassination," 917.

28. Bryan, *The Great American Myth*, 173.

29. Shepard, "Lincoln's Assassination," 917.

30. Du Barry, "Eyewitness Account of Lincoln's Assassination," 368.

31. Shepard, "Lincoln's Assassination," 917.

32. Reck, A. *Lincoln*, 86.

33. Williams, Dixon, and Beekman, "A Night to Remember," 144.

34. Roscoe, *Web of Conspiracy*, 536–37.

35. Shepard, "Lincoln's Assassination," 917.

36. Luthin, *The Real Abraham Lincoln*, 636.

37. *Boston Daily Globe*, April 11, 1920.

38. Burlingame, *Lincoln Observed*, 189; *Chicago Tribune*, April 17, 1865.

39. Rietveld, "An Eyewitness Account," 63.

40. Luthin, 637; Gerry, "Lincoln's Last Day," 528; J. E. Buckingham, Sr., *Reminis-*

cences and Souvenirs of the Assassination of Abraham Lincoln (Washington, D.C.: Rufus H. Darby, 1894), 13.

41. Statement of Jeannie Gourlay, Ford's Theater archive.

11. Terror on Lafayette Park

1. *New York Times*, May 20, 1865.
2. Ibid.
3. Van Deusen, *Seward*, 414.
4. *New York Times*, May 20, 1865.
5. Kunhardt and Kunhardt, *Twenty Days*, 53.
6. William H. Seward papers, Library of Congress.
7. Ibid.
8. *New York Times*, May 20, 1865; Kunhardt and Kunhardt, *Twenty Days*, 53.
9. *New York Times*, May 20, 1865.
10. William H. Seward papers.
11. Ibid.; *New York Times*, May 20, 1865.
12. Van Deusen, *Seward*, 414.
13. Seward papers.
14. *New York Times*, May 20, 1865.
15. Kunhardt and Kunhardt, *Twenty Days*, 53.
16. *New York Times*, May 20, 1865.
17. Reck, A. *Lincoln*, 134.
18. Seward papers.

12. The Last Bullet

1. Statement of James Ferguson, photocopy, Ford's Theater archives; Washington *Evening Star*, April 17, 1865.
2. Benn Pittman, *The Assassination of President Lincoln and the Trial of the Conspirators* (New York: Funk and Wagnalls, 1954), 76.
3. *Rochester* (N.Y.) *Daily Union and Advertiser*, April 17, 1865.
4. Reck, A. *Lincoln*, 98.
5. Ibid.
6. Washington *Evening Star*, April 17, 1865.
7. *Chicago Tribune*, April 17, 1865.
8. *New York Times*, April 18, 1865; *Harper's Weekly*, April 29, 1865, photocopy, Ford's Theater archive.
9. Statement of Harry Hawk, Ford's Theater archive.
10. Rietveld, "An Eyewitness Account," n. 65; Shaw, "The Assassination of Lincoln," 184.
11. "Two Letters on the Event of April 14, 1865," Illinois State Historical Society, Springfield.
12. Shaw, "Assassination of Lincoln," 184.
13. Statement of James Ferguson, Ford's Theater archives; Washington *Evening Star*, April 17,
14. Du Barry, "Eyewitness Account of Lincoln's Assassination," 367.
15. *New York Times*, April 15, 1865; William Kent letter, Ford's Theater archives; Statement of James Ferguson, Ford's Theater archives; Pittman, *The Assassination of*

President Lincoln, 76; DeMotte, "The Assassination of Abraham Lincoln," 425; Harry Read, "'A Hand to Hold While Dying': Dr. Charles A. Leale at Lincoln's Side," *Lincoln Herald*, Spring 1977, 22.

16. Statement of James Ferguson, Ford's Theater archive.

17. Reck, *A. Lincoln*, 109.

18. Pittman, *The Assassination of President Lincoln*, 79.

19. Markowitz, "Tragedy of an Age," 208.

20. Statement of William Elmendorf, Ford's Theater archive.

21. Ferguson, *I Saw Booth Shoot Lincoln*, 50.

22. Washington *Evening Star*, April 15, 1865; S. H. Bronson letter, April 16, 1865, Lincoln Museum, Fort Wayne, Indiana.

23. Ferguson, *I Saw Booth Shoot Lincoln*, 51.

24. Rietveld, "An Eyewitness Account," 64; Ferguson, *I Saw Booth Shoot Lincoln*, 51.

25. Ferguson, *I Saw Booth Shoot Lincoln*, 52.

26. Luthin, *The Real Abraham Lincoln*, 645–46.

27. *Rochester* (N.Y.) *Daily Union and Advertiser*, April 17, 1865; *Chicago Tribune*, April 21, 1865.

28. Ralph G. Newman, "The Mystery Occupant's Eyewitness Account of the Death of Abraham Lincoln," *Chicago History*, Spring 1975, 32.

29. Rietveld, "An Eyewitness Account," n. 66.

30. Turner, *Beware the People Weeping*, 25.

31. Bassett diary, Ford's Theater archives; Bryan, *The Great American Myth*, 210.

32. New Orleans *Daily Picayune*, April 29, 1865.

33. Reck, *A. Lincoln*, 114; Rietveld, "An Eyewitness Account," n. 66.

34. Washington *Evening Star*, April 15, 1865; Bryan, *The Great American Myth*, 210; Reck, *A. Lincoln*, 114.

35. Goodrich, *The Day Dixie Died*, 10.

36. Ibid., 11.

37. Shaw, "Assassination of Lincoln," 184; Warren Everhart, "Local Man Witnessed Lincoln's Assassination," Ford's Theater Archive.

38. Weik, "A New Story of Lincoln's Assassination," 562.

39. C. S. Taft, "Last Hours of Abraham Lincoln," *Medical and Surgical Reporter*, April 22, 1865.

40. Shaw, "Assassination of Lincoln," 184.

41. Clara Harris letter, photocopy, Ford's Theater archive.

42. Leale, "Lincoln's Last Hours," 4–5.

43. William Kent letter, Ford's Theater archive.

44. Leale, "Lincoln's Last Hours," 5.

45. Ibid., 5–6.

46. Buckingham, *Reminiscences and Souvenirs*, 15; Washington *Evening Star*, April 15, 1865.

47. Basler, *Walt Whitman's Memoranda*, 48.

48. Tucker, "Eyewitness to Lincoln's Last Hours," *Yankee Magazine*, April 1979, 145; Weichmann, *A True History of the Assassination*, 156.

49. Clara Harris letter, Ford's Theater archive.

50. Shaw, "Assassination of Lincoln," 184.

51. Ibid.

52. Ibid.

53. Reck, *A. Lincoln*, 124.

54. Shepard, *Lincoln's Assassination*, 917.

55. Reck, A. *Lincoln*, 126.

56. "Two Letters," Illinois State Historical Society, Springfield.

57. Shaw, "Assassination of Lincoln," 184.

58. Kunhardt and Kunhardt, *Twenty Days*, 1, 2; Sheldon P. McIntyre letter, Ford's Theater archives; Letter of "Lucian," April 18, 1865, Ford's Theater archive.

59. Ross, *President's Wife*, 242.

13. Murder in the Streets

1. Tarbell, "Death of Abraham Lincoln," 382.

2. *Chicago Tribune*, April 21, 1865.

3. Mose Sandford letter, Ford's Theater archive.

4. Howard H. Peckham, "James Tanner's Account of Lincoln's Death," *Abraham Lincoln Quarterly*, March 1942, 176, 178.

5. "Remarks of Hon. James A. Frear," Ford's Theater Archive.

6. *Chicago Tribune*, April 17, 1865.

7. Kunhardt and Kunhardt, *Twenty Days*, 75.

8. M. Helen Palmes Moss, "Lincoln and Wilkes Booth As Seen on the Day of the Assassination," *The Century Magazine*, April 1909, 951–53.

9. James Tanner and Norman R. Brown, "The First Testimony Taken in Connection with the Assassination of Abraham Lincoln," 19, Ford's Theater archives; Peckham, "James Tanner," 177.

10. Randall, *Orville Hickman Browning*, 20.

11. Moorfield Storey, "Dickens, Stanton, Sumner, and Storey," *Atlantic Monthly*, April 1930, 464–65.

12. *Diary of Gideon Welles*, 283; Kunhardt and Kunhardt, *Twenty Days*, 64.

13. Storey, "Dickens, Stanton, Sumner, and Storey," 463.

14. Kunhardt and Kunhardt, *Twenty Days*, 66; Nicolay and Hay, *Abraham Lincoln*, 301.

15. "What Tom Pendel Saw April 14, 1865," *Magazine of History* 34, no. 1 (1950): 18–19.

16. Ibid., 19.

17. Nicolay and Hay, *Abraham Lincoln*, 301; Storey, "Dickens, Stanton, Sumner, and Storey," 463.

18. *Diary of Gideon Welles*, 284–85.

19. *New York Herald*, April 15, 1865.

20. *New York Times*, May 18, 1865.

21. Nicolay and Hay, *Abraham Lincoln*, 305.

22. William H. Seward papers.

23. Roscoe, *Web of Conspiracy*, 145; *New York Times*, May 18, 1865.

24. *Diary of Gideon Welles*, 285.

25. Roscoe, *Web of Conspiracy*, 145.

26. William H. Seward papers.

27. Ibid.

28. *Diary of Gideon Welles*, 285.

29. Roscoe, *Web of Conspiracy*, 145.

30. *New York Times*, May 18, 1865.

31. *Diary of Gideon Welles*, 285.

32. Roscoe, *Web of Conspiracy*, 181.

33. Castel, *Andrew Johnson*, 1.

34. *Diary of Gideon Welles,* 286.

35. *New York Times,* April 17, 1865.

36. Leale, *Lincoln's Last Hours,* 8; *Diary of Gideon Welles,* 287.

37. Reck, A. *Lincoln,* 132; Kunhardt and Kunhardt, *Twenty Days,* 48; Ross, *The President's Wife,* 242; David Miller DeWitt, *The Impeachment and Trial of Andrew Johnson* (New York: Macmillan, 1903), 304.

38. Leale, *Lincoln's Last Hours,* 8.

39. Taft, *Last Hours of Abraham Lincoln,* 20.

40. Pittman, *The Assassination of President Lincoln,* 79.

41. Reck, A. *Lincoln,* 132.

42. Ibid.

43. *Philadelphia Inquirer,* April 17, 1865.

44. *New York Times,* April 17, 1865.

45. *Diary of Gideon Welles,* 287.

46. Shepard, "Lincoln's Assassination," 917–18.

47. de Chambrun, *Impressions of Lincoln,* 98.

14. A Spirit So Horrible

1. *New York Times,* April 15, 1865.

2. Moss, "Lincoln and Wilkes Booth," 953.

3. C. T. Allen, "Sixteen Years Ago: Washington City on the Night of Mr. Lincoln's Assassination," *Southern Bivouac,* 1 (Wilmington, N.C.: Broadfoot, 1992), 20.

4. Statement of Sergeant Albert Boggs, Ford's Theater archive.

5. *New York Times,* April 15, 1865.

6. Reck, A. *Lincoln,* 136.

7. Wilmington *Delaware Republican,* May 4, 1865. William Kent letter, Ford's Theater archive.

8. Albert Daggett, "Within the Last 12 Hours This City Has Been the Scene of the Most Terrible Tragedies . . . ," *Lincoln Lore,* April 1961, 4.

9. *Frank Leslie's Illustrated,* April 20, 1865; Wilmington *Delaware Republican,* May 4, 1865; Jay Winik, *April 1865: The Month That Saved America* (New York: Harper Collins, 2001).

10. Moss, "Lincoln and Wilkes Booth," 953.

11. Reck, A. *Lincoln,* 135.

12. Wilmington *Delaware Republican,* May 4, 1865.

13. Reck, A. *Lincoln,* 135.

14. Tarbell, "The Death of Abraham Lincoln," 384.

15. Good, *We Saw Lincoln Shot,* 36.

16. E. A. Chaplin letter, Ford's Theater archive.

17. Turner, *Beware the People Weeping,* 49.

18. Frederick C. Drake, "A Letter on the Death of Abraham Lincoln, April 16, 1865," *Lincoln Herald,* Winter 1982, 237.

19. *Syracuse* (N.Y.) *Herald,* October 3, 1915.

20. H. G. Hannaman letter and E. A. Chaplin letter, Ford's Theater archive; Mose Sandford letter, Ford's Theater archive; Turner, *Beware the People Weeping,* 27; Rietveld, "An Eyewitness Account," 68.

21. Goodrich, *The Day Dixie Died,* 22; Wilmington *Delaware Republican,* May 4, 1865; Thomas Sanders reminiscence, Lincoln Museum, Fort Wayne, Indiana.

22. Allen, "Sixteen Years Ago," 20.

23. Ibid., 21.

24. Ibid.

25. Seaton Munroe, "Recollections of Lincoln's Assassination," *North American Review,* April 1896, 426.

26. Rhodehamel and Taper, *Right or Wrong,* 152; Turner, *Beware the People Weeping,* 25–26.

27. Basler, *Walt Whitman's Memoranda,* 49.

28. Katherine Meader collection, Ford's Theater archive.

15. The Darkest Dawn

1. "Remarks of Hon. James A. Frear," 4; Peckham, "James Tanner," 178.

2. Tanner and Brown, "The First Testimony," 17.

3. Luthin, *The Real Abraham Lincoln,* 651.

4. Kunhardt and Kunhardt, *Twenty Days,* 49.

5. *New York Herald,* April 15, 1865.

6. *Chicago Tribune,* April 21, 1865.

7. *New York Herald,* April 15, 1865.

8. *Diary of Gideon Welles,* 286–87.

9. Rietveld, "An Eyewitness Account," n. 67; Weichmann, *A True History of the Assassination,* 157.

10. Leale, *Lincoln's Last Hours,* 10.

11. Lesley A. Leonard, "Abraham Lincoln and the 'Rubber Room,'" *Surratt Courier,* February 1986, 8.

12. Weichmann, *A True History of the Assassination,* 157; Raleigh (N.C.) *Daily Progress,* April 27, 1865.

13. John P. Usher letter, April 16, 1865, Library of Congress.

14. Ross, *President's Wife,* 243; Reck, *A. Lincoln,* 139.

15. Usher letter.

16. Raleigh (N.C.) *Daily Progress,* April 27, 1865.

17. Williams, Dixon, and Beekman, "A Night to Remember," 143.

18. *Chicago Tribune,* April 17, 1865.

19. Ibid.

20. Ross, *President's Wife,* 242.

21. Springfield *Illinois State Journal,* April 19, 1865.

22. *Diary of Gideon Welles,* 288; Washington *Evening Star,* April 15, 1865.

23. Tanner and Brown, "The First Testimony," 17.

24. Ibid., 17–18.

25. Reck, *A. Lincoln,* 144.

26. Tanner and Brown, "The First Testimony," 18.

27. Turner, *Beware the People Weeping,* 55.

28. Leale, *Lincoln's Last Hours,* 11.

29. Ulysses S. Grant, *Personal Memoirs* (New York: Charles L. Webster, 1886), 508.

30. Simon, *Julia Dent Grant,* 156.

31. John Y. Simon, ed., *The Papers of Ulysses S. Grant,* 14 (Carbondale: Southern Illinois University Press, 1985), n. 390.

32. Ibid.

33. Simon, *Julia Dent Grant,* 156.

34. Ibid.

35. Lamon, *Recollections of Abraham Lincoln,* 278.

36. Helen Grover, "Lincoln's Interest in the Theater," *The Century Magazine*, April 1909, 949.

37. Springfield *Illinois State Journal*, April 17, 1865.

38. Kunhardt and Kunhardt, *Twenty Days*, 78.

39. Tucker, "Lincoln's Last Hours," 146.

40. Springfield *Illinois State Journal*, April 17, 1865.

41. Bryan, *The Great American Myth*, 187.

42. Reck, *A. Lincoln*, 146–47.

43. Kunhardt and Kunhardt, *Twenty Days*, 83.

44. Reck, *A. Lincoln*, 149.

45. *Diary of Gideon Welles*, 288.

46. Smith Stimmel, "Experiences as a Member of President Lincoln's Bodyguard," Otto Eisenschiml collection, box 7, Illinois State Historical Library, Springfield.

47. Raleigh (N.C.) *Daily Progress*, April 27, 1865.

48. *Chicago Tribune*, April 17, 1865.

49. Taft, "Last Hours of Abraham Lincoln," 22.

50. Williams, Dixon, and Beekman, "A Night to Remember," 143.

51. Reck, *A. Lincoln*, 148.

52. Williams, Dixon, and Beekman, "A Night to Remember," 143.

53. Leale, *Lincoln's Last Hours*, 11.

54. Luthin, *The Real Abraham Lincoln*, 658.

55. *Frank Leslie's Illustrated*, April 20, 1865.

56. *New York Times*, April 17, 1865.

57. *Chicago Tribune*, April 17, 1865.

58. "James A. Frear," 7.

59. Taft diary, 36.

60. Ibid.

61. Reck, *A. Lincoln*, 157.

62. Ibid.

63. Kunhardt and Kunhardt, *Twenty Days*, 80.

64. *Chicago Tribune*, April 17, 1865.

65. *New York Times*, April 17, 1865.

66. Ibid.

67. Taft diary, 28.

68. "James A. Frear," 7.

69. *New York Times*, April 16, 1865.

70. Leale, *Lincoln's Last Hours*, 13.

16. Hemp and Hell

1. Brooks, *Washington, D.C. in Lincoln's Time*, 230–31.

2. Wilmington *Delaware Republican*, May 4, 1865.

3. Burlingame, *Lincoln Observed*, 192; Brooks, *Washington, D.C. in Lincoln's Time*, 231–32.

4. "The Most Solemn Easter," *Lincoln Lore*, April 10, 1933, 1.

5. *Hartford Daily Times*, April 15, 1865; St. Joseph (Mo.) *Morning Herald and Daily Tribune*, April 16, 1865.

6. John M. Taylor, *Garfield of Ohio: The Available Man* (New York: W. W. Norton, 1970), 103.

7. Barbara Marinacci, *O Wondrous Singer! An Introduction to Walt Whitman* (New York: Dodd, Mead, 1970), 236.

8. Kaplan, *Walt Whitman*, 302.

9. San Francisco *Daily Alta California*, April 16, 1865.

10. Ibid.

11. Ibid.

12. Edith Parker Hinckley, *Frank Hinckley: California Engineer and Rancher, 1838–1890* (Claremont, Calif.: Saunders, 1946), 57.

13. San Francisco *Daily Alta California*, April 17, 1865.

14. Marilyn Mayer Culpepper, *Trials and Triumphs: Women of the American Civil War* (East Lansing: Michigan State University Press, 1991), 372.

15. George Buckley letter, April 15, 1865, Buckley Family papers, Indiana Historical Society, Indianapolis.

16. Mackenzie, "*Maggie!*," April 15, 1865.

17. *Chicago Times*, April 17, 1865.

18. David Donald, "The Folklore Lincoln," *Journal of the Illinois Historical Society*, December 1947, 378.

19. *New York Times*, April 28, 1865.

20. *Philadelphia Inquirer*, April 22, 1865.

21. Searcher, *The Farewell to Lincoln*, 39; Washington *Evening Star*, May 12, 1865.

22. Detroit *Advertiser and Tribune*, April 16, 1865.

23. Donald O. Dewey, ed., "Hoosier Justice: The Journal of David M. Donald, 1864–1868," *Indiana Magazine of History*, September 1966, 199.

24. *Bangor* (Maine) *Daily Evening Times*, April 15, 1865.

25. Goodrich, *The Day Dixie Died*, 22; *Brooklyn* (N.Y.) *Daily Eagle*, April 17, 1865.

26. San Francisco *Daily Alta California*, May 16, 1865.

27. *Cleveland Morning Leader*, April 19, 1865.

28. *New York Times*, May 1, 1865.

29. Ibid., April 16, 1865; Detroit *Advertiser and Tribune*, April 16, 1865.

30. Edmond Beall, "Recollections of the Assassination and Funeral of Abraham Lincoln," *Journal of the Illinois State Historical Society*, January 1913, 488; Springfield *Illinois State Journal*, April 18, 1865; *Saint Louis Dispatch*, April 18, 1865; Letter, April 15, 1865, *Chicago History*, Spring 1947.

31. *Indianapolis Daily Journal*, April 21, 1865; New Orleans *Daily Picayune*, April 19, 1865; Springfield *Illinois State Journal*, April 17, 1865.

32. *Council Bluffs* (Iowa) *Bugle*, June 1, 1865; *New York Times*, April 21, 1865; *Denver Daily Rocky Mountain News*, April 17, 1865.

33. *New York Times*, April 16, 1865.

34. *Philadelphia Inquirer*, April 24, 1865.

35. *New York Times*, April 26, 1865; Virginia (Nev.) *Daily Territorial Enterprise*, April 18, 1865; *Lafayette* (Ind.) *Daily Courier*, April 17, 1865; San Francisco *Daily Alta California*, April 16, 1865; *Chicago Tribune*, April 17, 1865; *Bridgeport* (Conn.) *Evening Standard*, April 22, 1865; *Newark* (N.J.) *Daily Advertiser*, April 29, 1865.

36. *New York Times*, April 22, 1865.

37. Ibid., April 16, 17, 25; *New York Times*, April 21, 1865; Washington *Evening Star*, May 6, 1865.

38. *Indianapolis Daily Journal*, April 16, 1865; F. B. Miller collection, Redin Robins to "Dear liby," April 16, 1865, Kansas State Historical Society, Topeka.; T. R. Patton letter, Lincoln Museum, Fort Wayne, Indiana.

39. Robert Huston Milroy diary, Indiana Historical Society, Indianapolis.

40. William Henry Younts autobiography, Indiana State Historical Society, Indianapolis.

41. Indianapolis *Daily State Sentinel,* April 24, 1865; Springfield *Illinois State Journal,* May 3, 1865.

42. San Francisco *Daily Alta California,* April 17, 1865.

43. *New York Times,* April 22, 1865; *Hartford* (Conn.) *Daily Times,* April 21, 1865; *Chicago Tribune,* April 17, 20, 22, 1865; *Providence Daily Journal,* April 17, 1865; Martin Abbott, "Southern Reaction to Lincoln's Assassination," *Abraham Lincoln Quarterly,* September 1952, 117.

44. Boston *Daily Journal,* April 15, 1865.

45. Springfield (Ohio) *Daily News and Republic,* May 3, 1865.

46. *Hartford* (Conn.) *Daily Times,* April 24, 1865.

47. Goodrich, *The Day Dixie Died,* 24; *Montgomery* (Ala.) *Daily Mail,* May 15, 1865; Randall, *Mary Lincoln,* 204; New Orleans *Daily Picayune,* May 3, 1865.

48. Washington *Evening Star,* April 18, 1865; Edmund N. Hatcher, *The Last Four Weeks of the War* (Columbus, Ohio, 1891), 246–47; Indianapolis *Daily State Sentinel,* April 17, 1865; *New Orleans Times,* May 2, 1865.

49. *Indianapolis Daily Journal,* April 21, 1865.

50. Indianapolis *Daily State Sentinel,* April 24, 1865.

51. Detroit *Advertiser and Tribune,* April 16, 1865.

52. Goodrich, *The Day Dixie Died,* 23–24.

53. *Hartford* (Conn.) *Daily Times,* April 21, 1865.

54. Clipping, Lexington (Ky.) *Herald-Leader,* March 8, 1964, Kentucky Historical Society, Frankfort.

55. *Cincinnati Daily Commercial,* April 17, 1865.

56. *Chicago* Tribune, April 17, 1865.

57. Clipping, Lexington (Ky.) *Herald-Leader,* March 8, 1865, Kentucky Historical Society, Frankfort.

58. Nicholas Wainwright, ed., *A Philadelphia Perspective: The Diary of Sidney George Fisher Covering the Years 1834–1871* (Philadelphia: Historical Society of Pennsylvania, 1967), 493.

59. San Francisco *Daily Alta California,* April 16, 17, 1865.

60. Ibid., April 16, 1865.

61. Kathe van Winden, "The Assassination of Abraham Lincoln: Its Effect in California," *Journal of the West,* April 1965, 218.

62. San Francisco *Daily Alta California,* May 1, 4, 1865.

63. *Chicago Tribune,* May 3, 1865; Washington *Evening Star,* April 26, 1865.

64. Springfield *Illinois State Journal,* April 21, June 6, 1865.

65. Ibid., May 3, 1865.

66. *Cincinnati Daily Commercial,* April 17, 1865.

67. San Francisco *Daily Alta California,* April 20, 1865.

17. This Sobbing Day

1. Lewis Baldwin Parsons, "General Parsons Writes of Lincoln's Death," *Journal of the Illinois State Historical Society,* Winter 1951, 355.

2. Bryan, *The Great American Myth,* 192.

3. Leale, "Lincoln's Last Hours," 14.

4. *Diary of Gideon Welles,* 290.

5. *New York Times,* June 2, 1865.

6. Weichmann, *A True History of the Assassination,* 180.

7. Ivory G. Kimball, *Recollections from a Busy Life* (Washington, D.C.: Carnahan, 1912), 71.

8. Two Letters," April 18, 1865; Boston *Daily Advertiser*, April 17, 1865.

9. "Two Letters," April 18, 1865.

10. Weichmann, *A True History of the Assassination*, 180.

11. Boston *Daily Advertiser*, April 17, 1865.

12. Rhodehamel and Taper, *Right or Wrong*, 145.

13. Ibid.

14. Booth, *The Unlocked Book*, 200–01.

15. Hammond, *Diary of a Union Lady*, 346.

16. "Edwin Booth and Lincoln, with an Unpublished Letter by Edwin Booth," *Century Magazine*, April 1909, 920.

17. Booth, *The Unlocked Book*, 202.

18. "Edwin Booth and Lincoln," 920.

19. *Albany* (N.Y.) *Evening Journal*, April 21, 1865.

20. Turner, *Beware the People Weeping*, 27; Washington *Evening Star*, April 21, 1865.

21. Bryan, *The Great American Myth*, 202.

22. Mrs. McKee Rankin, "The News of Lincoln's Death," 262, Carrie A. Hall Collection, Kansas State Historical Society, Topeka.

23. Morris, "Some Recollections of John Wilkes Booth," 303.

24. Ibid.

25. Mary Elizabeth Massey, *Bonnet Brigades* (New York: Alfred A. Knopf, 1966), 320.

26. Washington *Evening Star*, April 15, 17, 1865.

27. Williams, Dixon, and Beekman, "A Night to Remember," 143.

28. Keckley, *Behind the Scenes*, 188, 189, 190, 191.

29. Edward Curtis statement, Ford's Theater archive.

30. Randall, *Diary of Orville Browning*, 20.

31. Curtis statement.

32. Ibid.

33. Niven, *Salmon P. Chase Papers*, 30.

34. Ibid.

35. Washington *Evening Star*, April 15, 1865.

36. Niven, *Salmon P. Chase Papers*, 31.

37. Castel, *Johnson*, 17; *Saint Louis Dispatch*, April 15, 1865.

38. Keckley, *Behind the Scenes*, 191–92.

39. *Diary of Gideon Welles*, 290.

40. Ibid.

41. Shepard, "Lincoln's Assassination," 918.

42. W. Emerson Reck, "Spring Cleaning Brings Lincoln Item to Light," Ford's Theater archives.

43. Clara Harris letter to "Dear Mary," April 25, 1865, Ford's Theater archives.

44. Turner and Turner, *Mary Todd Lincoln*, 222.

45. Henry Rathbone statement, Ford's Theater archive.

46. *Chicago Tribune*, April 17, 1865.

18. Black Easter

1. J. C. Power, *Abraham Lincoln, His Great Funeral Cortege, from Washington City to Springfield, Illinois, with a History and Description of the National Lincoln Monument* (Springfield, Ill., 1872), 13; Springfield *Illinois State Journal*, April 17, 1865.

2. John Downing, Jr. letter, Ford's Theater archives.

3. Burlingame, *Lincoln Observed*, 193.

4. Parsons, "General Parsons Writes of Lincoln's Death," 356.

5. Power, *Abraham Lincoln*, 127.

6. Stewart, "Lincoln's Assassination," 285.

7. San Francisco *Daily Alta California*, April 20, 23, 1865.

8. Weichmann, *A True History of the Assassination*, 180.

9. Richard N. Current, *The Lincoln Nobody Knows* (New York: McGraw-Hill, 1958), 282–83.

10. "The Most Solemn Easter," *Lincoln Lore*, April 10, 1933, 1.

11. Louis Philip Fusz diary, 71; Leroy P. Graf, ed., *The Papers of Andrew Johnson*, vol. 7 (Knoxville: University of Tennessee Press, 1986), 557; "The Truth Plainly Spoken," pamphlet, Illinois State Historical Library, Springfield.

12. *Albany* (N.Y.) *Evening Journal*, April 17, 1865.

13. Graf, *Papers of Andrew Johnson*, 570.

14. *Boston Daily Advertiser*, April 17, 1865.

15. Clara Harris letter to "Dear Mary," April 25, 1865, Ford's Theater archive.

16. Brooks, *Washington, D.C. in Lincoln's Time*, 66.

17. Washington *Evening Star*, April 17, 1865.

18. Ibid., April 15, 1865.

19. *New York Times*, April 18, 1865; Washington *Daily Times*, April 18, 1865.

20. Washington *Evening Star*, April 15, 17, 1865.

21. *Hartford* (Conn.) *Daily Times*, April 15, 1865; *Boston Daily Advertiser*, April 17, 1865.

22. Benjamin B. French papers, letter of Francis O. French, April 23, 1865, Library of Congress.

23. *Syracuse* (N.Y.) *Herald*, October 3, 1915.

24. Washington *Evening Star*, April 17, 1865.

25. Ibid.; *Philadelphia Inquirer*, April 17, 1865; "Two Letters," April 18, 1865, Illinois State Historical Society.

26. *Providence Daily Journal*, April 18, 1865; Washington *Evening Star*, April 17, 1865.

27. R. A. Camm, "From Sailor's Creek to Johnson's Island, Lake Erie," *Southern Bivouac*, vol. 2 (Wilmington, N.C.: Broadfoot, 1992), 444.

28. John James letter, to "Dear Parents," April 17, 1865, Ford's Theater archive.

29. Beverly Wilson Palmer, ed., *The Selected Letters of Charles Sumner* (Boston: Northeastern University Press, 1990), 294.

19. A Double Disaster

1. *Chicago Tribune*, April 21, 1865.

2. Margie Riddle Bearss, "Messenger of Lincoln's Death Herself Doomed," *Lincoln Herald*, Spring 1978, 50.

3. Abbott, "Southern Reaction," 115–16.

4. Margaret MacKay Jones, ed., *The Journal of Catherine Devereux Edmonston, 1860–1866* (Frankfort: Kentucky Historical Society), 104.

5. Emma LeConte, *When the World Ended: The Diary of Emma LeConte* (New York: Oxford University Press, 1957), 92–93.

6. Myrta Lockett Avary, *Dixie after the War: An Exposition of Social Conditions Existing in the South, during the Twelve Years Succeeding the Fall of Richmond* (New York: Doubleday, 1906), 83.

7. Bryan, *The Great American Myth*, 384.

8. Steers, *Blood on the Moon*, 45.

9. Hanchett, *The Lincoln Murder Conspiracies*, 33–34; Paul H. Bergeron, ed., *The Papers of Andrew Johnson*, vol. 8 (Knoxville: University of Tennessee Press, 1989), 28; James O. Hall, "The Dahlgren Papers: A Yankee Plot to Kill President Davis," *Civil War Times Illustrated*, November 1983, 33, 35.

10. Amanda Virginia Chappelear diary, Virginia Historical Society, Richmond.

11. Raleigh (N.C.) *Daily Progress*, May 17, 1865.

12. Turner, *Beware the People Weeping*, 96.

13. O. S. Barton, *Three Years with Quantrill: A True Story Told by His Scout John McCorkle* (1914; rpt., Norman: University of Oklahoma, 1992), 204–05.

14. James R. James, *To See the Elephant: The Civil War Letters of John A. McKee, 1861–1865* (Kansas City, Mo.: Leathers, 1998), 146.

15. Goodrich, *The Day Dixie Died*, 47.

16. Abbott, "Southern Reaction," 126.

17. *Frankfort* (Ky.) *Commonwealth*, June 13, 1865.

18. Avary, *Dixie after the War*, 82.

19. Spencer Bidwell King, Jr., ed., *The War-time Journal of a Georgia Girl, 1864–1865* (Macon, Ga.: Ardivan, 1960), 172–73.

20. Glenn Hodges, *Fearful Times: A History of the Civil War Years in Hancock County,Kentucky* (Hawesville, Ky.: Hancock County Historical Society, 1986), 75.

21. J. Winston Coleman, Jr., *Lexington during the Civil War* (Lexington, Ky.: Henry Clay, 1968), 43.

22. Edward W. Morley papers, "Dear Father," April 18, 1865, Library of Congress.

23. George Andrew Huron collection, "Recollection of Lincoln," Kansas State Historical Society, Topeka.

24. 1865 diary, Northcott Collection, Kentucky Museum, Bowling Green.

25. Carolyn L. Harrell, *When the Bells Tolled for Lincoln* (Macon, Ga.: Mercer University, 1997), 43.

26. Jedediah Hotchkiss papers, Library of Congress.

27. Mary B. Ford diary, Filson Club Historical Society, Louisville, Kentucky.

28. Abbott, "Southern Reaction," 113.

29. George Cary Eggleston, *A Rebel's Recollections* (Bloomington: Indiana University, 1959), 184.

30. Harrell, *When the Bells Tolled for Lincoln*, 41, 42.

31. Ibid., 39.

32. Searcher, *The Farewell to Lincoln*, 46.

33. James P. Jones, "Lincoln's Avengers: The Assassination and Sherman's Army," *Lincoln Herald*, Winter 1962, 187.

34. Charles Deamude letter, Illinois State Historical Library, Springfield.

35. Bearss, "Messenger of Lincoln's Death," 50.

36. Ibid.

37. Springfield *Illinois State Journal*, May 23, 1865.

38. John N. Ferguson diaries, Library of Congress.

39. Mary E. Kellogg, ed., *Army Life of an Illinois Soldier, Including a Day-by-Day Record of Sherman's March to the Sea: Letters and Diary of Charles W. Wills* (Carbondale: Southern Illinois University Press, 1996), 371.

40. Jones, "Lincoln's Avengers," 188; Solomon B. Childress journal, Missouri Historical Society, St. Louis.

41. Mary Iona Chadick diary, Alabama State Archives, Montgomery.

42. Louis Filler, ed., "Waiting for the War's End: An Ohio Soldier in Alabama after Learning of Lincoln's Death," *Ohio History*, Winter 1965, 56.

43. Filler, "Waiting for the War's End," 56.

44. Ivan Barr letter, April 24, 1865, Buckley Family papers, Library of Congress.

45. New Orleans *Daily Picayune*, April 23, 1865.

46. Harrell, *When the Bells Tolled*, 51.

47. New Orleans *Daily Picayune*, April 30, 1865.

48. Richard L. Troutman, ed., *The Heavens Are Weeping: The Diaries of George Richard Browder, 1852–1886* (Grand Rapids, Mich.: Zondervan, 1987), 197.

49. John E. Wilkins diary, Lincoln Museum, Fort Wayne, Indiana; *New York Times*, May 2, 1865; Charles East, ed., *The Civil War Diary of Sarah Morgan* (Athens: University of Georgia Press, 1991), 608; *New Orleans Tribune*, April 20, 1865.

50. *Recollections and Reminiscences, 1861–1865*, vol. 3 (South Carolina Division, United Daughters of the Confederacy, 1992), 301.

51. Matthew Jack Davis memoir, Sherman, Texas, Public Library; E. L. Cox diary, Virginia Historical Society, Richmond.

52. New Orleans *Daily Picayune*, May 5, 1865; *The War of the Rebellion*, Series, 1, XLVI, pt. 3, 787.

53. *War of the Rebellion*, ser. 1, XLVI, pt. 3, 787.

54. Charles H. Pierce letters, April 19, 1865, Indiana Historical Society, Indianapolis.

55. Searcher, *The Farewell to Lincoln*, 47.

56. Rosenblatt, *Hard Marching Every Day*, 324.

57. Harrell, 49; Turner, *Beware the People Weeping*, 50.

58. *Chicago Tribune*, April 22, 1865.

59. Ibid.

60. Ibid.

61. Ibid.

62. Coe, *Mine Eyes Have Seen the Glory*, 224.

63. *Chicago Tribune*, April 22, 1865; Graf, *Papers of Andrew Johnson*, 560.

64. *Chicago Tribune*, April 22, 1865.

65. *Providence Daily Journal*, April 10, 1865.

66. East, *Civil War Diary of Sarah Morgan*, 608.

67. George A. Hudson letters, "Dear Mother," April 28, 1865, Library of Congress.

68. J. G. Davis letter, Illinois State Historical Library, Springfield.

69. Culpepper, *Trials and Triumphs*, 371.

70. Mary Iona Chadick diary, Alabama State Archives, Montgomery.

71. McGaughy-Wallace diary, Kentucky Historical Society, Frankfort.

72. Goodrich, *The Day Dixie Died*, 25–26.

20. In Dungeons Dreadful

1. *New York Times*, April 27, 1865.

2. Henry Lawrence Burnett, "Assassination of President Lincoln and the Trial of the Assassins," 3, 4, online edition at http://www.tiac.net/users/ime/famtree/burnett/lincoln.htm (original ms. at Goshen, N.Y., Library).

3. New Orleans *Daily Picayune*, April 30, 1865.

4. *War of the Rebellion*, ser. 1, XLVI, pt. 3, 885.

5. Simon, *Papers of Ulysses Grant*, 396.

6. *Chicago Tribune*, April 28, 1865.

7. *New York Times*, May 7, 1865.

8. Williams, Dixon, and Beekman, "A Night to Remember," 143; *Lafayette* (Ind.) *Daily Courier*, May 3, 1865.

9. New Orleans *Daily Picayune*, April 22, 1865.

10. Van Deusen, *Seward*, 414.

11. Townsend, *John Wilkes Booth*, 12.

12. Ibid.

13. *Boston Daily Advertiser*, April 21, 1865.

14. Ibid., April 26, 1865.

15. Ibid.

16. Burnett, *Assassination of President Lincoln*, 8.

17. Bryan, *The Great American Myth*, 238.

18. Washington *Evening Star*, April 17, 1865.

19. Ibid., April 20, 1865.

20. Kunhardt and Kunhardt, *Twenty Days*, 187.

21. John Ford papers, manuscript, Maryland Historical Society, Baltimore.

22. Ibid.

23. Harry Ford, "The Lincoln Assassination: A Reminiscence by the Manager of Ford's Opera-House," Ford's Theater archive.

24. Statement of John Ford, Ford's Theater archive.

25. Mary Ferren letter, April 18, 1865, Solomon Smith collection, Missouri Historical Society, St. Louis.

26. Morris, "Some Recollections," 304.

27. *Chicago Tribune*, April 22, 1865.

28. Washington *Evening Star*, May 5, 1865.

29. *Philadelphia Inquirer*, April 22, 1865.

30. *New York Times*, April 18, 1865.

31. Washington *Evening Star*, May 5, 1865; Kunhardt and Kunhardt, *Twenty Days*, 187.

32. Kunhardt and Kunhardt, *Twenty Days*, 98.

33. Roscoe, *Web of Conspiracy*, 269–70.

34. *New York Times*, May 2, 1865.

35. Kunhardt and Kunhardt, *Twenty Days*, 196.

36. William Owner diary, May 2, 1865, Library of Congress.

37. Washington *Evening Star*, April 21, 22, 1865.

38. Goodrich, *The Day Dixie Died*, 53; Bryan, *The Great American Myth*, 246.

39. Harry Ford statement, Ford's Theater archive.

40. John T. Ford statement, Ford's Theater archive.

41. Ford, "Behind the Curtain of a Conspiracy," 484.

42. Harry Ford statement, Ford's Theater archive.

43. *Boston Daily Advertiser*, April 19, 1865.

44. Roscoe, *Web of Conspiracy*, 243.

45. *New York Times*, April 19, 1865; *Boston Daily Advertiser*, April 19, 1865.

46. *Boston Daily Advertiser*, April 19, 1865; Washington *Evening Star*, April 22, 1865; *New York Times*, April 19, 1865.

47. Washington *Evening Star*, April 22, 1865; Roscoe, 244; New Orleans *Daily Picayune*, May 12, 1865; *New York Times*, May 15, 1865.

48. Weichmann, *A True History of the Assassination*, 187.

49. Ibid., 219.

21. The Wrath of God and Man

1. Bryan, *The Great American Myth*, 200.
2. Graf, *Papers of Andrew Johnson*, 597.
3. Roscoe, *Web of Conspiracy*, 310.
4. Ibid.
5. *New York Times*, May 2, 1865.
6. Bryan, *The Great American Myth*, 284.
7. Ibid., 285.
8. *Philadelphia Inquirer*, April 25, 1865.
9. Ibid., April 20, 1865; *Chicago Tribune*, April 20, 1865; Washington (D.C.) *Evening Star*, April 20, 1865.
10. *New York Times*, April 22, 1865.
11. Downey, *Schuykill County*, 14.
12. Ibid., 15.
13. Ibid.
14. Roscoe, *Web of Conspiracy*, 300; New Orleans *Daily Picayune*, May 3, 1865.
15. *Hartford* (Conn.) *Daily Times*, April 24, 1865.
16. *New York Times*, May 1, 2, 1865; *Philadelphia Inquirer*, April 19, 25, 1865; Munroe, "Recollections of Lincoln's Assassination," 427; Bryan, *The Great American Myth*, 228–29; *Albany* (N.Y.) *Evening Journal*, April 21, 1865; Washington *Evening Star*, April 20, 1865.
17. Goodrich, *The Day Dixie Died*, 29–30.
18. Rathbun, "The Rathbone Connection."
19. *Leavenworth* (Kans.) *Daily Conservative*, April 23, 1865.
20. Bryan, *The Great American Myth*, 229.
21. Washington (D.C.) *Daily Times*, April 18, 1865.
22. Roscoe, *Web of Conspiracy*, 311.
23. Ibid.
24. L. B. Baker, "An Eyewitness Account of the Death and Burial of J. Wilkes Booth," *Journal of the Illinois State Historical Society*, December 1946, 427.
25. Weichmann, *A True History of the Assassination*, 61.
26. *New York Times*, May 1, 1865; Roscoe, 331; *Hartford* (Conn.) *Daily Times*, April 24, 1865.
27. Bryan, *The Great American Myth*, 197–98.
28. Virginia (Nev.) *Daily Territorial Enterprise*, April 18, 1865.
29. E. Jonas letter, Lincoln Museum, Fort Wayne, Indiana.
30. Edward Bates papers, Library of Congress.
31. *Chicago Tribune*, April 28, 1865.
32. Ibid.
33. Mortimer Blake, "Human Depravity: Sermon on John Wilkes Booth," vol. 14, Rare Book and Special Collections, Library of Congress.
34. Roger L. Rosentreter, "Our Lincoln Is Dead," *Michigan History*, March/April 2000, 36.

22. The Curse of Cain

1. Clarke, *The Unlocked Book*, 179; Rhodehamel and Taper, *Right or Wrong*, n. 156; Nicolay and Hay, *Abraham Lincoln*, 308–09.
2. Burnett, "Assassination of President Lincoln," 6.

3. *New York Times*, May 1, 1865.

4. Ibid.; Washington *Evening Star*, April 20, July 7, 1865.

5. *New York Times*, May 1, 1865; Nicolay and Hay, *Abraham Lincoln*, 308–09.

6. Roscoe, *Web of Conspiracy*, 216, 217; Weichmann, *A True History of the Assassination*, 194.

7. Roscoe, *Web of Conspiracy*, 217.

8. New Orleans *Daily Picayune*, April 25, 1865.

9. Ibid., April 30, 1865.

10. Goodrich, *The Day Dixie Died*, 51.

11. San Francisco *Daily Alta California*, April 16, 1865.

12. Rhodehamel and Taper, *Right or Wrong*, 157.

13. Ibid., 154, 155.

14. Clarke, *The Unlocked Book*, 110.

15. Ibid., 129.

16. Ibid., 131.

17. Ibid., 132.

18. Asia Booth Clarke letter, "Dear Jean," May 22, 1865, Ford's Theater archive.

19. Washington *Evening Star*, April 21, 1865.

20. Goodrich, *The Day Dixie Died*, 30.

21. *New Orleans Times*, May 2, 1865; *Chicago Tribune*, April 22, 1865.

22. *New Orleans Times*, May 2, 1865.

23. "Lincolniana," *Journal of the Illinois State Historical Society*, March 1948, 66.

24. Bryan, *The Great American Myth*, 243.

25. Clark, *The Assassination*, 116.

26. Judson Bemis letter, April 19, 1865, Bemis Collection, Missouri Historical Society, St. Louis.

27. Randall, *Mary Lincoln*, 347.

28. Luthin, *The Real Abraham Lincoln*, 662.

29. Virginia Jeans Laas, ed., *Wartime Washington: The Civil War Letters of Elizabeth Blair Lee* (Urbana: University of Illinois Press, 1991), 499.

30. Turner and Turner, *Mary Todd Lincoln*, 282.

31. Laas, *Wartime Washington*, 498.

32. Ibid., 497, 499.

33. Kunhardt and Kunhardt, *Twenty Days*, 119.

34. Randall, *Mary Lincoln*, 346.

35. Kunhardt and Kunhardt, *Twenty Days*, 120.

23. The Mid-week Sabbath

1. *Boston Daily Advertiser*, April 19, 1865.

2. "Two Letters," Charles Sanford letter, April 18, 1865.

3. Helen Varnum Hill McCalla diary, Library of Congress.

4. Randall, *Diary of Orville Hickman Browning*, 22.

5. Boston *Evening Standard*, April 22, 1865.

6. Ibid.

7. Du Barry, "Eyewitness Account of Lincoln's Assassination," 370.

8. Brooks, *Washington, D.C. in Lincoln's Time*, 234; "Two Letters," Charles Sanford letter.

9. Letter from "Lucian," April 18, 1865, to "Abbie," Ford's Theater archives; Brooks, *Washington, D.C. in Lincoln's Time*, 233.

10. Brooks, *Washington, D.C. in Lincoln's Time*, 234; Townsend, *The Life, Crime and Capture of John Wilkes Booth*, 17.

11. Luthin, *The Real Abraham Lincoln*, 667; Brooks, *Washington, D.C. in Lincoln's Time*, 233.

12. Nicolay and Hay, *Abraham Lincoln*, 317; Brooks, *Washington, D.C. in Lincoln's Time*, 234; Luthin, *The Real Abraham Lincoln*, 667; Washington *Evening Star*, April 20, 1865.

13. Van Deusen, *William Henry Seward*, 415; Springfield *Illinois State Journal*, April 18, 1865.

14. Brooks, *Washington, D.C. in Lincoln's Time*, 235; *Diary of Gideon Welles*, 293.

15. Brooks, *Washington, D.C. in Lincoln's Time*, 236.

16. Springfield *Illinois State Journal*, April 22, 1865.

17. Searcher, *The Farewell to Lincoln*, 66.

18. *Boston Daily Advertiser*, April 20, 1865.

19. Gardner Brewer letters, Illinois State Historical Society, Springfield.

20. New Orleans *Daily Picayune*, April 29, 1865.

21. Nellie Blow letter, April 21, 1865, Blow Family papers, Missouri Historical Society, St. Louis.

22. New Orleans *Daily Picayune*, April 28, 1865.

23. Francis French letter, April 23, 1865, Benjamin B. French Family papers, Library of Congress.

24. *Boston Daily Advertiser*, April 24, 1865.

25. *Abilene* (Kans.) *Journal*, February 3, 1887.

26. Ibid.; *New York Times*, May 18, 1865; Edgar Langsdorf, "The Mad Hatter of Kansas," *Prairie Scout*, vol. 4 (Abilene: Kansas Corral of the Westerners, 1981), 59.

27. Wilmington *Delaware Republican*, May 11, 1865; Langsdorf, "The Mad Hatter of Kansas," 59.

28. Earl C. Kubicek, "The Case of the Mad Hatter," *Lincoln Herald*, Fall 1981, 708.

29. Ibid., 709; Wilmington *Delaware Republican*, May 11, 1865.

30. *New York Times*, May 2, 1865.

31. Baltimore *American*, May 3, 1865.

32. *Newark* (N.J.) *Daily Advertiser*, May 1, 1865.

33. William C. Norton testimony, Boston Corbett pension files, National Archives; Kubicek, "The Case of the Mad Hatter," 708; Langsdorf, "The Mad Hatter of Kansas," 60.

34. Kubicek, "The Case of the Mad Hatter," 708.

35. *Newark* (N.J.) *Daily Advertiser*, May 1, 1865.

36. Wilmington *Delaware Republican*, May 11, 1865.

37. *New York Times*, May 2, 1865.

38. Wilmington *Delaware Republican*, May 11, 1865.

39. *New York Times*, May 2, 1865.

40. Byron Berkeley Johnson, *Abraham Lincoln and Boston Corbett with Personal Recollections of Each* (Waltham, Mass., 1914), 48.

41. *New York Times*, May 2, 1865.

42. Ibid; Boston Corbett letter to "Dear Brother Eddy," May 13, 1865, Boston Corbett papers, Kansas State Historical Society, Topeka.

43. Johnson, *Abraham Lincoln and Boston Corbett*, 50.

24. Oh! Abraham Lincoln!

1. George C. Maynard, "That Evening at Ford's," Ford's Theater archive.

2. Luthin, *The Real Abraham Lincoln*, 668.

3. Power, *Abraham Lincoln*, 34.

4. Ibid., 35; Kunhardt and Kunhardt, *Twenty Days*, 141; *Chicago Tribune*, April 22, 1865.

5. *New York Tribune*, April 22, 1865.

6. Kunhardt and Kunhardt, *Twenty Days*, 143.

7. Power, *Abraham Lincoln*, 35; Ozias Hatch letters, to "Julia," April 22, 1865, Sangamon Valley Collection, Lincoln Library, Springfield, Illinois.

8. Kunhardt and Kunhardt, 143; Power, 36.

9. *Philadelphia Inquirer*, April 24, 1865.

10. Kunhardt and Kunhardt, *Twenty Days*, 144.

11. Washington *Evening Star*, April 28, 1865.

12. Kunhardt and Kunhardt, *Twenty Days*, 144.

13. Boston *Daily Advertiser*, April 24, 1865; Ozias Hatch letter, April 22, 1865.

14. Peskin, "Putting the 'Baboon' to Rest," 26.

15. Ibid.

16. Kunhardt and Kunhardt, *Twenty Days*, 144; Power, *Abraham Lincoln*, 37.

17. Power, *Abraham Lincoln*, 37.

18. Searcher, *The Farewell to Lincoln*, 111.

19. Boston *Daily Advertiser*, April 24, 1865.

20. Ibid.

21. Undated, untitled newspaper clipping, Ford's Theater archives; Boston *Daily Advertiser*, April 24, 1865.

22. Jessie Ames Marshall, ed., *Private and Official Correspondence of Gen. Benjamin F. Butler during the Period of the Civil War*, vol. 5 (Norwood, Mass.: The Plimpton Press, 1917), 598.

23. *Chicago Tribune*, April 24, 1865.

24. Ibid.

25. Boston *Daily Advertiser*, April 24, 1865; W. Springer Menge and J. August Shimrak, eds., *The Civil War Notebook of Daniel Chisholm: A Chronicle of Daily Life in the Union Army, 1861–1865* (New York: Orion, 1989), 158.

26. *Chicago Tribune*, April 24, 1865.

27. New York *World*, April 25, 1865.

28. *Chicago Tribune*, April 24, 1865.

29. Henry S. Wilson letter, Ford's Theater archive.

30. *Philadelphia Inquirer*, April 24, 1865; Searcher, *The Farewell to Lincoln*, 117; New York *World*, April 25, 1865; Kunhardt and Kunhardt, *Twenty Days*, 150.

31. *Chicago Tribune*, April 24, 1865.

32. *Philadelphia Inquirer*, April 24, 1865; Boston *Daily Advertiser*, April 24, 1865.

33. New York *World*, April 25, 1865.

34. Ibid.

35. *Philadelphia Inquirer*, April 24, 1865; *Chicago Tribune*, April 24, 1865.

36. *Philadelphia Inquirer*, April 24, 1865; Kunhardt and Kunhardt, *Twenty Days*, 150.

37. Boston *Daily Advertiser*, April 24, 1865.

38. Undated, untitled article, Ford's Theater archive.

39. Boston *Daily Advertiser*, April 24, 1865; undated, untitled article, Ford's Theater archive.

40. Searcher, *The Farewell to Lincoln*, 113.

25. The Fox and the Hounds

1. *Chicago Tribune*, April 22, 1865.
2. *New York Times*, April 27, 1865.
3. Washington *Evening Star*, June 5, 1865.
4. Roscoe, *Web of Conspiracy*, 148.
5. *Chicago Tribune*, April 28, 1865.
6. Ibid., May 3, 1865.
7. Ibid., April 28, 1865; Washington *Evening Star*, April 28, 1865.
8. Wainwright, *A Philadelphia Perspective*, 496.
9. Goodrich, *The Day Dixie Died*, 144.
10. Washington *Evening Star*, April 28, 1865.
11. Goodrich, *The Day Dixie Died*, 142–43; *New York Times*, May 2, 1865.
12. Burnett, *Assassination of President Lincoln*, online edition.
13. Ibid.
14. Ibid.
15. Roscoe, *Web of Conspiracy*, 274.
16. Randall, *Diary of Orville Hickman Browning*, 28.
17. Weichmann, *A True History of the Assassination*, 227.
18. Roscoe, *Web of Conspiracy*, 265.
19. Ibid., 268.
20. Ibid., 265; Washington *Evening Star*, July 7, 1865. Steers, *Blood on the Moon*, 209.
21. Washington *Evening Star*, July 7, 1865.
22. Roscoe, *Web of Conspiracy*, 264–65; James L. Swanson and Daniel R. Weinburg, *Lincoln's Assassins: Their Trial and Execution* (Santa Fe, N.M.: Arena Editions, 2001), 17; George L. Porter, "How Booth's Body Was Hidden: The True Story Told for the First Time in the Columbian," box 7, Otto Eisneshiml collection, Illinois State Historical Library, Springfield.
23. Roscoe, *Web of Conspiracy*, 265.
24. Bryan, *The Great American Myth*, 235.
25. Ibid., 235.
26. Roscoe, *Web of Conspiracy*, 148.
27. Graf, *The Papers of Andrew Johnson*, 578–79.
28. Turner, *Beware the People Weeping*, 113.
29. Untitled newspaper clipping, June 10, 1865, Ford's Theater archive; *The War of the Rebellion*, series 1, XLVI, pt. 1, 1318.
30. Baker, "An Eyewitness Account," 429.

26. Blade of Fate

1. Betsy Fleet, ed., "A Chapter of Unwritten History: Richard Baynham Garrett's Account of the Flight and Death of John Wilkes Booth," *Virginia Magazine of History and Biography*, October 1963, 393.
2. Washington *Evening Star*, May 6, 1865.

3. Hanchett, *The Lincoln Murder Conspiracies*, 152.

4. Edwina Booth Grossman, *Edwin Booth: Recollections by His Daughter* (New York: Century, 1894), 227.

5. Clarke, *The Unlocked Book*, 43.

6. Rhodehamel and Taper, *Right or Wrong*, 4.

7. Clarke, *The Unlocked Book*, 31.

8. Ibid., 34, 102.

9. Reck, *A. Lincoln*, 63.

10. Ibid.

11. Clarke, *The Unlocked Book*, 56–57.

12. Ibid., 57.

13. Ibid., 57, 73, 91.

14. *Chicago Tribune*, April 25, 1865.

15. *New York Times*, April 21, 1865.

16. Boston *Daily Advertiser*, April 26, 1865; Kunhardt and Kunhardt, *Twenty Days*, 169.

17. *New York Times*, April 25, 1865.

18. Ibid., April 26, 1865.

19. Springfield *Illinois State Journal*, May 5, 1865.

20. Boston *Daily Advertiser*, April 26, 1865.

21. Charles and Ellen Tree Kean letter, May 4, 1865, Sol Smith collection, Missouri Historical Society, St. Louis.

22. Boston *Daily Advertiser*, April 26, 1865.

23. Searcher, *The Farewell to Lincoln*, 126–27.

24. Boston *Daily Advertiser*, April 26, 1865.

25. Undated, untitled newspaper clipping, Ford's Theater archive.

26. *New York Times*, April 25, 1865.

27. Kunhardt and Kunhardt, *Twenty Days*, 166.

28. Springfield *Illinois State Journal*, May 3, 1865.

29. *New York Times*, April 26, 1865.

30. *Chicago Tribune*, April 25, 1865; *War of the Rebellion*, ser. 1, XLVI, pt. 3, 952, 965.

31. Kunhardt and Kunhardt, *Twenty Days*, 166.

32. Searcher, *The Farewell to Lincoln*, 134.

33. *New York Times*, April 26, 1865.

34. Boston *Daily Advertiser*, April 26, 1865.

35. Ibid.; *New York Times*, April 26, 1865.

27. The Bad Hand

1. Louis Savage affidavit, Edward P. Doherty collection, Illinois State Historical Library, Springfield; Pittman, *The Assassination of President Lincoln*, 91; Tidwell, Hall, and Gaddy, *Come Retribution*, 476.

2. Weichmann, *A True History of the Assassination*, 216.

3. Baker, "An Eyewitness Account," 433.

4. *New York Times*, April 29, 1865.

5. Untitled newspaper clipping, June 10, 1865, Ford's Theater archives; Pittman, *The Assassination of President Lincoln*, 91.

6. Pittman, *The Assassination of President Lincoln*, 91.

7. Baker, "An Eyewitness Account," 433.

8. Untitled newspaper clipping, June 10, 1865, Ford's Theater archive.

9. William McQuade statement, Edward P. Doherty collection, Illinois State Historical Library, Springfield.

10. *New York Times*, January 18, 1895.

11. Pittman, *The Assassination of President Lincoln*, 91–92; Baker, "An Eyewitness Account," 434.

12. "The Death of John Wilkes Booth, 1865," 3, online edition, http://www.ibiscom.com/booth.htm.

13. Baker, "An Eyewitness Account," 434.

14. Ibid.

15. Washington *Evening Star*, April 28, 1865.

16. Baker, "An Eyewitness Account," 435–36.

17. William H. Garrett, "True Story of the Capture of John Wilkes Booth," *Confederate Veteran* 29 (1921): 129.

18. Ibid., 129–30.

19. Baker, "An Eyewitness Account," 436.

20. Pittman, *The Assassination of President Lincoln*, 92.

21. David Barker statement, Edward P. Doherty collection, Illinois State Historical Library, Springfield.

22. Washington *Evening Star*, April 28, 1865.

23. Pittman, *The Assassination of President Lincoln*, 94.

24. Herman Newgarten statement, Edward P. Doherty collection, Illinois State Historical Library, Springfield; John W. Millington, "A Cavalryman's Account of the Chase and Capture of John Wilkes Booth," online edition, Abraham Lincoln Research Site, 3.

25. Garrett, "True Story of the Capture," 129.

26. Pittman, *The Assassination of President Lincoln*, 95.

27. Ibid., 92.

28. Baker, "An Eyewitness Account," 436.

29. David Barker statement, Edward P. Doherty collection, Illinois State Historical Library, Springfield.

30. Weichmann, *A True History of the Assassination*, 216–17.

31. Baker, "An Eyewitness Account," 436.

32. Kubicek, "The Case of the Mad Hatter," 712.

33. Pittman, *The Assassination of President Lincoln*, 92.

34. Baker, "An Eyewitness Account," 436, 437.

35. Ibid., 437.

36. Ibid., 440.

37. Ibid.

38. Ibid.

39. Frank G. Carpenter, "John Wilkes Booth: A Talk with the Man That Captured Him," *Lippincott's Magazine*, September 1887, 451; *New York Times*, May 18, 1865.

40. Ibid.

41. Ibid.; Bryan, *Great American Myth*, 269.

42. L. K. B. Holloway reminiscence, John Wilkes Booth file, Espionage Items collection, Museum of the Confederacy, Richmond.

43. Ibid.

44. Millington, "A Cavalryman's Account," 3.

45. Pittman, *The Assassination of President Lincoln*, 95.

46. Millington, "A Cavalryman's Account," 3.

47. Roscoe, *Web of Conspiracy*, 401.

48. Bryan, *Great American Myth*, 269.

49. Baker, "An Eyewitness Account," 439.

50. Bryan, *The Great American Myth*, 270.

51. Baker, "An Eyewitness Account," 439.

52. Ibid.

53. *Chicago Tribune*, May 3, 1865.

54. Baker, "An Eyewitness Account," 441; Goodrich, *The Day Dixie Died*, 53.

55. Goodrich, *The Day Dixie Died*, 53.

56. Horace Bushnell testimony, Boston Corbett Pension files, National Archives.

28. The Hate of Hate

1. Washington *Evening Star*, April 28, 1865.

2. Ibid.; *New York Times*, May 1, 1865; *New Orleans Times*, May 3, 1865.

3. Clarke, *The Unlocked Book*, 128.

4. *Newark* (N.J.) *Daily Advertiser*, May 1, 1865.

5. Asia Booth Clarke letter, May 22, 1865, to "dear Jean," Ford's Theater archive.

6. Springfield *Daily Illinois State Journal*, May 4, 1865.

7. *New York Times*, May 2, 1865.

8. Washington *Evening Star*, April 27, 1865; *Chicago Tribune*, April 27, 1865; Lattimer and Alford, "Eyewitness to History," 97.

9. *Chicago Tribune*, April 28, 1865.

10. Washington *Evening Star*, July 7, 1865; Roscoe, *Web of Conspiracy*, 412–13; Baker, "An Eyewitness Account," 444.

11. Roscoe, *Web of Conspiracy*, 413.

12. Washington *Evening Star*, July 7, 1865.

13. Byron B. Johnson, pamphlet, "Boston Corbett, Who Shot John Wilkes Booth," Rare Books and Special Collections, Library of Congress.

14. Johnson, *Abraham Lincoln and Boston Corbett*, 38.

15. Johnson, "Boston Corbett, Who Shot John Wilkes Booth."

16. Ibid.

17. Ibid.; Washington *Evening Star*, April 27, 1865; Langsdorf, "The Mad Hatter of Kansas."

18. Bryan, *The Great American Myth*, 270.

19. *Abilene* (Kans.) *Journal*, February 3, 1887.

20. *Newark* (N.J.) *Daily Advertiser*, May 1, 1865.

21. Baltimore *American*, May 3, 1865.

22. *New York Times*, April 28, 1865.

23. *Chicago Tribune*, May 10, 1865.

24. Peskin, "Putting the 'Baboon' to Rest," 28.

25. Menge and Shimrak, *Civil War Notebook of Daniel Chisholm*, 158; Fusz diary, April 30, 26. *Chicago Tribune*, April 28, 1865.

27. Hanchett, *The Lincoln Murder Conspiracies*, 125.

28. Turner, *Beware the People Weeping*, 121.

29. *Chicago Tribune*, May 10, 1865.

30. Ibid.

31. Washington *Evening Star*, April 28, 1865.

32. *New York Times*, May 2, 1865.

33. Washington *Evening Star*, May 1, 1865.

34. Charles O. Paullin, "The Navy and the Booth Conspirators," *Journal of the Illinois State Historical Society*, September 1940, 275.

35. John Frederick May, "The Positive Identification of the Body of John Wilkes Booth," online edition, http://www.geocities.com/CapitolHill/Lobby/1510/booth.txt.

36. Roscoe, *Web of Conspiracy*, 413.

37. Munroe, "Recollections of Lincoln's Assassination," 432.

38. May, "The Positive Identification of the Body."

39. Washington *Evening Star*, April 28, 1865; Steers, *Blood on the Moon*, 263.

40. Munroe, "Recollections of Lincoln's Assassination," 431–32.

41. *New York Times*, May 1, 1865; William H. Townsend, *Lincoln and His Wife's Home Town* (Indianapolis: Bobbs-Merrill, 1929), 371.

42. *Chicago Tribune*, April 28, 1865.

29. The Heart of Israel

1. Undated, unnamed newspaper clipping, "Mob Attacked Gloater over Lincoln Death," Michigan State Archives, Lansing; Power, *Abraham Lincoln*, 71; Peskin, "Putting the 'Baboon' to Rest," 28.

2. Peskin, "Putting the 'Baboon' to Rest," 28.

3. Power, *Abraham Lincoln*, 59.

4. *Chicago Tribune*, 26, 1865.

5. Nicolay and Hay, *Abraham Lincoln*, 321.

6. *Chicago Tribune*, April 26, 1865.

7. Power, *Abraham Lincoln*, 63; Nicolay and Hay, *Abraham Lincoln*, 321; Mary Louise Coffin memoir, Lincoln Museum, Fort Wayne, Indiana.

8. Kunhardt and Kunhardt, *Twenty Days*, 173.

9. Untitled newspaper clipping, May 1, 1865, Ford's Theater archive.

10. Ozias Hatch letter, April 27, 1865.

11. Power, *Abraham Lincoln*, 66–67.

12. "Death and Funeral of Abraham Lincoln: A Contemporary Description by Mrs. Ellen Kean," Illinois State Historical Library, Springfield; Ellen Tree Kean letter, May 4, 1865, Sol Smith collection, Missouri Historical Society, St. Louis.

13. Searcher, *The Farewell to Lincoln*, 186, 218.

14. Power, *Abraham Lincoln*, 66–67.

15. Hatch letter, April 27, 1865.

16. Nicolay and Hay, *Abraham Lincoln*, 321; undated, untitled newspaper clipping, Ford's Theater archive.

17. Nicolay and Hay, *Abraham Lincoln*, 321.

18. *New York Times*, April 29, 1865.

19. Washington *Evening Star*, April 28, 1865.

20. "Lincoln's Funeral in Cleveland," *Lincoln Lore*, April 1968, 2.

21. Ibid.

22. Nicolay and Hay, *Abraham Lincoln*, 347.

23. "Lincoln's Funeral in Cleveland," 1.

24. *New York Times*, April 26, 1865; Wilmington *Delaware Republican*, May 4, 1865.

25. Luthin, *The Real Abraham Lincoln*, 663.

26. Ibid.

27. Undated, untitled newspaper clipping, Ford's Theater archive.

28. "Lincoln's Funeral in Cleveland," 3; Henry S. Wilson letter, April 21, 1865, Ford's Theater archive.

29. *Chicago Tribune*, April 28, 1865.

30. *New York Times*, April 25, 1865.

31. *Philadelphia Inquirer*, April 24, 1865.

32. *New York Times*, April 22, 1865.

33. *Chicago Tribune*, April 22, 1865.

34. Washington, D.C. police blotter, 1865, National Archives.

35. *New York Times*, April 25, 1865; New York *World*, April 25, 1865; Boston *Daily Advertiser*, April 24, 1865.

36. Kunhardt and Kunhardt, *Twenty Days*, 222.

37. Ibid., 226; Undated, untitled newspaper clipping, Ford's Theater archives; Levi R. Hiffner letter, Indiana Historical Society, Indianapolis; S. N. Kephart statement, Ross-Kidwell papers, Indiana Historical Society, Indianapolis.

38. John Jefferson diary, Filson Club Historical Society, Louisville, Kentucky.

39. Undated, untitled newspaper clipping, Ford's Theater archive.

40. Ellen Tree Kean letter, May 4, 1865, Sol Smith collection, Missouri Historical Society, St. Louis.

41. *Chicago Tribune*, April 28, 1865.

42. Springfield *Daily Illinois State Journal*, May 4, 1865; "Lincoln's Funeral in Cleveland," 2.

43. Charles C. Appel diary, Historical Society of Pennsylvania, Philadelphia.

44. Undated, untitled newspaper clipping, Ford's Theater archive.

45. Power, *Abraham Lincoln*, 98–99.

46. Undated, untitled newspaper clipping, Ford's Theater archive.

47. Chicago *Evening Journal*, May 3, 24, 1865.

48. Undated, untitled newspaper clipping, Ford's Theater archive.

49. Ibid.

50. Ibid.

30. Dust to Dust

1. Porter, "How Booth's Body Was Hidden," 71.

2. Ibid., 70; Washington *Evening Star*, July 7, 1865.

3. Baker, "An Eyewitness Account," 445.

4. Ibid.; Washington *Evening Star*, July 7, 1865.

5. Baker, "An Eyewitness Account," 455.

6. Ibid.

7. Porter, "How Booth's Body Was Hidden," 71.

8. Baker, "An Eyewitness Account," 446.

9. *Chicago Tribune*, April 29, 1865.

10. Mildred Lewis Rutherford, "Miss Rutherford's Scrapbook: Valuable Information about the South—The Assassination of Abraham Lincoln," vol. 2 (Athens, Ga., 1924), 9.

11. Baker, "An Eyewitness Account," 446.

12. John Q. Anderson, ed., *Brokenburn: The Journal of Kate Stone, 1861–1868* (Baton Rouge: Louisiana State University Press, 1955), 341.

13. *Chicago Tribune*, May 10, 1865; Cora Owens Hume diary, Filson Club Historical Society, Louisville, Kentucky.

14. Blake, *Human Depravity*, 4.

15. Theodore Edgar Saint John letter, May 4, 1865, Library of Congress.

16. *Alton* (Ill.) *Telegraph*, May 12, 1865; Springfield *Daily Illinois State Journal*, May 4, 1865.

17. James T. Hickey, "Springfield, May, 1865," *Journal of the Illinois State Historical Society* 58 (Spring 1965): 33.

18. Elbridge Atwood letter, May 7, 1865, Atwood Family letters, Illinois State Historical Library, Springfield.

19. Springfield *Daily Illinois State Journal*, May 8, 1865.

20. Kunhardt and Kunhardt, *Twenty Days*, 256.

21. Octavia Roberts Corneau, ed., "A Girl in the Sixties: Excerpts From the Journal of Anna Ridgely," *Journal of the Illinois State Historical Society* 22 (October 1929): 444–45.

22. Springfield *Daily Illinois State Journal*, May 3, 5, 1865.

23. Beall, "Recollections of the Assassination and Funeral," 490.

24. Springfield *Daily Illinois State Journal*, May 2, 6, 1865; W. W. Sweet, "Bishop Matthew Simpson and the Funeral of Abraham Lincoln," *Journal of the Illinois State Historical Society* 7 (April 1914): 66, 67.

25. Luthin, *The Real Abraham Lincoln*, 674; Kunhardt and Kunhardt, *Twenty Days*, 248.

26. Luthin, *The Real Abraham Lincoln*, 674.

27. Ibid.

28. Undated, untitled newspaper clipping, Ford's Theater archives; Springfield *Daily Illinois State Journal*, May 4, 1865.

29. *Alton* (Ill.) *Telegraph*, May 12, 1865; Power, *Abraham Lincoln*, 114–15; Beall, *Recollections*, 492.

30. Luthin, *The Real Abraham Lincoln*, 674.

31. *Chicago Tribune*, May 6, 1865.

32. Elbridge Atwood letter, May 7, 1865; Kunhardt and Kunhardt, *Twenty Days*, 257.

33. Beall, *Recollections*, 492.

34. Kunhardt and Kunhardt, *Twenty Days*, 301; Luthin, *The Real Abraham Lincoln*, 675–76.

35. *Chicago Tribune*, May 6, 1865.

36. Springfield *Daily Illinois State Journal*, May 6, 1865.

37. Goodrich, *The Day Dixie Died*, 63.

38. George Buckley letter, May 1, 1865, Buckley Family papers, Indiana Historical Society, Indianapolis.

31. Old Scores

1. Springfield *Daily Illinois State Journal*, May 3, 1865.

2. John Armstrong letter, Illinois State Historical Library, Springfield.

3. Horatio Nelson Taft diary, Library of Congress.

4. Springfield *Daily Illinois State Journal*, May 15, 1865.

5. Ibid.

6. Franklin, *Diary of James T. Ayers*, 101.

7. Ibid.

8. Jaquette, *South after Gettysburg*, 182.

9. William C. Davis, *An Honorable Defeat: The Last Days of the Confederate Government* (New York: Harcourt, 2001), 302.

10. *Chicago Tribune*, May 15, 22, 1865.

11. Julia Trumbull letters, May 16 and May 17, 1865, box 1, folder 15, Lyman Trumbull collection, Illinois State Historical Library, Springfield.

12. Goodrich, *The Day Dixie Died*, 69.

13. *Council Bluffs* (Iowa) *Bugle*, June 22, 1865.

14. Edward Payson Goodwin letter, June 1, 1865, Illinois State Historical Library, Springfield.

15. Graf, *The Papers of Andrew Johnson*, 581.

16. *New York Times*, May 6, 1865.

17. Goodrich, *The Day Dixie Died*, 77.

18. Castel, *Andrew Johnson*, 24; Springfield *Daily Illinois State Journal*, May 3, 1865; *New York Times*, May 2, 1865.

19. Washington *Evening Star*, May 27, 1865.

20. Alexandria *Louisiana Democrat*, June 14, 1865.

21. Lucius W. Barber, *Army Memoirs* (Chicago: J. M. W. Jones, 1894), 211.

22. Mackenzie, "*Maggie!*," May 28, 1865.

23. Washington *Evening Star*, May 6, 1865; Springfield *Daily Illinois State Journal*, May 3, 1865.

24. Randall, *Mary Lincoln*, 346.

25. Keckley, *Behind the Scenes*, 196.

26. Laas, *Wartime Washington*, n. 500; Simon, *Memoirs of Julia Dent Grant*, 157.

27. Gerry, "Lincoln's Last Day," 527.

28. *Boston Evening Standard*, April 22, 1865.

29. Rhodehamel and Taper, *Right or Wrong*, n., 146; Turner and Turner, *Mary Todd Lincoln*, 226; Keckley, *Behind the Scenes*, 193–94.

30. Turner and Turner, *Mary Todd Lincoln*, 228–29.

31. Ross, *The President's Wife*, 246.

32. Gerry, "Lincoln's Last Day," 527; Keckley, *Behind the Scenes*, 208.

33. Washington *Evening Star*, May 22, 1865.

34. Kunhardt and Kunhardt, *Twenty Days*, 98, 99.

35. *Chicago Tribune*, April 28, May 2, 1865.

36. Alexandria *Louisiana Democrat*, July 12, 1865.

37. Luthin, *The Real Abraham Lincoln*, 663.

38. A. Daggett letter, April 16, 1865, Ford's Theater archive.

39. Washington *Evening Star*, July 7, 1865.

40. *New York Times*, July 21, 1865.

41. Kunhardt and Kunhardt, *Twenty Days*, 97.

42. "Erroneous Assassination Reports," *Lincoln Lore*, April 1957, 2.

43. Mose Sandford letter, Ford's Theater archive.

44. *Portsmouth* (N.H.) *Journal*, May 27, 1865.

45. Roscoe, *Web of Conspiracy*, 404, 405.

46. Ben Graf Henneke, *Laura Keene: A Biography* (Tulsa, Okla.: Council Oak Books, 1990), 218.

47. Sandford letter, Ford's Theater archives.

48. Daggett letter, Ford's Theater archives.

49. Springfield (Ohio) *Daily News and Republic*, May 9, 1865.

50. Washington *Evening Star*, May 11, 1865.

51. Maggie Robinson letter, April 16, 1865, Buckley Family papers, Indiana Historical Society, Indianapolis.

52. *Portsmouth* (N.H.) *Journal*, July 15, 1865.

53. Langsdorf, "The Mad Hatter of Kansas."

54. Ibid.

55. Ibid.

56. Francis E. Leupp, *The True Story of Boston Corbett: A Lincoln Assassination Mystery Fifty Years After* (Putnam, Conn.: Privately printed, 1916), 10, 12.

57. *Lafayette* (Ind.) *Daily Courier*, May 4, 1865.

58. *Newark* (N.J.) *Daily Advertiser*, May 1, 1865.

59. "Courtmartial of Sergeant Boston Corbett," Boston Corbett collection, Kansas State Historical Society, Topeka.

60. Leupp, *The True Story of Boston Corbett*, 12.

61. Fusz diary, April 30, 1865.

62. Washington *Evening Star*, May 11, 1865.

63. Ibid., May 27, 1865.

64. *Chicago Tribune*, May 6, 1865.

65. Francis Tumblety, *A Few Passages in the Life of Dr. Francis Tumblety, the Indian Herb Doctor, etc.* (Cincinnati: Francis Tumblety, 1866), 25.

66. Ibid., 25, 26.

67. Washington *Evening Star*, June 10, 1865.

68. *Newark* (N.J.) *Daily Advertiser*, May 1, 1865; Washington *Evening Star*, May 2, 6, 1865.

32. The Living Dead

1. Washington *Evening Star*, July 7, 1865.

2. Ibid.

3. Ibid.

4. Turner, *Beware the People Weeping*, 159; Paullin, "The Navy and the Booth Conspirators," 273.

5. Washington *Evening Star*, May 9, 1865.

6. Mrs. Burton Harrison, *Recollections, Grave and Gay* (New York: Charles Scribner's Sons, 1911), 230–31.

7. Henry Kyd Douglas, *I Rode with Stonewall* (Chapel Hill: University of North Carolina Press, 1940), 343.

8. *Philadelphia Inquirer*, July 7, 1865; Washington *Evening Star*, April 28, 1865.

9. Brooks, *Washington, D.C. in Lincoln's Time*, 238; Edward Goodwin letter, to wife, June 1, 1865, Edward Payson Goodwin collection, Illinois State Historical Library, Springfield; "The Executions at Washington," *Monthly Religious Magazine*, August 1865.

10. Washington *Evening Star*, May 19, 1865.

11. Brooks, *Washington, D.C. in Lincoln's Time*, 239.

12. Ibid., 239.

13. Goodwin letter, June 1, 1865.

14. *New York Times*, July 8, 1865.

15. David Miller DeWitt, *The Assassination of Abraham Lincoln, and Its Expiation* (New York: Macmillan, 1909), 122.

16. *Pittsburgh Chronicle*, undated clipping, online edition, "The Trial of the Conspirators"; Goodwin letter, June 1, 1865.

17. *New York Times*, May 18, 1865; Washington *Evening Star*, May 19, 1865.

18. *Chicago Tribune*, May 15, 1865.

19. *New York Times*, July 8, 1865.

20. Turner, *Beware the People Weeping*, 158.

21. Ibid., 199.

22. *New York Times,* May 18, 1865.

23. Goodwin letter, June 1, 1865.

24. Washington *Evening Star,* June 5, 1865.

25. Ibid., June 13, 1865.

26. Ibid., July 7, 1865.

27. *Philadelphia Inquirer,* undated clipping, online edition, "The Trial of the Conspirators."

28. *Philadelphia Inquirer,* July 7, 1865.

29. Brooks, *Washington, D.C. in Lincoln's Time,* 238.

30. *Philadelphia Inquirer,* July 7, 1865.

31. Ibid.

32. Albany (N.Y.) *Evening Journal,* May 26, 1865.

33. John A Gray, "The Fate of the Lincoln Conspirators: The Account of the Hanging, Given by Lieutenant-Colonel Christian Rath, the Executioner," *McClure's,* October 1911, 633.

34. *Philadelphia Inquirer,* undated clipping, online edition, "The Conspiracy Trials."

35. *Lafayette* (Ind.) *Daily Courier,* May 22, 1865.

36. Swanson and Weinburg, *Lincoln's Assassins,* 19.

37. Roscoe, *Web of Conspiracy,* 442; Ford, "Behind the Curtain of a Conspiracy," 486.

38. David Miller Dewitt, *The Judicial Murder of Mary E. Surratt* (Baltimore, Md.: John Murphy, 1895), 18–19.

39. Harrison, *Recollections, Grave and Gay,* 232.

40. Douglas, *I Rode with Stonewall,* 341–42.

41. Edward Goodwin letter, June 1, 1865.

42. Brooks, *Washington, D.C. in Lincoln's Time,* 241; Washington *Evening Star,* May 29, 1865.

43. Washington *Evening Star,* July 7, 1865.

44. Richard Watts memoir, Lincoln Museum, Fort Wayne, Indiana.

45. William Spangler letter, John Ford Papers, Maryland Historical Society, Baltimore.

46. Washington *Evening Star,* June 5, 1865.

47. Gray, "The Fate of the Lincoln Conspirators," 634.

48. Harrison, *Recollections, Grave and Gay,* 232, 234.

33. The Most Dreadful Fate

1. Van Deusen, *William Henry Seward,* 416; Washington *Evening Star,* June 21, 1865.

2. Charles C. Appel diary.

3. Washington *Evening Star,* June 15, 1865; Washington *Daily Times,* May 4, 1865.

4. Washington *Evening Star,* July 7, 1865.

5. *New York Times,* July 18, 1865.

6. Washington *Evening Star,* June 5, 6, 1865.

7. *New York Times,* July 18, 1865.

8. Goodrich, *The Day Dixie Died,* 31, 77; Columbia *Missouri Statesman,* July 7, 1865.

9. *Council Bluffs* (Iowa) *Bugle,* May 25, 1865.

10. Ibid.

11. Goodrich, *The Day Dixie Died*, 170.

12. New Orleans *Daily Picayune*, May 7, 1865; Washington *Evening Star*, May 10, 1865.

13. Goodrich, *The Day Dixie Died*, 172.

14. Paul H. Bergeron, ed., *The Papers of Andrew Johnson*, vol. 8 (Knoxville: University of Tennessee Press, 1989), 11.

15. A. C. Proctor letter, Library of Congress.

16. John W. Tuttle diary, Kentucky Historical Society, Frankfort.

17. Ibid.

18. Goodrich, *The Day Dixie Died*, 174.

19. Thomas Goodrich, *Black Flag: Guerilla Warfare on the Western Border, 1861–1865* (Bloomington: Indiana University Press, 1995), 164.

20. Goodrich, *The Day Dixie Died*, 173.

21. Donald O. Dewey, ed., "Hoosier Justice: The Journal of David McDonald, 1864–1868," *Indiana Magazine of History*, September 1966, 204.

22. *Council Bluffs* (Iowa) *Bugle*, June 1, 1865; *Alton* (Ill.) *Telegraph*, May 26, 1865; Gus Frey letter, June 11, 1865, A. G. Frey collection, Illinois State Historical Library, Springfield.

23. *Alton* (Ill.) *Telegraph*, June 2, 1865.

24. Louis Philip Fusz diary.

25. Washington *Evening Star*, July 5, 1865.

26. *Philadelphia Inquirer*, July 7, 1865.

27. *New York Times*, July 8, 1865.

28. *Philadelphia Inquirer*, July 7, 1865; Washington *Evening Star*, July 6, 1865.

29. Washington *Evening Star*, July 6, 1865; *Philadelphia Inquirer*, July 7, 1865.

30. *Philadelphia Inquirer*, July 7, 1865; Swanson and Weinburg, *Lincoln's Assassins*, 25.

31. *New York Times*, July 8, 1865.

32. *Philadelphia Inquirer*, July 7, 1865; Washington *Evening Star*, July 6, 1865.

33. *Philadelphia Inquirer*, July 7, 1865.

34. Ibid.

35. Swanson and Weinburg, *Lincoln's Assassins*, 25.

36. *New York Times*, July 8, 1865.

37. Washington *Evening Star*, July 7, 1865.

38. *Providence Daily Journal*, July 10, 1865.

39. Washington *Evening Star*, July 7, 1865.

40. Ibid.

41. Dewitt, *The Judicial Murder of Mary E. Surratt*, 120.

42. *Providence Daily Journal*, July 10, 1865.

43. Ibid.

44. Ibid.; untitled clipping, July 8, 1865, Ford's Theater archive.

45. *New York Times*, July 8, 1865.

46. Undated, untitled clipping, box 8, Otto Eisenshiml collection, Illinois State Historical Library, Springfield.

47. Gray, "The Fate of the Lincoln Conspirators," 635.

48. Ibid.; Dewitt, *The Judicial Murder of Mary E. Surratt*, 141.

49. Harrison, *Recollections, Grave and Gay*, 234.

34. Beads on a String

1. *Philadelphia Inquirer*, July 8, 1865; Swanson and Weinburg, *Lincoln's Assassins*, 24.

2. Washington *Evening Star*, July 7, 1865; *New York Times*, July 8, 1865.

3. *New York Times*, July 8, 1865.

4. Washington *Evening Star*, July 7, 1865.

5. Ibid.

6. Ibid.; *Philadelphia Inquirer*, July 8, 1865.

7. Washington *Evening Star*, July 7, 1865.

8. Swanson and Weinburg, *Lincoln's Assassins*, 24.

9. Washington *Evening Star*, July 7, 1865.

10. Ibid.

11. *Philadelphia Inquirer*, July 8, 1865.

12. Washington *Daily Times*, July 8, 1865; Alexandria *Louisiana Democrat*, July 26, 1865.

13. Washington *Daily Times*, July 8, 1865.

14. *Providence Daily Journal*, July 10, 1865.

15. *Philadelphia Inquirer*, July 8, 1865; *New York Times*, July 8, 1865.

16. *New York Times*, July 8, 1865.

17. Alexandria *Louisiana Democrat*, July 26, 1865.

18. Washington *Evening Star*, July 7, 1865.

19. Alexandria *Louisiana Democrat*, July 26, 1865.

20. Washington *Evening Star*, July 7, 1865; "The Clemency Plea Debate," *Surratt Courier*, May 1986.

21. Washington *Evening Star*, July 7, 1865.

22. Ibid.; Washington *Daily Times*, July 8, 1865.

23. *Providence Daily Journal*, July 10, 1865.

24. Kunhardt and Kunhardt, *Twenty Days*, 214.

25. Ibid., 208.

26. Mary E. Trindal, "History at Its Worst," *Surratt Courier*, June 1991, Ford's Theater archive.

27. *Philadelphia Inquirer*, July 8, 1865.

28. Trindal, "History at Its Worst."

29. *Philadelphia Inquirer*, July 8, 1865.

30. Ibid.

31. Kunhardt and Kunhardt, *Twenty Days*, 209.

32. *Philadelphia Inquirer*, July 8, 1865.

33. Washington *Evening Star*, July 7, 1865; Daniel Pearson, ed., "One of the Grimmest Events I Ever Participated In: William E. Coxshall and the Execution of the Lincoln Conspirators," *The Lincoln Ledger*, November 1995, 5.

34. Pearson, "One of the Grimmest Events," 4.

35. Ibid., 5.

36. *Philadelphia Inquirer*, July 8, 1865.

37. Undated, untitled newspaper clipping, Ford's Theater archive.

38. Dewitt, *The Assassination of Abraham Lincoln*, 140.

39. Trindal, "History at Its Worst."

40. Washington *Evening Star*, July 7, 1865; Swanson and Weinburg, *Lincoln's Assassins*, 25.

41. *Philadelphia Inquirer*, July 8, 1865.

42. Ibid.

43. *Providence Daily Journal*, July 10, 1865; Washington *Evening Star*, July 7, 1865.

44. Swanson and Weinburg, *Lincoln's Assassins*, 28.

45. Washington *Evening Star*, July 10, 1865.

46. Abram Dunn Gillette, "The Last Days of Payne," Ford's Theater archives.

47. *New York Times,* July 8, 1865; Washington *Evening Star,* July 7, 1865; *Philadelphia Inquirer,* July 8, 1865.

48. Untitled clipping, July 8, 1865, Ford's Theater archive.

49. "Hanging the Conspirators Told by an Eyewitness in an Old Letter," Ford's Theater archive.

50. Alexandria *Louisiana Democrat,* July 26, 1865; Turner, *Beware the People Weeping,* 171; Weichmann, *A True History of the Assassination,* 283; Washington *Evening Star,* July 7, 1865.

51. Washington *Daily Times,* July 8, 1865; Washington *Evening Star,* July 7, 1865.

52. "Hanging the Conspirators," Ford's Theater archive.

53. Trudeau, *Out of the Storm,* 374.

54. *Providence Daily Journal,* July 10, 1865; *New York Times,* July 8, 1865.

55. *New York Times,* July 8, 1865.

56. Washington *Evening Star,* July 7, 1865.

57. Ibid.; *Philadelphia Inquirer,* July 8, 1865.

58. *Philadelphia Inquirer,* July 8, 1865.

59. *New York Times,* July 8, 1865.

60. Washington *Evening Star,* July 7, 1865.

61. Swanson and Weinburg, *Lincoln's Assassins,* 31.

62. *New York Times,* July 8, 1865.

63. Porter, "How Booth's Body Was Hidden," Eisenshiml collection, box 7, Illinois State Historical Library, Springfield.

64. Swanson and Weinburg, *Lincoln's Assassins,* 31.

65. Turner, *Beware the People Weeping,* 171.

66. Hanchett, *The Lincoln Murder Conspiracies,* 70–71.

67. Washington *Evening Star,* July 7, 1865.

68. Ibid.

69. *Providence Daily Journal,* July 10, 1865.

70. *New York Times,* July 8, 1865; *Philadelphia Inquirer,* July 8, 1865.

71. *Providence Daily Journal,* July 10, 1865.

72. Alexandria *Louisiana Democrat,* July 26, 1865.

73. Ibid.; Washington *Evening Star,* July 10, 1865; Pearson, 6; *Philadelphia Inquirer,* July 8, 1865; Gray, 636; *Milwaukee Free Press,* February 1, 1914; Undated *New York Press* clipping, "Hangman of President Lincoln's Assassins Tells His Story," Otto Eisenshiml collection, box 8, Illinois State Historical Library, Springfield.

74. *Philadelphia Inquirer,* July 8, 1865.

75. Washington *Evening Star,* July 7, 1865; Swanson and Weinburg, *Lincoln's Assassins,* 29; *New York Times,* July 8, 1865.

76. *Philadelphia Inquirer,* July 8, 1865; Washington *Evening Star,* July 7, 1865.

77. Washington *Evening Star,* July 7, 1865.

78. John J. Toffey letter, Ford's Theater archive.

79. *Providence Daily Journal,* July 10, 1865; Washington *Evening Star,* July 7, 1865.

80. Swanson and Weinburg, *Lincoln's Assassins,* 30.

81. Washington *Evening Star,* July 7, 8, 1865.

82. Trindal, "History at Its Worst."

83. Washington *National Tribune,* October 22, 1903.

84. Ibid.

85. Swanson and Weinburg, *Lincoln's Assassins,* 30; Washington *Evening Star,* July 10, 1865; Undated *New York Press* article, "Hangman," Eisenshiml collection.

86. Washington *Daily Times*, July 8, 1865.
87. Burnett, "Assassination of President Lincoln," online edition.
88. Swanson and Weinburg, *Lincoln's Assassins*, 26.
89. "Killing Women," photocopy, Ford's Theater archive.
90. "Eyewitness Accounts," binder, Ford's Theater archives.
91. Washington *Evening Star*, July 8, 1865.
92. Harrison, *Recollections, Grave and Gay*, 235.
93. Ibid.

Epilogue

1. Swanson and Weinburg, *Lincoln's Assassins*, 30.
2. Anna Surratt letter, Edwin Stanton papers, Library of Congress.
3. Bryan, *The Great American Myth*, 291.
4. Ibid., 297; Washington *Evening Star*, July 10, 11, 1865.
5. Randall, *The Diary of Orville Hickman Browning*, 37–38.
6. Ibid., 38.
7. Washington *Evening Star*, June 10, 1865.
8. Bryan, *The Great American Myth*, 297.
9. *New York Times*, July 17, 1865.
10. Letter to Ford, July 9, 1865, John Ford papers.
11. Hyman and Thomas, *Stanton*, 435.
12. Alexandria *Louisiana Democrat*, July 12, 1865.
13. Ibid.
14. *Memphis Daily Avalanche*, April 4, 1866.
15. Baker, "An Eyewitness Account," n., 427.
16. *Boston Daily Advertiser*, August 9, 1865; Leupp, *The True Story of Boston Corbett*, 11.
17. Undated clipping, *Cleveland Leader*, Ford's Theater archives.
18. Leupp, *The True Story of Boston Corbett*, 12.
19. M. V. B. Sheafor statement, Boston Corbett pension files, National Archives; Kubicek, "The Case of the Mad Hatter," 713–14; Langsdorf, "The Mad Hatter of Kansas," 63.
20. Langsdorf, "The Mad Hatter of Kansas," 64–65; Kubicek, "The Case of the Mad Hatter," 714.
21. Langsdorf, "The Mad Hatter of Kansas," 65–66.
22. Kubicek, "The Case of the Mad Hatter," 714–15; Langsdorf, "The Mad Hatter of Kansas," 66.
23. Kubicek, "The Case of the Mad Hatter," 715.
24. Ibid.
25. Kubicek, "The Case of the Mad Hatter," 716; Langsdorf, "The Mad Hatter of Kansas," 67.
26. Bryan, *The Great American Myth*, 307.
27. Fleet, "A Chapter of Unwritten History," n., 404.
28. Asia Booth letter, May 22, 1865, Ford's Theater archives.
29. Clarke, *The Unlocked Book*, 183, 185.
30. Ibid., 186; Bryan, *The Great American Myth*, 310.
31. Bryan, *The Great American Myth*, 92.
32. Ibid., 307.

33. Roscoe, *Web of Conspiracy*, 516; undated, untitled article, Ford's Theater archives.

34. Nicolay and Hay, *Abraham Lincoln*, 295.

35. "Major Rathbone and Miss Harris Guests of the Lincolns in the Ford's Theater Box," *Lincoln Lore*, August 1971, 3.

36. Rathbun, "Rathbone Connection"; *New York Times*, December 30, 1883.

37. "Major Rathbone and Miss Harris," 3; *New York Times*, December 28, 30, 1883; Reck, "The Tragedy of Major Rathbone," 205.

38. Reck, "The Tragedy of Major Rathbone," 205.

39. Ibid., 205, 206; undated, untitled newspaper clippings, Ford's Theater archives; Nicolay and Hay, *Abraham Lincoln*, 295.

40. Turner and Turner, *Mary Todd Lincoln*, 258.

41. Ibid., 225; Burlingame, *Lincoln Observed*, 197.

42. Neely and McMurtry, *The Insanity File*, 5; Turner and Turner, *Mary Todd Lincoln*, 238–39.

43. Keckley, *Behind the Scenes*, 212–13.

44. Randall, *Mary Lincoln*, 392–93.

45. Turner and Turner, *Mary Todd Lincoln*, 291, 295.

46. Randall, *Mary Lincoln*, 413.

47. Undated, untitled clipping, Ford's Theater archives.

48. David B. Chesebrough, "His Own Fault: Rev. Charles H. Ellis of Bloomington Sermonizes on the Assassination of Abraham Lincoln," *Illinois Historical Journal*, Autumn 1993, 146.

49. Undated, untitled clipping, Ford's Theater archives.

50. Washington *Daily Morning Chronicle*, April 20, 1865.

51. Nicolay and Hay, *Abraham Lincoln*, 354.

52. Randall, *Mary Lincoln*, 391.

53. Kunhardt and Kunhardt, *Twenty Days*, 257.

54. Marinacci, *O Wonderous Singer!*, 240.

55. Ibid.

BIBLIOGRAPHY

Books

Anderson, John Q., ed. *Brokenburn: The Journal of Kate Stone, 1861–1868*. Baton Rouge: Louisiana State University Press, 1955.

Avary, Myrta Lockett. *Dixie after the War: An Exposition of Social Conditions Existing in the South, during the Twelve Years Succeeding the Fall of Richmond*. New York: Doubleday, Page, 1906.

Barber, Lucius W. *Army Memoirs*. Chicago: J. M. W. Jones, 1894.

Barton, O. S. *Three Years with Quantrill: A True Story Told by His Scout John McCorkle*. 1914; reprint, Norman: University of Oklahoma, 1992.

Basler, Roy P., ed. *Walt Whitman's Memoranda during the War and Death of Abraham Lincoln*. Bloomington: Indiana University Press, 1962.

Bergeron, Paul H., ed. *The Papers of Andrew Johnson*. Knoxville: University of Tennessee Press, 1989.

Berry, Mary Clay. *Voices from the Century Before: The Odyssey of a Nineteenth-Century Kentucky Family*. New York: Arcade, 1997.

Brooks, Noah. *Washington, D. C. in Lincoln's Time*. New York: Rinehart, 1958.

Bryan, George S. *The Great American Myth*. New York: Carrick and Evans, 1940.

Buckingham, J. E. *Reminiscences and Souvenirs of the Assassination of Abraham Lincoln*. Washington, D.C.: Rufus H. Darby, 1894.

Burlingame, Michael. *The Inner World of Abraham Lincoln*. Urbana: University of Illinois Press, 1994.

Burlingame, Michael, ed. *Lincoln Observed: The Civil War Dispatches of Noah Brooks*. Baltimore, Md.: Johns Hopkins University Press, 1998.

Castel, Albert. *The Presidency of Andrew Johnson*. Lawrence: Regents Press of Kansas, 1979.

Clark, Champ. *The Assassination: Death of the President*. Alexandria, Va.: Time/Life, 1987.

Clarke, Asia Booth. *The Unlocked Book: A Memoir of John Wilkes Booth by His Sister, Asia Booth Clarke*. New York: Benjamin Blom, 1971.

Coe, David, ed. *Mine Eyes Have Seen the Glory: Combat Diaries of Union Sergeant Hamlin Alexander Coe*. Rutherford, N.J.: Fairleigh Dickinson University Press, 1975.

Coleman, J. Winston, Jr. *Lexington during the Civil War*. Lexington, Ky.: Henry Clay, 1968.

Culpepper, Marilyn Mayer. *Trials and Triumphs: Women of the American Civil War.* East Lansing: Michigan State University Press, 1991.

Current, Richard N. *The Lincoln Nobody Knows.* New York: McGraw-Hill, 1958.

Davis, William C. *An Honorable Defeat: The Last Days of the Confederate Government.* New York: Harcourt, 2001.

de Chambrun, Adolphe. *Impressions of Lincoln and the Civil War: A Foreigner's Account.* New York: Random House, 1952.

DeWitt, David Miller. *The Assassination of Abraham Lincoln, and Its Expiation.* New York: Macmillan, 1909.

———. *The Impeachment and Trial of Andrew Johnson.* New York: Macmillan, 1903.

———. *The Judicial Murder of Mary E. Surratt.* Baltimore, Md.: John Murphy, 1895.

DiLorenzo, Thomas J. *The Real Lincoln: A New Look at Abraham Lincoln, His Agenda, and an Unnecessary War.* New York: Prima, 2002.

Donald, David. *Lincoln.* New York: Simon and Schuster, 1995.

———. *Lincoln's Herndon.* New York: Alfred A. Knopf, 1948.

Douglas, Henry Kyd. *I Rode with Stonewall.* Chapel Hill: University of North Carolina Press, 1940.

Downey, Edgar. *Schuykill County and Some of Its People When Abraham Lincoln Was Assassinated.* Pottsville, Pa., 1952.

East, Charles, ed. *The Civil War Diary of Sarah Morgan.* Athens: University of Georgia Press, 1991.

Eggleston, George Cary. *A Rebel's Recollection.* Bloomington: Indiana University Press, 1959.

Ferguson, W. J. *I Saw Booth Shoot Lincoln.* Austin, Tex.: Pemberton, 1969.

Franklin, John Hope, ed. *The Diary of James T. Ayers, Civil War Recruiter.* Springfield: Illinois State Historical Society, 1947.

Good, Timothy S., ed. *We Saw Lincoln Shot: One Hundred Eyewitness Accounts.* Jackson: University Press of Mississippi, 1995.

Goodrich, Thomas, *Black Flag: Guerilla Warfare on the Western Border, 1861–1865.* Bloomington, Indiana University Press, 1995.

———. *Bloody Dawn: The Story of the Lawrence Massacre.* Kent, Ohio: Kent State University Press, 1991.

Goodrich, Thomas, and Debra Goodrich. *The Day Dixie Died: Southern Occupation, 1865–1866.* Mechanicsburg, Pa.: Stackpole, 2001.

Graf, Leroy P. *The Papers of Andrew Johnson.* Knoxville: University of Tennessee Press, 1986.

Grossman, Edwina Booth. *Edwin Booth: Recollections by His Daughter.* New York: Century, 1894.

Hale, Laura Virginia. *Four Valiant Years in the Lower Shenandoah Valley, 1861–1865.* Front Royal, Va.: Hathaway, 1986.

Hammond, Harold Earl, ed. *Diary of a Union Lady, 1861–1865.* New York: Funk and Wagnalls, 1962.

Hanchett, William. *The Lincoln Murder Conspiracies.* Urbana: University of Illinois Press, 1986.

Harrell, Carolyn L. *When the Bells Tolled for Lincoln.* Macon, Ga.: Mercer University, 1997.

Harrison, Mrs. Burton. *Recollections Grave and Gay.* New York: Charles Scribner's Sons, 1911.

Hatcher, Edmund N. *The Last Four Weeks of the War.* Columbus, Ohio, 1891.

Henneke, Ben Graf. *Laura Keene: A Biography.* Tulsa, Okla.: Council Oak Books, 1990.

Hinckley, Edith Parker. *Frank Hinckley: California Engineer and Rancher, 1838–1890.* Claremont, Calif.: Saunders, 1946.

Hodges, Glenn. *Fearful Times: A History of the Civil War Years in Hancock County, Kentucky.* Hawesville, Ky.: Hancock County Historical Society, 1986.

Holzer, Harold. *Dear Mr. Lincoln: Letters to the President.* Reading, Mass.: Addison/Wesley, 1993.

Hyman, Harold, and Benjamin Platt Thomas. *Stanton: The Life and Times of Lincoln's Secretary of War.* New York: Alfred A. Knopf, 1962.

Jaquette, Henrietta Stratton. *South after Gettysburg: Letters of Cornelia Hancock, 1863–1868.* New York: Thomas Y. Crowell, 1956.

James, James R. *To See the Elephant: The Civil War Letters of John A. McKee, 1861–1865.* Kansas City, Mo.: Leathers, 1998.

Johnson, Byron Berkeley. *Abraham Lincoln and Boston Corbett with Personal Recollections of Each.* Waltham, Mass., 1914.

Jones, Jenkin Lloyd. *An Artilleryman's Diary.* Madison: Wisconsin History Commission, 1914.

Kaplan, Justin. *Walt Whitman: A Life.* New York: Simon and Schuster, 1980.

Keckley, Elizabeth. *Behind the Scenes.* New York: G. W. Carleton, 1868.

Kellogg, Mary, E., ed. *Army Life of an Illinois Soldier, Including a Day-by-Day Record of Sherman's March to the Sea: Letters and Diary of Charles W. Wills.* Carbondale: Southern Illinois University Press, 1996.

Kimball, Ivory G. *Recollections from a Busy Life.* Washington, D.C.: Carnahan, 1912.

King, Spencer Bidwell, Jr., ed. *The War-time Journal of a Georgia Girl, 1864–1865.* Macon, Ga.: Ardivan, 1960.

Kunhardt, Dorothy Meserve, and Philip B. Kunhardt, Jr. *Twenty Days: A Narrative in Text and Pictures of the Assassination of Abraham Lincoln.* New York: Harper and Row, 1965.

Kunhardt, Philip B. Jr., and Peter W. Kunhardt. *Lincoln: An Illustrated Biography.* New York: Alfred Knopf, 1992.

Laas, Virginia Jeans, ed. *Wartime Washington: The Civil War Letters of Elizabeth Blair Lee.* Urbana: University of Illinois Press, 1991.

Lamon, Ward Hill. *Recollections of Abraham Lincoln, 1847–1865.* Washington, D.C.: Dorothy Lamon Teillard, 1911.

LeConte, Emma. *When the World Ended: The Diary of Emma LeConte,* New York: Oxford University Press, 1957.

Leech, Margaret. *Reveille in Washington, 1860–1865.* New York: Harper's Brothers, 1941.

Leupp, Francis E. *The True Story of Boston Corbett: A Lincoln Assassination Mystery Fifty Years After.* Putnam, Conn., 1916.

Loftin, Tee. *Stranger's Guided Tour to Washington, D. C.: 1865: The Civil War City As Mr. Lincoln Knew It.* Washington, D.C., 1967.

Luthin, Reinhard H. *The Real Abraham Lincoln: A Complete One Volume History of His Life and Times.* Englewood Cliffs, N.J.: Prentice Hall, 1960.

Mackenzie, Muriel Davies. *Maggie! Maggie Lindsley's Journal.* Southbury, Conn., 1977.

Marinacci, Barbara. *O Wonderous Singer! An Introduction to Walt Whitman.* New York: Dodd, Mead, 1970.

Marshall, Jessie Ames, ed. *Private and Official Correspondence of Gen. Benjamin F. Butler during the Period of the Civil War.* Norwood, Mass.: Plimpton Press, 1917.

Marshall, John A. *American Bastille: A History of the Illegal Arrests and Imprisonment of American Citizens During the Late Civil War.* Philadelphia: Thomas W. Hartley, 1870.

Massey, Mary Elizabeth. *Bonnet Brigades*. New York: Alfred A. Knopf, 1966.

Menge, W. Springer, and J. August Shimrak, eds. *The Civil War Notebook of Daniel Chisholm: A Chronicle of Daily Life in the Union Army, 1861–1865*. New York: Orion, 1989.

Neely, Mark E., Jr. *The Fate of Liberty: Abraham Lincoln and Civil Liberties*. New York: Oxford University Press, 1991.

Neely, Mark E., Jr., and R. Gerald McMurtry. *The Insanity File: The Case of Mary Todd Lincoln*. Carbondale: Southern Illinois University Press, 1986.

Nicolay, John G., and John Hay. *Abraham Lincoln: A History*. New York: Century, 1890.

Niven, John, ed. *The Salmon P. Chase Papers*, vol. 5. Kent, Ohio: Kent State University, 1998.

Painter, Ruth Randall. *Mary Lincoln: Biography of a Marriage*. Boston: Little, Brown, 1953.

Palmer, Beverly Wilson, ed. *The Selected Letters of Charles Sumner*. Boston: Northeastern University Press, 1990.

Paludin, Phillip Shaw, *The Presidency of Abraham Lincoln*. Lawrence: University Press of Kansas, 1995.

Pittman, Benn. *The Assassination of President Lincoln and the Trial of the Conspirators*. New York: Funk and Wagnalls, 1954.

Power, J. C. *Abraham Lincoln, His Great Funeral Cortege, from Washington City to Springfield, Illinois, with a History and Description of the National Lincoln Monument*. Springfield, Ill., 1872.

Randall, James G., ed. *The Diary of Orville Hickman Browning, 1865–1881*. Springfield: Illinois State Historical Library, 1933.

Reck, W. Emerson. *A Lincoln: His Last 24 Hours*. Jefferson, N.C.: McFarland, 1987.

Recollections and Reminiscences, 1861–1865. South Carolina Division, United Daughters of the Confederacy, 1992.

Rhodehamel, John and Louise Taper, eds. *Right or Wrong, God Judge Me: The Writings of John Wilkes Booth*. Urbana: University of Illinois Press, 1997.

Roscoe, Theodore. *The Web of Conspiracy: The Complete Story of the Men Who Murdered Abraham Lincoln*. Englewood Cliffs, N.J.: Prentice Hall, 1959.

Rosenblatt, Emil and Ruth, eds. *The Civil War Letters of Private Wilbur Fisk, 1861–1865*. Lawrence: University of Kansas Press, 1992.

Ross, Ishbel. *The President's Wife: Mary Todd Lincoln—A Biography*. New York: G. P. Putnam's Sons, 1973.

Schwartz, Gerald, ed. *A Woman Doctor's Civil War*. Columbia: University of South Carolina Press, 1989.

Searcher, Victor. *The Farewell to Lincoln*. New York: Abingdon, 1965.

Sherman, John. *Recollections of Forty years in the House, Senate and Cabinet: An Autobiography*. Chicago: Werner, 1895.

Simon, John Y., ed. *The Personal Memoirs of Julia Dent Grant*. Carbondale: Southern Illinois University Press, 1975.

Steers, Edward, Jr. *Blood on the Moon: The Assassination of Abraham Lincoln*. Lexington: University Press of Kentucky, 2001.

Swanson, James L., and Daniel R. Weinberg. *Lincoln's Assassins: Their Trial and Execution*. Santa Fe, N.M.: Arena Editions, 2001.

Taylor, John M. *Garfield of Ohio: The Available Man*. New York: W. W. Norton, 1970.

Tidwell, William A. *April '65: Confederate Covert Action in the American Civil War*. Kent, Ohio: Kent State University Press, 1995.

Tidwell, William A., James O. Hall, and David Winfred Gaddy. *Come Retribution: The Confederate Secret Service and the Assassination of Lincoln*. Jackson: University Press of Mississippi, 1988.

Townsend, George Alfred. *The Life, Crime, and Capture of John Wilkes Booth*. New York: Dick and Fitzgerald, 1865.

Townsend, William H. *Lincoln and His Wife's Home Town*. Indianapolis: Bobbs-Merrill, 1929.

Troutman, Richard L., ed. *The Heavens Are Weeping: The Diaries of George Richard Browder, 1852–1886*. Grand Rapids, Mich.: Zondervan, 1987.

Trudeau, Noah Andre. *Out of the Storm: The End of the Civil War, April–June 1865*. Baton Rouge: Louisiana State University Press, 1994.

Tumblety, Francis. *A Few Passages in the Life of Dr. Francis Tumblety, the Indian Herb Doctor, etc.* Cincinnati: Francis Tumblety, 1866.

Turner, Thomas Reed. *Beware the People Weeping: Public Opinion and the Assassination of Abraham Lincoln*. Baton Rouge: Louisiana State University Press, 1982.

Van Deusen, Glyndon G. *William Henry Seward*. New York: Oxford University, 1967.

Wainwright, Nicholas, ed. *A Philadelphia Perspective: The Diary of Sidney George Fisher Covering the Years 1834–1871*. Philadelphia: Historical Society of Pennsylvania, 1967.

Weichmann, Louis J. *A True History of the Assassination of Abraham Lincoln and the Conspiracy of 1865*. New York: Alfred A. Knopf, 1975.

Welles, Gideon. *Diary of Gideon Welles: Secretary of the Navy under Lincoln and Johnson*. Vol. 2. Boston: Houghton Mifflin, 1911.

Werner, Emmy E. *Reluctant Witnesses: Children's Voices from the Civil War*. Boulder, Colo.: Westview, 1998.

Wilson, Douglas, L. and Rodney O. Davis. *Herndon's Informants: Letters, Interviews, and Statements about Abraham Lincoln*. Urbana: University of Illinois Press, 1998.

Winik, Jay. *April 1865: The Month That Saved America*. New York: Harper Collins, 2001.

Articles

Abbott, Martin. "Southern Reaction to Lincoln's Assassination." *Abraham Lincoln Quarterly*, September 1952, 111–27.

Alfriend, Edward M. "Recollections of John Wilkes Booth." *The Era*. October 1901, 603–05.

Allen, C. T. "Sixteen Years Ago: Washington City of the Night of Mr. Lincoln's Assassination." In *Southern Bivouac*, vol. 1, 18–22. Wilmington, N.C.: Broadfoot, 1992.

Baker, L. B. "An Eyewitness Account of the Death and Burial of J. Wilkes Booth." *Journal of the Illinois State Historical Society*, December 1946, 425–46.

Beall, Edmond. "Recollections of the Assassination and Funeral of Abraham Lincoln." *Journal of the Illinois State Historical Society*, January 1913, 488–92.

Bearss, Margie Riddle. "Messenger of Lincoln's Death Herself Doomed." *Lincoln Herald*, Spring 1978, 49–51.

Burnett, Henry Lawrence. "Assassination of President Lincoln and the Trial of the Assassins." Online edition: http://www.tiac.net/users/ime/famtree/burnett/lincoln.htm.

Camm, R. A. "From Sailor's Creek to Johnson's Island, Lake Erie." In *Southern Bivouac*, 443–46 Wilmington, N.C.: Broadfoot, 1992.

Carpenter, Frank G. "John Wilkes Booth: A Talk with the Man That Captured Him." *Lippincott's Magazine*, September 1887, 449–51.

Chesebrough, David B. "His Own Fault: Rev. Charles H. Ellis of Bloomington Sermonizes on the Assassination of Abraham Lincoln." *Illinois Historical Journal*, Autumn 1993, 146–58.

"The Clemency Plea Debate." *Surratt Courier*, May 1986.

Corneau, Octavia Roberts, ed. "A Girl in the Sixties: Excerpts from the Journal of Anna Ridgely." *Journal of the Illinois State Historical Society*, October 1929, 401–46.

Daggett, Albert. "Within the Last 12 Hours this City has been the Scene of the Most Terrible Tragedies. . . ." *Lincoln Lore*, April 1961, 1–4.

"The Death of John Wilkes Booth, 1865." Online edition at: http://www.ibiscom.com/booth.htm.

DeMotte, William H. "The Assassination of Abraham Lincoln." *Journal of the Illinois State Historical Society*, October 1927, 422–28.

Dewey, Donald O., ed. "Hoosier Justice: The Journal of David M. Donald, 1864–1868." *Indiana Magazine of History*, September 1966.

Donald, David. "The Folklore Lincoln." *Journal of the Illinois Historical Society*, December 1947.

Drake, Frederick C. "A Letter on the Death of Abraham Lincoln, April 16, 1865." *Lincoln Herald*, Winter 1982, 237–38.

Du Barry, Helen. "Eyewitness Account of Lincoln's Assassination." *Journal of the Illinois State Historical Society*, September 1946, 366–70.

"Edwin Booth and Lincoln, with an Unpublished Letter by Edwin Booth." *Century Magazine*, April 1909, 919–20.

"Erroneous Assassination Reports." *Lincoln Lore*, April 1957.

"The Executions at Washington." *Monthly Religious Magazine*, August 1865, 116.

"Eye Witness Describes Lincoln Assassination in Letter to Brother." *Baltimore and Ohio Magazine*, February 1926.

Filler, Louis, ed. "Waiting for the War's End: An Ohio Soldier in Alabama After Learning of Lincoln's Death." *Ohio History*, Winter 1965, 55–62.

Fleet, Betsy, ed. "A Chapter of Unwritten History: Richard Baynham Garrett's Account of the Flight and Death of John Wilkes Booth." *Virginia Magazine of History and Biography*, October 1963, 387–407.

Ford, John T. "Behind the Curtain of a Conspiracy." *North American Review*, April 1889, 484–93.

Garrett, William H. "True Story of the Capture of John Wilkes Booth." *Confederate Veteran*, 1921, 129–30.

Gerry, Margarita Spalding. "Lincoln's Last Day: New Facts Now Told for the First Time by William H. Crook (His Personal Body-Guard)." *Harpers Monthly Magazine*, September 1907, 519–30.

Gray, John A. "The Fate of the Lincoln Conspirators: The Account of the Hanging, Given by Lieutenant-Colonel Christian Rath, the Executioner." *McClure's*, October 1911, 626–36.

Grover, Helen. "Lincoln's Interest in the Theater." *The Century Magazine*, April 1909, 948–50.

Hall, James O. "The Dahlgren Papers: A Yankee Plot to Kill President Davis." *Civil War Times Illustrated*, November 1983, 30–39.

Hall, Wade, and Debra C. Reynolds. "Mary Todd Lincoln: A Life of Loss." *Louisville (Ky.) Courier-Journal Magazine*, July 11, 1982.

Hickey, James T. "Springfield, May, 1865." *Journal of the Illinois State Historical Society*, Spring 1965.

Jones, James P. "Lincoln's Avengers: The Assassination and Sherman's Army." *Lincoln Herald*, Winter 1962, 185–90.

Knox, James S. "A Son Writes of the Supreme Tragedy." *Saturday Review*, February 11, 1956, 11.

Kubicek, Earl C. "The Case of the Mad Hatter." *Lincoln Herald*, Fall 1981, 708–19.

Langsdorf, Edgar. "The Mad Hatter of Kansas." In *Prairie Scout*, 59–73. Abilene: Kansas Corral of the Westerners, 1981.

Leonard, Lesley A. "Abraham Lincoln and the 'Rubber Room.'" *Surratt Courier*, February 1986.

"Lincoln's Funeral in Cleveland." *Lincoln Lore*, April 1968, 1–3.

"Lincoln's Second Inaugural: A Gala Event in Washington Society." *Lincoln Lore*, February 1959, 1–3.

MacCulloch, Campbell. "This Man Saw Lincoln Shot." *Good Housekeeping*, February 1927, 20–21, 114–18.

Maione, Michael, and James O. Hall. "Why Seward? The Attack on the Night of April 14, 1865." *Lincoln Herald*, Spring 1998, 29–34.

"Major Rathbone and Miss Harris Guests of the Lincolns in the Ford's theater Box." *Lincoln Lore*, August 1971, 1–3.

Markowitz, Arthur, M. "Tragedy of an Age: An Eyewitness Account of Lincoln's Assassination." *Journal of the Illinois State Historical Society*, Summer 1973, 205–11.

May, John Frederick. "The Positive Identification of the Body of John Wilkes Booth." Online edition at: http://www.geocities.com/CapitolHill/Lobby/1510/booth.txt.

McBride, Robert W. "Lincoln's Body Guard: The Union Light Guard of Ohio with Some Personal Recollections of Abraham Lincoln." *Indiana Historical Society* 5, no. 1 (1911).

Millington, John W. "A Cavalryman's Account of the Chase and Capture of John Wilkes Booth." Online edition at: http://members.aol.com/RVSNorton/Lincoln.html.

Morris, Clara. "Some Recollections of John Wilkes Booth." *McClure's Magazine*, February 1901, 299–304.

Moss, M. Helen Palmes. "Lincoln and Wilkes Booth As Seen on the Day of the Assassination." *The Century Magazine*, April 1909.

"The Most Solemn Easter." *Lincoln Lore*, April 10, 1933.

Munroe, Seaton. "Recollections of Lincoln's Assassination." *North American Review*, April 1896, 424–34.

Newman, Ralph G. "The Mystery Occupant's Eyewitness Account of the Death of Abraham Lincoln." *Chicago History*, Spring 1975, 32–33.

Palmer, F. W. "Death of President Lincoln." *Annals of Iowa*, July 1900.

Parsons, Lewis Baldwin. "General Parsons Writes of Lincoln's Death." *Journal of the Illinois State Historical Society*, Winter 1951, 355–57.

Paullin, Charles O. "The Navy and the Booth Conspirators." *Journal of the Illinois State Historical Society*, September 1940, 269–77.

Pearson, Daniel, ed. "One of the Grimmest Events I Ever Participated In: William E. Coxshall and the Execution of the Lincoln Conspirators." *Lincoln Ledger*, November 1995, 1–6.

Peckham, Howard H. "James Tanner's Account of Lincoln's Death." *Abraham Lincoln Quarterly*, March 1942, 176–83.

Peskin, Allan. "Putting the 'Baboon' to Rest: Observations of a Radical Republican on Lincoln's Funeral Train." *Lincoln Herald*, Spring 1977, 26–28.

"The President's Office." *Lincoln Lore*, June 12, 1939.

Read, Harry. " 'A Hand to Hold While Dying': Dr. Charles A. Leale at Lincoln's Side." *Lincoln Herald*, Spring 1977, 21–25.

Rietveld, Ronald D. "An Eyewitness Account of Abraham Lincoln's Assassination." *Civil War History: A Journal of the Middle Period*, March 1976, 60–69.

Rosentreter, Roger L. "Our Lincoln Is Dead." *Michigan History*, March/April 2000.

Shaw, E. R. "The Assassination of Lincoln: The Hitherto Unpublished Account of an Eyewitness." *McClure's Magazine*, December 1908, 181–85.

Shepard, Julia Adelaide. "Lincoln's Assassination Told by an Eyewitness." *Century Magazine*, April 1909, 917–18.

Stern, Philip Van Doren. "The President Came Forward and the Sun Burst through the Clouds." *American Heritage* 9, no. 2 (February 1958), 10–15, 94–97.

Stewart, Charles J. "Lincoln's Assassination and the Protestant Clergy of the North." *Journal of the Illinois State Historical Society*, Autumn 1961, 268–93.

Storey, Moorfield. "Dickens, Stanton, Sumner, and Storey." *Atlantic Monthly*, April 1930, 463–65.

Sweet, W. W. "Bishop Matthew Simpson and the Funeral of Abraham Lincoln." *Journal of the Illinois State Historical Society*, April 1914, 62–71.

Taft, C. S. "Last Hours of Abraham Lincoln." *Medical and Surgical Reporter*, April 22, 1865, 20–23.

Tanner, James, and Norman R. Brown. "The First Testimony Taken in Connection with the Assassination of Abraham Lincoln." Copy at Ford's Theater Archives, Washington, D.C., 17–19.

Tarbell, Ida M. "The Death of Abraham Lincoln." *McClure's*, December 1896, 374–84.

Temple, Wayne C, ed. "The Civil War Letters of Henry C. Bear: A Soldier in the 116th Illinois Volunteer Infantry." *Lincoln Herald*, Spring 1961, 3–18.

Trindal, Mary E. "History at Its Worst." *Surratt Courier*, June 1991, 5–6.

Tucker, Louis Leonard. "Eyewitness to Lincoln's Last Hours." *Yankee Magazine*, April 1979, 144–47.

Turner, Justin G., ed. "April 14, 1865: A Soldier's View." *Lincoln Herald*, Winter 1964, 178–80.

Unnamed, untitled article. *Journal of the Illinois State Historical Society*, Autumn 1958, 324.

van Winden, Kathe. "The Assassination of Abraham Lincoln: Its Effect in California." *Journal of the West*, April 1965, 211–30.

"What Tom Pendel Saw April 14, 1865," *Magazine of History* 34, no. 1 (1927): 17–20.

Weik, Jesse W. "A New Story of Lincoln's Assassination: An Unpublished Record of an Eyewitness." *Century*, February 1903, 559–62.

Williams, Henry, Elizabeth Dixon and Daniel Dean Beekman. "A Night to Remember." *Yankee Magazine*, February 1973, 140–45.

Woodward, George A. "The Night of Lincoln's Assassination." *United Service*, May 1889, 471–76.

Diaries, Letters, Manuscripts, Statements, Clippings, Etc.

· Abraham Lincoln File. Kansas State Historical Society, Topeka.

Adams, James A. Letters. Indiana Historical Society, Indianapolis.

Appel, Charles C. Diary. Historical Society of Pennsylvania, Philadelphia.

Armstrong, John. Letter. Illinois State Historical Library, Springfield.

"The Assassination of Lincoln." Undated, untitled clipping. Ford's Theater Archive, Washington, D.C.

Atwood, Elbridge. Letter. Illinois State Historical Library, Springfield.

Barker, David. Statement. Edward P. Doherty Collection, Illinois State Historical Library, Springfield.

Bassett. Diary. Ford's Theater Archives, Washington, D.C.

Bates, Edward. Papers. Library of Congress.

Bell Collection. Delaware Public Archives, Dover.

Bemis Collection. Letter. Missouri Historical Society, St. Louis.

Blake, Mortimer. "Human Depravity: Sermon on John Wilkes Booth." Rare Books and Special Collections, Library of Congress.

Blow Family. Papers. Missouri Historical Society, St. Louis.

Boggs, Albert. Statement. Ford's Theater Archive, Washington, D.C.

Brewer, Gardner. Letters. Illinois State Historical Library, Springfield.

Bronson, S. H. Letter. Lincoln Museum, Fort Wayne, Indiana.

Buckley Family. Papers. Indiana Historical Society, Indianapolis.

Chadick, Mary Iona. Diary. Alabama State Archives, Montgomery.

Chaplin, E. A. Letter. Ford's Theater Archives, Washington, D.C.

Chappelear, Amanda Virginia. Diary. Virginia Historical Society, Richmond.

Childress, Solomon B. Journal. Missouri Historical Society, St. Louis.

Clarke, Asia Booth. Letters. Copies at Ford's Theater Archive, Washington, D.C.

Coffin, Mary Louise. Memoir. Lincoln Museum, Fort Wayne, Indiana.

Colyer, Henry. Letter. Ford's Theater Archive, Washington, D.C.

Corbett, Boston. Papers. Kansas State Historical Society, Topeka.

Cox, E. L. Diary. Virginia Historical Society, Richmond.

Curtis, Edward. Statement. Ford's Theater Archives.

Davis, J. G. Letter. Illinois State Historical Library, Springfield.

Davis, Matthew Jack. Memoir. Sherman, Tex., Public Library.

Deamude, Charles. Letter. Illinois State Historical Library, Springfield.

"Death and Funeral of Abraham Lincoln: A Contemporary Description by Mrs. Ellen Kean." Illinois State Historical Library, Springfield.

Downing, John, Jr. Letter. Ford's Theater Archive, Washington, D.C.

Eades, Harvey L. Diary. Shaker Collection, Kentucky Museum, Bowling Green.

Eisenschiml, Otto. Collection. Illinois State Historical Library, Springfield.

Elmendorf, William. Statement. Ford's Theater Archive, Washington, D.C.

Everhart, Warren. "Local Man Witnessed Lincoln's Assassination." Ford's Theater Archive, Washington, D.C.

Ferguson, James. Statement. Ford's Theater Archive, Washington, D.C.

Ferguson, John N. Diaries. Library of Congress.

Fish, Hamilton. Diary. Library of Congress.

Ford, Harry. "The Lincoln Assassination: A Reminiscence by the Manager of Ford's Opera-House." Ford's Theater Archive, Washington, D.C.

Ford, John. Papers. Maryland Historical Society, Baltimore.

Ford, John. Statement. Ford's Theater Archive, Washington, D.C.

Ford, Mary B. Diary. Filson Club Historical Society, Louisville, Kentucky.

French, Benjamin. Papers. Library of Congress.

Frey, Gus. Letter. Illinois State Historical Library, Springfield.

Fusz, Louis Philip. Diary. Missouri Historical Society, St. Louis.

Gillette, Abram Dunn. "The Last Days of Payne." Ford's Theater Archive, Washington, D.C.

Goodwin, Edward Payson. Letter. Illinois State Historical Library, Springfield.

Gourlay, Jeannie. Statement. Ford's Theater Archive, Washington, D.C.

Granniss, Sarah. Letter. Illinois State Historical Library, Springfield.

"Hanging the Conspirators Told by an Eyewitness in an Old Letter." Ford's Theater Archive.

"Hangman of President Lincoln's Assassins Tells His Story." Otto Eisenshiml Collection, Illinois State Historical Library, Springfield.

Hannaman, H. G. Letter. Ford's Theater Archive, Washington, D.C.

Harris, Clara. Letter. Ford's Theater Archive, Washington, D.C.

Hatch, Ozias. Letters. Sangamon Valley Collection, Lincoln Library, Springfield, Illinois.

Hawk, Harry. Statement. Ford's Theater Archive, Washington, D.C.

Hiffner, Levi R. Letter. Indiana Historical Society, Indianapolis.

Holloway, L. K. B. Reminiscence. John Wilkes Booth File, Museum of the Confederacy, Richmond.

Hotchkiss, Jedediah. Papers. Library of Congress.

Hudson, George A. Letters. Library of Congress.

Hume, Cora Owens. Diary. Filson Club Historical Society, Louisville, Kentucky.

Huron, George Andrew. Collection. Kansas State Historical Society, Topeka.

James, John. Letter. Ford's Theater Archives, Washington, D.C.

Jefferson, John. Diary. Filson Club Historical Society, Louisville, Kentucky.

Johnson, Byron B. "Boston Corbett, Who Shot John Wilkes Booth." Rare Books and Special Collections, Library of Congress.

Jonas, E. Letter. Lincoln Museum, Fort Wayne, Indiana.

Jones, Margaret MacKay, ed. *The Journal of Catherine Devereux Edmonston, 1860–1866.* Manuscript. Kentucky Historical Society, Frankfort.

Kean, Ellen Tree. Letter. Solomon Smith Collection, Missouri Historical Society, St. Louis.

Kent, William. Letter. Ford's Theater Archive, Washington, D.C.

Kephart, S. N. Statement. Ross-Kidwell Papers, Indiana Historical Society, Indianapolis.

"Killing Women." Ford's Theater Archive, Washington, D.C.

Lattimer, John K. and Terry Alford. "Eyewitness to History: Newton Ferree, the Lincoln Assassination and the Close of the Civil War in Washington." Undated, untitled copy at Ford's Theater Archive, Washington, D.C.

Leale, Charles A. "Lincoln's Last Hours." Illinois State Historical Library, Springfield.

Letter. April 15, 1865. *Chicago History*, Spring 1947.

Lexington (Ky.) *Herald-Leader.* March 8, 1865. Clipping. Kentucky Historical Society, Frankfort.

Lockwood, Jeremiah T. Papers. Library of Congress.

Lucian. Letter. Ford's Theater Archives, Washington, D.C.

Maynard, George C. "That Evening at Ford's." Ford's Theater Archives, Washington, D.C.

McCalla, Helen Varnum Hill. Diary. Library of Congress.

McGaughy-Wallace. Diary. Kentucky Historical Society, Frankfort.

McIntyre, Sheldon P. Statement. Ford's Theater Archive, Washington, D.C.

McQuade, William. Statement. Edward P. Doherty Collection, Illinois State Historical Library, Springfield.

Mead, Rufus, Jr. Papers. Library of Congress.

Meader, Katherine. Collection. Ford's Theater Archive, Washington, D.C.

Meyer, Benjamin. Letter. Missouri Historical Society, St. Louis.

Miller, F. B. Collection. Kansas State Historical Society, Topeka.

"Mob Attacked Gloater over Lincoln Death." Undated newspaper clipping, Michigan State Archives, Lansing.

Morley, Edward W. Papers. Library of Congress.

Moss, Helen. Memoir. Library of Congress.

"Mrs. Rutherford's Scrapbook: Valuable Information about the South: The Assassination of Abraham Lincoln." Athens, Ga., 1924.

Newgarten, Herman. Statement. Edward P. Doherty Collection, Illinois State Historical Library, Springfield.

Northcott Collection. Diary, 1865. Kentucky Museum, Bowling Green.

Noyes, Edward. *Wisconsin's Reaction to the Assassination of Abraham Lincoln.* Rare Book Collection, Library of Congress.

Owner, William. Diary. Library of Congress.

Patton, T. R. Letter. Lincoln Museum, Fort Wayne, Indiana.

Philips, Henry B. Statement. Ford's Theater Archive, Washington, D.C.

Pierce, Charles H. Letters. Indiana Historical Society, Indianapolis.

Poole, Edmund Leicester. Letter. Library of Congress.

Proctor, A. C. Letter. Library of Congress.

Rathbone, Henry. Statement. Ford's Theater Archive, Washington, D.C.

Rathbun, Frank. "The Rathbone Connection." Ford's Theater Archive, Washington, D.C.

Reck, W. Emerson. "Spring Cleaning Brings Lincoln Item to Light." Ford's Theater Archives, Washington, D.C.

"Remarks of Hon. James A. Frear." Ford's Theater Archive, Washington, D.C.

Robinson, Maggie. Letter. Buckley Family Papers, Indiana Historical Society, Indianapolis.

Saint John, Theodore Edgar. Letter. Library of Congress.

Sanders, Thomas. Reminiscence. Lincoln Museum, Fort Wayne, Indiana.

Sandford, Mose. Letter. Ford's Theater Archives. Washington, D.C.

Savage, Louis. Affidavit. Edward P. Doherty Collection, Illinois State Historical Library, Springfield.

Seward, William H. Papers. Library of Congress.

Smith, Solomon. Collection. Missouri Historical Society, St. Louis.

Spangler, William. Letter. John Ford Papers, Maryland Historical Society, Baltimore.

Stanton, Edwin. Letter. Copy at Ford's Theater Archive, Washington, D.C.

Surratt, Anna. Letter. Edwin Stanton Papers, Library of Congress.

Taft, Horatio Nelson. Diary. Library of Congress.

Toffey, John J. Letter. Ford's Theater Archive, Washington, D.C.

Torrey, Charles Oscar. Papers. Library of Congress.

Trumbull, Julia. Letter. Lyman Trumbull Collection, Illinois State Historical Library, Springfield.

"The Truth Plainly Spoken." Pamphlet. Illinois State Historical Library, Springfield.

Tuttle, John W. Diary. Kentucky Historical Society, Frankfort.

"Two Letters on the Event of April 14, 1865." Illinois State Historical Society, Springfield.

Wilkins, John E. Diary. Lincoln Museum, Fort Wayne, Indiana.

Willett, Gordon Arthur. Letters. Historical Society of Washington, D.C.

Wilson, Henry. Letter. Ford's Theater Archives, Washington, D.C.

Newspapers

Abilene (Kans.) *Journal*, 1887.
Albany (N.Y.) *Evening Journal*, 1865.
Alexandria *Louisiana Democrat*, 1865.
Alton (Ill.) *Telegraph*, 1865.
Baltimore *American*, 1865.
Bangor (Maine) *Daily Evening Times*, 1865.
Belleville (Ill.) *Advocate*, 1865
Boston Daily Advertiser, 1865.
Boston Daily Globe, 1920.
Boston *Daily Journal*, 1865.
Boston *Evening Standard*, 1865.
Boston *Herald*, 1897.
Bridgeport (Conn.) *Evening Standard*, 1865.
Brooklyn (N.Y.) *Daily Eagle*, 1865.
Chicago *Evening Journal*, 1865.
Chicago Times, 1865.
Chicago Tribune, 1865.
Cincinnati Daily Commercial, 1868.
Cleveland Morning Leader, 1865.
Columbia *Missouri Statesman*, 1865.
Concord *New Hampshire Statesman*, 1865.
Council Bluffs (Iowa) *Bugle*, 1865.
Denver Daily Rocky Mountain News, 1865.
Detroit *Advertiser and Tribune*, 1865.
Dover *Delawarean*, 1865.
Frankfort (Ky.) *Commonwealth*, 1865.
Frank Leslie's Illustrated, 1865.
Harper's Weekly, 1865.
Hartford (Conn.) *Daily Times*, 1865.
Indianapolis Daily Journal, 1865.
Indianapolis *Daily State Sentinel*, 1865.
Lafayette (Ind.) *Daily Courier*, 1865.
Lynchburg Virginian, 1864.
Memphis Daily Avalanche, 1866.
Milwaukee Free Press, 1914.
Montgomery (Ala.) *Daily Mail*, 1865.
Newark (N.J.) *Daily Advertiser*, 1865.
New Orleans Daily Picayune, 1865.
New Orleans Times, 1865.
New Orleans Tribune, 1865.
New York Herald, 1865.
New York Times, 1865.
New York Tribune, 1865.
New York *World*, 1865.
Philadelphia Inquirer, 1865.
Portsmouth (N.H.) *Journal*, 1865.
Providence Daily Journal, 1865.
Raleigh (N.C.) *Daily Progress*, 1865.

Rochester (N.Y.) *Daily Union and Advertiser,* 1865.
Saint Louis Dispatch, 1865.
San Francisco *Daily Alta California,* 1865.
Springfield *Daily Illinois State Journal,* 1865.
Springfield (Ohio) *Daily News and Republic,* 1865.
St. Joseph (Mo.) *Morning Herald and Daily Tribune,* 1865.
Syracuse (N.Y.) *Herald,* 1915.
Trenton (N.J.) *State Daily Gazette,* 1865.
Virginia (Nev.) *Daily Territorial Enterprise,* 1865.
Washington, *Daily Constitutional Union,* 1865.
Washington, *Daily Morning Chronicle,* 1865.
Washington, *Daily National Intelligencer,* 1865.
Washington, *Daily Times,* 1865.
Washington *Evening Star,* 1865.
Wilmington *Delaware Republican,* 1865

Federal Documents

Boston Corbett Pension Files. National Archives.
The War of the Rebellion: A Compilation of the Official Records of the Union and Confederate Armies. Washington, D.C.: Government Printing Office, 1894.
Washington, D.C. Police Blotter, 1865. National Archives.

INDEX

━━━

Note: Numbers in **boldface** indicate photos.

Tom Goodrich is author of *Black Flag: Guerilla Warfare on the Western Border, 1861–1865* and *The Day Dixie Died: Southern Occupation, 1865–1866* (with Debra Goodrich).